The ESSENTIAL DICTIONARY of INTERNATIONAL TRADE

JERRY M. ROSENBERG

BARNES
&NOBLE
BOOKS
NEW YORK

Text design by Lundquist Design, New York

ISBN: 0-7607-4617-6

04 05 06 07 08 TP 10 9 8 7 6 5 4 3 2 1

To Liz, Jon, and Celia
"A beautiful and loving family of tomorrow"

PREFACE

Almost 25 years ago, the first edition of the *Dictionary of International Trade* appeared, originally published by John Wiley & Sons. This dictionary, now in its third edition, testifies to significant changes in the world of international trade and global business.

The war against Iraq has created the Trade Bank of Iraq. The ascension of new nations of central Europe to the European Union has elevated the challenges for international trade with the United States. New regulations of the World Trade Organization present opportunities for the expansion of global cross-border activities. The debate over subsidies and the pressure to balance government deficits add to the turmoil and the creation of new terminology. The ever-growing presence of China as a force is central to the future of international trade. Prospects for peace in the Middle East have elevated world trade as a means for becoming the glue for stability and peace. Free-trade accords are proliferating, presenting both opportunities and barriers to a more prosperous world. Anti-globalization continues to be a cry for many nations around the world. And yet, international interdependency and the global village remain the promising hope for the almost 6.5 billion people of the world.

With this new edition, I have attempted to incorporate

those phrases and concepts that are ever-present in the headlines and daily events, integrating the latest thinking with the more traditional, in order to clarify for the user how the terminology can be translated into comprehension, action, and reward.

A lifetime of pursuing the proper and meaningful usage of business words has found support from those individuals that are most important to me. There is my precious wife, Ellen, who after 44 years of marriage remains a partner in all of our activities. Sharing my interest in lexicography are others in my family, my daughters, Liz and Lauren, respectively married to Jon and Bob, and my three grandchildren, Bess, Ella, Celia. Watching these girls advance from one stage of development to another is sheer delight. Their exchange of love is the greatest of rewards.

To my audience and users, I continue to appreciate the effort spent communicating with me as to suggestions for new entries and/or corrections of definitions found in this volume.

Jerry M. Rosenberg, Ph.D.
September 2004
New York, New York

INTRODUCTION

This *Essential Dictionary of International Trade* incorporates traditional terms used in the world of international trade. Over time, issues and practices of global business have drastically shifted and been altered by current geopolitics, the search for new resources, and for less-costly labor. Therefore, a library of concepts and terms has mushroomed in the past 50 years as this discipline has received its rightful place as an independent and proper course of inquiry and activity.

This work of more than 4,000 entries has been prepared with the hope that awareness of the accepted meanings of terms may enhance the process of sharing information and ideas. Though it cannot eliminate the need for the user to determine how a writer or speaker treats words, such a dictionary shows what usages exist. It should assist in stabilizing terminology. Most important, it should aid people in saying and writing precisely, with greater clarity, what they intend.

A word can take on different meanings in different contexts. There may be as many meanings as there are areas of specialty. A goal of this lexicon is to be broad and to establish core definitions that represent the variety of individual meanings, to enhance parsimony and clearness in the communication process. Many terms are used in different ways. I have tried to unite them without giving one advantage or dominance over another. Whenever possible (without creating a controversy), I have stated the connection among multiple usages. Commonly used symbols, acronyms, and abbreviations are included. Foreign words and phrases are given only if they have become an integral part of our English vocabulary.

This work reaches throughout all departments within global business and international trade, both private and public, by acknowledging that the sum of an organization is greater than any of its individual parts. The result is an all-inclusive lexicon of international trade.

ORGANIZATION
& FORMAT

This is a defining work rather than a compilation of facts. The line is not easy to draw, because in the final analysis meanings are based on facts. Consequently, factual information is used when necessary to make a term more readily understood. All entries are presented in the language of those who use them. The level of complexity needed to define will vary with the user; one person's complexity is another's precise and parsimonious statement. Several meanings are sometimes given—relatively supplied, both general and specialized entries—to make this dictionary an unusually useful reference source.

Alphabetization. Words are presented alphabetically. Compound terms are placed where the reader is most likely to look for them. They are entered under their most distinctive component, usually nouns. Should you fail to locate a word or phrase where you initially search for it, turn to a variant spelling, a synonym, a shortened form, or a different word of a compound term.

Headings. The current popular term is usually given as the principal entry, with other terms cross-referenced to it. Some terms have been included for historical significance, even though they are no longer in common use.

Cross-References. Cross-references go from the general to the specific. Occasionally "See" references from the specific to the general are used to inform the user of words related to particular entries. "See" references to currently accepted terminology are made wherever possible. The use of "Cf." suggests words to be compared with the original entry.

Synonyms. The phrase "Synonymous with" following a definition does not imply that the term is exactly equivalent to the principal entry under which it appears. Frequently, the term only approximates the primary sense of the original entry.

Disciplines. Many words are given multiple definitions based on their utilization in various fields of activity. The definition with the widest application is given first, with the remaining definitions listed by area of specialty. Since the areas may overlap, the reader should examine all multiple definitions.

The ESSENTIAL
DICTIONARY of
INTERNATIONAL
TRADE

A

AA (always afloat): a contractual statement to avoid hull damage, providing that a chartered ship will always be afloat during the charter period, whether at port or at sea.

AAEI: see *American Association of Exporters and Importers.*

AAIB: see *Arab-African International Bank.*

abandon: a proceeding wherein a rail carrier seeks authority to abandon all or part of its line.

abandonment:

(1) the elimination from use of a fixed asset.

(2) a surrender of property by the owner to the insurer in order to claim a total loss, when, in fact, the loss may be less than total.

(3) a request by a carrier for permission to stop service over all or part of its route or to give up ownership or control of the cargo or carrier; a refusal to accept delivery of badly damaged items.

Abatement Forfaitaire: synonymous with *Montant Forfaitaire.*

ABC: see *American Business Center.*

ABEDA: see *Arab Bank for Economic Development in Africa.*

ABN (Authorité du Basin du Niger): see *NBA.*

above the line:

(1) the promotional expenses associated with advertising in one of the media.

(2) that portion of a nation's budget dealing with revenue, mainly taxes and expenditure.

(3) for firms, all income and expenses before tax. See *autonomous transactions.*

above-the-line items: see *autonomous transactions.*

ABS: see *American Bureau of Shipping.*

absolute advantage:

(1) theory of Adam Smith; an advantage of one nation or area over another in the costs of manufacturing an item in terms of used resources. Cf. *comparative advantage.*

(2) the advantage enjoyed by a country because it can produce a product at a lower cost than other countries.

absolute form of purchasing parity: suggests that prices of two products of different countries should be equal when measured by a common currency.

absolute quotas: government limitation on the amount of items that can enter into the commerce of a nation within a given time frame. When the absolute quota is filled, no additional items are permitted in during the stated time period.

absorption: the assumption by one carrier of switching or other special charges of another, generally without increasing the rate to the shipper.

absorption costing: a type of product costing that assigns fixed manufacturing overhead to the units produced as a product cost.

absorption of charges on freight: the payment by a carrier, out of its revenue on a shipment, of the charges assessed by others for switching, lighterage, wharfage, or other service incidental to transportation.

abstract: an abridged summary of information omitting unessentials.

abstract of waybills: a brief or synoptical statement of waybills, distinguished as to waybills received or waybills forwarded; a report of freight received and dispatched from a station.

Abu Dhabi Fund for Economic Development (ADFAED): fund to promote economic development in African, Arab, and Asian nations; founded in 1971, with headquarters in Abu Dhabi, United Arab Emirates.

abuses: unfair practices by one nation against another following the completion of a trade agreement. Examples are: (a) directly or indirectly imposing unfair purchase or selling prices or other unfair trading conditions; (b) limiting production, markets, or technical development, to the prejudice of consumers; (c) applying dissimilar conditions to equivalent transactions with other trading parties, thereby placing them at a competitive disadvantage; (d) making the conclusion of contracts subject to acceptance by the other parties of supplementary obligations which, by their nature or according to commercial usage, have no connection with the subject of such contracts. Rectifying such abuses may require the assistance of an international trade court or commission.

ACC: see *Arab Cooperation Council.*

accelerated tariff elimination: mutual agreement between nations to increase the speed of tariff reduction within the framework of international accords.

acceptance:

(1) a time draft (or bill of exchange) that the drawee has accepted

and is unconditionally obligated to pay at maturity. The draft must be presented first for acceptance—the drawee becomes the acceptor—then for payment. The word "accepted" and the date and place of payment must be written on the face of the draft.

(2) the drawee's act in receiving a draft and thus entering into the obligation to pay its value at maturity.

(3) any agreement to purchase goods under specified terms. An agreement to purchase goods at a stated price and under stated terms.

acceptance, clean: see *clean acceptance*.

acceptance credit: a means by which commercial banks and foreign banking institutions establish credit with a bank so they can participate in the acceptance practice to assist in financing import-export and domestic transactions. See *acceptance house*.

acceptance facility: a bank line of credit extended to finance imports or exports. A lending bank can require a borrower to pledge a warehouse receipt, bill of lading, or other evidence of title to the underlying items.

acceptance financing: a means of securing short-term credit used by exporters. Should an exporter require working capital and offer a draft for payments in advance of its maturity date, the bank may choose to accept the request.

acceptance house: a financial institution lending funds on the security of bills of exchange. The house may lend funds to an exporter to cover the gap between the production of goods and the receipt of proceeds from their sale. The house may also lend money on a bill or add its name to a bill drawn on another party, especially in foreign trade. See *acceptance credit*.

acceptance, trade: see *trade acceptance*.

accepted: see *acceptance*.

accepted bill of exchange: synonymous with *trade acceptance*.

accepting bank: see *acceptance financing*.

acceptor: the drawee of a note for acceptance, who agrees, upon signing the form, to pay a draft or bill when due.

accession:

(1) the act of becoming a member of a community common market, such as becoming a new member of the European Union. For example, 10 countries ascended into the European Union in the spring 2004.

(2) the process of a country joining the GATT, now the WTO. During accession to the WTO, a country accords tariff and other concessions that are its "price of admission" to the WTO.

accessions: goods affixed to and part of other items.

accessorial service: a service rendered by a carrier in addition to a transportation service, such as assorting, packaging, pre-cooling, heating, storage, or substitution of tonnage.

accidental exporting: an export business obtained through no effort of the exporter.

accommodating transactions: international transactions that are exchanges in official reserve assets of, and of foreign official assets in, a nation that must balance international cash flows. Cf. *autonomous transactions*.

accommodation bill of lading: a bill of lading issued by a common carrier before receipt of items for shipment.

accommodation paper: a promissory note, endorsed by individuals, allowing the original signer of the note to receive bank credit; thus the second or other signer(s) accepts the guarantee of credit.

account: a record of all the transactions, and the date of each, affecting a particular phase of a business, expressed in debits and credits, evaluated in money, and showing the current balance, if any.

accountability controls: control procedures that fix responsibility for the custody of assets, documents, accounting records, and elements of electronic data bases.

accountancy: British term for accounting practices.

accounting exposure: expressed in a foreign currency, risks of depreciation or appreciation that may impact on an accounting statement, or any entries within the statement.

account party: importer, for purposes of the letter of credit.

accounts receivable: amounts owed to an entity, primarily by its trade customers.

accounts receivable financing: the exporter provides indirect financing for the importer by exporting goods and allowing for payments to be made at a later date.

ACH: see *automated clearing house*.

ACM: see *Arab Common Market*.

ACP (states): the nations from Africa, the Caribbean, and the Pacific signatory to the European Community's Lomé Convention. In July 1989, the European Community agreed on a revised offer for a new five-year trade and aid pact to the ACP group of nations to replace the Lomé Convention, including a plan to compensate these original 66 nations for losses in earnings from commodity exports because of world market fluctuations. See *Lomé Conventions.*

acquired advantage: form of trade advantage due to technology rather than to the availability of natural resources, climate, etc.

acquisition: the purchase of one company by another company.

acquisition strategy: form of foreign direct investment involving the purchase of existing assets in a foreign country.

across-the-board tariff negotiations: negotiations involving uniform percentage reductions or increases in duties on primary categories of goods.

ACT: see *Amazonian Cooperation Treaty.*

Acta de Barahona: an agreement, of January 1, 1992, providing for the establishment of a free-trade area between Venezuela, Colombia, and Bolivia, with Peru and Ecuador joining on July 1, 1992. See *Andean Pact.*

active income: income of a controlled foreign corporation that is derived from the active conduct of a trade or business, as specified by the U.S. Internal Revenue Code.

active trade balance: a balance of trade that is favorable.

ACTN: see *Advisory Committee on Trade Policy and Negotiations.*

act of God: in contractual language, an irresistible superhuman cause, such as no reasonable human foresight, prudence, diligence, and care can anticipate or prevent. See *force majeure.*

act of state doctrine:

(1) a principle of international law advancing the concept that every sovereign nation can legally do what it likes within its own borders and that other nations will not sit in judgment over these acts of state.

(2) a jurisdictional principle of international law which holds that all acts of other governments are considered to be valid by U.S. courts, even if such acts are illegal or inappropriate under U.S. law.

actual owner: the party having legal title to a vessel, as listed in the ship's registry papers.

actuals: merchandise and other items available for immediate purchase and subsequent sale.

actual total loss: a loss that occurs when an item is totally destroyed or destroyed sufficiently to become useless. In shipping, it implies that the vessel is a total loss.

actual valuation: the true value of a shipment at the time of delivery to the carrier.

actual value rate: a freight rate applicable to some commodities, where, depending on the actual items, value can vary considerably.

ACU:

(1) see *Artificial Currency Unit.*

(2) see *Asian Currency Unit.*

AD: see *antidumping.*

adaption: a global marketing approach where the manufacturer adapts goods and services to the requirements of foreign consumers.

adaptive perspective: assumes that adaptive cultures enhance a firm's financial performance.

ADB:

(1) see *African Development Bank.*

(2) see *Asian Development Bank.*

added-value tax: see *value-added tax.*

address commission: the commission paid to a charterer's agent for arranging the loading of a vessel.

ADFAED: see *Abu Dhabi Fund for Arab Economic Development.*

ADIBOR: Abu Dhabi Interbank Offered Rate. See *London Interbank Offered Rate.*

adjudication: the legal mechanism for settling international disputes when parties to the conflict submit them to an appropriate court.

adjustable peg: a system permitting changes in the par rate of foreign exchange after a country has had long-run disequilibrium in its balance of payments. It allows for short-run variations within a narrow range of a few percentage points around the par value.

adjustment:

(1) a change in an account to correct an incorrect entry or for some other sound reason.

(2) the change in an official currency rate or in internal economic policies to correct a payments imbalance.

adjustment assistance: financial and technical assistance to workers, firms, and communities to help them adjust to import competition.

adjustment process: an international system and mechanism for payments adjustment policies; for example, exchange rate alignment, shifts in national expenditures, exchange controls.

adjustment trigger: an objective measure impelling exchange rate or economic policy changes.

administrative agency: the appropriate government unit responsible for and authorized to implement legislation.

administrative coordination: strategic formulation and implementation in which an *MNC* makes strategic decisions based on the merits of the individual situation rather than using a predetermined economically or politically driven strategy.

administrative protections: a type of trade barrier in the form of various rules and regulations that make it more difficult for foreign firms to conduct business in a particular nation.

administrator ad colligendum: an administrator appointed to collect foreign assets.

admiralty: jurisdiction over causes of action occurring in connection with contracts to transport by water; also, other marine matters.

admission temporoire: see *ATA carnet.*

adoption notice: a statement by a carrier that it is lawfully accepting an obligation (usually the freight tariffs) of a predecessor.

ADR (Agreement on Dangerous Goods): the European Community's Agreement on the International Carriage of Dangerous Goods by Road. It became effective in 1968 and was signed by 14 nations, including all EC countries. ADR ensures that dangerous goods being conveyed by road can cross international frontiers without hindrance provided that the goods are packed and labeled in accordance with the Agreement. Tanker vehicles carrying inflammable substances are subject to technical inspection. Cf. *advance determination ruling.*

AD-REF: see *ad referendum.*

ad referendum (AD-REF): an expediency used during the process of negotiating agreements or concessions. Generally, if a concession is agreed to ad referendum, it is understood to mean that the concession is agreed to pending the final approval of a higher governmental authority.

ADS: see *agent/distributor service.*

aduana: (Spanish) *customs,* or customers duty.

ad valorem:
> (1) (Latin) according to value. See *duty*.
>
> (2) a tax or duty levied as a fixed percentage of an item's value.

ad valorem equivalent (AVE): a duty assessed on a specific basis that is expressed as a percentage of the value of an import. See *specific duty*.

ad valorem tariff: a tariff based on a percentage of the value of the goods imported.

advance against documents: a loan made on the security of the documents covering the shipment.

advance bill:
> (1) a bill of exchange drawn prior to the shipment of goods.
>
> (2) the invoice presented before the items or services itemized have been delivered or carried out. It is usually requested by purchasers for tax reasons.

advanced charge: the amount of freight or other charge on a shipment advanced by one transportation line to another, or to the shipper, to be collected from the consignee.

advance determination ruling (ADR): an application to the U.S. Internal Revenue Services to determine if a transfer price policy of a multinational firm is appropriate. Cf. *American Depository Receipt*.

Advanced Technology Products (ATP): a major category within the U.S. Commerce Department of exports. In 1992, ATPs exceeded $100 billion, with the nation's ATP surplus at $38 billion, annualized. ATP exports to the developing nations were up 15 percent in 1992.

advance freight: freight paid for in advance. It permits the shipper to endorse the bill of lading with a freight release, and the importer to take immediate delivery.

advance import deposit: a deposit prior to the release of foreign exchange, required by some governments.

adventure: in marine insurance, a peril.

advising bank: a bank, operating in the exporter's nation, that handles letters of credit for a foreign bank by notifying the exporter that the credit has been opened in his or her favor. The advising bank fully informs the exporter of the conditions of the letter of credit without necessarily bearing responsibility for payment.

advisory capacity: a position indicating that a shipper's agent or representative is not empowered to make definitive decisions or adjustments without approval of the group or individual represented. Cf. *without reserve.*

Advisory Committee on Trade Policy and Negotiations (ACTPN): a group appointed by the U.S. President to advise him on matters of trade policy and related issues, including trade agreements.

advocacy center: Washington-based center, created in November 1993 to aid high-level U.S. official advocacy to aid companies negotiating projects worldwide.

AED: the international standard code for the currency of the United Arab Emirates—the UAE dirham.

AEF: see *African Enterprise Fund.*

AELE (Association Européene de Libre Échange): see *European Free Trade Association.*

AEX: see *Amsterdam Exchanges.*

AFA: the international standard code for the currency of the Afghanistan—the Afghani.

AfDB: see *African Development Bank.*

AFESD: see *Arab Fund for Economic and Social Development.*

affiant: one who makes an affidavit.

affidavit: a written statement sworn to before a notary public.

affiliate: a unit, either partially or wholly owned by a multinational enterprise. This includes subsidiaries, branches, joint ventures, and any other legal form implying at least partial control over the entity.

affiliated bank: partly owned, separately incorporated, overseas banking operation of a home country bank.

affiliated foreign group: group that is either a foreign parent organization or is controlled by a foreign individual(s) having more than fifty percent ownership.

affirmative dumping decision: the decision that a nation has deliberately marketed products below their fair market value and is therefore subject to antidumping duty orders or other measures.

affreightment: the act of hiring or contracting, by which a vessel or space is engaged for the transportation of freight.

Afghani: the monetary unit of Afghanistan.

afianzadoraz: bonding company of Mexico allowing the importer in Mexico to guarantee payment to the foreign exporter.

AFIDA (Agricultural Foreign Investment Disclosure Act of 1978): Federal legislation requiring foreign investors in U.S. agricultural lands to report investments to the U.S. Department of Agriculture. All AFIDA reports are available for public inspection.

afloat: items on the oceans and seas en route to their destinations. It does not apply to arrivals ready for unloading.

aforos: a customs value for computing ad valorem levies in some South American nations. The customs value is different from market value and is applied to designated classes of imports.

AFRA (average freight rate assessment): an assessment determined monthly by the London Tanker Brokers Panel of the average cost for transporting oil in several different sizes of tankers.

African and Mauritian Common Organization: see *OCAM.*

African, Caribbean, and Pacific countries: see *ACP.*

African Development Bank (ADB) (AfDB): an organization formed in 1964 with the objective of helping to provide development capital for Africa. The headquarters are at Abidjan, Ivory Coast. The bank is responsible for stimulating regional economic growth by granting loans and providing technical assistance to its members, which include 50 regional African countries and 25 nonregional nations.

African Enterprise Fund (AEF): fund, part of International Finance Corporation to aid small and medium-sized firms in sub-Sahara Africa to stimulate economic/business growth. Commenced operations in 1989.

African Groundnut Council (AGC): established in 1964, in Lagos, Nigeria; an international commodity group purporting to promote consumption of the product, exchange data on efficient production and marketing, and stimulate potential customers to attain consistently predictable and profitable prices for producers of the commodity. Members are Gambia, Mali, Niger, Nigeria, Senegal, Sudan, and Burkina Faso. Synonymous with *Conseil Africain de l' Arachide (CAA).*

African Growth and Opportunity Act (AGOA): U.S. trade pact legislation which runs until 2008; a duty-free program.

African Timber Organization (ATO): formed in 1975 and headquartered in Libreville, Gabon; coordinates methods among producer-member countries for influencing the prices of wood in the global marketplace. Producer members include Cameroon, Central African Republic, Congo, Equatorial Guinea, Gabon, Ghana, Côte d'Ivoire, Liberia,

Malagasy Republic, Tanzania, and Zaire. Synonymous with *Organisation Africaine du Bois (OAB)*.

African Union: a long-term projected concept for the nations of Africa; to be modeled after the European Union. After nearly four decades of the Organization of African Unity, the 53-nation changed its name to African Union commencing in 2002. It will have an African Central Bank, African Investment Bank, and African Monetary Fund. See *Afro*.

Afro: a suggested currency for all of Africa. See *African Union*.

AFTA (ASEAN Free Trade Area): the South-East Asia free trade area. On October 22, 1992, the economic ministers of the six states of ASEAN—Indonesia, Singapore, Thailand, Malaysia, the Philippines, and Brunei—met in Manila to discuss the creation of a group that would bring together 320 million consumers, with the aim of starting a round of tariff cuts on January 1, 1993, to a maximum of 5 percent, creating a free market in at least 15 industrial products over 15 years. Cement, rubber, wooden furniture, and textiles are included in an initial list of 15 products. See *Association of South-East Asian Nations*.

after market: the secondary market, in the fixed-interest and Eurobond markets; the time between the issue of the security and the lifting of syndicate restrictions.

AG:

(1) see *Aktiengesellschaft*.

(2) Arabian Gulf.

against all risks: insured against all generally accepted risks in marine insurance.

AGC: see *African Groundnut Council*.

agency:

(1) in the United States, the debt of an agency of the U.S. government.

(2) form of banking operation that cannot accept public deposits.

agency fee: the charge by a ship's agent or owner for services while the vessel is in port.

Agency for International Development (AID): an agency in the U.S. Department of State charged with coordinating overseas economic assistance.

Agency for International Trade Information and Cooperation: based in Geneva, Switzerland; provides trade-related technical assistance in developing countries to assist them to participate actively in the work of the World Trade Organization and in negotiations under its auspices. In 2003, it changed its status from a Swiss Government–funded NGO to an intergovernmental organization with 30 members whose are providing funding of 18 million Swiss francs for five years. See *World Trade Organization*.

agency office: an office of a foreign bank in the United States that cannot accept domestic deposits. It seeks business for the bank when a U.S. firm operates internationally.

agency tariff: a tariff issued by a publishing agent for one or more transportation lines.

agent: a person authorized to transact business for and in the name of another. See *foreign sales agent*.

agent bank:
(1) a bank acting for a foreign bank.
(2) in the Eurocredit market, a bank appointed by other banks within the syndicate to handle the administration of a loan. The agent is usually a lead bank, but the agent function starts with the signing of the loan when the lead bank function terminates.

agent de change: a member of the Paris Bourse (stock exchange).

agent/distributor service (ADS): an export promotion service to industry of the U.S. Department of Commerce's International Trade Administration; its goal is to locate foreign companies to serve as agents and distributors of American products.

agent for exporter: duly authorized forwarding agent of an exporter.

aggregate demand:
(1) the total spending within an economy.
(2) the total of personal consumption expenditures, business investments, and government spending.

aggregated shipment: a sum of cargo, bound for a single consignee, which has been assembled over time by a carrier at his or her premises from smaller lots shipped in from one or more sources. The entire lot can be shipped on to the consignee as a single load.

aggregate limit of liability: the total amount of the insurers' liability under a Foreign Credit Insurance Association insurance policy.

aggregate risk: the full exposure of a bank to a customer for both spot and forward contracts.

aggregate supply: the capacity of a country's total resources to produce real goods and services.

agio:
(1) a premium paid for the exchange of one nation's currency for that of another's. Cf. *disagio.*
(2) the rate of exchange among differing countries.

AGOA: see *African Growth and Opportunity Act.*

agreed valuation: the value of a shipment agreed on to secure a specific rating and/or liability.

agreed weight: the weight prescribed by agreement between carrier and shipper for goods shipped in certain packages or in a certain manner.

Agreement Corporation: synonymous with *Edge Act.*

Agreement on Anti-Dumping Practices: a 1980 international agreement, following the Tokyo Round of GATT; established conditions under which anti-dumping duties can be legally imposed by a nation as its defense against what it claims are "dumped" imports. See *Agreement on Implementation of Article VI; dumping.* Synonymous with *Anti-Dumping Code.*

Agreement on Customs Valuation: a 1980 international agreement, following the Tokyo Round of GATT; replaced numerous systems of customs valuation with transparent regulations to afford participating members a fair, neutral, and uniform process of valuing items for the purpose of levying customs duties. The Agreement harmonized numerous goods. See *Tokyo Round.* Synonymous with *Customs Valuation Code.*

Agreement on Dangerous Goods: see *ADR.*

Agreement on Government Procurement: a 1988 international agreement, following the Tokyo Round of GATT; approved by 12 nations to create a uniform set of worldwide practices applicable to government procurement so as to allow all bidders to have a fairer chance to tender for such contracts, free of discrimination. See *Tokyo Round.* Synonymous with *Government Procurement Code.*

Agreement on Implementation of Article VI: the 1979 multilateral trade negotiations agreement that replaced a similar agreement negotiated in 1967 as part of the Kennedy Round. This is the only MTN agreement to have such a precedent; it aims to ensure the greatest possible uniformity in signatories' antidumping practices by specifying the basis for the imposition, collection, and duration of antidumping duties.

Agreement on Import Licensing: a 1988 international agreement, following the Tokyo Round of GATT; approved by 27 nations to help ensure that international licensing procedures per se do not evolve as trade barriers and that transparent licensing methods are incorporated in a clear and nondiscriminatory fashion. See *Tokyo Round*. Synonymous with *Import Licensing Code*.

Agreement on Interpretation and Application of Articles VI, XVI, and XXIII: see *Subsidies Code*.

Agreement on Technical Barriers to Trade: synonymous with *Standards Code*.

Agreement on the International Carriage of Dangerous Goods by Road: see *ADR*.

Agreement on Trade in Civil Aircraft (ATCA): a 1988 international agreement, following the Tokyo Round of GATT. Twenty-two civil-aircraft manufacturing nations agreed to eliminate all duties on aircraft and their parts, liberalize government procurement procedures for civil aircraft, and agree on principles for the production of airplanes. See *Tokyo Round*. Synonymous with *Aircraft Agreement*.

Agricultural Foreign Investment Disclosure Act of 1978: see *AFIDA*.

agriculture: see *Common Agricultural Policy*.

AIB: see *Arab International Bank*.

AIBD: see *Association of International Bond Dealers*.

AID: see *Agency for International Development*.

aide-memoire: a brief summary of verbal statements made to a foreign government representative and left with that person.

AIH: the ports of Antwerp and Hamburg.

AIOEC: see *Association of Iron Ore Exporting Countries*.

airbill: see *air waybill*.

Aircraft Agreement (ATCA): formally known as the *Agreement on Trade in Civil Aircraft*, this MTN agreement is the only major sector-specific agreement. It established a framework of rules governing the conduct of trade in civil aircraft, based on commercially competitive practices. Under its provisions, signatories have: (a) eliminated tariffs on civil aircraft, engines, parts, and components; (b) established rules addressing government involvement in civil-aircraft procurements; and (c) built upon MTN codes on standards for the aircraft sector. Synonymous with *Agreement on*

Trade in Civil Aircraft.

airline exchange rail order: a standard form of order issued by airline companies and drawn on agents of rail carriers to furnish rail, parlor, or sleeping car tickets and sometimes cash, etc., to grounded airline passengers and to airline company employees.

air waybill (AWB): a transport document that covers both domestic and international flights transporting goods to a specified destination. This is a nonnegotiable instrument of air transport that serves as a receipt for the shipper, indicating that the carrier has accepted the goods listed and obligates itself to carry the consignment to the airport of destination according to specified conditions.

AKA: see *Ausfuhrkredit Gmbh.*

Aktiebolag: in Sweden, a business incorporation requiring an initial minimum capitalization of 5,000 kroner, with two thirds of the firm's directors Swedish citizens.

Aktiengesellschaft (AG): in Germany, a business incorporation. The original designation applied to large publicly held firms capitalized at a minimum of 100,000 deutsche marks. The initials *AG* follow the corporation's name.

ALADI (Asociación Latino-Americana de Integración): Latin American Integration Association; headquartered in Montevideo, with 11 nations. Its objective is to form reciprocal trade agreements in the area.

ALAT: see *Latin American Association of International Trading Companies.*

alien: an individual residing in a nation although a citizen of another.

alien company: an incorporated company formed and operating under the regulations of a foreign nation.

ALL: the international standard code for the currency of Albania—the lek.

all-commodity rate: a freight rate applying, with certain restrictions, on any and all commodities.

allfinanz: (German) for mergers between banks and insurers.

Alliance for Progress: this agreement was signed in 1961 at Punta del Este, Chile, by 20 North, South, and Central American nations, giving a more comprehensive institutional expression to the attempt by the United States to stimulate economic cooperation in Latin America through multilateral assistance. This was the goal of the Inter-American Development Bank, founded in 1958, with the Inter-American Investment Corporation, formed in 1986 as the Bank's affiliate, to encourage the creation, expansion, and modernization of the private sector. See *Punta del Este.*

all in: in pricing, indicating that a quoted rate includes all cargo charges.

allocate: to distribute, assign, or allot.

Allocations Under Lines of Credit: Canada's Export Development Corporation agreement of lines of credit with private banks and public institutions in foreign nations, to facilitate medium and long-term export financing to foreign purchasers of Canadian capital goods and services; provides financial incentives for foreigners. See *Export Development Corporation.*

allonge: a paper affixed to a bill on which further endorsements are written.

all ordinaries index: Australian stock index, representing 330 of the most-active listed firms.

all or none order:

(1) a stipulation that a request to purchase or sell as security must be achieved in total or not at all.

(2) a stipulation that all securities sold by a broker or underwriter of a new issue become final only when the entire issue is purchased within a stated time period.

allotment:

(1) an assignment of pay for the benefit of dependents.

(2) the separation of anticipated revenues among specific classes of expenditures.

allowance:

(1) a sum granted as a reimbursement or repayment.

(2) a deduction from the gross weight or value of goods.

(3) extra payments to expatriate employees to meet the higher costs they incur abroad.

all purposes: a charter party provision giving the time allotted for loading and unloading freight.

all rail: shipment entirely by rail transportation.

all-risks insurance: marine insurance that protects the insured from direct loss arising from any fortuitous cause other than the perils or causes specifically excluded by name. Synonymous with *floater policy.*

all told: the total deadweight capacity of a vessel, including water, stores, and fuel, in addition to cargo-carrying capacity.

all water: entirely by water transportation.

alongside (the side of a ship): placement of goods on the dock or barge within reach of the transport ship's tackle so that the goods can be loaded aboard the ship.

Alpen-Adria: a grouping of nations covering much of the area of the old Austria-Hungary. Slovenia and Croatia have been members since it was formed in 1978, along with Austria's Lander's provinces, three of Hungary's western regions, and the German land of Bavaria. It attempts to promote regional cooperation.

alternative rates: two or more rates, of which the one that produces the lowest charge is applicable.

alternative tariff: a tariff containing two or more rates from and to the same points, on the same goods, with authority to use the one that produces the lowest charge. See *sectional tariff.*

always accessible: a charter party provision indicating that a loading or unloading facility will be available when a carrier arrives.

always afloat: see *AA.*

Amazonian Cooperation Treaty (ACT): a 1978 accord among Amazon Basin nations to cooperate in the economic development of the region. Headquartered in Brasilia, its signatories are Bolivia, Brazil, Columbia, Ecuador, Guyana, Peru, Surinam, and Venezuela. Synonymous with *Amazon Pact.*

Amazon Pact: synonymous with *Amazonian Cooperation Treaty.*

AMCO (African and Mauritian Common Organization): see *OCAM.*

amendments:
(1) alterations to an original agreement.
(2) within the GATT, now WTO, Agreement, the provision of Article XXX that amendments (which become effective upon acceptance by two-thirds of the contracting parties) are to be effective only for those parties accepting them.

American Association of Exporters and Importers (AAEI): a lobbying group, formed in 1921; deals with federal regulations on international trade; based in New York City.

American Bureau of Shipping (ABS): formed in 1862, a private certification society that sets standards of seaworthiness and classifies vessels and marine equipment for the insurance industry.

American Business Center (ABC): U.S. Commerce department effort; provides assistance to U.S. firms to network with other countries; under direction of the U.S. Agency for International Development.

American Depository Receipt: see *Depository Receipt.*

American Free Trade Area (AFTA): obsolete term. Now referred to as *Free Trade (Agreement) Area for the Americas.*

American goods returned: a provision of the U.S. Tariff Schedules that allows duty-free return of merchandise of American manufacture. The goods must not have been manipulated or advanced in value, except for the packaging of the item.

American sector: that part of the globe having as its focal center the United States with its boundary neighbors Canada and Mexico. Not far away are both Central and South America, along with Caribbean states. See *New American Community.* Cf. *Asian sector; European sector.*

American selling price (ASP): the price charged by U.S. producers for goods, used to determine the duty to be paid on a similar item brought into the United States, rather than determining the duty on the actual cost of the item to an importer.

American terms: an exchange rate expressed as a number of currency units per dollar.

Americas: the 33 countries found in North, Central, and South America.

Americas Initiative: see *Enterprise for the Americas Initiative.*

AMF: see *Arab Monetary Fund.*

Amman Middle East/North Africa Economic Summit: held in Amman, Jordan, October 29–31, 1995; goals were to facilitate the expansion of private-sector investment in the region, to cement a public-private partnership which will ensure that end, and to work to enhance regional cooperation and development. Agreed to create a Bank for Economic Cooperation and Development, a Regional Tourism Board, a Regional Business Council, and an Executive Secretariat in Rabat. Cf. *Cairo Middle East/North Africa Economic Conference; Casablanca Middle East/North Africa Economic Summit; Doha Middle East/North Africa Economic Conference.*

amortization:

(1) an attempt to liquidate a future obligation slowly by making charges against a capital account or by adding monies to cover the debt.

(2) the gradual reduction of a debt by means of equal periodic payments sufficient to meet current interest and to liquidate the debt at maturity. When the debt involves real property, the periodic payments often include a sum sufficient to pay taxes and insurance on the property.

Amount of Support: see *Montant de Soutien.*

Amstel Club: finance houses from 15 European nations that make reciprocal arrangements for trade finance. The full name is *Amstel Finance International AG.*

Amstel Finance International AG: see *Amstel Club.*

Amsterdam Exchanges (AEX): formed by the 1997 merger of the Amsterdam Stock Exchange and the European Options Exchange and Necigef (the Dutch Central Institution for Girosecurities transactions).

Amsterdam Treaty: see *European Union—Amsterdam Treaty.*

AMU (Arab Mahgreb Union): see *MCM.*

anchorage:

(1) duties to be paid for anchoring in some harbors and ports.

(2) the place where a vessel waits for its berth.

Andean Community (CAN): in 1997, the name Andean Pact was changed to Andean Community (CAN). Its objectives remain as the promotion of "the balanced and harmonious development of the member countries under equitable conditions…through integration and economic and social cooperation." See *Andean Pact.*

Andean Pact: in November 1969, the Cartagena Agreement, signed in Cartagena, Colombia, established the basic framework of the pact. Venezuela joined in 1974, while Chile withdrew in 1976, resulting in the Pact's current membership of Venezuela, Colombia, Peru, Bolivia, and Ecuador. From its inception, the Pact sought to harmonize its members' trade and investment regimes through a preferential tariff structure for Pact members, a common external tariff, and decrees on investment and intellectual property rights.

Until 1990, the Pact experienced little to no success in guiding its members' commercial policies. By that time, each of the Pact countries had embarked on individual trade and investment liberalization programs. At the November 1990 Pact meeting in La Paz, Bolivia, the five Andean presidents agreed on the creation of an Andean common market by 1996.

At the December 4–5, 1991, Pact presidents' meeting in Cartagena, final approval was granted to more trade liberalization reforms in two days than in the previous 22 years of the Pact's existence. The historic *Acta de Barahona* provided for the establishment of a free trade area between Venezuela, Colombia, and Bolivia on January 1, 1992. Peru and Ecuador received a six-month delay in their free trade zone participation, with both fully acceding on July 1, 1992.

Each member is permitted a list of exceptions receiving protected status (Venezuela, Colombia, and Peru, 50 products each; Bolivia and Ecuador, 100 products each), with duties phased out on January 1, 1993. See *Buenos Aires Consensus*; *Decision 313*; *Acta de Barahona*; *Free Trade Area of Americas.* Cf. *Acta de Barahona*; *Mercosur.* Synonymous with *Community of Andean Nations*; *El Pacto Andino.*

Andean Reserve Fund: see *Andean Pact.*

Andean Trade Initiative (ATI): established by the U.S. government in 1990 to parallel the Caribbean Basin Initiative of 1984 by stimulating business in the region. In addition to opening up competitive sources for U.S. imports, this initiative encourages strong demand for U.S. exports-particularly equipment, machinery, and other inputs for the productive sector—and offers attractive investment possibilities. Provides duty-free access for most products exported from the Andean countries.

Andean Trade Preference Act (ATPA): this unilateral trade benefit U.S. program is similar to the Caribbean Basin Initiative (CBI) and is designed to promote economic development through private sector initiative in the four Andean countries of Bolivia, Colombia, Ecuador, and Peru. As the trade component to President George H. W. Bush's war on drugs, one goal is to encourage alternatives to coca cultivation and production by offering broader access to the U.S. market. Another goal is to stimulate investment in nontraditional sectors and diversify the Andean countries' export base. The primary provision of the program is expanded duty-free entry into the United States granted by Congress. *ATPA* went into effect on December 4, 1991, and lasted for a period of 10 years.

In the summer of 1992, President George H. W. Bush signed proclamations making Bolivia and Colombia beneficiaries under the Andean Trade Preferences Act, thus permitting duty-free access to the U.S. market to certain goods in the Andean region for up to 10 years. Since 1997, called the Andean Community (CAN). See *Andean Community.* See *Caribbean Basin Initiative.*

ANG: the international standard code for the currency of Netherlands Antilles—the Netherlands Antillian guilder.

ANRPC: see *Association of Natural Rubber Producing Countries.*

ansvarlig selskap: a Norwegian unlimited general partnership.

anticipated bunker price: the fuel-cost freight factor stipulated in a charter party allocating the cost or benefit of fuel price increases or decreases occurring during the life of a charter party.

anti-dumping (AD): the reason(s) for seeking redress against foreign producers by alleging unfair competition in the domestic market. Claims must prove unfair pricing and/or injury to the domestic industry. See *Agreement on Anti-Dumping Practices*; *Anti-Dumping Act of 1974.*

Anti-Dumping Act of 1974: legislation designed to prevent the sale of goods at a lower price than exists in the goods' country of origin. The U.S. Treasury Department determines whether imported products are being sold at "less than fair value" in this country. Should it be determined that the domestic industry is harmed by the imports, extra duties can be imposed. See *Super 301.*

Anti-Dumping Code: see *Agreement on Implementation of Article VI.* Synonymous with *Agreement on Anti-Dumping Practices.*

anti-dumping duty: a tariff designed to prevent imports of goods for sale at a price in the importing country lower than the price in the country of origin of the goods.

anti-dumping order: see *anti-dumping duty.*

anti-globalization: see *globalization.*

antitrust laws: laws to prevent business from engaging in such practices as price fixing or market sharing.

any-quantity rate: a rate applying on a weight basis but without regard to carload minimum weights, and applicable to any quantity of freight tendered:

AOK: the international standard code for the currency of Angola— the Kwanza Angola.

APC: see *Asian and Pacific Council.*

APCC: see *Asian and Pacific Coconut Community.*

APEC (Asia-Pacific Economic Cooperation Forum): formed in November 1989, with 12 members: Australia, Brunei, Canada,

Indonesia, Japan, the Republic of Korea, Malaysia, New Zealand, the Philippines, Singapore, Thailand, and the United States. The three Chinas—the People's Republic of China, Hong Kong, and Chinese Taipei—were added later.

Collectively, they constitute the most powerful regional economies of the world, with a combined gross regional product of more than $14 trillion. The APEC members' share of world trade approaches 35 percent, or about $2.3 trillion. Members constitute the U.S.'s most important economic partners. Its goals are to sustain regional growth and development, to strengthen the multilateral trading system, and to reduce barriers to investment and trade without detriment to other economies, thus encouraging increased interaction between our Asian and Pacific economic partners and all three members of NAFTA.

APEMF: see *Association of Iron Ore Exporting Countries.*

APO: see *Asian Productivity Organization.*

apparent good order: the undamaged packaging of freight delivered to a carrier for shipment to a stated destination.

appraiser: one who determines the value of goods.

appreciation:

(1) the increase in the value of an asset in excess of its depreciable cost, due to economic and other conditions; the increase of present value over the listed book value.

(2) the increase in market value of a currency's exchange rate, a capital asset, or financial paper. Cf. *depreciation.*

appropriability theory: that companies will favor foreign direct investment over such nonequity operating forms as licensing arrangements so that potential competitors will be less likely to gain access to proprietary information.

approximation: see *harmonization.*

Arab-African International Bank (AAIB): established in 1964, and headquartered in Cairo, Egypt. Banks of varying Arab nations maintain the bank, whose function is to serve as a financial and economic link between Arab and African countries.

Arab Authority for Agricultural Investment and Development: A regional Arab organization involving 15 member countries, including five Gulf States; concerned with investment in and development of agriculture and the related fields, with the view to enhance production of foods in its member countries; headquarter in Khartoum, Sudan.

Arab Bank for Economic Development in Africa (ABEDA): headquartered in Khartoum, Sudan; founded in 1973. Its purpose is to spread Arab capital into non-Arab Africa for development projects. Synonymous with *Banque Arabe pour le Développement Économique en Afrique (BADEA)*.

Arab Common Market (ACM): a 1965 customs union between Egypt, Iraq, Sudan, Syria, the United Arab Emirates, and Yemen under the guidance of the Council of Arab Economic Unity. To reinvigorate the stalled ACM, on December 22, 2000, President Mubarek of Egypt called for an Arab Common Market or Islam Common Market. The hope is to have all 22 Arab League nations become members; remains to be implemented. Synonymous with *Arab Common Trade Market; Islamic Common Market.*

Arab Common Trade Market: Synonymous with Arab Common Market.

Arab Cooperation Council (ACC): established in 1989 by Egypt, Iraq, Jordan, and Yemen; terminated in August 1990 following Iraq's invasion of Kuwait. Formed in Baghdad with Arab nations not members of the Gulf Cooperation Council that gave aid to Iraq during its war with Iran.

Arab Fund for Economic and Social Development (AFESD): formed in 1968 to finance joint Arab programs in Arab nations that may be of general Arab interest; headquartered in Kuwait.

Arab International Bank (AIB): established in 1971, with headquarters in Cairo, Egypt. Its purpose is to assist in the financing of development and of overseas trade, particularly for member nations and other Arab countries.

Arab Investment Company: formed in 1974 as a joint stock company. Headquartered in Saudi Arabia, its functions include promoting the investment of Arab capital by undertaking investment projects itself and by operating in the financial markets.

Arab League: founded in 1945, with headquarters in Egypt. Provides for mutual support, cooperation in social and economic programs, and coordination in mutual defense. Members include Algeria, Bahrain, Djibouti, Egypt, Iraq, Jordan, Kuwait, Lebanon, Libya, Mauritania, Morocco, Oman, the Palestine Liberation Organization, Qatar, Saudia Arabia, Somalia, Sudan, Syria, Tunisia, and Yemen. Synonymous with *The League of Arab States.*

Arab Mahgreb Union (AMU): see *MCM*. Synonymous with *Mahgreb Common Market*.

Arab Monetary Fund (AMF): an international financial organization, created in 1977 and headquartered in Abu Dhabi. Twenty countries, plus the Palestine Liberation Organization, are represented. It maintains close ties to the IMF, the World Bank, and the Bank for International Settlements.

arb: short for *arbitrager*.

arbitrage: the process of buying foreign exchange, stocks, bonds, and other commodities in one market and immediately selling them in another market at slightly higher prices. The term has evolved to also describe any large-scale speculation in securities.

arbitrager (arbitrageur): an individual who engages in the activity of arbitrage. See *arbitrage*.

arbitraries: specific amount allowed for bridge or other service in the division of interline fares or rates.

arbitrary:
(1) a fixed amount that a transportation line agrees to accept in dividing joint rates.
(2) a fixed amount added to or deducted from one station to make a rate from another station.
(3) a fixed amount added to or deducted from a rate to one station to make a rate to another station.

arbitrary prorate: a division of revenue on interline traffic that bears no discernible relation to the comparative lengths of haul, services, or local rates of the participating carriers. Arbitrary divisions may also include provisions by which one carrier may receive its local rates and the other carrier receives the remainder of the through rate.

arbitration: the process whereby parties to a conflict agree to present their dispute before, and have the matter adjudged by, an independent third party that is not a court of law.

arbitration clause: a clause within the sales contract between an exporter and an importer that specifies the method under which disputes relevant to the contract in question will be settled.

Arbitration Convention: a measure approved by the Council of the European Community, now Union, on July 23, 1990. It provides for the introduction of an arbitration procedure to resolve the differences of opinion of the kind that may arise between the tax authorities of different member states when they reassess transfer prices between associated enterprises for tax purposes.

arbitration of exchange: when prices of bills of exchange payable in foreign currency vary throughout financial centers in the world. Consequently, an individual from country A may find it profitable to purchase a bill of exchange from country B for payment in still another country.

Arcru: a unit of account first used in 1974; based on the movement of 12 Arab currencies against the U.S. dollar.

Area Control List: see *Export-Import Permits Act*.

Arrangement Regarding Bovine Meat: resulting from the Tokyo Round of GATT, now WTO; with 27 member nations plus the European Community. It purports to promote liberalization of world beef trade, to discourage the use of voluntary restraint agreements, and to oversee usage of unnecessarily restrictive trade measures by producer-exporter nations. See *voluntary restraint agreements*.

arrival draft: an instrument that must be accepted on or near the date of a vessel's arrival and is usually payable without further documentation.

arrival notice: a notice, furnished to consignee, of the arrival of freight.

arrivals: imported items that are located in a bonded warehouse for which duty has not been paid.

arrived ship: a vessel that has docked and is ready for loading and unloading. In addition, the exporter or consignee must have been informed, usually in writing, of the vessel's readiness for loading and unloading.

ARS: the international standard code for the currency of Argentina—the peso Argentina.

Article Eight currency: a senior currency according to the *International Monetary Fund* that is both convertible and free of controls.

articles of mixed status: items manufactured within a free trade zone of components of more than one status (the product of several factors). Upon withdrawal of the items fabricated within a zone, the finished item is assessed duties in accordance with the status of the merchandise from which it was composed.

Artificial Currency Unit (ACU): a financial accounting unit established by international accord and based on a basket of national currencies; for example, the European Currency Unit, Special Drawing Rights. ACUs are traded among official bodies and for accounts held by major international banks. They cannot be used in private transactions.

AsDB: see *Asian Development Bank.*

ASE: see *Athens Stock Exchange.*

ASEAN: see *Association of South-East Asian Nations.*

ASEAN Free Trade Area: see *AFTA.*

as freighted: a method for calculating ocean freight surcharges indicating that those surcharges are to be set by the same method used to compute the basic freight charge. See *base freight.*

Asialease: the Asian Leasing Association, established in 1982 as a federation of the leasing firms and association that function in the Asian market. It has in excess of 40 members from 10 nations.

Asian and Pacific Coconut Community (APCC): established in 1969 to share data on increasing the efficiency of the production, processing, and research of coconut (and its byproducts) among producer member nations. It is headquartered in Jakarta, Indonesia, with India, Indonesia, Malaysia, Papua New Guinea, the Philippines, Solomon Islands, Sri Lanka, Thailand, Vanuatu, and Western Samoa as members.

Asian and Pacific Council (APC): created in 1966 by Australia, Japan, New Zealand, the Philippines, the Republic of Korea, the Republic of China, and Thailand. It purports to bring together regional members to discuss economic, social, and cultural issues.

Asian CD: any certificate of deposit issued by a bank located in Asia; usually denominated in U.S. currency.

Asian Clearing Union: a joint arrangement for settling international payments imbalance between Bangladesh, Burma, India, Iran, Nepal, Pakistan, and Sri Lanka. See *Asian Monetary Unit.*

Asian Currency Unit (ACU): the separate accounting entity by which the Asian dollar deposit market was created. The market emerged from a Bank of America proposal. See *Artificial Currency Unit.*

Asian Development Bank (ADB) (AsDB): established in 1966 to help provide development capital for Asia. Headquartered in Manila.

Asian dollars: U.S. dollar bank deposits traded outside the United

States in Asia and the Pacific Rim. See *Asian Currency Unit*. Cf. *Eurodollars*.

Asian Free Trade Area (AFTA): on October 22, 1992, economic ministers of AFTA met in Manila to discuss the creation of a trade group that would bring together 320 million consumers in one of the world's fastest growing regions. They started a round of tariff cuts on January 1, 1993, creating a free market in at least 15 industrial products over 15 years. AFTA's aim is to reduce most tariffs to a maximum of 5 percent in a series of cuts. Cement, rubber, wooden furniture, and textiles are included in its list. In November 2002, South-East Asia leaders and China met to create the world's largest trade area, encompassing 1.7 billion people (nearly 1/3 of the world's population) and trade valued in that year at $1.2 trillion. AFTA is expected to take 10 years to implement.

Asian Leasing Association: see *Asialease*.

Asian Monetary Unit: the accounting unit for the Asian Clearing Union with a value equal to the Special Drawing Rights (SDRs) issued by the IMF. See *Asian Clearing Union*.

Asian nations: see *Association of South-East Asian Nations*.

Asian Productivity Organization (APO): formed in 1971, with headquarters in Tokyo and 14 members; dedicated to increasing the productivity of industry for participating nations, and the Asian economic area.

Asian sector: that part of the globe has Japan as its nucleus but on the periphery, and coming on strong, are countries of EANIC (East Asian Newly Industrialized Countries: Hong Kong, Singapore, South Korea, and Taiwan). Standing by with high hopes are China and other neighbors.

This Asian area represents that part of the world with the greatest growth potential. Six of the world's 10 largest ports are still in Asia. Many experts believed that sometime in the next century, Asia would eclipse North America as the world's most powerful region. Some predict that in 25 years, the combined GNP of East Asia will be larger than all of Europe's and twice that of the United States. There is China's economic boom and the resilience of economic growth throughout the region. With a population 10 times that of North America and 6 times that of Europe, and with faster growth rates than either North America or Europe, Asia at some point may overtake the other two regions economically, in total output if not per-capita. Many specialists say Asia's economic output could overtake North America's as early as 2010 or as late as 2020. Cf. *American sector; European sector; Pacific Rim.*

Asia-Pacific Economic Cooperation: see *APEC.*

Asia-Pacific Economic Cooperation Forum: see *APEC.*

Asia-Pacific Economic Cooperation Group (APEC): see *Pacific Economic Cooperation Group.*

asked price:
(1) the price that is officially offered by a seller.
(2) the price at which a stock is offered for sale.

asking quote: the price at which a foreign exchange dealer is willing to sell.

ASKI system: an exchange control system under which payment for imported goods is made in marked funds usable only to purchase goods of the importing country. The term is the abbreviation of the German phrase for "foreigners' special accounts for domestic payments."

as laytime: a condition in a vessel charter agreement stipulating that time was lost to the vessel because the shipper, charterer, or consignee cannot provide a berth for the ship.

Asociación Latino-Americana de Integración: see *ALADI.*

Asociación Latino-Americano de Traficantes (ALAT): see *Latin American Association of International Trading Companies.*

ASP: see *American selling price.*

assailing thieves: in marine insurance contracts, coverage of losses due to the use of force or violence by thieves.

assembly service: a service provided by a common carrier whereby small lots of cargo for a given consignee are shipped to the carrier's terminal to be aggregated into a single shipment.

assessment: antidumping duties imposed on imported items.

asset exposure: the total of assets which will be adversely affected by a depreciation or devaluation of a currency.

assign: to transfer or make over to another party.

assigned arrangement: management arrangement in which one partner in a strategic alliance assumes primary responsibility for the operations of the alliance.

assigned siding: a sidetrack owned by a transportation line and assigned for the use of one or more firms or individuals in loading or unloading cars.

assignee: one to whom a right or property is transferred.

assignment:

(1) the transfer in writing of property title from one individual to another.

(2) the transfer in writing of the legal right in a policy to another party.

(3) the transfer of stock title.

assignor: one by whom a right or property is transferred.

assists: product components exported from the United States for insertion or inclusion in foreign-manufactured exports to the United States. A duty is levied against assists by the U.S. Customs Service on first re-importation into the United States. U.S. inputs falling into the assists category, but consisting entirely of research and design outputs, are exempted from duties.

Associated Company: in the United Kingdom, a firm in which at least 20 percent but not more than 50 percent of its controlling interest is owned by another firm. Synonymous with *Related Company.*

association agreements: a special kind of relationship between nations that goes beyond the mere regulation of trade and involves close economic cooperation and financial assistance. There can be an agreement that maintains special links between certain member nations and nonmember nations, and there can be agreements in preparation for the establishment of a customs union. Cf. *cooperation agreements.*

Association Cambiste Internationale: the international organization of foreign exchange dealers, consisting of national Forex clubs affiliated throughout the world; headquartered in Paris.

Association des Pays Exportateurs de Mineral de Fer: see *Association of Iron Ore Exporting Countries.*

Association Européenne de Libre-Échange: see *European Free Trade Association.*

Association of International Bond Dealers (AIBD): headquartered in Zurich; dealers' professional organization that recommends procedures and policies; a self-regulatory body that represents the primary and secondary Eurobond markets.

Association of Iron Ore Exporting Countries (AIOEC): established in 1975, with headquarters in Geneva; created a mechanism for collaboration by export members (Algeria, Australia, India,

Liberia, Mauritania, Peru, Sierra Leone, Sweden, and Venezuela) in the fields of exploration and processing of iron ore and to set higher and more profitable world prices. Synonymous with *Association des Pays Exportateurs de Minerai de Fer (APEMF)*.

Association of Natural Rubber Producing Countries (ANRPC): headquartered in Kuala Lumpur, Malaysia, after it was created in 1970, with India, Indonesia, Malaysia, Papua New Guinea, Singapore, Sri Lanka, and Thailand. Its purported aim is to stabilize prices and provide for fair and continuing profit for exporters of the product.

Association of South-East Asian Nations (ASEAN): an association formed in 1967 by Indonesia, Malaysia, the Philippines, Singapore, and Thailand agreeing to work together to accelerate economic growth, social progress, and cultural development, and to promote peace and stability within the area. The Sultanate of Brunei joined on January 7, 1984. In its first serious attempt at economic integration, ASEAN completed, in October 1992, recommendations to implement a free-trade agreement, which took effect January 1, 1993. It provides for preferential, gradually reduced tariffs to expand intra-ASEAN trade. See *AFTA*. See *Asian Free Trade Area*.

ASSUC: Association des Organisations Professionnelles de Commerce des Sucres pour les pays de la CEE; the Association of Sugar Trade Organizations for the EC countries.

assured: the person who has insured a shipment and has title to the goods.

astray freight:
(1) less-than-carload freight that is marked for destination and that becomes separated from the regular revenue waybill.
(2) freight that is destined for a particular location and owner but does not arrive. See *overfreight*.

astray freight waybill: a waybill used for astray freight. See *free-astray*.

Asuncion Treaty: see *Mercosur*.

ASX: see *Australian Stock Exchange*.

ATA (admission temporoire) carnet: an international customs temporary importation document that is used for exhibits for international trade fairs, samples, and professional equipment. It can be used in all European Union member nations and many other countries in the world. Since January 1, 1993, carnets are not needed for movement between EU member states. The ATA Carnet is therefore only used for temporary exports outside the European Union.

at and from: marine insurance covering a vessel in port or at sea.

at best: the instruction with a buying or selling order indicating that it should be carried out quickly at the best possible price. Synonymous with *at the market*.

ATCA: see *Agreement on Trade in Civil Aircraft*.

ATDONSHINC: anytime day or night, Sundays and holidays inclusive.

Athens Stock Exchange (ASE): primary stock exchange in Greece; based in Athens.

ATI: see *Andean Trade Initiative*.

ATO: see *African Timber Organization*.

at or better: in placing a purchase order for securities, buying at the price specified or under; in a selling request, selling at the price given or above.

ATP: see *Advanced Technology Products*.

ATPA: see *Andean Trade Preference Act*.

Atri: a customs form used to facilitate preferential rates of customs duty on EU-originating goods to be imported into Turkey.

at the market: synonymous with *at best*.

AUD: the international standard code for the currencies of Australia, Christmas Island, Cocos (Keeling) Islands, Gilbert Islands, Heard and Mcdonald Islands, Kiribati, Nauru, Norfolk Island, and Tuvalu—the Australian dollar.

au jour le jour: the rate for money lent from day to day on the French money market. Rates vary according to whether the loan is made against the security of Treasury or private bills.

Auksfuhrkredit Gmbh (AKA): an export credit firm created by a consortium of German commercial banks to provide medium- and long-term export finance.

Austral: the monetary unit of the Argentines.

Australia: See *U.S.-Australia Free Trade Agreement*.

Australian dollar: unit of currency for Australia, Kiribati, Nauro, and Tuvalu.

Australian Stock Exchange (ASX): the combined stock exchanges in Australia.

Austrian School: the milieu in which 19th-century theorists developed a theory of value and theories of interest and capital. Later analysts stressed the dangers of government intervention in the economy.

Austrian shilling: former monetary unit of Austria.

autarky: an attempt to minimize a nation's dependence on other countries by substituting national manufacturing imports of goods.

Authorité du Basin du Niger (ABN): see *NBA*.

authority to purchase: in Far Eastern trade, a substitute for a commercial letter of credit; this instrument permits a bank to which it is directed to purchase drafts drawn on an importer rather than on a bank.

authorized dealer: banks allowed by their regulating body to deal in foreign exchange.

automated clearing house (ACH): a computerized facility used by member depository institutions to process (i.e., combine, sort, and distribute) payment orders in computer-readable form.

automatic adjustment mechanism: the economic response that occurs when a balance of payments imbalance arises. When a trade deficit exists under flexible exchange rates, a currency devaluation usually occurs to stimulate exports and reduce imports. Under fixed exchange rates, domestic inflation is expected to be lower than foreign inflation, leading to relatively lower domestic prices and again increased exports and reduced imports.

automatic funds transfer: the efficient and accurate transfer of funds, often global, from one account or investment vehicle to another without direct management.

automatic standard: a monetary standard where the amount and value of money is consciously managed but is the result of the working of demand and supply for a precious metal or foreign currency that follows on differences in trading volume between nations.

Automotive Products Trade Agreement: signed in 1965 by the United States and Canada to provide both countries with the duty-free entry of new cars and original automotive machine parts. Synonymous with *Auto Pact*.

autonomous duty: a unilateral levy imposed by national law.

autonomous transactions: international transactions that take place for profit and are thereby included in the current account and capital account of a nation. They are independent of balance-of-payments considerations since they exclude unilateral transfers. See *above the line*. Cf. *accommodating transactions*.

Auto Pact: synonymous with *Automotive Products Trade Agreement*.

aval: payment of a bill of exchange or promissory note that has been endorsed by the signature of a third party (usually a bank) appearing on the bill guaranteeing that it will cover any default of payment by the buyer.

AVE: see *ad valorem equivalent*.

average agreement: document signed by the owners of cargo wherein they agree to pay to the carrier any general average contribution due so that the cargo can be released after a general average has occurred.

average bond: a bond given by an individual in receipt of freight, stating that the receipt will contribute to any standard claim.

average demurrage agreement: an agreement made between a shipper and a transportation line whereby the shipper is debited for the time cars are held for loading or unloading beyond a certain period and credited for the time cars are released by him within a certain period, demurrage charges being assessed by the transportation line, usually at the end of the month, for any outstanding debits. See *demurrage*.

average freight rate assessment: see *AFRA*.

average haul: as applied to freight, the average distance in miles one ton is carried, computed by dividing the number of ton miles by the number of tons carried.

average load: the average number of tons of freight per loaded vehicle, obtained by dividing the total number of tons by the number of vehicle loads originated.

average load per car:
(1) the average number of tons of freight per loaded car, obtained by dividing the number of tons originated by the number of carloads originated.
(2) the average number of net ton miles per loaded car-mile, the miles of all loaded freight cars being used as a divisor.

average, particular: see *particular average*.

average rate: the average foreign exchange rate over a period of time; e.g., the annual or quarterly average.

average revenue per ton mile: freight revenue divided by revenue ton miles (revenue tons multiplied by miles hauled).

average speed: in freight trains, the average distance traveled in one hour, computed by dividing the total freight-train miles by the total freight-train hour.

average weight of rail: the average weight in pounds per yard of rail.

averaging: in international securities, methods used in an attempt to improve the average price paid or received for securities by buying or selling at a variable rate as prices climb or drop.

away: U.S., for trade, quotes or markets that do not approximate current market levels.

AWB: see *air waybill*.

AWG: the international standard code for the currency of Aruba—the Aruban guilder.

B

BAA: see *Buy American Act.*

back: shortened form of backwardation. See *backwardation.*

backed note: a note authorizing a ship's master to take on water-borne items and evidence that freight charges are covered.

back freight: freight payable when delivery is not taken within a reasonable period at the discharge point; the executive in charge deals with the items at the owner's expense.

back haul: to haul a shipment back over part of a route that it has traveled.

back letter:

(1) a retroactive clarification of the terms or conditions of a charter party.

(2) a letter of indemnity issued by a shipper of cargo to a steamship firm to secure issuance of a clean bill of lading where one would not be issued otherwise.

backspread: a condition that exists when the price difference for identical items in two markets is less than the normal difference (e.g., a stock selling for $50 on the New York Stock Exchange and for the equivalent of $55 on the London Stock Exchange, the difference being due to shipping costs, insurance).

back-to-back credit:

(1) operations where a loan is made in one currency in one nation against a loan in another currency in another nation. The foreign importer provides the finance house with appropriate documents, on the strength of which a credit is opened in favor of the exporter. These can be used to back another credit for the exporter.

(2) credit opened by a bank on the strength of another credit.

back-to-back letters of credit: two letters of credit with identical documentary requirements and validity, except for a difference in the price of merchandise as shown by the invoice and the draft.

backwardation:

(1) a basic pricing system in commodity futures trading. A price structure in which the nearer deliveries of a commodity cost more than contracts that are due to mature many months in the future.

(2) on the London Stock Exchange, fees and interest due on short sales of delayed delivery securities.

backward vertical integration: establishing facilities to manufacture inputs used in the production of a firm's final products.

BACS: see *Bankers' Automated Clearing House.*

BADEA: see *Banque Arabe pour le Développement Économique en Afrique.*

BAF (bunker adjustment factor): a surcharge imposed by shipping conferences to cover bunker fuel price fluctuations.

bagged cargo: a commodity classification referring to goods that are placed in individual shipping sacks made of canvas, jute, or synthetic material.

Bahamas dollar: monetary unit of the Bahamas.

Bahrain: See *U.S.-Bahrain Free Trade Agreement.*

Bahraini dinar: monetary unit of Bahrain.

Baht: monetary unit of Thailand.

bail bond:
(1) a bond guaranteeing the appearance in court of the principal named in the bond.
(2) a bond given to a court to secure the release of an arrested ship.

bailee receipt: a document used in import financing evidencing title to goods.

bailment:
(1) a delivery of goods by one party to another, to be held according to the purpose of the delivery and to be returned or delivered when that purpose is accomplished.
(2) a transfer of possession without transfer of title.

Baker Plan: plan developed in 1985 by U.S. Treasury Secretary James Baker to solve the international debt crisis; stressed debt rescheduling, tight controls over domestic monetary and fiscal policies, and continued loans to debtor nations. Cf. *Brady Plan.*

baksheesh (bakshish): (Arab) an unethical, often illegal, gratuity, to facilitate a business arrangement. In Middle Eastern nations, it is considered appropriate and customary. See *bribery.*

balance commerciale: (French) balance of trade in merchandise.

balanced budget: a budget in which forward expenditures for a set period are matched by expected revenues for the same period.

balanced economic growth: economic expansion throughout a nation at approximately the same geometric rate for all items manufactured.

balanced economy: a condition of national finances in which imports and exports are equal.

balance des paiements courants: (French) current account of the balance of payments.

Balance for Official Financing: in the United Kingdom, includes current account balance, total investment, and other capital flows plus a balancing item for errors and omissions.

balance of concessions: see *reciprocity.*

balance of payments (BOP):
(1) a statement identifying all financial transactions of a country and its population with other nations of the world.
(2) a financial statement that compares all reported payments by residents of one country to residents of other countries with payments to domestic residents by foreign residents. If more money has been paid out than received, the BOP is in deficit. If the opposite condition exists, the BOP is in surplus. Cf. *balance of trade.*

balance of payments adjustment: the automatic response of an economy to an imbalance in a country's international transactions. If a trade deficit occurs, it usually leads to a currency devaluation and/or reduction of domestic prices relative to prices in other countries.

balance of payments consultations: the coordination between the GATT, now the WTO, and the IMF to ensure that trade and payments implications of trade restrictions imposed for balance of payments reasons are taken fully into account. Under GATT Articles XII and XVIII countries may temporarily deviate from certain GATT rules to remedy serious balance of payments problems.

balance of payments deficit: a situation in which a nation is spending more abroad than it earns abroad.

balance of payments surplus: an imbalance in the balance of payments that exists when a country exports more than it imports.

balance of trade: the difference between a country's total imports and exports; if exports exceed imports, a favorable balance of trade exists; if not, a trade deficit is said to exist. See *invisible trade balance.* Cf. *balance of payments.*

balance of trade deficit: a situation in which the value of a country's imports exceeds the value of its exports for a specific period of time.

balance on goods and services: the algebraic sum of exports and imports of goods and services. It includes merchandise trade (exports and imports of goods) and the so-called invisible items: shipping charges, income on investments, rents, royalties, payments for insurance, donations, and travel. A surplus balance on goods and services is compatible with an export of capital or an accumulation of foreign exchange reserves. On the other hand, a deficit balance on goods and services must be financed by an import of capital or a drawing down of foreign exchange reserves.

balance on goods, services, and unilateral transfer: the balance on current account that—except for errors and omissions—must be counterbalanced by capital movements, a change in official reserves, or both. All transactions involving transfers of goods and services are included in the current account, with the exception of monetary gold transactions, which are recorded as a component part of U.S. official reserve assets. The balance on goods, services, and unilateral transfers is net foreign investment by the United States.

balance on services trade: difference between a country's service exports and imports.

balboa: the monetary unit of Panama.

balcony group: a group of underwriters whose commitments are smaller than those of the major bracket underwriters, but significantly greater than those of the sub-major underwriters.

balespace: a vessel's interior capacity.

ballast: unnecessary stock used for stabilizing an ocean carrier operating below its stowage capacity.

ballast bonus: see *BB*.

balloon: a loan repayment method where the last repayment is greater than the previous repayments.

balloon freight: light, low-density, and bulky cargo.

ballooning: price manipulation used to send prices beyond safe or real values.

balloon loan: see *balloon*.

Baltic Common Market: an economic community formed after the West recognized the independence efforts of Estonia, Latvia, and Lithuania on August 27, 1991. These liberated Baltic countries took their first steps to develop a common market, modeled on the free-trade area and customs union that formed the present-day European Union. Dissolved when these nations joined the

European Union on May 1, 2004.

Baltic Exchange: headquartered in London; has the major responsibility for matching cargoes to ships, and vice versa.

Baltic Freight Index (BFI): an index based on a given number of dry cargo voyages, each weighted according to its importance in the market and historical data.

Baltic International Freight Futures Exchange Ltd.: see *BIFFEX*.

banana republics: (slang) derogatory, referring to Central American nations.

bancassurance: (French) for mergers between banks and insurers.

Banco Centroamericano de Integracion Economica: see *Central American Bank for Economic Integration*.

Banco de la Republica Oriental del Uruguay: import/export Bank of Uruguay.

Banco InterAmericano de Desarollo: see *Inter-American Development Bank*.

Banco LatinoAmerican de Exportaciones: incorporated in 1978; headquartered in Panama City, Panama. A multinational bank providing short- and medium-term years of financing; primarily for Latin American commercial banks.

Banco Nacional de Comercio Exterior: Mexico's national foreign trade bank.

Banco National de Mexico: largest private bank in Mexico.

band: under the Bretton Woods agreement, the range within which a currency is permitted to move under freely floating exchange rates. See *currency band; European Monetary System; value-added tax*.

Bangladesh Bank: the central bank of Bangladesh.

bankable charter: a charter party where the shipper is of such creditworthiness or financial status that the ship owner can use the charter contract as collateral for loans.

bank affiliate: an export trading company totally or partially owned by a banking institution as provided under the 1982 Export Trading Company Act.

bank bill: synonymous with *bank note*.

bank currency: synonymous with *bank note*.

Bank Documentary Credit Insurance (BDCI): an insurance program of the Canadian Export Development Corporation providing cover for banks that are involved in export credit financing.

banker's acceptance:
(1) a bill of exchange drawn on or accepted by a bank to pay specific bills for one of its customers when the bills become due.
(2) a negotiable time draft drawn on and accepted by a bank that adds its credit to that of an importer of items. It usually results from letters of credit in foreign trade.

Bankers' Automated Clearing House (BACS): established in 1968, the United Kingdom's system of electronic funds transfer operated by the clearing banks.

banker's bill: a bill of exchange drawn by an exporter on the importer's bank.

banker's credit: synonymous with *letter of credit*.

banker's draft:
(1) a check drawn by one bank against funds deposited to its account in another bank.
(2) in international trade, a draft payable on demand and drawn by or on behalf of the bank itself. It is regarded as cash and cannot be returned unpaid.

banker's payment: an order or draft drawn by one bank in favor of another bank.

Bank for International Settlements (BIS): an international institution founded in Basle (Basel), Switzerland, in 1930. BIS is designed to foster cooperation among world central banks, to seek opportunities for development of financial activity among governments, and to serve as an agent involving the transfer of payments.

bank guarantee: an assurance from a bank by a foreign purchaser that the bank will pay an exporter up to a given amount for items shipped if the foreign purchaser defaults.

bank letter of credit policy: enables banks to confirm letters of credit by foreign banks supporting U.S. exports.

bank note: a promissory note released by an authorized bank that is payable on demand to the bearer and can be used as cash. Such notes, as established by law, are redeemable as money and are considered to be full legal tender. Synonymous with *bank bill; bank currency*.

bank notes: the actual paper currency of a nation.

Bank of Central African States (BCAS): formed in 1955 as a regional international financial organization serving as the exclusive issuer of bank notes and coins within subscriber-member nations of Cameroon, Central African Republic, Chad, Congo, and Gabon. BCAS is headquartered in Yaoundé, Cameroon. Synonymous with *Banque des États de l' Afrique Centrale (BEAC)*.

bank post remittance: the conversion into cash or a money form of a foreign bill of exchange, and subsequent mailing of the latter to the payee.

bank rate:
(1) the rate of discount established by the national bank of a country for rediscounting of eligible paper.
(2) the rate charged by the national bank of a country on advances on specific collateral to banks.

bank release: negotiable time draft drawn on and accepted by a bank that adds its credit to that of an importer of good, thus permitting the purchaser of goods to take delivery.

bank return: a statement of a check clearinghouse.

bank swap: the purchase of a foreign currency with the forward sale of the same foreign currency on deposit at a future date coinciding with the maturity date of the deposit. Synonymous with *bankswapped deposit; currency swap; foreign-exchange swap transactions; swapped deposit.*

bank-swapped deposit: synonymous with *bank swap*.

Banque Arabe pour le Développement Économique en Afrique (BADEA): see *Arab Bank for Economic Development in Africa*.

Banque Centrale des États de l'Afrique de l'Ouest (BCEAO): bank functioning as a Central Bank authority of the West African Monetary Union, issuing common currency for its member states.

Banque d'Affaires: a French bank involved in long-term financing and in the ownership of companies, usually industrial firms.

Banque de Developpement des États de l'Afrique Centrale: see *Central African States Development Bank*.

Banque de France: the central bank of France, created by Napoleon Bonaparte in 1800.

Banque des États de l'Afrique Centrale (BEAC): see *Bank of Central African States*.

Banque Éuropeene d'Investissement: see *European Investment Bank*.

Banque Francaise du Commerce Exterieur: French government-owned agency that is the lender for officially supported export credits at preferential interest rates, providing financing for international trade.

Banque Ouest-Africaine de Developpement: see *West African Development Bank.*

Bardepot: a German regulation requiring a percentage of foreign borrowings by German residents to be deposited in cash in a non-interest-bearing account with the Bundesbank.

bareboat charter:

(1) charter of a ship without the crew. Cf. *demise charter.*

(2) a ship charter arranged for a given time period where the charterer in effect takes control of the vessel, paying all operating and voyage costs.

bargaining school theory: that the negotiated terms for foreign investors depend on how much investors and host countries need each other's assets.

barge-aboard-catamaran: in the Scandinavian nations, a system of hauling cargo. It is the practice of placing a barge preloaded with cargo aboard a catamaran, or a twin-hulled vessel, for transport to a destination point.

barratry:

(1) the action of officers or crews of a ship in willfully destroying or injuring a ship or its cargo.

(2) the practice of exciting and encouraging quarrels and lawsuits.

Barre Plan: one of the steps toward economic and monetary union within the European Community. It was presented to the Council of Ministers in February 1969 by Raymond Barre, then vice-president of the Commission. The Plan advocated that each member nation undertake to place part of its reserves at the disposal of the other members so that, should difficulties arise, any member could call on its partners for assistance up to a fixed amount. It advanced the concept that negotiations and arrangements were to be between the central banks rather than with governments. The Plan was approved by the Council of Ministers in July 1969.

barriers: see *frontier barriers; nontariff barrier; priority practices.*

barter: the direct exchange of one commodity for another without the transfer of money. Barter is an important means of trade with nations using currency that is not readily convertible.

barter agreement: an agreement between two nations providing for the exchange of given quantities or values of specified commodities.

base currency: currency against which exchange rates are usually quoted in a given nation; e.g., the sterling, the U.S. dollar.

base freight: in ocean freight pricing, the price of shipping items to be determined by weight or measurement.

Basel (Basle) Agreement of 1967: signed between Great Britain and the major nations of the West. This agreement determined the repayment of advances for funds given to the United Kingdom during its sterling crisis. The agreement is important since it represents the first time that a nation agreed to a dollar guarantee on its debt to other nations.

Basel (Basle) Convention of 1989: multilateral treaty restricting trade in hazardous waste, solid wastes, and incinerator ash; sponsored by 116 nations.

base rate: an annual interest rate on which graduated lending charges are determined by U.K. banks.

basic balance: the sum of the balance-of-payments current account plus long-term capital movements.

basic price: used in conjunction with price supports applying to fruit, vegetables, and pork. Once the average market price is below the basic, or cost of production, price, action is taken to support the market by buying in surplus output. See *intervention price*.

basing rate: a rate used only for the purpose of constructing other rates. Cf. *proportional rate*.

basis:

(1) the yield to maturity of bonds at a given price, as shown by bond tables.

(2) in calculating capital gains or losses, the value employed as the original property cost, which may or may not be the true cost.

(3) the difference between the cash price of a money market instrument that is hedged and a futures contract.

basis point: 1/100 of 1 percent, a minimal measure in finance and trade.

basis swap: see *interest rate swap*.

basket of currencies: see *Units of Account*.

basket pegger: a nation maintaining a fixed exchange rate utilizing an average of a combination of foreign currencies rather than a single currency.

Basket Units of Account: see *Units of Account*.

Basle Accord: see *Basel Agreement*.

Basle credits: the ad hoc mutual arrangements between central banks for rendering each other foreign exchange assistance.

European and certain other central bankers gather regularly at Basle for *Bank for International Settlement* meetings.

BB (ballast bonus): a lump-sum figure paid to cover a voyage in ballast, i.e., without cargo.

BBD: the international standard code for the currency of Barbados—the Barbados dollar.

BC: bulk cargo

BCAS: see *Bank of Central African States.*

BCEAO: see *Central Bank of West African States.*

BC-NET: see *Business Cooperation Network.*

BCP: see *Buyer Credit Protocol.*

BDCI: see *Bank Documentary Credit Insurance.*

BDR: see *bearer depositary receipt.*

BDT: the international standard code for the currency of Bangladesh—the taka.

BEAC: see *Bank of Central African States.*

bearer depositary receipt (BDR): a depositary receipt made out in bearer form; used to assist in the trading of foreign corporations.

bear squeeze: a strategy by central banks that know uncovered "bears"—those who seek to capitalize on a depressed market—have sold their currency "short." By temporarily bidding up the currency until the time comes for the bears to deliver the currency they had contracted to sell, the central bank forces the bears to take a loss. Cf. *short selling.*

beggar-thy-neighbor policy: an attempt to discourage imports by increasing tariffs or using other effective means. See *free trade.*

behavioral economics: an approach to economic research that uses behavioral sciences (psychology, sociology, management, and decision theories) and findings in explaining and predicting economic behavior, including that of international trade and commerce. The pioneering work can be found in the *Handbook of Behavioral Economics,* edited by B. Gilad and S. Kaish (JAI Press, 1986).

BEI (Banque Éuropeene d'Investissement): see *European Investment Bank.*

Belgian franc: former monetary unit of Belgium.

Belgium-Netherlands-Luxembourg Customs Union: see *Benelux.*

Belgo-Luxembourg Economic Union: see *BLEU.*

belt line: in exporting and importing, a railway that moves items between railways and shipping ports.

benchmarking: competitive benchmarking has been used by industry for decades. It compares the performance of products and processes with those of world leaders. Benchmarking includes (a) determining what aspects of activities need improvement; (b) tracking down a country or Free Trade Agreement (FTA) that is the world leader in performing the process, making the product, or paralleling the economy of the inquiring nation; (c) working with the other nations or FTA groups of countries, visiting with them, talking with executives, and measuring exactly how they perform as well as they do.

bends: short for "both ends." It is used when the load and discharge of a vessel are the same, or when the description is the same for both the load and discharge.

beneficial interest (owner): an individual who is not the true owner of property but who enjoys all or part of the benefits to it by reason of a trust or private arrangement.

beneficiary:

(1) the person in whose favor a letter of credit is issued or a draft is drawn.

(2) in international trade, the exporter.

beneficiary developing country: part of the U.S. Trade Act of 1974; any country or possession of a country authorized by the President to be accorded duty-free entry of merchandise into the United States.

Benelux (Belgium-Netherlands-Luxembourg Customs Union): a portmanteau word, formed from "Belgium, the Netherlands, and Luxembourg," to describe the customs union of these nations and subsequently applied to their concerted actions. A customs union between the Kingdom of Belgium and the Grand Duchy of Luxembourg was concluded at Brussels on July 25, 1921, and ratified on March 5, 1922, and the customs frontier between the two countries was abolished on May 1, 1922. The union was dissolved in 1940 but was reestablished on May 1, 1945. A customs union was signed between Belgium and Luxembourg on March 14, 1947, and then by the Netherlands. The total union became effective on January 1, 1948, known as the Benelux Economic Union. A joint tariff was adopted and import licenses were still needed. A total economic union came into practice on November 1, 1960.

Benelux Economic Union: see *Benelux*.

BERD: see *European Bank for Reconstruction and Development*.

Berlaymont: the name of the European Union's headquarters, built in the 1960s in Brussels.

Bermuda dollar: monetary currency of Bermuda.

Berne Union (Convention):

(1) an International Convention dealing with copyright, initially prepared in 1886. Literary or artistic works published in a nation that is a signatory to the Convention enjoy copyright in the territories of the other signatories.

(2) a second Union that was established in 1934, with 26 member nations, to work for "the international acceptance of sound principles of export credit and investment insurance." There are now 36 export and credit and investment insurers in the Union who work toward the maintenance of credit insurance in international trade.

berth bill of lading: a bill of lading issued by the master of a vessel belonging to a regular shipping line.

berth terms: terms under which the ship owner pays loading and discharge costs. Synonymous with *gross terms*.

best efforts offering: the public offering of a new stock where underwriters agree to use their best efforts to sell the entire issue by a given date.

best-information available: procedure of WTO when a respondent in an antidumping/countervailing duty system case either declines to offer data or provides inadequate information. The investigator then may seek other data.

BFA: see *bilateral framework agreement*.

BFI: see *Baltic Freight Index*.

BGL: the international standard code for the currency of Bulgaria— the lev.

B/H: the ports of Bordeaux /Hamburg.

BHD: the international standard code for the currency of Bahrain— the Bahraini dinar.

BIBOR: the abbreviation for Bahrain Interbank Offered Rate. See *LIBOR*.

bid:

(1) general: an offering of money in exchange for property (items, goods, etc.) put up for sale.

(2) international business: the amount a trader is willing to pay for foreign exchange.

bid-ask spread: difference between the price at which a bank is willing to buy a currency versus the price at which it will sell that currency.

bid bond: guarantee dealing with international tenders; provides fulfillment of an offer.

bid guaranty coverage: guaranties issued by the Overseas Private Investment Corporation on behalf of the U.S. exporter of merchandise and/or services in favor of a foreign government buyer.

BIF: the international standard code for the currency of Burundi—the Burundi franc.

BIFFEX (Baltic International Freight Futures Exchange Ltd.): one of several markets constituting the Baltic Futures Exchange; trades dry cargo shipping futures.

big bangers: people who advocate abrupt, sweeping moves toward a Western-style market economy. For example, those within the former Soviet bloc nations who argue for rapid adaptation of industrialized nations' methods of free trade. Cf. *gradualists.*

Big Bankers Syndicate: a Swiss bond-issuing syndicate that issues a majority of new Swiss franc bonds.

big figure: used by foreign exchange dealers to denote the first three digits of an exchange rate.

Big Security Guarantees (BSGs): a Canadian Export Development Corporation program whereby the EDG covers a bank that has financed a bid by an exporter and provides the foreign purchaser with bid security on behalf of the Canadian exporter.

bilateral agreement: an accord signed between two countries.

bilateral assistance: foreign aid provided by one country directly to another rather than channeled via an international (multilateral) agency such as the United Nations.

bilateral clearing: an international trade system designed to economize on the use of scarce foreign exchange by routing all payments through a central bank. This takes the place of routing through foreign trade banks or their equivalent that demand the nations involved exactly balance their mutual trade every year.

bilateral framework agreement (BFA): provides a mechanism for nations to consult about trade and investment issues but is not a binding commitment to eliminate trade or investment barriers. A BFA may be the first major step prior to a negotiation of a free trade accord.

Bilateral Investment Treaty: see *BIT.*

bilateralism: an international policy having as its object the achievement of particular balances of trade between two nations by means of discriminatory tariff, exchange, or other controls. The initiative is usually taken by a country having an "unfavorable" balance of trade.

bilateral payments agreement: an agreement between two countries or their central banks to channel all or specified settlements between themselves through special accounts, normally subject to a reciprocal credit margin (swing). Arrangements of this nature usually imply that the use of convertible foreign currencies or gold between the partner countries is avoided except when the credit margin is exceeded or net balances are settled.

bilateral restraint agreement: any agreement or activity involving government authorities or private participants and their counterparts in another nation to control or limit trade in specified items. See *voluntary restraint agreement.*

bilateral safeguard: see *snap-back.*

bilateral tax accord: agreement between a foreign government and the U.S. establishing the personal tax liability of a U.S. citizen assigned to a foreign nation.

bilateral trade: any transaction between two countries.

bilateral trade agreement (pact): the formal exchange agreement between two nations. See *protectionism.*

bill broker: any financial dealer in bills of exchange. In the United Kingdom, synonymous with *discount house.*

billed weight: the weight shown in a waybill and freight bill.

bill of credit: an individual's written request to a bank asking for the delivery of money to the bearer on the credit or account of the writer.

bill of exchange: an unconditional written order calling on the party to whom it is addressed to pay on demand or at a future date a sum of money to the order of a named party or to the bearer. Examples are acceptances or the commercial bank check. See *draft.* Synonymous with *documentary draft.*

bill of lading (B/L): a document that establishes the terms of a contract between a shipper and a transportation company under which freight is to be moved between specified points for a specified charge. Usually prepared by the shipper or his agent on forms issued by the carrier, it serves as a document of title, a contract of carriage, and a receipt for goods. See *air waybill; booking number; data-freight receipt; forward exchange; inland bill of lading; letter of indemnity; minimum bill of lading; ocean bill of lading; on-board bill of lading; on-deck bill of lading; optional bill of lading; order bill of lading; seabridge; short-form bill of lading; straight bill of lading; superimposed clause; through bill of lading; York-Antwerp Rules.*

bill of parcels: listing sent with a shipment that provides descriptions and prices for included items.

bill of sale: a contract for the sale of goods.

bill of sight: a temporary entry permit, authorized by a customs official, for imported items, allowing the goods to be unloaded from a carrier to permit examination by a customs agent to identify their true character.

bill of sufferance: a document given by customs authorities to coastal ships authorizing the movement of items in bond.

bill to party: party designated on a bill of lading as the one responsible for the payment of freight charges.

bimetallism: monetary system using two metals, e.g., silver and gold, to serve as backing for a nation's money supply.

Binational Dispute-Settlement Mechanism: see *Binational Dispute-Settlement Panel.*

Binational Dispute-Settlement Panel: as provided in the 1989 FTA between the United States and Canada, a five-member panel (at least two from Canada and two from the United States) to expedite the resolution of cases and disputes dealing with the trade agreement's antidumping and countervailing duty disputes. See *Binational Secretariat.*

Binational Secretariat: a permanent secretariat with offices in Washington, D.C., run by a U.S. Secretary, and another in Ottawa, run by a Canadian Secretary, as stipulated by the U.S.-Canada free-trade accord. Review procedures are made for examination of disputes. See *Binational Dispute-Settlement Panel.*

bind: a country's promise not to increase its tariff; used during trade negotiations.

binding agreement: any instrument of formal agreement between two or more countries where each nation complies with the terms and conditions of it.

bindings: a provision by GATT, now WTO, that signatories may bind tariff rates by including them in schedules appended to the

GATT. Once a duty is bound, it may not be raised beyond that bound level without compensating affected parties. See *bound rates; tariff bindings.*

binding tariff: a nation that agrees to maintain tariffs at a stated level.

Binding Tariff Classification ruling: a formal conclusion as to an item's classification of good(s) being imported to the U.S. Such rules become binding at all ports of entry unless revoked by the Customs Services.

birdyback: the shipping of containerized cargo on aircraft.

Birmingham Declaration: a declaration in response to the unpopularity of the Maastricht Treaty for Economic Union among the then 12-member European Community nations. It was formulated at a meeting held in Birmingham, England, on October 16, 1992. "The Community must develop together as twelve, on the basis of the Maastricht treaty, while respecting, as the treaty does, the interests and diversity of member states." This unusual summit meeting sought to repair damage done by the earlier financial crisis, impacting on exports and imports. Ultimately it had little impact once passage of the Maastricht Treaty took place. See *Maastricht Treaty.*

Birr: the monetary unit of Ethiopia.

BIS: see *Bank for International Settlements.*

BISNIS (Business Information Service for the Newly Independent States): a Center of the U.S. Department of Commerce; opened on June 16, 1992; serves as a clearinghouse for information on commercial and trade opportunities in Russia and the other states of the former Soviet Union.

BIT (Bilateral Investment Treaty): guarantees U.S. firms nondiscriminatory treatment in their entry and operations where firms are also guaranteed nondiscriminatory treatment with respect to activities associated with investment, such as access to public utilities at nondiscriminatory prices, the right to hire or act as an agent, and access to financial institutions; guarantees U.S. investors the right to convert overseas currencies (i.e., rubles) profit earnings to dollars and transfer them abroad; guarantees transfers for contract payments, such as debt service payments or payments for imported inputs; guarantees U.S. investors that their investments will not be expropriated by foreign governments except for a public purpose; and in the case of a dispute between an

American investor and a foreign government, the Treaty guarantees the investor access to international arbitration. See *Calvo Doctrine*.

B/L: see *bill of lading*.

black economy: that part of a country's output of goods and services which illegally escapes taxation. See *informal economy*.

black list: in international trade, a list of individuals and firms of another country with whom the domestic nation forbids commerce by its nationals.

black market: buying or selling products and commodities or engaging in exchange of foreign currencies in violation of government restrictions. Cf. *gray market*.

black money: (slang) illegal funds earned through the international drug trade.

Black Sea Economic Cooperation: a group formed by Turkey, Bulgaria, Romania, and the former Soviet Union to promote regional cooperation, in trade and other matters of mutual interest. Reinvigorated in January 1998, now eleven nations—Russia, Ukraine, Turkey, Georgia, Romania, Bulgaria, Albania, Armenia, Azerbaijan, Moldova, and Greece—to create a market of 350 million people and develop mutually advantageous economic/trade cooperation.

Black Sea Trade and Development Bank (BSTDB): an international financial institution established with the participation of 11 countries in the Black Sea region with the purpose of promoting intraregional trade, financing projects, and promoting investment in the member states.

Black Tuesday: name for economic impact of the September 11, 2001, attacks on the World Trade Towers in New York City and the Pentagon in Washington, D.C. In one week following the reopening of the stock market, the U.S. economy lost more than $1 trillion worth of investments. The Dow dropped 14.2 percent, its largest since the Great Depression.

blading: (slang) a contraction of bill of lading, used often in documents and when speaking.

blanket certificate of origin: a government document that is completed by the exporter and covers continuous shipments of items from the same exporter to the same importer, with all falling under the same customs classification, thus eliminating the need for separate documents for each identical shipment.

blanket rate:
   (1) a rate applicable from and/or to a group of points.
   (2) a special rate applicable on several different articles in a single shipment.

blanket tariff supplement: a single publication containing additions to or changes in two or more tariffs.

blanket waybill: a waybill covering two or more consignments of freight.

BLEU (Belgo-Luxembourg Economic Union): a union founded in 1921, to integrate the two diminutive economies of Belgium and Luxembourg. It includes a common currency, a common economic policy, the elimination of internal trade barriers, and the formation of a common external tariff wall. Although modified twice, to accommodate the Benelux and the European Community, BLEU still exists as Europe's most complete economic union.

block:
   (1) a bundle of checks deposited for credit with a bank, along with their relative deposit slips.
   (2) a large holding or transaction of stock, popularly considered to be 10,000 shares or more.

blockade: the act of preventing commercial exchange with a country or port, usually during wartime, by physically preventing carriers from entering a specific port or nation. Cf. *embargo.*

blocked account: financial assets that cannot be transferred into another currency or out of the country without the government's permission.

blocked currency: currency whose conversion into another foreign currency is prohibited by law.

Block Exemptions: broad categories of agreement providing exemption from the ban on restrictive trade agreements. They were identified by the European Union's Commission acting under the Council of Ministers.

block positioner: a firm that acquires stocks in blocks so as to facilitate the handling of customer orders.

blue finger: effective and profitable international trade activity resulting from all participants being directly or indirectly members of the same family. For example, the exporter works and lives in one country, while the importer, a close relative, works in another importing nation. Synonymous with *jebble.*

Blueprint for Cooperation: see *Single European Act.*

BMD: the international standard code for the currency of Bermuda—the Bermudan dollar.

BND: the international standard code for the currency of Brunei—the Brunei dollar.

boa: a system of jointly floated currencies whose exchange rates are allowed to fluctuate against each other within limits that are wider than in the snake. See *snake.*

BOB: the international standard code for the currency of Bolivia—the boliviano.

bolivar: the monetary unit of Venezuela.

boliviano: the monetary unit of Bolivia.

bolsa: (Spanish) stock exchange.

Bolsa De Commercio de Santiago: Chile's major stock exchange.

Bolsa de Madrid: see *Madrid Stock Exchange.*

Bolsa De Valores de Sao Paulo: largest of Brazil's nine stock exchanges, accounting for nearly 70 percent of all stock activity.

Bolsa Mexicana de Valores: see *Mexican Stock Exchange.*

bona fide: (Latin) in good faith.

bond:

(1) an interest-bearing certificate of debt, usually issued in series, by which the issuer obligates itself to pay the principal amount at a specified time, usually five years or more after date of issue, and to pay interest periodically, usually semi-annually.

(2) an obligation to answer for the debt of another person.

bonded:

(1) a bond posted as security that a tax or tariff will be paid on time.

(2) goods in a government-supervised storage facility where items are stored without payment of duties or taxes until they are removed.

bonded storage: synonymous with *free trade zone.*

bonded warehouse: synonymous with *free trade zone.*

bonds:

(1) **Eurobonds:** a long-term bond marketed internationally in countries other than the country of the currency in which it is denominated. This issue is not subject to national restrictions.

(2) **zero-coupon bonds:** pay no periodic interest; the total yield is obtained entirely as capital gain on the final maturity date.

(3) **dual-currency bonds:** denominated in one currency but pay interest in another currency at a fixed rate of exchange. Can also pay redemption proceeds in a currency different from the currency of denomination.

(4) **floating rate bonds:** the most commonly issued instrument, the interest coupons on which are adjusted regularly according to the level of some base interest rate plus a fixed spread.

bonus scheme: an export incentive found in some nations. Exporters can increase their earnings on a yearly basis and receive a percentage of the incremental value of annual imports. The incentive has been authorized by GATT, now WTO, if the bonus is used to supplement the cost of importing raw materials for production for the domestic market.

booking: an arrangement with a steamship company for the acceptance and carriage of freight.

booking number: the Arabic number given to a contract of affreightment to serve as an identifying reference on a bill of lading. See *bill of lading.*

book investment: the amount at which assets are recorded in the accounts of a carrier. Synonymous with *ledger value.*

book squaring: the lowering of market exposure to zero by foreign exchange brokers

book value:

(1) the amount of an asset found in the company's records, not necessarily that which it would bring in the open market.

(2) determined from a company's records by adding all assets, then deducting all debts and other liabilities, plus the liquidation price of any preferred issues. The sum arrived at is divided by the number of common shares outstanding, and the result is "book value per common share."

boom:

(1) a time when business expands and the value of commodities and securities increases.

(2) a period of rapidly rising prices and increased demand for goods and services, usually accompanied by full employment.

boomerang: an international program to minimize the practice of goods dumping, by returning such items duty free and exempt of quantity restrictions.

BOP: see *balance of payments.*

border barriers: the physical barriers encountered at borders between nations, affecting both goods and individuals. Border customs controls carry out a number of commercial functions: they make border collections of duties viable; they control the flow of farm items, allowing different price levels for the same products to exist across member nations; they check plants and animals to preserve different health levels in different nations; they check trucks for road transport licenses; and they protect the trade regimes that individual nations may have with countries that are not participants in a community or trade accord.

However one analyzes the value of border crossings and the funds collected there, such customs posts are in fact a matter of taxes. Since taxes are the primary civilian prerequisite of sovereignty, this issue has given nations their right to independence and justified their existence over and over again. Therefore, reducing and eventually eliminating customs throughout an internal market would put an end to much of this. Borders do not divide markets, they separate different nations that they protect.

border tax adjustment: a rebate of sales, value-added, or other indirect taxes paid on merchandise prior to export. Permitted by WTO.

BOT: see *Buono Ordinario Del Tesoro*.

both ends: see *bends*.

both-to-blame clause: within an ocean bill of lading, a statement addressing the responsibilities of the ship to the cargo interests in the event of a sea collision.

bottom-fishing: buying stocks in countries whose currencies are lowest against the U.S. dollar.

bottomry: a funding method employed by a carrier's owner to finance transport activities by pledging the ship as collateral.

bottomry bond: a bond used when a ship's master requires funds urgently to complete a voyage. The shipper borrows on the security of the ship and cargo with this bond. Credit is required.

bound rates: tariff rates resulting from GATT; negotiations or accession that are appended to the GATT in the form of a loose-leaf tariff schedule and are enforceable under Article II of GATT, now WTO. See *bindings*.

bounty: added payments offered by a government as an incentive for a specific industry or the export of certain items.

bourse: (French) stock exchange.

boycott: an attempt to prevent the carrying on of a business by urging people not to buy from the firm being boycotted; frequently used on the international scene for political or economic reasons; illustrated by appeals, threats, and so on, to secure redress of a grievance.

boycottage:

(1) in Europe, a commercial boycott.

(2) an agreement for the purpose of damaging the competitive interest of another country or private entity.

boycottage d'aggression: a boycott directed by a trade combination against a nonmember company.

boycottage sanction: in Western Europe, a lawful boycott directed against a member of a trade combination as a penalty for departing from the combination's rules or otherwise failing to perform.

bracket: groupings determined by underwriting amounts in a new issue or loan.

Brady Plan: plan developed in 1989 by U.S. Treasury Secretary Nicholas Brady to solve the international crisis; involves writing off a portion of the debtor nation's debt or repurchase of the debts at less than face value. Cf. *Baker Plan.*

branch: a foreign operation of a company that is not a separate entity from the parent that it owns.

branch bank: overseas banking operation of a home country bank that is not separately incorporated.

branch house: a manufacturer's location away from headquarters, used almost exclusively for purposes of stocking, selling, shipping, and servicing the company's products.

branch office: an office or department of a company at a location away from headquarters. It is a part of the company and not a separate legal entity.

BRE: the international standard code for the currency of Brazil—the cruzeiro real.

break:

(1) a discount.

(2) an unexpected drop in the price of stocks and commodities.

(3) in a Eurocredit, a clause that passes on to a borrower the risk that certain events may curtail the lender's activity or close the Eurocurrency market.

(4) any discrepancy in the accounts of brokerage houses.

break bulk:
(1) to unload and distribute a portion or all of the contents of a car.
(2) usually, cargo conventionally kept as opposed to bulk, unitized, or containerized cargo, or items that have been stripped from containers for forwarding to final destination.

break bulk point: a point at which a portion or all of the contents of a railcar are unloaded and distributed.

breaking bulk:
(1) the practice of some middlemen to take a large, economical shipment from a manufacturer and divide it into smaller units to sell for greater profit.
(2) the point when cargo is first unloaded.

break out: when a specific security climbs above a level where strong selling resistance exists, or drops below a level of strong purchasing support.

Bretton Woods: a resort in the White Mountains of New Hampshire, where the United Nations Monetary and Financial Conference convened in 1944. Those assembled agreed to establish the International Monetary Fund and the International Bank for Reconstruction and Development, also known as the World Bank. Articles of agreement were adopted by the international monetary conference of 44 nations. The fund's major responsibility is to maintain orderly currency practices in international trade, while the bank's function is to facilitate extension of long-term investments for productive purposes. Periodic meetings are held at Bretton Woods to amend the original agreement. See *International Bank for Reconstruction and Development; International Monetary Fund.*

bribery: the payment resulting in the payer receiving some right, benefit, or preference to which he or she has no legal right and that he or she would not have obtained except by paying the money. In the United States, a bribe is a criminal offense. See *baksheesh; Foreign Corrupt Practices Act of 1977.*

bridge: synonymous with *overhead traffic.*

bridge toll: a charge made for transporting traffic over a bridge.

brief: a written abstract of testimony and pleadings in a case, and commentaries thereon.

British Overseas Trade Board: composed of industry and government representatives; located within the British Department of Trade and Industry; advises the government on international trade and guides the export promotion program.

British pound: monetary unit of the United Kingdom.

broadcast system: syndicating Eurocredits whereby a bank (or banks) receives a mandate to provide the funds and then offers participation in the loan, more or less indiscriminately, to other banks, by letter or telex.

broadline global competition: the competitive strategy that implies production of a wide range of products in one or more industries with sales in many countries.

broken period: a forward foreign exchange arrangement that is not for a standard maturity period.

broken stowage: cargo space lost because of packages of uneven size.

broker:

(1) a person who prepares contracts with third parties, as with a freight broker and customs broker, on behalf of a principal.

(2) a specialist who represents buyers of property and liability insurance and deals with either agents or companies in arranging for the coverage required by the customer.

(3) a state-licensed individual who acts as a middleman in property transactions between a buyer and a seller.

brokerage:

(1) the fee or commission charged by a broker.

(2) in the United States, a brokerage firm.

brown items:

(1) in the United Kingdom, furniture.

(2) in the United States and Canada, durables.

Bruges Group: a bipartisan group of British lawmakers and prominent European economists opposed to a federal Europe formed this association to prevent the single-market impulse from being transformed into a program for political and trade centralization.

Brunei dollar: monetary unit of Brunei.

Brussels Definition of Value: a system for valuing imports to assess ad valorem duties. This approach determines customs value based on the normal price of goods, or an estimated price reached according to predetermined conditions. It was adopted in 1953 by the Convention on the Valuation of Goods for Customs Purposes and was significantly replaced by the Customs Valuation Agreement. It is not officially used in the United States.

Brussels Stock Exchange: founded in 1801; covers most stock transactions within Belgium.

Brussels Tariff Nomenclature: see *BTN*.

BSD: the international standard code for the currency of the Bahamas—the Bahamian dollar.

BSTDB: see *Black Sea Trade and Development Bank*.

BTN: the international standard code for the currency of Bhutan—the ngultrum.

BTN (Brussels Tariff Nomenclature):

(1) established in 1950, the standard classification of goods for custom tariff purposes used by the majority of nations. In 1987, the European Union's Council of Ministers adopted a new harmonized system of customs classification replacing the BTN; it has been used since then in the Union and other nations around the world. The new system also serves as the basis of the integrated Community tariff known as TARIC, which was introduced in January 1988. See *NIMEXE; TARIC*.

(2) the widely used international tariff classification system that preceded the current *Customs Cooperation Council Nomenclature*.

BTP: see *Buono Del Tesoro Poliennale*.

bucket shop:

(1) an institution engaged in securities dealings of doubtful legality.

(2) an unlicensed, dishonest business.

Buenos Aires Consensus: a 1991 agreement calling for open markets and economies among Latin American countries.

buffer stock:

(1) merchandise kept on hand to prevent a shortage resulting from an unexpected increase in demand for items.

(2) a supply of a commodity that the executive of a commodity agreement tries to accumulate and hold so that when the price of the commodity begins to rise above desirable levels, sales can be made from that stock to dampen the price rise.

BUK: the international standard code for the currency of Burma—the kyat.

bulk freight: freight not in packages or containers.

bulkhead:

(1) a partition separating one part of a ship between decks from another part.

(2) a structure to resist the pressure of earth or water.

bulk items: goods sold and delivered in loose form, such as grain.

bulk stowage: the shipment of unpackaged items.

bulldog bond: a bond denominated in sterling issued by a non-UK resident in the UK market.

bullet: a borrowing that is not to be repaid gradually but in a lump sum at the end of its term.

bullet bond: a bond, usually a Eurobond, having no early redemption, but redeemed at full maturity.

bullionism: the monetary policy of mercantilism that called for direct regulation of transactions in foreign exchange and in precious metals to maintain a favorable balance in the home country.

bunching: the accumulation and tender of railcars for loading or unloading in excess of orders or contrary to customary schedules.

Bundesbank: the central bank of Germany; established in 1875; located in Frankfurt.

bundling: where a government packages several export receivables and transfers them to a commercial bank, which in turn converts the bulk receivables into commercial paper and sells the paper on the open market.

bunds: German government bonds.

bunker adjustment factor: see *BAF.*

bunker charge: a charge for loading into the bunkers of a vessel coal used by the vessel (does not include the cost of coal).

Buono Del Tesoro Poliennale (BTP): Polyannual, i.e., medium-term, fixed-rate Italian Treasury bill with maturities of more than one year.

Buono Ordinario Del Tesoro (BOT): Italian Treasury bills with maturities of three, six, or 12 months.

burden: a ship's carrying capacity.

burden of proof: proving disputed facts at issue in a proceeding.

Bureau of Export Administration (BXA): created in 1987, an operating arm of the U.S. Department of Commerce to distinguish the function of export control from that of export promotion. See *Export-Import Permits Act.*

Bureau Veritas: see *BV.*

Burundi franc: monetary unit of Burundi.

Business Cooperation Network (BC-NET): a European Union electronic service aimed at bringing together firms from different nations in mergers and joint ventures.

business cycle: any interval embracing alternating periods of economic prosperity and depression.

Business Information Service for the Newly Independent States: see *BISNIS*.

Buy American Act (BAA): federal legislation of 1933, as amended, seting up the basic principals of a general buy-national policy. It applies to government supply and construction contracts and requires that federal agencies procure only domestically unmanufactured supplies for public use which have been mined or produced in the United States and only manufactured goods with a substantial local content of a minimum of 50 percent.

The Executive Order of 1954, as amended, expands the scope of the Act to allow procuring entities to set aside procurement for small business and firms in labor surplus areas, and to reject foreign bids either for national interest reasons or national security reasons.

Exemption from the Act is provided for public-interest reasons. The Act obligations do not apply to the procurement of goods to be used outside the United States, to goods which are not available on the domestic market, and to goods whose cost is determined to be unreasonable.

The application of the legislation may be waived in order to give a preferential or less favorable treatment for certain countries, for example on the basis of the Trade Agreements Act of 1979 in the case of Free Trade Agreements signed by the United States with Canada, Mexico, and Israel. See *buy local legislation; Exon-Florio Amendment.*

buy at best: to bid higher and higher prices without any limit until the required quantity is bought.

buy-back:

(1) a provision in a sales contract stating that the seller will repurchase the property within a specified period of time, usually for the selling price, if the purchaser is transferred from the area.

(2) a form of countertrade transaction; an agreement between the importer and exporter covering the export of particular capital items under one contract, and the agreement by the importer to pay for them with the resultant output yielded by the capital goods that the exporter will buy back or assign under a separate contract.

buyer credit: a financial arrangement under which a bank or export credit agency in the exporting country extends a loan directly to a foreign buyer or to a bank in the importing country.

Buyer Credit Protocol (BCP): an export financing facility of the Canadian Export Development Corporation, to create an incentive for foreigners to buy Canadian goods and services on credit by providing a guarantee for export loans to qualified foreign purchasers.

buying agent: see *purchasing agent.*

buy local legislation: laws that are intended to favor the purchase of domestically sourced goods
or services over imported ones, even though it has sold to another firm. See *Buy American Act.*

buy national:

(1) any discriminatory government procurement procedures or policies that offer preferential margins for national versus foreign suppliers.

(2) any discriminatory slogan, promotion, or other form of propaganda that suggests favoring domestic versus foreign items and suppliers, based on perceived or real threats from imported items, e.g., the U.S. slogan, Buy American. See *Buy American Act.*

buy quote: the foreign exchange rate at which a foreign exchange dealer is willing to purchase a currency, and therefore the price at which a vendor can sell foreign exchange to that dealer.

BV:

(1) *Bureau Veritas,* French ship classification society and inspection agency.

(2) abbreviation in the Netherlands to refer to a privately held, limited-liability firm.

BWP: the international standard code for the currency of Botswana—the pula.

BXA: see *Bureau of Export Administration.*

BZD: the international standard code for the currency of Belize—the Belize dollar.

C

C$: Canadian dollar.

CAA: see *African Groundnut Council.*

CABEI: see *Central American Bank for Economic Integration.*

cable: (slang) the dollar/sterling spot exchange rate.

cable transfer: use of a cablegram to place funds in the hands of an individual in a foreign country. Funds are deposited with a local (domestic) bank, which cables instructions to a correspondent bank abroad to make the funds available to the payee.

CABNIS (Consortia of American Business in the Newly Independent States): a U.S. Department of Commerce program designed to help U.S. firms establish a commercial presence in NIS. See *BIT.*

cabotage: an issue of considerable importance in international air-trade. Currently, U.S. airplanes can start in Santiago, continue to Caracas, and then fly on to New York or Miami. The stretch between Santiago and Caracas is cabotage, meaning that American carriers can operate in the internal market of another nation. See *double-disapproval principle.*

CACM: see *Central American Common Market.*

CACTUS: an acronym for a European Union project that tests the feasibility of developing computerized data based on import and export regulations to assist EU traders.

CAD:

(1) the international standard code for the currency of Canada—the Canadian dollar.

(2) See *cash against documents.*

CADDIA (Cooperation in the Automation of Data Documentation for Import/Export and Agriculture): the European Community's Commission pioneered an action plan, launched in 1985, that replaces paper documentation with more efficient and cost-effective electronic data interchange. This EC project is designed to establish the infrastructure and data-processing hardware that provides the EC with the information essential for the smooth functioning of the customs union and the common trade policies. See *Harmonized System; Single Customs Document.*

CAEU: see *Council of Arab Economic Unity.*

CAF:
(1) see *cost and freight.*
(2) see *currency adjustment factor.*

Cairns Group: composed of 14 farm exporting nations: Australia, Argentina, Brazil, Canada, Chile, Colombia, Fiji, Hungary, Indonesia, Malaysia, New Zealand, the Philippines, Thailand, and Uruguay. It has been a forceful leader in the Uruguay rounds of the GATT, now WTO. See *General Agreement on Tariffs and Trade; World Trade Organization.*

Cairo Middle East/North Africa Economic Conference: held in Cairo, Egypt, November 12–14, 1996. President Mubarak urged that regional cooperation does not revolve around Israel, that there was plenty of room for consolidating inter-Arab ties and Arab relations with other countries. Cf. *Amman Middle East/North Africa Economic Summit; Casablanca Middle East/North Africa Economic Summit; Doha Middle East/North Africa Economic Conference.*

Caisse Centrale de Cooperation Economique (CCCE): within the French Ministry of Cooperation and Development; provides assistance and cooperation in developing nations. Established in 1941; headquartered in Paris.

calendar: the dates of forthcoming issues of securities.

calendar day period: see *fast track authority.*

calendar spreading: the simultaneous purchase and sale of options within the same class having different expiration dates.

call:
(1) to demand payment of a loan secured by collateral because of failure by a borrower to comply with the terms of the loan.
(2) to demand payment of an installment of the price of bonds or stocks that have been subscribed.
(3) the right to redeem outstanding bonds prior to their scheduled maturity.

callable capital: that portion of a company's capital not paid up and on which the firm's directors can call for payments to be made.

call money:
(1) currency lent by banks, usually to stockbrokers, for which payment can be demanded at any time.
(2) interest-bearing deposits repayable at call, on demand. Includes both domestic money market and Euromarket funds. Synonymous with *day-to-day money.*

call option: an option contract that entitles the purchaser to buy a fixed amount of foreign exchange at a fixed price in the future.

call price: the price at which a callable bond is redeemable; used in connection with preferred stocks and debt securities having a fixed claim. It is the price that an insured must pay to voluntarily retire such securities. Often the call price exceeds the par or liquidating price in order to compensate the holder of the called security for his or her loss of income and investment position resulting from the call.

call protection: convertibles issued in recent years offering protection of two to three years. After that, the company can force conversion of the bonds into stock. It usually does so when the convertible trades at 25 to 30 percent above its call price. While the protection is in place, though, the convertible's price has unlimited potential and will continue to trade at a premium over the conversion value. If a bond is called, the investors run the risk of losing some accrued interest.

Calvo Doctrine: a Latin American tradition that favors the adjudication of instances of confiscation and other investment disagreements in the local country's courts rather than under international arbitration. Retaining such a posture tends to discourage new investment in the country supporting this Doctrine. Some South American countries have and are quickly moving to renounce this Doctrine. See *BIT*.

cambism: engaging in the sale of foreign monies.

cambist:

(1) an individual who buys and sells foreign currencies.

(2) a handbook in which foreign currencies are converted into currency tables of the country for which the handbook is issued.

cambistry: the study of exchange of foreign currencies, with emphasis on identifying the least expensive procedure for remitting to a foreign nation.

CAN: see *Andean Community*.

Canada: see *Canada Free Trade Agreement; North American Free Trade Agreement*.

Canada Account: as provided under the Canadian Export Development Act, legislation allowing the extension of export credits and export insurance to nations commercially rejected by the Canadian Export Development Corporation. Synonymous with *Government Account*.

Canada Export Awards: a 1983 program aimed at promoting international trade by communicating with Canadian exporters how their government can be of assistance in their efforts to market overseas.

Canada Free Trade Agreement (CFTA): in early November 1988, Canadian voting citizens were in the midst of the most rancorous general election in their 121-year history. Advocates of a free trade accord saw a continental marketplace of 267 million people in which Canadian and American entrepreneurs would be equal competitors. The United States and Canada are the world's largest trading partners, and each country has invested far more in each other than in any other country in the world.

A free trade agreement took effect on January 1, 1989. The agreement was expected to reduce both countries' cost of doing business, increasing their productivity and competitiveness, at the same time reducing inflation, creating more jobs, and, in general, strengthening their economies.

Canada would get increased access to a market ten times its size. In return, Canada would make bigger tariff cuts because its tariffs were three to four times higher than those of the United States. In addition to being the world's largest trading partners, the United States and Canada are each other's largest investment partners.

All tariffs, which are the most obvious form of trade restriction, were to be eliminated incrementally by 1998. Other types of agricultural trade restrictions to be eliminated included import licenses, technical barriers such as package and labeling standards, and regulations that cannot be justified from a food safety or phytosanitary perspective. Those changes were to boost U.S. exports of fruits, vegetables, wines, and wood products, as well as improve prospects for increased exports of grain and oilseed products.

CFTA was dissolved when Canada became a formal partner to NAFTA on December 17, 1992. See *NAFTA; North American Secretariats; Trade Commission (Canada Free Trade Agreement).* Synonymous with *Canada-U.S. Free Trade Agreement.*

Canada-Israel Free Trade Agreement: signed in the fall 1996 and implemented in January 1997.

Canada-U.S. Free Trade Agreement: synonymous with *Canada Free Trade Agreement.*

Canadian bill: Canadian Treasury bills denominated in U.S. dollars.

Canadian Export Association: based in Ottawa, a private association, created in 1943, to represent and encourage exports of Canadian companies.

Canadian International Development Agency (CIDA): an official government agency formed in 1968 to provide loans and grants throughout the world. In part, modeled after the U.S. International Development Cooperation Agency.

Canadian International Trade Tribunal (CITT): a Canadian governmental unit that was given its powers by the Special Import Measures Act. It is responsible for issues of dumping and countervailing duties, providing its capital, Ottawa, with findings that may impact on Canada's import policy. Its functions are similar to the U.S. International Trade Commission.

canceling: the date a ship owner and charterer agree a vessel must be prepared to load at latest or the charter may be canceled.

canceling date: see *canceling.*

CAP: see *Common Agricultural Policy.*

cap: a limit on the upward movement of an interest rate.

capacity:

(1) the volume of space within a container or other space, expressed in units.

(2) the amount of cargo that can be handled by a freight car, truck, or other carrier.

(3) competency or legal authority.

cape-sized ships: bulk carriers and combos of about 100,000 to 150,000 deadweight.

capital: the amount invested in a venture; a long-term debt plus owners' equity; the net assets of a firm, partnership, and so on, including the original investment, plus all gains and profits.

capital account:

(1) an account maintained in the name of the owner or owners of a business and indicating the equity in that business usually at the close of the last accounting period.

(2) balance of payment items not included in a current account, including investment and deposit monies, aid, and military expenditure.

capital account balance: foreign government and private investment in the U.S., netted against similar U.S. investment in foreign countries.

capital controls: restrictions interfering with the movement of international capital, including tariffs, duties, quotas, etc.

capital exports: the outflow of monies from a capital account; i.e., those items not included in a nation's current account balance of payments, including investment and deposit funds, aid, and military expenditure. If these exports are significant over a short time period, they are referred to as capital flight.

capital flight: see *capital exports.*

capital inflow:

(1) increase in a nation's foreign assets located in that country.

(2) reduction in a nation's assets outside the country.

capital intensive: processes that require a high concentration of capital relative to labor per unit of output and products produced by such processes.

capitalism:

(1) an economic system under which the means of production are owned and controlled by the private sector of the population, with a minimum of government involvement.

(2) an economic system based on freedoms of ownership, production, exchange, acquisition, work, movement, and open competition.

capitalize:

(1) to include in an investment account expenditures for purchase or construction of property, or for organization.

(2) to issue securities to represent such investment.

(3) to divide income by a rate of interest to obtain principal.

capital lease: synonymous with *export finance lease.*

capital movements: the shifts in indebtedness and in gold stocks serving as balancing items when determining the international payments of a nation.

Capital Movements Code: synonymous with *Code of Liberalization of Capital Movements.*

capital outflow:

(1) the decrease in a country's foreign assets held in the country.

(2) the increase in a country's assets held outside the country.

capital risk: a risk created when a bank has to pay out funds to a counterpart in a deal without knowing whether the counterpart is able to meet its side of the bargain.

capital stock:

(1) amounts contributed or to be contributed for the prosecution

of the business and benefit of creditors represented by certificates or receipts, with or without par value.

(2) the total of transferable interests of the owners of a corporation.

captain's protest: a document prepared by the captain of a vessel on arriving at port, showing conditions encountered during the voyage, generally for purpose of relieving the ship owner of any loss to the cargo, thus requiring cargo owners to look to the insurance company for reimbursement.

CARDIS (Cargo Data Interchange System): an electronic system to facilitate the exchange of trade information by substituting computer printouts for paper documents.

caretaker: a person accompanying a shipment requiring special attention while en route.

cargo: the lading of a vessel, car, or vehicle. Synonymous with *freight*.

cargo broker: a broker representing the charterer in finding a ship to hire.

Cargo Data Interchange System: see *CARDIS*.

cargo manifest: list of a ship's items or passengers and without any list of charges.

cargo preference: a policy by which a nation gives its own vessels priority in the ocean carriage of its exports and imports before permitting ships of other nations a share. An agreement to share cargo, normally made with a liner conference, is referred to as cargo sharing.

cargo selectivity system: within the U.S. Custom Service, an automated commercial system; identifies the particular type of screening, either general or intensive, for imported merchandise. Has been upgraded since the September 11, 2001, attacks in the U.S.

cargo sharing: see *cargo preference*.

cargo tonnage: the weight ton in the United States is 2,000 or 2,240 pounds; in British countries, it is the English long or gross ton of 2,240 pounds. In France and other countries having the metric system, the weight ton is 2,204.62 pounds (1,000 kg). The measurement ton is usually 40 cubic feet, but in some instances, a larger number of cubic feet is taken as a weight ton. Cf. *volume of freight; weight/measure; gross tonnage*.

Caribbean Basin: composed of islands in the Atlantic Ocean; with a population of approximately 30 million. See *Caribbean Basin Initiative.*

Caribbean Basin Economic Recovery Act (CBERA): U.S. government legislation of 1983 to provide nonreciprocal tariff preferences, i.e., duty-free entry, to developing nations in the Caribbean Basin. Terminated on September 30, 1995.

Caribbean Basin Initiative (CBI): the U.S. government established the CBI in 1984 to stimulate business in the Caribbean, to open up competitive sources for U.S. importers, and to stimulate strong demand for U.S. exports.

CBI provides duty-free access for most CBI exports to the United States in an effort to encourage economic development in Central America and the Caribbean. Major goals of the CBI are: (a) to provide a stimulus for private investment, particularly in nontraditional sectors, with the aim of diversifying the beneficiary countries' economic base; and (b) to encourage host country governments to adopt reforms conducive to business and general market liberalization.

The main features of the CBI include: (a) duty-free entry to the United States for a broad range of eligible products from CBI beneficiary countries, excluding most textiles and apparel, canned tuna, petroleum, most footwear, and certain watches and watch parts from former communist countries. Leather flat goods produced in CBI nations receive a lower than normal duty rate, but are not duty free; (b) to qualify for duty-free entry, eligible products must be substantially transformed in the CBI beneficiary country(ies) and have a minimum of 35 percent value added in that country(ies). Up to 15 percent of this 35 percent value added can be made up of U.S. components; (c) duty free treatment for products, excluding textiles and apparel, assembled in the CBI beneficiary countries from 100 percent U.S. components, without regard for substantial transformation of value-added criteria.

Since the establishment of the CBI, nontraditional exports from the CBI nations to the United States surged, led by apparel, frozen shrimp and lobster, jewelry, medical instruments, pineapple, melon, electronic apparatus, frozen vegetables, and sports equipment. See *Guaranteed Access Level program.*

Caribbean-Canadian Economic Trade Development Program (CARIBCAN): a multilateral Canadian program of 1986 granting preferential, one-way, duty-free entry of goods to Canada from Caribbean nations that were former British colonies.

Caribbean Common Market (CARICOM): CARICOM was established in 1973 to form a common market for trade and to promote other forms of economic cooperation among its member states. It is composed of 13 English-speaking countries: Antigua/Barbuda, the Bahamas, Barbados, Belize, Dominica, Grenada, Guyana, Jamaica, Monserrat, St. Kitts-Nevis, St. Lucia, St. Vincent-the Grenadines, and Trinidad and Tobago. Although Bahamas is a member of the organization, it is not a signatory to CARICOM trade agreements.

CARICOM's common external tariff has been adopted by all member states except Monserrat, St. Kitts-Nevis, St. Lucia, and Antigua/Barbuda. The CARICOM common external tariff ranges from 5 to 45 percent. CARICOM also seeks to complete its mission to eliminate all barriers to intraregional trade.

These nations have a combined population of only 5.5 million. As a model for use in NAC negotiations, the United States and CARICOM signed a Trade and Investment Framework Agreement in July 1991. The first meeting of the bilateral Trade and Investment Council established by the framework agreement was held on April 2, 1992.

Trade links between South America and the English-speaking nations of the Caribbean were also strengthened. For example, effective January 1, 1993, under an accord between the Caribbean Community and Venezuela, some CARICOM exports entered the country duty free, with tariffs declining gradually over five years. In return, Venezuelan exports received Caricom's most favorable terms.

At its October 1992 meeting, heads of government of member countries committed to phase down the common external tariff (CET) from the current maximum rate of 45 percent to 20 percent over five years, ending January 1, 1998. The scheduled phase-down allowed for some individual country discretion, and certain products, particularly luxury goods. Agricultural products are subject to a 5 percent surcharge.

The first reduction to a maximum CET of 30 to 35 percent was implemented on January 1, 1993, by Jamaica, Trinidad and Tobago, Barbados, Guyana, Dominica, Granada, and St. Vincent and the

Grenadines. The nations of Antigua and Barbuda, Monserrat, St. Kitts-Nevis, and St. Lucia, which previously had not joined the CET, agreed to participate beginning with a 35 percent maximum tariff on June 30, 1993. Belize was authorized to delay implementation of the reduced CET for two years at all stages.

Caribbean Development Bank (CDB): created in 1970, with headquarters in Barbados, to finance economic development and integration in the Caribbean.

Caribbean Free Trade Association (CARIFTA): a predecessor to the Caribbean Common Market; formed in 1968 with 12 members to aid in the development of the region's economy. See *Caribbean Common Market.*

Caribbean Group for Cooperation in Economic Development (CGCED): the regional planning unit of the Caribbean Common Market.

CARIBCAN: see *Caribbean-Canadian Economic Trade Development Program.*

CARICOM: see *Caribbean Common Market.*

CARIFTA: see *Caribbean Free Trade Association.*

carload:
(1) in rail shipments, the quantity of freight required for the application of a carload rate.
(2) a car loaded to its carrying capacity.

carload minimum weight: the least weight at which a shipment is handled at a carload rate.

carload rate: a rate applicable to a carload quantity of goods.

carnet: a document of international customs that permits temporary duty-free importation of specific items into certain nations. See *admission temporoire; covered under carnet.*

carriage and insurance paid to (CIP): a term of sale, identifying that carriage and insurance is paid to the named place of destination; applies in lieu of cost, insurance, and freight for shipment by means other than water.

carriage character: the charge made by a carrier of freight for carrying items from one place to another.

carrier: in transportation, an individual or organization, usually without a permit of public franchise, that is engaged in transporting products or people. Cf. *common carrier.*

carrier's certificate: a document from a steamship company, airline, or other mode of transportation carrying imported merchandise, certifying to the customs authorities that the party named is the proper and legitimate recipient of the items and is authorized to effect clearance through customs.

carrier's lien: right of a carrier to retain property that it has transported as security for the collection charges. Cf. *stoppage in transit*.

carry:

(1) to enter or post.

(2) the interest cost of financing the holding of securities.

(3) the act of a broker in providing money to customers who trade by margin accounts; to hold stocks.

cartage: the charge made for hauling freight on carts, drays, or trucks.

Cartagena Agreement: see *Andean Pact*.

cartage to shipside: the charge made for carting, draying, or trucking freight to alongside a vessel.

cartel: a group of separate business organizations or nations that have agreed to institute approaches to alter competition by influencing prices, production, or marketing. A cartel is rarely as effective as a monopoly.

carting: the hauling of freight on carts, drays, or trucks.

carting to shipside: the carting, draying, or trucking of freight to alongside a vessel.

Casablanca Middle East/North Africa Economic Summit: held in Casablanca from October 30 to November 1, 1994. An historic event, as it brought citizens and leaders from the Arab world together with Israeli counterparts. A Middle East Development Bank was proposed (never fulfilled). Cf. *Amman Middle East/North Africa Economic Summit; Cairo Middle East/North Africa Economic Conference; Doha Middle East/North Africa Economic Conference*.

case of need: instructions given by an exporter when drawing a bill on a foreign importer; e.g., "Refer to XYZ Co. in case of need." "XYZ Co." is usually an agent or subsidiary, with power to act, or may serve merely as a source of advice. Should something go wrong, the bank collecting the bill proceeds to contact the agent.

cash against documents (CAD): payment for goods on presentation of documents evidencing shipments.

cash before delivery (CBD): a requirement to pay prior to delivery of goods. Cf. *cash on delivery*.

cash delivery: same-day delivery of traded securities.

cash in advance (CIA): payment for goods in which the price is paid in full before shipment is made. This method is usually used only for small purchases or when the goods are built to order.

Cash Management Bill: U.S. Treasury bills introduced in 1975 to raise funds quickly for a short period; ranging from nine to 20 days to maturity, with notice of their offering given up to 10 days ahead. All payments must be made in federal funds.

cash on delivery (COD): any purchase made with the expectation that the item(s) will be paid for on delivery. Cf. *collection on delivery; franco delivery.*

cash payment: the portion of the contract price on medium- and long-term credits that the foreign purchaser pays the U.S. exporter on or before delivery of the goods or services. The minimum cash payment is 15 percent of the contract price.

cash position:
(1) the percentage of cash to the total net assets; the net amount after the deduction of current liabilities.
(2) for a trade of foreign exchange, indicates whether the trader has cash on hand for immediate use.

cash ratio:
(1) the ratio of cash and related assets to liabilities.
(2) in Great Britain, deposits required by the Bank of England.

cash with order (CWO): payment for goods in which the buyer pays when ordering and in which the transaction is binding on both parties.

Cassis de Dijon Case: a 1979 European Community precedent-setting case that developed from difficulties by a German firm wishing to import Cassis liqueur into West Germany. Cassis is a low-proof black-currant liqueur that failed to meet the requirements of German law that only drinks containing at least 32 percent alcohol by volume could be sold as liqueurs. The European Court of Justice concluded that an importing Community country cannot justify prohibiting the sale of a product from another Community nation simply on the ground that the way it applies regulations affecting consumer protection is different from that imposed on a domestic product. The Commission believed that the idea of the Euro-product (e.g., Euro-beer, Euro-loaf) was negated. No longer can member states keep out competing products from another member state because they are slightly different from their own. Decision impacts significantly on the exporting and importing of goods throughout the European Union. See *mutual recognition; nontariff barrier.*

casus major: significant casualty, most often accidental, by an Act of God, a ship or plane crash.

CBD: see *cash before delivery.* In the United States and Canada, synonymous with *payment in advance.*

CBERA: see *Caribbean Basin Economic Recovery Act.*

CBI: see *Caribbean Basin Initiative.*

CBLC: see *Lake Chad Basin Commission.*

CBWAS: see *Central Bank of West African States.*

CCC:
(1) see *Commodity Credit Corporation.*
(2) see *Customs Cooperation Council.*

CCCE: see *Caisse Centrale de Cooperation Economique.*

CCCN: see *Customs Cooperation Council Nomenclature.*

CCT:
(1) see *Certificato Di Credito Del Tesoro.*
(2) see *Common Customs Tariff.*

CCTH: see *Council of Canadian Trading Houses.*

CDA: see *Cuban Democracy Act.*

CDB: see *Caribbean Development Bank.*

CEAO (Communauté Économique de l'Afrique de l'Ouest): see *West African Economic Community.*

CECA (Communauté Européenne du Charbon et de l'Acier): see *European Coal and Steel Community.*

ceding company: the original insurance company that has accepted the risk cedes part of that risk to a reinsurer.

CEFCO (Cooperative Export Financing Corporation): a U.S. plan for a co-op to borrow money cheaply, usually by using tax breaks or by obtaining funds in low-interest money markets abroad and then relending it to foreign buyers of U.S. exports.

CEM: see *combination export manager.*

CE mark: a method of the European Union to create a system for marking goods. In this approach to industrial standards, member states of the European Union agreed on a number of governing principles for the CE mark—the mark that indicates a product's compliance with EU technical regulations. The CE stamp, important to exporters, signifies a product's conformity to EU rules on technical harmonization.

CEN (Comité Européen de Normalisation): see *European Committee for Standardization.*

CENELEC (Comité Européen de Normalisation Electrotechnique): see *European Commission for Electrotechnical Standardization.*

Central African Customs and Economic Union: created in 1966 to encourage the establishment of a Central African Common Market, with a common external tariff.

Central African States Development Bank: created in 1974; headquartered in Brazzaville, Congo; provides loans for economic development and supports cross-border projects.

Central American Bank for Economic Integration (CABEI): an autonomous body intended to serve as the primary central financial institution of the *Central American Common Market.*

Central American Clearing House: created in 1961 to establish a multilateral mechanism for clearing international payments between the Central American central banks.

Central American Common Market (CACM): founded when Guatemala, Honduras, Nicaragua, and El Salvador signed the General Treaty of Central American Economic Integration on December 13, 1960, with Costa Rica joining in 1962. This Treaty established a number of measures aimed at an eventual economic union, namely a common customs tariff (in 1988, more than 90 percent complete), a degree of unity in productive investments, and the coordination of economic policies and monetary schemes. Synonymous with *Mercado Común Centroamericano.*

Central American Free Trade Agreement: See *U.S.-Central America Free Trade Agreement.*

central bank: a "banker's bank." This bank holding institution is the main body of bank reserves of a nation and the prime reservoir of credit (e.g., Bank of England, Bank of France). A central bank will effect monetary policy, regulate not just banking but a whole range of financial services and markets, encourage economic innovation and legal infrastructure, and possess proper links with other global financial centers.

Central Bank of West African States (CBWAS): headquartered in Dakar, Senegal, a financial institution, becoming operational in 1962, that serves as the only issuer of notes and coins (CFA franc) for members of the West African Monetary Union (WAMU). Participating nations are Benin, Côte d'Ivoire, Niger, Senegal,

Togo, and Burkina Faso. See *CFA franc.* Synonymous with *Banque Centrale des États de l'Afrique de l'Ouest (BCEAO).*

central bank swaps: exchanges of currencies between central banks of different nations providing transferable currency to member nations that enable them to protect their own rates of inter-and extra-community exchange. Synonymous with *swap arrangements.*

Central European nations: at one time called Eastern Europe, composed of former Soviet bloc nations of Bulgaria, Czechoslovakia, Hungary, Poland, Romania, and Yugoslavia. By January 1991, Central Europe accounted for only 7 percent of the European Community's total trade, but this should increase rapidly. Effective April 2004, most of the Central European nations will be joining the European Union as full members.

central exchange rate:

(1) exchange rate established between two European currencies through the European Monetary System arrangement.

(2) the exchange rate between two currencies is allowed to move within bands around that central exchange rate.

Central Government Borrowing Requirement: see *CGBR.*

centralization: the situation in which decision making is done at the home office rather than at the country level.

centralized cash depository: entity controlled by a parent corporation that coordinates worldwide cash flows of its subsidiaries and pools their cash reserves.

centrally planned economy: governments plan and direct almost all economic activity and usually own the factors of production.

centrally planned markets: markets in which there is almost no free market activity and the government owns all major factors of production, controls labor, and tries to plan all activity.

central rate: a currency rate established under a temporary regime (based on an International Monetary Fund executive board decision of December 18, 1974) by a country that temporarily does not maintain rates based on a par value in accordance with the relevant fund rules but does maintain transactions in its territories. Central rates are in certain respects treated as par values; the concept was introduced primarily so that fund members (who, prior to August 15, 1971, had an effective par value) could base their exchange rates on a stable rate subject to specified margin requirements during the period when the par value of the U.S. dollar was not effective. Since the change in the par value of the U.S. dollar in 1974, a number of countries have replaced their central rates with new par values.

central reserve assets: Gold, SDRs, ECUs, or hard foreign currencies held in a nation's treasury.

CEPGL: see *Economic Community of Great Lakes Countries.*

certain: (French) indirect quotation.

certificate: any written or printed document of truth that can be used as proof of a fact.

certificate of analysis: a document required by an importer or governmental authority, attesting to the quality or purity of commodities purchased overseas.

certificate of health: a document completed by exporters of goods to ensure the importing nation that the items exported meet established standards of safety, purity, or cleanliness.

certificate of inspection: a document certifying that merchandise (such as perishable goods) was in good condition immediately prior to its shipment.

certificate of manufacture: in foreign trade, a statement signed by an exporter that goods ordered by the importer have been finished and set aside for shipment. This document is used with a letter of credit for the benefit of the exporter.

certificate of origin: a certificate declaring that goods purchased from a foreign country have indeed been produced in that country and not in another. Under U.S./Canada/Mexico free-trade accords, traders are required to submit duly completed certificates of origin to their international counterparts to claim full or partial exemption from customs duties.

certificate of product origin: see *certificate of origin.*

certificate of public convenience and necessity: a document issued to a common carrier by an appropriate regulatory agency authorizing the carrier to haul specified cargoes between designated points under established rates.

Certificate of Review: a legal document issued by the U.S. Department of Commerce that grants immunity from state and federal antitrust prosecution to export trading firms.

certificate of weight: an authoritative statement of the weight of a shipment.

certification: an administrative task that awards a product a certificate if it satisfies special tests. See *conformance testing; standards.*

Certificato Di Credito Del Tesoro (CCT): a long-term variable-interest-rate credit certificate issued by the Italian Treasury.

certified trade mission: trade mission organized by government agencies, trade associations, chambers of commerce, etc., to provide export-import opportunities and interfacing with potential partners.

CES: see *Comprehensive Export Schedule.*

cession of goods: the surrender of merchandise.

CET (Common External Tariff): see *Common Customs Tariff.*

CEUCA: see *Customs and Economic Union of Central Africa.*

C&F: see *cost and freight.*

CFA franc (Communauté Financiere Africaine franc): monetary unit used primarily in former French Central and West African colonies; having a fixed parity against the French franc. See *Central Bank of West African States; franc zone.*

CFC: see *controlled foreign corporation.*

C&F FO: see *cost and freight, free out.*

CFI: see *Court of First Instance.*

CFP Franc (French Pacific Community franc): monetary unit used in departments and overseas territories in the Pacific. Exchangeable with the *CFA franc.*

CFS: container freight station.

CFTA (Canada-U.S. Free Trade Agreement): see *Canada Free Trade Agreement.*

CFZ: see *Colón Free Zone.*

CGBR (Central Government Borrowing Requirement): the difference in the United Kingdom between the government's expenditure and revenue, excluding the local authority sector.

CGCED: see *Caribbean Group for Cooperation in Economic Development.*

CGRT: see *compensated gross registered tonnage.*

chaebol: Korean for giant group; the Korean system of vertical business integration that unites a group of manufacturers, suppliers, and distributors into a single unit. According to Western nations, chaebol restrains competition. Cf. *Keiretsu.*

chamber of commerce: traditionally, a national trade-promoting organization serving its members with information and reports on increasing international trade.

Chancellor of the Exchequer: the official in the United Kingdom in charge of the receipts and payments of the government. A function similar to the Secretary of the Treasury in the United States.

channel manager: the international marketing manager who attempts to minimize price increases in a competitive market environment.

CHAPS: see *Clearing House Automated Payments Systems*.

chargeable weight: weight of a shipment used for determining freight charges.

charges forward: charges involved with exporting merchandise into a country; includes trade commission, brokerage fees, legal costs and fees, and pilotage dues and charges.

charter: see *chartered ship*.

chartered ship: a ship leased by its owner or agent for a stated time, voyage, or voyages.

charterer's liability: the legal liability assumed by the charterer of a ship.

charter hire: the freight paid by the charterer of a ship to the ship's owner.

chartering agent: a specialized broker involved in securing cargo space on ships.

Charter of Paris: signed on November 21, 1990, by the leaders of 34 countries; marked the final denouement of World War II and the end of the Cold War.

charter party: a written contract, usually on a special form, between the owner of a vessel and a charterer who rents use of the vessel or of a part of its freight space. The contract generally includes the freight rates and the ports involved in the transportation.

charter party assignment: the legal agreement that assigns the monies the ship owner receives from the charterer to a bank as security for a loan to the owner, often for the construction of a ship.

checker: the worker designated by an ocean carrier line to inspect shipments and issue receipts for freight delivered to a port for export.

check rate: the basic rate for foreign exchange trades, used to calculate all other rates. Synonymous with *demand rate*.

cheese war: the European Community, bowing to U.S. Administration requests, temporarily suspended export refunds on two U.S.-bound cheeses April 23, 1975. The suspensions, on Gruyere and Emmenthal, were the last in a complex series requested by the United States following the Commission's February 5 reintroduction of export refunds on certain cheeses destined for U.S. markets. The refunds had earlier been suspended in July 1974 after a U.S. complaint that EC export refunds had caused a large loss in U.S. domestic cheese sales. See *restitution payments.*

cheque: chiefly British variation of "check," used in Canada and other countries where French or English is spoken.

CHF: the international standard code for the currencies of Liechtenstein and Switzerland—the Swiss franc.

Chicago Board of Trade: the world's largest grain exchange where spot or futures contracts are completed in a host of agricultural products.

Chile: see *U.S.-Chile Free Trade Agreement.*

Chilean peso: monetary unit of Chile.

China trade: after Mao Zedong's death in 1976, Deng Xiaoping took charge in 1978 and began a series of structural reforms that liberalized the economy. By 2003, China's population was 1.31 billion (22% of the world's population), with 36% living in urban areas and 64% in rural locations. China's economy has grown 8% per year, doubling every decade with exports doubling every five years. In 2003, Asia and Europe make up 83% of China's total imports, with 9% from North America. Asia, Europe, and North America received 93% of China's total exports.

CHIPS: see *Clearing House Interbank Payment Systems.*

CHOPT: charterer's option.

CI: see *Consortium Insurance.*

CIA: see *cash in advance.*

CIDA: see *Canadian International Development Agency.*

CIF: see *cost, insurance, and freight.*

CIP: see *carriage and insurance paid to.*

circle: a practice whereby a customer indicates an interest in buying and an underwriter agrees to provide a given quantity of a new issue subject to pricing.

circuitous route: an extremely indirect route.

CIT: see *Court of International Trade.*

CITES: Convention on International Trade in Endangered Species.

CITT: see *Canadian International Trade Tribunal.*

CIUTS: see *Unit Trusts.*

C.K.D. (completely knocked down):

(1) commodities to be handled and shipped in disassembled form.

(2) a marking applied on the side of shipping containers to be exported noting that the contents are in disassembled form.

(3) in freight forwarding overseas, designates commodities in disassembled form. Such items are imported to take advantage of low tariff classifications, as contrasted with assembled imports, which usually have higher value.

claim: a demand made on a transportation line for payment on account of a loss sustained through its negligence.

claim tracer: a request for advice concerning the status of a claim.

classification (freight): a publication containing a list of articles and the classes to which they are assigned for the purpose of applying class rates, together with governing rules and regulations. See *Lloyds*.

classification register: see *classification (freight)*.

classification territory: defined areas within which a particular freight classification applies.

classification yard: the place where railcars are segregated by the carriers according to their destinations or deliveries and made ready for proper train movement or duty.

claused bill of exchange: a bill of exchange bearing on its face a clause specifying the underlying transaction or the rate of exchange to be used.

claused bill of lading: notation on a bill of lading noting a deficient condition of the
merchandise or the packaging.

clause paramount: a uniform contract that incorporates national laws and international accords into ocean bills of lading.

clean:

(1) without documents, as in clean versus documentary drafts.

(2) in Great Britain, a price quoted excluding accrued interest.

clean acceptance: a formal acknowledgment by a principal in negotiations for the charter of a ship that he or she accepts the offer submitted, without additional modification, and that he or she is bound to execute the charter party.

clean bill of lading: a bill of lading received by the carrier for goods received in appropriate condition (no damages or missing items); does not bear the notation "Shippers Load and Count." Cf.

dirty bill of lading. See *over, short, and damaged (OS&D).*

clean collection: the presentation to a bank, by an exporter, of only the financial documents needed to secure payment for items already shipped.

clean credit: any letter of credit from a bank against which the foreign seller can draw a bill without documentary support. This credit is available only to firms having the best credit reputation.

clean draft: a draft to which no documents have been attached.

clean float: the increase or decrease in the price of a currency because of market forces and uninfluenced by government intervention in the market for the purpose of administering the float. See *floating currency.*

clean report of findings: a document from a recognized inspection agency certifying that certain items were examined and found to be in order.

clearance:
(1) an act of clearing customs.
(2) a certificate of authority by a customs official, permitting a ship to leave or enter port after having met customs requirements.

clear customs: see *clearance.*

clear days: business days free from weather interference, strikes, or government restraints.

clearing:
(1) the physical transfer of cash and securities between the purchasers and sellers.
(2) a procedure through which a clearinghouse becomes buyer to each seller of a future contract, and seller to each buyer, and assumes responsibility for protecting buyers and sellers from financial loss by assuring performance on each contract.

clearing account: an account designed to facilitate the distribution of certain items that usually affect more than one class of accounts, such as those for the production and distribution of power, the production and handling of materials and supplies, and for shop operations.

clearinghouse: an association of banks in a city, created to facilitate the clearing of checks, drafts, notes, or other items among the members. It also formulates policies and rules for the mutual welfare of all members.

Clearing House Automated Payments Systems (CHAPS): the

central United Kingdom money transfer mechanism for larger payments. CHAPS consists of a network of linked computers operated by the U.K. clearing banks.

clearinghouse exchanges: synonymous with *exchanges.*

clearinghouse funds:

(1) monies within the banking system that are transferable from bank to bank through the Federal Reserve System. Federal funds are available on a daily basis, whereas clearinghouse funds require three days to clear.

(2) funds used to settle transactions on which there is a one-day float.

Clearing House Interbank Payment Systems (CHIPS): an automated clearing facility operated by the New York Clearing House Association that processes international funds transfers among its members. CHIPS is a system that moves dollars between 100 New York financial institutions, mostly major U.S. banks and branches of foreign banks.

clearing member: a member of a clearinghouse who is also an exchange member. Since not all exchange members are members of a clearinghouse, they clear their transactions with a clearing member.

clearing union: an international clearinghouse made up of the central banks of member nations, where international payments are settled by means of each nation's trading surplus and/or deficit. It allows countries to concentrate on efficient output, free of worry about exporting to one nation while importing from another.

clear record: a record showing that a shipment was handled without any loss or damage being sustained.

close:

(1) to transfer the balances of revenue and expense accounts at the end of an accounting period.

(2) to sign a legal paper indicating that property has formally changed ownership.

(3) to conclude a sale or agreement.

(4) the short period before the end of the trading session when all trades are officially declared to have been confirmed "at or on the close."

closed economy: an economy closed to international trade having no exports, imports, or capital movements.

close-end fund: in investment firm whose shares are traded on a securities exchange or the over-the-counter market.

closing date: the deadline for delivery of cargo to a carrier for shipping.

CLP: the international standard code for the currency of Chile—the Chilean peso.

club:
(1) a grouping of nations involved in a financial arrangement, often a less-developed-country debt rescheduling. Cf. *Paris Club.*
(2) a Euromarket term for a loan syndication technique in which the lead bank and comanagers carry out various responsibilities. Fees are reduced using this approach.

CMEA: see *Council for Mutual Economic Assistance.*

CNR: charterer not reported.

CNY: the international standard code for the currency of China—the Yuan renminbi.

COA: see *contract of affreightment.*

coastal trade: trade carried out between ports of one country.

coastwise: by way of, or along the coasts, in transportation by water.

Cocoa Producers' Alliance (COPAL): an alliance founded in 1962, and headquartered in Lagos, Nigeria. This worldwide commodity group exchanges information among members, promotes the use of the commodity, and attempts to assure adequate supplies along with sound prices and profits for producer-members.

COCOM (Coordinating Committee for Multilateral Export Controls): a voluntary group of most NATO nations that administers a common set of export controls to prevent transfer of sensitive goods to former Soviet bloc nations. Based in Paris, its role has been diminished in recent years.

COD: see *cash on delivery.*

Code of Liberalization of Capital Movements: the agreement of all members of the Organization of Economic Cooperation and Development to an international standard of conduct in the free movement of capital among them, thus binding each nation to refrain from enacting restrictive measures against direct investment. Synonymous with *Capital Movements Code.*

codetermination: a system in which representatives of labor participate in the management of a company; more popular in Europe than in the United States.

COFACE (Compagnie Francaise d'Assurance pour le Commerce Exterieure): an export credit–granting agency of the French government.

cofinancing: financing a nation in parallel by institutions such as the International Monetary Fund, the World Bank, and commercial banks. May include situations where commercial lendings are made with cross-default clauses relating to IMF or World Bank loans. Default on the latter is taken as default on the commercial loans.

cohesion funds: means of funneling economic development aid to countries whose per capita GDP is less than 90 percent of the EU average.

coincident indicator: a measure of economic activity that traditionally moves in the same direction and during the same time period as total economic movement.

co-insurance:
(1) insurance held jointly with others.
(2) a provision in a policy that requires the insured to carry additional insurance equal to a certain specified percentage of the value of the property. The inclusion of the provision, whether mandatory or optional, usually gives to the insured rates lower than would otherwise apply.

collecting bank: a bank that collects payment on the bill sent by a remitting bank.

collection documents: see *collection papers.*

collection on delivery (COD): the request that the cost of merchandise and other charges be collected at the time the goods are delivered. Cf. *cash on delivery.*

collection papers: all documents submitted to a buyer for the purpose of receiving payment for a shipment.

collections:
(1) presentation for payment of an obligation, and the payment thereof.
(2) the gathering of money for presentation of a draft or check for payment at the bank on which it was drawn, or presentation of any item for deposit at the place at which it is payable.
(3) agreement by the exporter and importer to use the services of the exporter's bank to effect receipt of payment from the importer.

Collective Investment in Transferable Securities (UCITS): see *Unit Trusts.*

Collective Investment Undertakings: see *Unit Trusts*.

collective reserve unit (CRU): an international currency or unit of money for use along with currencies in the reserves of banks around the world.

collect shipment: a shipment for which freight charges and advances are made by the delivering carrier from the consignee.

collision insurance: coverage for damage to the insured object caused by collision with any object, stationary or moving.

Colombian peso: monetary unit of Colombia.

Colombo Plan: formed in 1950, thus making it one of the oldest and longest-standing development associations, with 26 members of Africa, plus Canada, the United Kingdom, and the United States. Headquartered in Colombo, Sri Lanka, the Plan promotes economic development by providing funds and assistance for development projects to member nations within the region.

colon: the monetary unit of Costa Rica and El Salvador.

Colón Free Zone (CFZ): established in 1948, the largest free zone in Latin America. Firms in the CFZ engage in warehousing, regional distribution, manufacturing, and wholesale trade. There are no import duties or taxes on goods entering the zone.

column 1 rates: U.S. import tariff rates that have been established through negotiation. They are congressionally approved and usually bound. These are most-favored-nation (MFN) rates and must apply equally to all countries receiving MFN tariff treatment from the United States, unless superseded by certain preferential tariff arrangements for developing countries. See *Statutory Rate of Duty*. Cf. *column 2 rates*.

column 2 rates: statutorily tariff rates dating back to the 1930s Smoot-Hawley period. They are substantially higher than column 1 rates. They are currently assessed only on imports from countries not receiving most favored nation treatment from the United States. See *Smoot-Hawley Act; Statutory Rate of Duty*. Cf. *column 1 rates*.

combination export manager (CEM): a person who serves as an export sales agent for more than one domestic exporter. CEM sells under its name to foreign-based companies and receives its revenue from commissions.

combination rate: a tariff rate made by combining two or more rates published in different tariffs.

combination through rate: a through rate made by combining two or more rates published in different tariffs.

combined bill of lading: a bill of lading covering a shipment of merchandise by more than one mode of transportation.

combined carrier: see *combo*.

combined transport bill of lading: a bill of lading covering the movement of items through more than one carrier, and often via several modes of transport; the issuer assumes responsibility for the goods throughout the journey, but legal liability for the cargo may be governed by the laws or bill of lading conditions of the underlying carriers hired to perform transport services.

combo: a combined carrier that can carry multiple cargoes; for example, ore and oil.

COMECON: see *Council for Mutual Economic Assistance*.

COMESA Free Trade Area: The Common Market for Eastern and Southern Africa (COMESA) agreement (2000) aims at scrapping tariffs and providing an export stimulus for state-members. COMESA is considered a prelude for Africa to evolve as a major economy and will consequently play an important role in enhancing competitiveness of trade exchange in a globally integrated economy. Twenty nations joined the accord in the year 2002.

Comité Européen de Normalisation (CEN): see *European Committee for Standardization*.

Comité Européen de Normalisation Electrotechnique (CEN-ELEC): see *European Committee for Electrotechnical Standardization*.

comity principles: where trading partners agree to take each other's legitimate interests into account; for example, when considering an antitrust action.

command economy: an economy where central planning determines policies of market supply and demand. Synonymous with *nonmarket economy*.

commerce: trade between states and nations.

Commercial Attaché: a representative of the U.S. Bureau of Foreign and Domestic Commerce located in a foreign country for the purpose of assisting and fostering the foreign trade of the United States.

commercial bank guarantee programs: of the Export-Import Bank of U.S.; provide repayment guarantees to eligible lenders for secured loans that would not be obtainable without a Eximbank guarantee.

commercial bank participation: the share of the financed portion lent by one or more commercial banks or similar institutions in transactions in which Eximbank is also a lender.

commercial bank retention: the percentage of the financed portion on which a bank retains the commercial risk. This percentage is calculated on the financed portion minus the exporter's retention.

commercial bill: a bill of exchange arising from the sale of merchandise in an international market.

commercial controls: restrictions imposed by countries on international trade.

commercial counterfeiting: a practice involving the manufacture or sale of goods that defraud the purchaser by falsely implying that the products are produced by a reputable manufacturer.

commercial invoice: an itemized list of goods shipped, usually included among an exporter's collection papers.

commercial paper: any notes, drafts, checks, or deposit certificates used in a business.

commercial policies: a country's regulations that impact on its international trade.

commercial risks: hazards or barriers that jeopardize exporters being paid.

commercial set: the four major documents covering a shipment: the invoice, the bill of lading, the certificate of insurance, and the bill of exchange or draft.

commercial treaty: an accord between two or more nations identifying conditions, rules, and regulations under which trade between members may be transacted.

commingled fund: a common fund in which the funds of several accounts are mixed.

commission agent: see *purchasing agent.*

Commission du Bassin du Lac Chad (CBLC): see *Lake Chad Basin Commission.*

Commission of the European Union: based in Brussels, the major administrative arm of the European Union.

Commission on Transnational Corporations: a United Nations agency that deals with multinational enterprises.

commitment fee: a fee charged when a bank has granted an overdraft or term loan which is not being fully used.

commodity: an item of commerce or trade.

commodity agreement: an agreement among producer nations to control the price and/or output of a primary product.

Commodity Control List: a listing of products subject to U.S. export controls administered by the Commerce Department.

Commodity Credit Corporation (CCC): formed in 1933, a unit of the U.S. Department of Agriculture that offers, via legislation, supports and protections for U.S. farmers and export credits for their foreign customers.

commodity eligibility: items that qualify for participation in the Agency for International Development; includes items that make a positive contribution to the evolution of the beneficiary nation.

commodity import programs: U.S. government programs created to assist the export of U.S. goods to U.S.-aid recipient nations.

commodity rate: a rate applicable on a specific commodity between certain specified points.

commodity standard: a suggested monetary system that proposes to substitute a commodity or commodities for the precious metal or other base of a currency.

commodity tariff: a tariff containing only commodity rates.

commodity terms of trade: the ratio of the price index of a country's exports to the price index of its imports, multiplied by 100. Synonymous with *net barter terms of trade*.

Common Agricultural Policy (CAP): a critical European Union policy, originally designed to improve productivity and fair living standards for farmers and farm workers; stabilize markets; and secure supplies at reasonable prices for the consumer. These were the objectives set by the Treaty of Rome in 1957. It was first adopted in January 1962 following the recommendations of the Stresa Conference. Its aims are to increase agricultural productivity, to ensure a fair standard of living for those who work in agriculture, to stabilize markets, and to ensure reasonable consumer prices. By 1992, CAP had become the center of a controversy between the European Community and the United States over subsidies, quotas, and the signing of the Uruguay Round of GATT.

By the summer of 2003, the EU, with resistance primarily from France, chose to deal with the issue of an excessive 50 percent of the budget going to CAP. Rather than subsidize farmers for production, curtailments will henceforth shift to quality of production, environmental concerns, etc. See *General Agreement on Tariffs and Trade; subsidies.*

common carrier: a carrier that moves people or goods for a price and without partiality.

Common Customs Tariff (CCT): a tariff that represents the duty paid on goods entering the EU Customs Union at any point. The level averages about 6 percent, but certain specific duties are levied on agricultural and other products. CCT required harmonization of national custom laws, and an ongoing process for which the European Commission is responsible with administrative power delegated to it by the Council of Ministers. See *European Free Trade Association; nontariff barrier.* Synonymous with *Common External Tariff (CET).*

Common External Tariff (CET) (CXT): synonymous with *Common Customs Tariff.*

common market: a trade interaction among nations that maintains a common external tariff and no internal customs. The most famous are the *European Coal and Steel Community,* the *European Economic Community,* and the European Atomic Energy Community. It is often applied to the entire European Union.

Common Market for Eastern and Southern Africa: See *COMESA Free Trade Area.*

common point: a point reached by two or more transportation lines.

common stock: securities that represent an ownership interest in a corporation. If the company has also issued preferred stock, both common and preferred stock holders have ownership rights. The common stock holders assume the greater risk but generally exercise a greater degree of control and may gain the greater reward in the form of dividends and capital appreciation.

common tariff: a tariff published by or for the account of two or more transportation lines as issuing carriers.

common technical specification: a part of the European Union standardization requirement. A technical specification is prepared with a view to uniform application in all nations agreeing to the accord.

Communal Bond: a bond issued by a German mortgage bank or public sector bank and secured by a loan to the public sector.

Communauté Économique de l'Afrique de l'Ouest (CEAO): see *West African Economic Community.*

Communauté Économique des États de l'Afrique Centrale (CEEAC): see *Bank of Central African States.*

Communauté Économique des Pays des Grands Lac (CEPGL): see *Economic Community of Great Lakes Countries.*

Communauté Financiere Africaine franc: see *CFA Franc.*

Community Customs Code: see *Common Customs Tariff.*

Community of Andean Nations (CAN): consists of Bolivia, Columbia, Ecuador, Peru, and Venezuela, as subregional common market mechanism. Synonymous with *Andean Pact.*

Community Patent Convention: see *European Patent Convention; Patent Law.*

community preference: a European Union concept that prices domestic agricultural products below imported items. Threshold prices or minimum import prices, together with subsidies for domestic production, are set at levels to guarantee that non-EU country imports will be somewhat more expensive than the domestic items.

Community Trademark: the European Commission commenced work on the harmonization or unification of industrial property law in 1959. In 1973, the Trade Mark Registration Treaty was signed. In November 1980, a proposal was made for legislation harmonizing national laws on trademarks, and for the establishment of a Community Trademark and a Community Trade Mark Office. It ensures that trademarks enjoy uniform protection under the laws of all member nations and indicates regulations governing registration of trademarks directly affecting the movement of goods and services within the Community. See *Company Law; trademark.*

Compagnie Francaise d'Assurance pour le Commerce Exterieure: see *COFACE.*

Company Law: refers to European Union legislation harmonizing company law. It stems from Article 54 of the Treaty of Rome as part of Union policy of the right of establishment and the removal of obstacles to cross-frontier cooperation. Legislation already adopted deals with company capitalization, mergers, company accounts, and stock exchanges. New directives permit existing companies to restructure across borders without suffering from differing national laws. By 1992, laws were harmonized so as to provide for cross-border mergers; ensure the separation of the functions of management and supervision of management in the interests of shareholders; ensure employee participation and bring member state laws closer together; and relieve foreign branches of firms of the need to publish separate branch accounts. See *European Economic Interest Grouping*.

comparable access: protectionist argument that companies and industries should have the same access to foreign markets as foreign industries and companies have to their markets.

comparative advantage:

(1) a theory first detailed by David Ricardo in 1817, holding that nations should export products that they can produce relatively more efficiently than other nations and import products for which they are relatively high-cost producers.

(2) a country's or area's advantage in the manufacture of a particular item when its social cost of production for that item is less than the social cost experienced by other countries or areas for the same item.

compensated gross registered tonnage (CGRT): a measurement based on the weight of a standard cargo ship; used for calculating the actual work involved in constructing all forms of vessels.

compensating product: an input or product secured by a manufacturer in a domestic market to substitute for an imported input or product used to produce items for export.

compensation: a GATT, now WTO, principle holding that if any member country raises a tariff above its bound rate, withdraws a binding, or otherwise violates a trade concession without GATT justification, the party must lower other tariffs or make other concessions to offset the disadvantage suffered by trading partners, or face offsetting actions (retaliation) by affected parties. See *retaliation*.

compensation deal: a semi-barter arrangement in which goods are bought partially in cash and partially with other goods.

compensation payments: synonymous with *restitution payments*.

compensation trading: an exporter's agreement to accept part payment in items from the purchaser's nation in lieu of cash.

compensatory duty: an extra duty imposed upon imports to offset some artificial trade advantage of those products.

compensatory financing: an IMF service providing short-term finance to compensate for shifts in a nation's export levels caused by circumstances frequently outside a nation's control.

compensatory official financing: a transaction carried out by an official agency to provide (or absorb) foreign exchange to (or from) an individual carrying on another transaction.

compensatory suspension: the suspension of trade concessions by a country in retaliation for the suspension of concessions by a trading partner. Cf. *compensatory withdrawal,*

compensatory trade: any transaction that involves asset transfer as a condition of purchase.

compensatory withdrawal: the cancellation of a trade concession by a country in retaliation for the withdrawal of a concession by a trading partner. Cf. *compensatory suspension.*

competitive alliance: cooperation between competitors for specific purposes.

competitive analysis: the process in which principal competitors are identified and their objectives, strengths, weaknesses, and product lines are assessed.

competitive benchmarking: see *benchmarking.*

competitive devaluation: any devaluation of currency to gain a competitive advantage in export markets.

competitive intelligence: see *competitor intelligence system; industrial espionage.*

competitive rate: a rate established by a transportation line to meet competition of another transportation line.

competitive traffic: traffic in the movement of which two or more transportation lines compete.

competitor intelligence system: the procedure for gathering, analyzing, and disseminating information about a firm's competitors.

complementation agreement: an accord between a commercial entity and two or more governments to lower or eliminate duties among themselves on given items produced by the firm in one or more of the signatory states, thus inducing a manufacturer to place a factory in one of the signatory nations to supply that nation and others with the output of the plant.

completely knocked down: see *C.K.D.*

compound duty: a duty, tax, or tariff expressed or calculated as a combination of an ad valorem and a specified duty. Synonymous with *mixed tariff.*

compound tariff: tax that combines elements of an ad valorem tariff and a specific tariff.

compradore: agent in a foreign country hired by a domestic businessperson to facilitate transactions with local businesses within the foreign country.

Comprehensive Export Schedule (CES): a list, prepared by the U.S. Bureau of Commerce, specifying those items the sale of which to buyers outside the jurisdiction of the United States requires an export permit. Cf. *Export-Import Permits Act*.

comptant: (French) spot settlement in foreign exchange.

concealed damage: damage to the contents of a package that is in good order externally.

concentration point: a place where less-than-carload shipments are united to be shipped as a carload.

concentration strategy: approach used when a multinational firm evolves a program for assessing and choosing nations to enter and commit resources.

concession: a tariff reduction, tariff binding, or other agreement to reduce import restrictions; usually accorded pursuant to negotiation in return for concessions by other parties.

concessional financing: credit extended by industrially developed nations to less-developed nations on terms that are less severe than those offered by competitive money markets. Cf. *near concessional financing*.

conditionality: those conditions imposed when a nation draws funds from the IMF related to its credit tranches. There are four tranches and borrowing under each tranche attracts its own conditions. Other conditions apply to borrowing in excess of regular credit tranches, such as where a nation borrows to replace finance lost because of a decline in exports. See *compensatory financing; International Monetary Fund; tranche*.

conditional most-favored-nation treatment: the according of most-favored-nation treatment, subject to compliance with specific terms or conditions. All members of GATT, now WTO, including the United States, accord unconditional MFN treatment to most other GATT members. The United States, however, accords annually renewable MFN treatment to a limited number of countries conditional on their compliance with the terms of Title IV of the Trade Act of 1974. See *most favored nation*.

conditional sale lease: synonymous with *export finance lease*.

condition precedent: a contract clause stating that immediate duties and rights will vest only upon the occurrence of an event.

It is not a promise; therefore, its breach is not grounds for action against damages. However, it is the basis for a defense.

conference: the coming together of international ocean shipping firms or lines that operate regular services, for the purpose of creating a framework for agreement on matters such as the setting of freight rates, the pooling of revenue, and the allocation of the number and frequency of individual company sailings. Synonymous with *shipping conference.*

conference lines: an association of ship-owning lines that operate on a specific route. Standard tariff rates are fixed and a regular service is operated for the mutual benefit of both the merchant trading on that route and the ship owner running the company.

conference rate: shipping rates arrived at by conference of carriers applicable to transportation, generally water transportation.

confirm: an act of a correspondent bank in the seller's country by which it agrees to honor the issuing bank's letter of credit.

confirmed letter of credit: a method of enhancing a foreign bank's credit status. A foreign bank wishing to issue a letter of credit to a local concern may request a local bank in the city in which the beneficiary is located to confirm this credit to the beneficiary. This confirmation lends the prestige and responsibility of the local bank to the transaction because the status of the foreign bank may be unknown to the beneficiary. The confirming bank assumes responsibility for the payment of all drafts drawn under the credit and usually charges a fee for doing so.

confirming: a financial service whereby an independent firm confirms an independent order in a seller's country and makes payment for the goods in the monetary unit of that nation.

confiscation: the seizure of private property, without compensation, usually by a governmental agency.

conformance testing: a technical task of testing products to determine whether or not they meet the requirements defined in a standard. The tests are conducted by the supplier of the product (first-party testing) or by an independent body (third-party testing). See *certification; standards.*

confrontation and justification: a strategy used during multinational trade negotiations to define the positions of the differing national delegations, where each group is confronted by the other with questions dealing with tariff cuts proposed, etc. The delegation confronted must justify its stand on the points raised.

connecting carrier: a carrier that has a direct physical connection with another or that forms a connecting link between two or more carriers.

consecutives: the number of voyages performed, one following another, on a single-voyage basis for the account of one charterer.

Conseil Africain de l'Arachide: see *African Groundnut Council*.

consign: the act of ordering, via a bill of lading, a carrier to deliver a lot of merchandise from a given point to a given destination.

consignee:

(1) the ultimate recipient of goods.

(2) the person to whom articles are shipped.

consignee marks: a symbol placed on packages for export, generally consisting of a square, triangle, diamond, circle, cross, etc., with designed letters and/or numbers, for the purpose of identification.

consignment:

(1) the act of entrusting goods to a dealer for sale but retaining ownership of them until sold. The dealer pays only when and if the goods are sold.

(2) items shipped by a producer or dealer to an agent on the understanding they will be sold at the best possible price or properly watched. The shipper retains ownership.

consignment note: an instrument given when goods are dispatched, providing details of the item, the sender, and the individual to whom they are sent. The latter signs it upon arrival, providing proof of delivery.

consignment terms: export trading on the basis that items exported on consignment remain the property of the exporter and are sold for the exporter by his or her agent.

consignor:

(1) the originator of a shipment; a person who delivers goods to an agent.

(2) the person by whom articles are shipped.

consol:

(1) a bond that will never reach maturity; a bond in perpetuity.

(2) the name given to a British government bond.

Consolidated Fund: funds in the United Kingdom standing to the account of the Exchequer; the revenue is paid from taxation and is used to finance government projects.

consolidation: synonymous with *make bulk.*

Consortia of American Businesses in the Newly Independent States: see *CABNIS.*

Consortium Insurance (CI): an Export Development Corporation insurance program to protect Canadian members of an export consortium against the call of a performance instrument where the other member(s) of the group may be unable to pay their respective shares.

conspiracy in restraint of trade: collusion; two or more competitors who conspire to restrain trade in some manner. The conspiracy may be directed at competing firms or may be aimed at customers or suppliers.

constant costs: the difference between the out-of-pocket, or variable, costs, and the total costs. Those costs, within the limits of the range of output under study, are unaffected by increases or decreases in production.

Constitution of the European Union: in June 2003, the EU's leaders met in Salonika, Greece, and broadly agreed to a European draft constitution, the first in its history.

constructed price: a value for customs purposes that ignores the invoice price of the goods but is derived by computing the cost inputs of the item, to which are added the normal costs associated with preparing the goods for export.

Construction Differential Subsidy: a subsidy by the U.S. government to ship operators, to encourage construction in American shipyards.

constructive delivery: acceptance by buyer and seller that possession and ownership have been transferred from one to another, although the purchased goods may not have been delivered.

constructive mileage: an arbitrary mileage allowed to a carrier in dividing joint rates, or mileage pro rata.

consul: a government official residing in a foreign country to care for the interests of his or her country.

consular declaration: a formal statement, made to the consul of a foreign country, describing goods to be shipped.

consular invoice: a document required by some countries showing exact information as to consignor, consignee, value, description, etc., of a shipment.

Consumer Consultative Council: effective January 1990, the

European Community established this group to ensure that consumers' interests are adequately represented in the formulation of other common policies for completion of the internal market. New measures were proposed, including comparative advertising, standards contracts with product guarantees after purchases, removing unfair contract terms in sales between member nations, and protecting consumers in general.

consumer price index: the measurement of the cost of living. See *inflation.*

consumer protection: see *product liability.*

consumption effect of a tariff: lowers consumer demand for imported items imposed as a result of a tariff imposed by the importing nation.

consumption entry: a customs entry where an importer pays the applicable dues and the merchandise is released from customs custody.

container:

(1) anything in which articles are packed.

(2) a large storage unit, which can easily be transferred to a trailer truck and can be neatly stacked on a train or ship.

container freight station: a warehouse or terminal licensed by the U.S. Customs to receive in-bound consolidations of containerized cargo.

containerization: using containers for international and domestic trade.

containment, conflict, common problems, and common management: these are the four C's of Jean Monnet—the father of the European Union—that he incorporated into a model for the reconstruction of post–World War II Europe.

contango:

(1) the cost factors when calculating from one given period to a future point.

(2) a basic pricing system in futures trading. A form of premium or carrying charge; for example, instead of paying for the cost of warehousing silver bullion, paying insurance finance charges and other expenses (silver users prefer to pay more for a futures contract covering later delivery).

content: see *rules of origin.*

continental rate: the rate charged in Europe for foreign exchange and on bills of exchange.

contingency protection: in Canada, all antidumping and counter-vailing duties and measures employed by the U.S. government and that the United States refers to as unfair trade practices when these retaliatory measures are used by third nations.

contingent assets: items without value to an accounting firm until the fulfillment of conditions regarded as uncertain.

contingent liabilities: items that may under certain conditions become obligations of the firm, but are neither direct nor assumed obligations on the date of the balance sheet.

contocurrent account: used in Germany and parts of Switzerland to identify what is called in the United States a checking account.

contraband: illegal or prohibited traffic.

contract carrier: a transportation firm that contracts with shippers to transport their goods. The price is negotiated between the carrier and the shipper. The contract carrier cannot accept shipments from the general public.

contract demurrage: liquidated damages payable by a charterer to a ship owner for holding up the vessel beyond the time allocated in the charter party; calculated on a per-day or per-hour basis.

contracting parties (CPs): the signatory countries to the GATT. These countries have accepted the specified obligations and benefits of the GATT agreement. See *World Trade Organization (WTO.)*

contract manufacturing: manufacturing of a product or component by one company for another company. The two companies may or may not be related by stock ownership, common parent, or otherwise.

contract of affreightment (COA):
(1) a provision of a specified tonnage capacity to transport bulk cargo during a given period between two ports or areas at agreed-on rates.
(2) an agreement by a shipping carrier to provide cargo space on a ship at a given price and at a specified time to accommodate a shipper, who then becomes liable for payment of the carrier even if the carrier cannot fulfill its responsibility to ship the items.

contract price: the sale price negotiated between the U.S. exporter and the foreign buyer payable in the United States for the export from the United States of U.S. goods and services. This price may include, among other things, freight and marine insurance, but it excludes any charges payable for non-U.S. goods and services unless otherwise permitted; certain engineering services; import duties or levies of a similar nature; charges for local costs; and any other charges not legally payable in the United States.

Contract Regarding a Supplement to Tanker Liability for Pollution (CRISTAL): a contract providing compensation on a worldwide basis for oil pollution caused by tankers, supplemental to that provided by ship owners. Cf. *Tanker Owners Voluntary Agreement on Liability for Oil Pollution.*

contracts in foreign currency: agreements to buy and sell an amount of one currency for another at an agreed rate of exchange.

contributions from other firms: amounts receivable from others to meet a firm's net deficit when, under terms of agreements or contracts, no obligation for subsequent reimbursement is incurred.

controllable forces: forces internal to the firm that management administers to adapt to changes in uncontrollable environmental forces.

controlled economy: an economy that is regulated and greatly influenced by government.

controlled facility: a free port facility that is a portion of a national territory.

controlled foreign corporation (CFC): a foreign corporation of which more than 50 percent of the voting stock is owned by U.S. shareholders.

controlled in fact: the authority of a domestic firm to establish general policy or to dominate daily operations over a foreign subsidiary, partnership, etc.

convenience statements: financial statements translated into the language of the foreign country statements where monetary units are expressed in the foreign country's currency.

conventional duty: a customs duty, or rate of duty, arising out of a treaty or other international agreement, as contrasted to an autonomous duty unilaterally imposed by a government, absent of any international agreement.

convergence: the movement of the price of a futures contract toward the price of the underlying cash commodity. Initially the price is higher, but as the contract approaches expiration, the futures price and the cash price converge.

convergence criteria: conditions that must be met by EUM members in order in order to participate in the EU's single currency program.

conversion:

(1) an appropriation of freight by a carrier.

(2) the exchange of one currency for another.

conversion exposure: the inherent risk in converting one currency into another or one balance sheet into a consolidated balance sheet.

conversion rate: an exchange rate from foreign to domestic currency.

conversion ratio: the number of shares of common stock received when a convertible bond or convertible preferred stock is exchanged with the same firm. The price is frequently given at the issue date of the bond or preferred stock and may not be the same as the market price when the conversion takes place.

conversion restrictions: limits on foreign investors by foreign governments in the conversion of remittances from one local currency to U.S. dollars and the transfer of these remittances outside of the host country.

convertibility: exists when a holder of a currency is able to transfer the money in question into a hard currency without restrictions. True convertibility occurs at a single free-market exchange rate, not one imposed by a government or by central banks. See *soft currency.*

convertibility clause: clause attached to some *Eurobonds* that allows them to be converted into a specified number of common stock shares.

convertible currency: a currency that can be bought and sold for other currencies at will.

convertible Eurobonds: fixed rate *Eurobonds* that can be exchanged either for shares of common stock or for currency.

cooperation agreements: one of the two kinds of trade agreements between nations of a structured group, for example, the European Union and nonmember nations. They are not as far-reaching as association agreements, being aimed solely at intensive economic cooperation. Cf. *association agreements.*

Cooperation in the Automation of Data Documentation for Import/Export and Agriculture: see *CADDIA.*

cooperative exporters: established international manufacturers who export other manufacturers' goods as well as their own.

Cooperative Export Financing Corporation: see *CEFCO*.

Coordinating Committee for Multilateral Export Controls: see *COCOM*.

COP: the international standard code for the currency of Colombia—the Colombian peso. See *custom of port*.

COPAL: see *Cocoa Producers' Alliance*.

coproduction: a form of counter-trade transaction where an exporter receives payment contingent on allowing the importer to locally produce a portion of the total export contract.
Synonymous with *direct offsets*.

cordoba: the monetary unit of Nicaragua.

corporate bond equivalent: the semiannual equivalent rate of return for a security with other than semiannual interest.

corporate dumping: activity of exporting banned or out-of-date items to a foreign market where restrictive rules on the specific items are not as severe.

corporate tax equivalent: a rate of return needed on a par bond to produce the same after-tax yield to maturity as a given bond.

correspondent bank: a bank that, in its own country, handles the business of a foreign bank.

corset: a strategy whereby the more money that banks accumulate for lending over six months, the bigger the deposits with a central bank will have to be.

cost:
(1) the value given up by an entity in order to receive goods or services.
(2) the value given up to obtain an item in the volume needed, shipped to the desired location. All expenses are costs, but not all costs are expenses.

cost and freight (C&F) (CAF): shipping term indicating that the seller will pay only freight charges to a location, not insurance.

cost and freight, free out (C&F FO): includes the cost of the goods, freight charges, and unloading. Most grain and sugar are traded on this basis.

cost-based transfer price:
(1) price at which a parent firm sells products to foreign affiliates.
(2) price at which a foreign affiliate sells items to its parent, based on the actual cost of the merchandise to the firm supplying the items.

cost, insurance, and freight (CIF): a quoted price that includes the handling charges, insurance, and freight costs to a named place of delivery, usually to a port of entry.

cost, insurance, freight, and exchange: the cost of goods, marine insurance, transportation charges, and exchange charges paid to the foreign point of delivery.

cost, insurance, freight, collection, interest: the cost of goods, marine insurance, transportation charges, and interest paid to the foreign point of delivery.

cost, insurance, freight, interest, and exchange: the cost of goods, marine insurance, transportation charges and interest, and exchange charges paid to the foreign point of delivery.

cost of goods sold: the purchase price of goods sold during a specified period, including transportation costs.

cost of production: the sum of the cost of materials, fabrication, and/or processing employed in making items sold in a home market or to a third country, together with appropriate allocations of general management and selling costs.

cost of reproduction new: the estimated cost of reproducing the existing property of a carrier under price levels of a specified period.

cost plus approach: transfer of items at a cost plus a fair markup to cover expenses for the company supplying the items to the foreign affiliate.

cottage industry: production away from a central factory, typically in the worker's own home or cottage; most popular in less-developed nations.

Council of Arab Economic Unity (CAEU): formed in 1957 by the Arab Economic Council of the *Arab League* to encourage economic cooperation and integration of the Arab national economies. Members are Iraq, Jordan, Kuwait, Libya, Mauritania, Somalia, Sudan, Syria, United Arab Emirates, Yemen, and the Palestine Liberation Organization.

Council of Canadian Trading Houses (CCTH): a national organization created by the Canadian Export Association to provide Canadian exporters with several activities, including data on, and referral, key accredited trading houses; and to determine the accreditation criteria for Canadian trading houses.

Council of the European Union: main decision-making body of the EU; composed of members (one for each member country) who represent the interests of their home governments in Council deliberations.

Council of Ministers: headquartered in Brussels, composed of one member from each nation of the EU, and entrusted with making major policy decisions.

Council for Mutual Economic Assistance (CMEA) (COMECON): after a meeting at its Moscow headquarters in January 1991, the executive committee of COMECON announced its intention to disband formally in February 1991. It was replaced by a market-oriented group, the Organization for International Economic Cooperation, whose members formally will be free to trade with any nation. On June 28, 1991, the nine member nations of COMECON signed an agreement to put the organization out of business, with a ceremony in Budapest. See *Organization for International Economic Cooperation.*

count certificate: a document confirming the count of merchandise at the time of shipment or delivery.

Counterfeit Code: a draft agreement addressing commercial counterfeit (i.e., trademark) problems in international trade. Initiated during the Tokyo Round, this code was never concluded. The issue of counterfeiting, as well as other intellectual property issues, was a major issue in the GATT *Uruguay Round.*

counterfeiting: the illegal use of a well-known manufacturer's brand name on copies of the firm's merchandise.

counterpart monies: local currency equivalents of dollar assistance given to nations by the United States following World War II that are, in turn, to purchase U.S. goods or services.

counterpurchasing:

(1) placing an order with a manufacturer in one country with the expectation that merchandise of equal value and/or quantity will be sold in the opposite direction to the other nation. See *countertrade.*

(2) a form of *countertrade* transaction; an agreement between the exporter and importer covering two linked contracts and two linked transactions.

counterspeculation: action by the government in a controlled economy, designed to counteract the power of buyers or sellers to influence price (and thus speculate) by estimating the price that would prevail in the absence of restrictions by sellers or buyers and then guaranteeing that estimated price. The guaranteed price is achieved by government purchases of sales.

countertrade:

(1) the sale of goods or services that are paid for in whole or in part by the transfer of goods or services from a foreign country. See *counterpurchasing; offset deals; overseas investment.*

(2) international trade where an export sale is contingent on a reciprocal purchase or undertaking by the exporter. Countertrade has spread to more than 100 nations since its emergence in East-West trade in the mid-1970s.

(3) a practice whereby a supplier commits contractually, as a condition of sale, to reciprocate and undertake certain specified commercial initiatives that compensate and benefit the buyer. See *Interagency Group on Countertrade.*

countervailing duty (CVD): import duty imposed over and above normal levels when an importing nation considers the export price to contain a subsidy. The WTO permits use of such duties if material injury to the importing country's producers occurs. See *countervailing duty investigations.* Synonymous with *punitive duty.*

Countervailing Duty Investigations: as provided in *NAFTA,* special provisions are provided for resolving disputes by a national panel, whose power is limited to whether decisions rendered by Mexico, the United States, or Canada are consistent with their domestic law, which may result in the payment of an import duty over and beyond normal levels. See *countervailing duty.*

country controlled buying agent: a government agency that is the primary or sole entity authorized to trade with foreign nations for the purchase of certain items.

country limitation schedule: conditions that a U.S. import bank places on its guarantees and insurance policies, respectively, listed by country.

country of dispatch: nation from which a seller has to send merchandise to the named place of destination.

country of export destination: nation where items are to be consumed, further processed, or manufactured, as known to a shipper at time of export.

country of origin: country where an item was grown, manufactured, or processed (in one country), or the last nation in which the item underwent a substantial change.

country risk:
(1) the risk of lending monies to or making an investment in a specific nation.
(2) evaluating the risks before lending or investing in a country.

country risk assessment: evaluating the risks before lending or investing in a country.

country similarity concept: theory that when a company develops a new item in response to a perceived need in its home market, it will look for overseas markets that are expected to be similar to those within the home market.

coupon: the portion of a bond that is redeemable at a given date for interest payments.

courriel: (French) e-mail.

courtier: (French) *broker.*

Court of Auditors: a court, known as the European Union Court; established in 1975 by amendment to the *Treaty of Rome.* It originally consisted of 10 members (one from each Community nation) appointed for a six-year term by the Council of Ministers in consultation with the European Parliament. The Court may comment on the accounts to all Community Institutions and can issue advisory opinions. Internal auditing, however, is carried out by each Institution's financial controller. Court members comment on a variety of issues, including international trade, within and external to EU nations.

Court of First Instance (CFI): a second-level court of the European Union. It hears employment disputes brought by EU employees and other relevant matters. Appeals are sent to the European Court of Justice. Established in October 1988 by formal decision of the European Community's Council of Ministers. The task of the Court of First Instance is to improve the judicial protection of some of its current workload so that the Court of Justice (the EU's highest court) can concentrate its activities on the fundamental task of ensuring uniform interpretation of Community law.
In September 1989, 12 new judges were appointed to man this junior branch of the tribunal, to be housed in two courtrooms of the European Court of Justice's headquarters on the Kirchberg Plateau in Luxembourg City. See *European Court of Justice.*

Court of International Trade (CIT): a U.S. court that hears appeals on parajudicial and administrative trade decisions and hears antidumping, product classification, and countervailing duty matters, in addition to unfair trade practice cases.

covenant: a contract pertaining to an undertaking, a promise, or an agreement to do or forbear from doing that which has legal validity and is legally enforceable.

covered arbitrage: arbitrage between financial instruments denominated in differing currencies, using forward cover to eliminate exchange risk.

covered investment: an investment in a second currency that is covered by a forward sale of the currency to protect against exchange rate fluctuations. The profit depends on interest rate differentials minus the discount or plus the premium on a forward sale.

covered margin: the interest rate margin between two instruments denominated in differing currencies, after taking account of the cost of forward cover.

covered under carnet: export items making temporary trips to overseas nations, then reexported from them, and ultimately being re-imported to their originating nation, under the authority of an International Chamber of Commerce (ICC) carnet. See *carnet.*

covering exchange risk: synonymous with *hedging.*

CPs: see *contracting parties.*

crawling peg: a foreign exchange rate that permits the par value of a country's currency to change automatically by small increments, upward or downward, if—in actual daily trading on the foreign exchange markets—the price in terms of other monies persists on the floor or ceiling of the established range for a given period.

CRC: the international standard code for the currency of Costa Rica—the Costa Rican colon.

Creditexport: a non-profit-making consortium of Belgian commercial banks and other public and private financial institutions to fund medium- and long-term export credit.

credit hedge: hedging by borrowing the currency of risk, converting it immediately to the ultimately desired currency, and repaying the loan when payment is received.

crédit mixte: a combination of conventional government export financing and concessionary loans that are made interest free or at very low rates.

creditor nation: a country with a balance of payments surplus. Cf. *debtor nation*.

credit protocol: a financial agreement, signed between official credit-granting agencies in different nations, that allows purchasers in one nation to use foreign credit to finance their imports. See *export financing*.

credit rating:
(1) the amount, type, and form of credit, if any, that a bank estimates can be extended to an applicant for credit.
(2) an estimate of the credit and responsibility assigned to mercantile and other establishments by credit-investigating organizations.

credit risk: the risk assumed for the possible nonpayment of credit extended.

credit risk insurance: insurance designed to cover risks of nonpayment for delivered goods. Cf. *marine insurance*.

credit tranche: one of the four conditional *International Monetary Fund* lines of credit against which a country can borrow after it has drawn its reserve tranche.

CRISTAL: see *Contract Regarding a Supplement to Tanker Liability for Pollution*.

cross-border factoring: factoring by a network of factors across borders. The exporter's factor can contact correspondent factors in other countries to handle the collection of accounts receivable.

cross-border lease: a lease in which the lessor and lessee are in two different countries.

cross-border lending: lending of funds by a U.S. bank to less-developed countries.

Cross-Border Transaction Tax: proposed by U.S. House Majority Leader Richard Gephardt to be included in the renegotiation of the North American Free Trade Agreement in the fall of 1992. He urged that as tariffs on trade with Mexico are cut, the United States should introduce this cross-border transaction tax to generate funds for retraining workers who lose jobs because of the trade accord and for cleaning up the environment. Became a supplemental ruling of the final draft of NAFTA. See *North American Free Trade Agreement*.

cross check: the placing of two diagonal lines across the front of a check and the addition of a term or series of words to determine the negotiability of the check, such as to one's banker if his or her name is inserted between the lines. Rarely used in the United States, but found in parts of Europe and Latin America.

cross-currency exposure: when a firm's debt-servicing requirements in a currency are not covered by its revenue-generating capabilities in that currency.

cross-default clause: a loan agreement clause stating that default on any other loans to the borrower will be regarded as default on this one.

cross investment: foreign direct investment made by large firms in each other's home country as a defense measure.

cross licensing: technology transfer between different firms.

cross rates of exchange: comparisons of exchange rates between currencies that reveal whether it would be profitable to exchange the first currency for a second, the second for a third, then the third for the first.

cross subsidization: a marketing method where a firm employs earnings in one foreign market to support its marketing activities in another foreign market.

cross trader: the provision of freight service between ports in two or more different nations by a shipping company that is not under the national flag of any of them.

crowding out: the negative impact of larger government deficits on economic growth.

Crown Corporation: a limited liability company owned at least 51 percent by the Canadian Government.

CRU: see *collective reserve unit.*

Cruzeiro: the monetary unit of Brazil.

CSK: the international standard code for the currency of Czech Republic—the koruna.

Cuban Assets Control Regulations: prohibits virtually all commercial and financial transactions with Cuba or Cuban nationals by U.S. companies, U.S.-owned or -controlled companies, and U.S. nationals, unless specifically licensed by the Department of the Treasury. See *Cuban Democracy Act.*

Cuban Democracy Act (CDA) of 1992: amends the Cuban Assets Control Regulations and further restricts licensed trade with Cuba to only humanitarian actions and food aid operations. The CDA lays down a number of trade prohibitions: (a) a prohibition of all commercial transactions and payments by U.S.-owned or -controlled foreign firms with Cuba. This does not affect contracts entered into before the date of enactment of the CDA; (b) 180-days landing ban on commercial vessels departing from Cuba, except pursuant a license issued by the U.S. Department of Treasury; (c) a landing ban on vessels carrying goods or passengers to or from Cuba or carrying goods in which Cuba has any interest, except pursuant a license issued by the U.S. Secretary of Treasury; (d) a prohibition on supplying ships carrying goods or persons to or from Cuba.

Cuban peso: monetary unit of Cuba.

CUF: see *customs user fees.*

cum coupon: international bond market terms for dealings in a bond where the purchaser acquires the right to receive the next due interest payment.

cum dividend: the dividend included. The purchaser of a stock cum dividend has the right to receive the declared dividend.

cumulative preferred: a stock whose holders are entitled, if one or more dividends are omitted, to be paid the omitted dividends before dividends are paid on the company's common stock.

CUP: the international standard code for the currency of Cuba—the Cuban peso.

currency: paper money and coin issued by a government or central bank, which circulate as the legal medium of exchange. See *vehicle(s) currency.*

currency abbreviation: prepared in English and adopted by the International Standardization Organization; the written, nonsymbolic, short-form, Arabic-letter spelling of the world's major currencies. For example, the deutsche mark is DEM; the Japanese yen is JPY; the U.S. dollar is USD.

currency adjustment factor (CAF): the charge imposed by shipping conferences to cover currency fluctuations.

currency area: the group of countries whose currencies are pegged to any one DC currency. Many LDCs peg the value of their currency to that of their major DC trading partner.

currency availability clause: a Euromarket clause providing that banks can switch their lending to a different currency should the original currency no longer be available.

currency band:
(1) a carefully defined area within which a nation's money fluctuates on both sides of its official parity. Set at 2.25 percent each side

of the parity at the 1971 Washington Smithsonian Agreement.
(2) margin within which a currency is allowed to shift. See *European Exchange Rate Mechanism.*

currency basket: assembled currencies individually weighted and whose combined value is the equivalent of a single unit. See *European Currency Unit.*

currency bloc: nations that use a common currency base (e.g., the British sterling bloc exists for Great Britain and many of her present and former colonies).

currency, blocked: see *blocked currency.*

currency clause: in contracts for setting a fixed rate between two currencies; to avoid the impact of devaluation or revaluation.

currency cocktail: a unit of account based on a number of currencies.

currency contract period: immediately after the devaluation of a currency, the time when contracts negotiated before the devaluation become due.

currency convertibility: the ability to exchange for gold, as well as for other currencies. See *convertible currency.*

currency depreciation: the decline in the relative value of a national currency under a flexible exchange rate system. See *depreciation.*

currency devaluation: any action by a government or by the marketplace to reduce the value of a currency in relation to the currencies of other nations.

currency exchange (swap): a long-term exchange of currency between two firms in different nations.

currency exchange controls: controls established by a government restricting how much foreign currency its residents or visitors can have and how much they must pay for it.

currency futures: contracts in the futures markets set for delivery in a major currency. Firms selling products throughout the world can hedge their currency risk with these futures.

currency inconvertibility: when a company is unable to convert local currency into a convertible currency and transfer remittances outside the host nation.

currency option clause: a statement permitting the payment of principal and interest on a Eurobond issued in one currency to be made in a different currency at the option of the buyer.

currency parities: parities that were agreed on by members of the International Monetary Fund; funds of all the world's major nations are set in relation to the U.S. dollar.

currency swap: synonymous with *bank swap*.

currency transferability: the ability of a currency to be easily exchanged for another currency by any and all its owners.

currency union: a region where rates of exchange are fixed.

current account:

(1) a running account between two companies, reflecting the movement of cash, merchandise, etc.

(2) the balance of payments embracing a nation's physical imports/exports and international transactions in invisible goods and services, such as shipping and banking.

current account balance: the difference between the nation's total exports of goods, services, and transfers and its total imports of them. It excludes transactions in financial assets and liabilities. See *balanced economy*.

current assets: includes cash and those assets that are readily convertible into cash or are held for current use in operations, current claims against others, and amounts accruing to the carrier that are subject to current settlement.

current liabilities: amounts payable within a comparatively brief period, usually not exceeding one year from the date of the balance sheet.

current rate method: the use of the exchange rate in effect on a balance sheet date when translating financial statements of a foreign subsidiary.

custody bill of lading: bill of lading issued by U.S. warehouses as a receipt for merchandise stored.

Customary Freight Unit: the unit on which freight is assessed on bulk or unpackaged cargoes, as defined by the U.S. Carriage of Goods by Sea Act. Loss or damage is limited to $500 per package.

customhouse: the place for the payment of import duties in the United States and for the payment of import and export duties in other nations.

customhouse bond: a bond required by the U.S. government in connection with payment of duties or for producing bills of lading.

customhouse broker: an individual or firm licensed to enter and clear goods through customs.

custom of port (COP): relates to customs and practices that have slowly been established for movements in a port, usually concerning loading and discharge of items.

customs: taxes imposed by a government on the import or export of items. Cf. *duty; tariff.*

Customs and Economic Union of Central Africa (CEUCA): formed in 1964 with Cameroon, Central African Republic, Chad, Congo, and Gabon as members, to establish a common market among Central African nations. Synonymous with *Union Douanière et Économique de l'Afrique Centrale (UDEAC).*

Customs and Trade Act of 1990: the United States imposes user fees with respect to the arrival of merchandise, vessels, trucks, trains, private boats and planes, as well as passengers. The Customs and Trade Act of 1990 extends and modifies these provisions, among other things, by considerably increasing the level of the fees, thus seeking to use fees rather than taxes as a source of revenue.

customs bond: a guarantee required by a foreign nation when it demands assurance that a firm will re-export equipment temporarily shipped into the country, rather than selling it locally.

customs broker: a firm whose activities are the preparation and processing of needed documentation for customs authorities so as to have goods cleared through customs at rates of duty most favorable to the party who hires the broker. Synonymous with *customs clearing agent.*

customs classification: the category where goods are placed for the purpose of levying a duty or tariff. See *BTN (Brussels Tariff Nomenclature).*

customs clearing agent: synonymous with *customs broker.*

Customs Cooperation Council (CCC): headquartered in Brussels, with more than 90 nations as members; studies issues relating to the development of a globally uniform customs classification system and to standardization approaches. See *Customs Cooperation Council Nomenclature.*

Customs Cooperation Council Nomenclature (CCCN): formally *BTN (Brussels Tariff Nomenclature);* a customs system, designed by the Customs Cooperation Council, for classifying goods for the purpose of customs valuation.

customs duty: a border tax usually levied on imports. See *duty.*

customs harmonization: the continuing activity to standardize customs procedures and nomenclatures worldwide. See *Harmonized System.*

customs import value: value of items appraisal by the U.S. Customs Service.

customs privileged facility: area set aside by a government to assist in the exchange, transfer, movement, or use of items between nations with international trade restrictions.

customs rate: the rate of exchange employed by U.S. Customs in converting foreign currency invoices for the purpose of arriving at a value, in U.S. dollars, for imported items.

customs tariff: a schedule of charges assessed by the government on imported or exported goods.

customs union:

(1) a form of a regional economic integration group that eliminates tariffs among member nations and establishes common external tariffs.

(2) an arrangement whereby European Union nations agreed to do away with customs barriers between themselves and apply a common tariff to nations outside the European Union so that the level of protection will be the same wherever a product enters the Community. It was formed by the six Community founder members in 1968 and was extended to include newer member nations of the European Community. See *duty-free allowances; European Monetary System; external trade; harmonization.*

customs user fees (CUF): see *Customs and Trade Act of 1990.*

customs valuation: the assignment by customs authorities of a value for duty purposes to imported goods. For example, Mexican Customs, as of January 1, 1993, began using the transaction value to calculate duties owed on imports. Previously, Mexico used the higher cost, insurance, and freight value as the basis for calculating duty and tax. As a result, U.S. exports are now subject to less duty and tax, since the cost basis is lower. See *Customs Valuation Code.*

Customs Valuation Code: synonymous with *Agreement on Customs Valuation.*

CVD: see *countervailing duty.*

CVE: the international standard code for the currency of Cape Verde—the Cape Verde escudo.

CWO: see *cash with order.*

CXT: *Common External Tariff.* See *Common Customs Tariff.*
CYP: the international standard code for the currency of Cyprus—the Cyprus pound.
Cyprus pound: monetary unit of Cyprus.

D

D (d): dollar.

DAA: see *documents against acceptance.*

DAC: see *Development Assistance Committee.*

D/A drafts: *documents on acceptance.* Time drafts (trade acceptances) payable at some time in the future.

daily hire: the fee paid by a charterer to a ship owner for each day that the vessel is under charter.

dalasi: the monetary unit of Gambia.

dangerous goods note: used instead of a standard shipping note to cover delivery of hazardous cargo to the docks.

Danish krone: monetary unit of Denmark.

Dansk Eksportfinansierungsfond (DEFC) (Danish Export Credit Finance Corporation): set up in 1975 by the Danish Central Bank and the commercial banking sector. It normally lends for two to five years at a preferential rate, but may lend for longer, especially to developing countries.

Danube Commission: constituted in 1949 and based on the Convention relating to navigation control on the river Danube, which was signed in Belgrade August 18, 1948. It is composed of representatives from the nations on the Danube; one each for Austria, Bulgaria, Hungary, Romania, Czechoslovakia, the former Soviet Union, and Yugoslavia. It checks that the Convention provisions are carried out; establishes a uniform buoying system on all the Danube's navigable waterways; and sees to the fundamental arrangement relating to navigation on the river. It is headquartered, since 1954, in Budapest.

DAP: see *documents against payment.*

data freight receipt: a document issued by vessel operators in lieu of a bill of lading on straight consignment shipments. The data-freight system cannot be used in transactions where an order bill of lading is called for.

date draft: draft that matures a specific number of days after the date is issued, without consideration to the date of acceptance.

date for value determination: the date when imported goods were exported from their country of origin. The value of the merchandise in effect on that date is used in setting duties.

date of maturity: the date on which a debt must be paid. Usually applied to those debts evidenced by a written agreement, such as a note or bond.

dawn raids: a reference to the right to raid companies for evidence of alleged price fixing. In 1989, the European Court of Justice upheld the European Community's Commission's right to raid companies for this purpose, confirming the Commission's extensive powers to enforce EC competition rules. Further, it boosts the drive to promote competition and trade in the Community in advance of the single market. The court backed the right for the Commission to investigate a firm's books immediately if it suspects a violation of competition law. In addition, the Commission has the right to seek information that it cannot necessarily identify in advance. With the assistance of national authorities, it can search for information even if the targeted firm is unwilling to cooperate. Should a firm resist, the investigators must secure a search warrant according to national law, but the company exposes itself to fines until the Commission actually begins the investigation. National authorities are not permitted to determine whether an investigation is justified, but may ensure that any enforcing measures are neither arbitrary nor out of proportion with the inquiry's aim.

daylight exposure: the total open position allowed to a bank's foreign exchange department during a business day.

day loan: a one-day loan, granted for the purchase of stock, for the broker's convenience. Upon delivery, securities are pledged as collateral to secure a regular call loan.

day order: an order, especially in commodities, to buy or sell that, if not executed, expires at the end of the trading day on which it was entered.

days of grace: the reasonable length of time allowed, without suffering a loss or penalty, for postponed payment or for the presentation for payment of certain financial documents.

day-to-day money: synonymous with *call money.*

DCE: see *Domestic Credit Expansion.*

DCR: see *Domestic Content Requirements.*

DDM: formerly the international standard code for the currency of Germany—the Deutsche mark; now absorbed as part of the single currency—the Euro.

dead freight: paid when a charterer does not provide a full cargo, and the ship owner charges freight for the space that would have been used.

deadheading:

(1) the movement of empty vehicles or railcars to a destination point.

(2) the practice of providing free transportation for workers of a transportation firm.

deadspace:

(1) unoccupied space.

(2) space engaged but not used by a shipper.

deadweight: weight that a ship is capable of carrying, plus bunkers, stores, and fresh water, when loading to the maximum permitted marks. The weight is measured in long tons (2,240lbs) or tonnes (2,204 lbs).

deadweight loss (of a tariff): synonymous with *protection cost (of a tariff)*.

dealer:

(1) a trader in securities, currencies, or other financial instruments.

(2) an organization, when it is taking positions for its own account.

debenture:

(1) indebtedness, usually in long-term obligations, which is unsecured.

(2) a corporate obligation that is sold as an investment.

(3) a voucher or certificate acknowledging that a debt is owed by the signer.

debenture certificate:

(1) a document authorizing payment of money granted as a bounty to an exporter of some domestic items.

(2) a customhouse document authorizing a rebate on duties paid on imported items to be exported.

debt: money, services, or materials owed to another person as the result of a previous agreement.

debt buy-backs: a debt-reduction method whereby a debtor nation purchases (buys back) its financial obligations, at either a discount or for cash.

debt capital: funds borrowed to finance the operations of a business.

debtee: a creditor.

debt-equity swaps: a debt-reduction method involving the exchange by a debtor nation of portions of its external debt for ownership in state-owned enterprises. The purchaser of the debt makes a loan to the debtor nation; the buyer then secures local currency at its face value; and the purchaser uses this local currency to purchase local equity in the nation.

debt financing: raising money or capital by borrowing.

debt forgiveness: the writing off of portions of the principal, interest, or both, by bankers to whom these amounts of debt are owed by foreign governments.

debt for nature swaps: reduction of debtor nations' debts in return for protection of sensitive environmental habits. See *debtor nation*.

debtor nation: a country whose citizens, companies, and government owe more to foreign creditors than foreign debtors owe them. Cf. *creditor nation*. See *debt for nature swaps*.

debt overhang: the payment of a nation's external debt by negotiation between the debtor nations and its creditors, with payments relating to the economic performance of the debtor nation instead of the original contractual terms.

debt reduction: see *debt*.

debt rescheduling: means for reducing the external debt owed to foreign nations by a debtor nation.

debt-service ratio:
(1) payments made by a country to foreign debt as a percentage of the country's export earnings.
(2) the ratio of debt to equity in a commercial enterprise.

debt servicing: capability to pay the principal and interest of a nation's foreign debt; requires cash payments to cover the interest and lower the total principal of a loan.

Decision 313: the countries of the Andean Pact passed legislation to implement an intellectual property rights agreement adopted in February 1992. These nations now offer a minimum of 15 years of patent protection for a variety of goods, including pharmaceuticals, although individual nations may offer even stronger protection. In addition, some protection is being given to biotech products, including microorganisms, with the exception of human genetics and animal species. See *Andean Pact*.

deck cargo: items stowed on the deck of a vessel.

declaration date: the date on which payment of a dividend is authorized by a corporation's board of directors.

declared value: the value of merchandise stated by the owner when the goods are delivered to the carrier.

DECs: see *District Export Councils.*

dedomiciling: relocating the headquarters of an international firm to a country where there is less or no taxation of foreign income and few restrictions on foreign investment.

deductive value: means of setting the value of imported goods if the transaction value of identical merchandise or of similar items cannot be determined.

deepening: the process of the 15 member nations of the European Union moving toward greater political, economic, and social union.

de facto protectionism: nontariff forms of protection used by countries to restrict imports. For example, the U.S. uses voluntary quotas on Japanese automobiles and has tried to convince other nations to reduce their exports to the U.S. and to increase their imports of U.S. goods. See *nontariff barrier; protectionism.*

default: the failure to do that which is required by law or to perform on an obligation previously committed. Commonly used when some legally constituted governing body fails to pay the principal or interest on its bond or fails to meet other financial obligations on maturity.

DEFC: see *Dansk Eksportfinansierungsfond.*

defeasance: a clause providing that performance of certain specified acts will render an instrument or contract void.

defer: to delay payment to a future time.

deferral rule: rule permitting U.S. companies to defer paying U.S. income taxes on profits earned by their foreign subsidiaries.

deferrals: cash collected before revenue is recognized as being earned, or cash disbursed before an expense is recognized as being incurred.

deferred payment credit: a type of letter of credit providing for payment some time following presentation of a shipping document by an exporter.

Deficiency Payment: a U.K. Exchequer payment to producers or agricultural marketing boards in the United Kingdom that is based on the difference between the guaranteed price and market prices.

deficit:
> (1) the excess of liabilities over assets.
>
> (2) indicating obligations or expenditures for items that are in excess of the amount allotted for those items in a financial budget.

deficit financing: when government expenditures exceed revenues, making up differences by borrowing. The objective is to expand business activity and yield an improvement in general economic conditions. The deficit is covered by the release of government bonds.

Deficit-Reduction Act: an August 1993 federal legislative package to lower the nation's deficit by raising personal income taxes, increasing gasoline taxes 4.3 cents per gallon, removing any business investment tax credit, offering $3.5 billion for enterprise zones, and providing $20.8 billion extra for earned-income tax credit. Rules on the taxation of foreign source income and the reduction in corporate retained earnings and investment encouraged a greater number of U.S. multinationals to invest more of their profits abroad.

deficit, trade: see *trade deficit.*

deindustrialize: capital outflows going from one developed country to another when investment returns are most advantageous. Will decapitalize a country's productive capacity.

delayed differentiation: a manufacturing strategy in which all products are manufactured in the same way for all countries until as late in the assembly process as possible, with differentiation of features or components introduced in the final stages of production.

del credere agent: in the U.K., when a third party serves as agent guaranteeing payment from a purchaser to a seller in an international trade transaction.

delegated authority: the authority of a commercial bank to commit Eximbank's guarantee for specified amounts and under certain conditions without prior approval from Eximbank; available in the working capital guarantee program and the medium-term bank guarantee program, and conferred only through a separate delegated authority letter of agreement with Eximbank.

delinquency: the failure to pay a debt when due.

delivered at frontier: when the seller is required to supply items that conform with the contract, at his or her own risk and expense, the seller must place the items at the disposal of the purchaser at the named place of delivery at the border at the specified time. The purchaser is responsible for complying with import formalities and duty payments.

delivered cost: the price at which goods are billed, including transportation charges.

delivered duty exempt: an obligation of the seller to pay the cost of the goods, insurance against loss, the freight charges to get them to the named port of destination, and any duties or surcharges or taxes levied on the items by the importing nation.

deliver-to party: individual or entity who physically receives shipped items.

delivery: the transfer of possession of an item from one person to another.

delivery date: the date by which a vendor must ship purchases to a store to comply with the agreed-on terms. Failure to meet this deadline is considered reason for cancellation of the order.

delivery risk: the risk that a counterpart will not be permitted to complete his or her side of the deal, although willing to do so.

delivery verification certificate: form used to trace imported items from the custody of the importer to the custody of the manufacturer, and used to substantiate a producer's drawback claim.

delivery versus payment (DVP): synonymous with *cash on delivery*.

DEM: deutsche mark, the former currency of Germany.

demand conditions: includes the composition of home demand, the size and pattern of home demand, and the internalization of demand. See *demand patterns*.

demand patterns: measures of the characteristics of goods and services purchased by consumers in different countries; tends to be similar in countries at the same stage of economic development. See *demand conditions*.

demand rate: synonymous with *check rate*.

Demand Sterling: used in London and other British banks; sight bills of exchange drawn in pounds.

demise charter: the charter of a vessel that transfers the ownership of the ship to the charterer for the duration. Cf. *bareboat charter*.

demonetization: the withdrawal of specified currency from circulation.

demurrage: the detention of a freight or a ship beyond the time permitted for loading or unloading, with additional charges for detention. See *average demurrage agreement; detention time; lay time.*

demurrage, contract: see *contract demurrage.*

denaturing: the act of making a commodity unfit for human consumption; by, for example, contaminating wheat with fish oil. To encourage the use of wheat as animal feed, a denaturing premium can be granted to authorized users that makes wheat competitive with less expensive coarse grains. Sugar can also be denatured to be used for animal feed.

density of a commodity: the weight of a commodity in pounds per cubic foot.

Department of Agriculture, U.S.: the federal department established in 1889 to conduct farm educational and research programs and to administer numerous federal agricultural-aid programs and other projects to aid farmers and ranchers.

Department of Commerce, U.S.: the federal department established in 1913 to promote domestic and foreign trade. Plays a key role in international trade accords and the enforcing of trade restrictions.

Department of the Treasury, U.S.: the federal agency created in 1789 to impose and collect taxes and customs duties, to enforce revenue and fiscal laws, to disburse federal funds, to manage the public debt, and to coin and print money.

dependent nations: nations that rely heavily on other nations for imports of essential goods.

depo: short for deposit.

deposit of estimated duties: antidumping duties that must be deposited upon entry of goods, which are the subject of an antidumping duty order for each manufacturer, producer, or exporter equal to the amount by which the foreign market value exceeds the U.S. price of the items.

Depository Receipt: a mechanism to allow for the trading of foreign stocks on U.S. stock exchanges when the overseas nation involved will not allow foreign ownership of the stock of domestic firms. The shares are therefore deposited with a bank in the country of incorporation and an affiliated or correspondent bank in the United States issues depository receipts for the securities. The major purpose of the instrument is to officially identify ownership of the stock in the foreign country. Short for *American Depository Receipt.*

deposit-taking company (DTC): a financial institution that can take deposits, make loans, discount bills, and issue letters of credit, but cannot be called a bank. The concept originated in Hong Kong.

depreciated currency: resulting from the lowering in the exchange value of currency, funds not accepted at face or par value.

depreciation: in accounting, charges against earnings to write off the cost, less salvage value, of an asset over its estimated useful life. See *currency depreciation*. Cf. *appreciation*.

depth of market: the extent of business that can be done in a market without causing a price disturbance.

derelict: a ship abandoned at sea.

derivative right of action: this strategy was proposed by U.S. Representative Richard Gephardt in the summer 1992, along with his concept for a transaction tax, to protect U.S. interests along the Mexican border. Prior to the heated debate that was expected over the North American Free Trade Agreement, he proposed that there should be a derivation right of action for U.S. shareholders to sue U.S. firms doing business in Mexico, or any other country. In this way Congressman Gephardt wanted the Environmental Protection Agency to treat the failure to abide by environmental laws as an unfair trade practice. This was fully absorbed as part of the supplemental NAFTA final negotiations. See *North American Secretariats*.

despatch money: the amount paid by a ship owner to the charter as an incentive for completing the loading or unloading operation in less than the time permitted under the charter party.

destabilizing speculation: making a profit by selling a foreign currency when the domestic exchange rate is low or is falling, in the expectation that the exchange rate will fall even further; or buying a foreign currency when the domestic exchange rate is high or is climbing, in the expectation that the exchange rate will rise still further.

destination: the place to which a shipment is consigned.

destination carrier: the carrier performing the line haul service nearest to the point of destination and not a carrier performing merely a switching service at the point of destination.

destination clauses: marketing contracts to permit an oil monopoly to stipulate which countries should receive oil, preventing the oil from being diverted to the spot market. See *spot market*.

Destination Control Statement: any of several statements that the U.S. government requires to be displayed on export shipments and that specify the destinations for which export of the shipment has been authorized.

detention time: additional charges made by the carrier when there is a lack of equipment or space on receiving docks to enable the carrier to unload merchandise, thus increasing work time. See *demurrage*.

determination: verification and certification for customs purposes of the origin of merchandise or property.

deutsche mark (DM): Germany's former currency, replacing the old reichsmark in 1948; now absorbed as part of the single currency—the euro.

devaluation: an action taken by the government to reduce the value of the domestic currency in terms of gold or foreign monies. See *J-curve*. Cf. *revaluation*.

devanning: unloading of merchandise from a container.

developed countries: nations characterized by a relatively high standard of living as measured by per-capita income, life expectancy, infant mortality, high literacy rates, and high per-capita levels of education. Cf. *less-developed countries*.

developing countries: see *less-developed countries*. Cf. *developed countries*.

development assistance: see *Development Assistance Committee*.

Development Assistance Committee (DAC): a committee of the *Organization for Economic Cooperation and Development* whose function is to encourage the flow of funds from member nations to the developing countries.

development bank: a bank that aids less developed nations (LDCs) in economic development. Such banks may lend or invest money and encourage local ownership. They may be worldwide, regional, or national. See *Bank for Europe*.

development contribution: a contribution of a proposed *Overseas Private Investment Corporation* project to the economic and social development of the host country.

Development Finance Companies (DFCs): the financing of development finance companies by the World Bank, which commenced in 1950 with a loan of $2 million to the Development Bank of Ethiopia. See *International Bank for Reconstruction and Development*.

deviation: any departure by a vessel from the scope or route of the planned voyage.

DFA: see *Draft Final Act*.

DFCs: see *Development Finance Companies*.

DFP (duty-free port): see *free trade zone*.

DFZ (duty-free zone): see *free trade zone*.

differential tariff: a tariff that gives preference to, discriminates against, or a combination of both, certain items from a nation or group of nations.

Dillon Round: one of the multinational trade rounds of GATT running from 1960 to 1962. The Common External Tariff was adopted, with the United States granting significant concessions on agricultural exports. Named after Douglas Dillon, the then U.S. under-secretary of state. See *General Agreement on Tariffs and Trade*.

DIN: the German Standard Institute.

dinar: the monetary unit of Abu Dhabi, Aden, Algeria, Bahrain, Iraq, Jordan, Kuwait, Libya, South Yemen, Tunisia, and Yugoslavia.

DIP: Direct Investment Position.

direct exporting: activities involving the sale and transmittal of items directly from an exporter to an importer. It does not exist where any intermediary takes title to the goods for reprocessing, repackaging, consolidation, transhipment, and/or warehousing for the purpose of resale.

direct foreign investment: see *direct investments*.

direct identification drawback: provision that permits U.S. companies to use imported components in the manufacturing process without having to include the duty paid on the imported goods in costs and sales prices.

direct investments:

(1) investments in foreign corporations when the investors have a controlling interest in the overseas firm.

(2) capital flow into a nation by private people or by organizations that claim ownership over the use of the invested capital. See *foreign direct investment*.

directional rate: a freight rate reduced for cargo moving in a direction where cargo is light, so as to stimulate movements. Often shipments in an opposite direction have higher freight rates.

direct offsets: synonymous with *coproduction*.

direct quote: a method of quoting exchange rates that reports the number of the home currency given for one unit of a foreign currency.

direct selling: sale of items by an exporter directly to distributors or final customers rather than to trading firms or other intermediaries, in order to achieve greater control over the marketing function and to earn higher profits.

dirham: the monetary unit of Morocco.

dirty bill of lading: a bill of lading that qualifies the items being carried. Synonymous with *foul bill of lading.* Cf. *clean bill of lading.*

dirty cargo: goods in an unclean or unsanitary condition that are transported either as bulk cargo or as cargo in containers with disposable linings.

dirty float: a currency that floats in value in terms of other currencies but is not free of government intervention. Governments intervene to smooth or manage fluctuations or to maintain desired exchange rates.

dirty money: currency acquired via criminal, illicit, or unlawful international business activities.

disagio: the charge made for exchanging depreciated foreign monies. Cf. *agio.*

disaster clause: a Eurocredit loan agreement clause containing provisions for repayment of the loan if the Euromarket should disappear.

disbursement: an actual payment of funds toward the full or partial settlement of an obligation.

DISC: see *Domestic International Sales Corporation.*

disclaimer: a document, or a clause in a contract, that renounces or repudiates the liability of an otherwise responsible party in the event of (a) noncompliance by such other party to certain conditions described in the instrument, (b) named external conditions, or (c) losses incurred because of a discrepancy in the goods delivered or the weight or count made by the shipper.

discount:
(1) the amount of money deducted from the face value of a note.
(2) the relationship of one currency to another. For example, Canadian currency may be at a discount to U.S. currency.
(3) in foreign exchange, a margin by which the forward rate drops below spot.

discount house: synonymous with *bill broker.*

discounting of drawings under a letter of credit: see *purchase of drawings under a documentary credit.*

discount margin: where the forward value of a currency is less than the spot price. Synonymous with *negative premium*.

discount rate:

(1) in the United States, the interest rate charged by the Federal Reserve System to its members; an interest rate used in evaluating expenditures that measures the relative value of benefits or returns obtained now, as compared with later.

(2) the interest rate at which a central bank will discount governmental paper or lend money against government paper collateral.

discrepancy: a situation where documents presented to an advising bank by an exporter do not conform to the letter of credit.

discretionary cargo: cargo exempt from the controls of cargo preference legislation requiring that specified items can only be shipped on vessels of the home country or other nations having received special arrangements.

discretionary fund: discretionary income enlarged by the amount of new credit extensions, which also may be deemed spendable as a result of consumer decision relatively free of prior commitment or pressure of need.

discretionary income: the amount of income remaining after paying taxes and making essential purchases.

discrimination:

(1) in the trade sense, reflects restrictive trade measures that favor one nation at the expense of another.

(2) unequal treatment of internationally traded goods or services according to their source or destination. WTO members are generally prohibited from applying discriminatory treatment either to imports or exports. See *most-favored nation; national treatment*.

disequilibrium:

(1) a condition in which incentives to change exist; usually in reference to markets in which either purchasers or producers, or both, have not yet adjusted prices and quantities to their satisfaction.

(2) the imbalance of national or world payment. Under the Bretton Woods agreement, nations were theoretically obliged to adjust their exchange rate or economies when their payments balances moved into fundamental disequilibrium. See *fundamental disequilibrium*.

disinvestment: the reduction of capital goods.

dispatch: an amount paid by a vessel's operator to a charterer if loading or unloading is completed in less time than stipulated in the charter party.

dispatch earning: a saving in shipping costs arising from rapid unloading at the point of destination.

dispatcher: an agent responsible for efficiently routing and sending merchandise to its destined location.

dispatching: the control and flow of pickups and deliveries of freight and the movement of cargo.

Dispute-Settlement System: in the *General Agreement on Tariffs and Trade,* now *WTO,* the procedures and regulations that have been agreed to by all parties, where differences and disagreements between contracting parties can be reconciled amicably.

distance rate: a rate that is applicable according to distance.

distress freight: cargo carried by a vessel at a depressed freight rate due to the ship's sailing empty, or nearly so, to its next port.

distribution license: license permitting its holder to make multiple exports of stated commodities to overseas consignees who are approved of in advance by the U.S. Bureau of Export Administration.

distributor: a foreign-based business that works under contract for an exporter in an offshore target market. The distributor imports directly from the exporter, and, where needed, performs the marketing activities of sales, service, promotion, and distribution. Synonymous with *wholesaler.*

District Export Councils (DECs): groups of volunteer businesspeople in every state that are appointed by the U.S. Department of Commerce to assist exporters; principal functions include direct counseling of infrequent exporters and coordination of export promotion ventures. See *Public and Private Programs.*

divergence indicator: an indicator purporting to measure which member currency of the European Monetary System diverges from its central parity against the European Currency Unit. See *European Monetary System.*

diversification strategy: approach whereby an international firm produces or sells in many nations to avoid relying on one particular market.

diversion: any change in the billing after a shipment has been received by a carrier at its point of origin and prior to delivery at its destination.

diversionary dumping: when a foreign producer sells to a third-country market at less than fair value and the product is then further processed and shipped to another country. See *dumping*.

dividend: a portion of the net profits that has been officially declared by the board of directors for distribution to stockholders. A dividend is paid at a fixed amount for each share of stock held by the stockholder.

DKK: the international standard code for the currencies of Denmark, Faeroe Islands, Greenland-the Danish kroner.

DM: former currency of Germany. See *deutsche mark*.

DO: the international standard code for the currency of Djibouti—the Djibouti franc.

DOA: see *documents on acceptance*.

dobra: the monetary unit of San Tomé and Principe.

dockage: synonymous with *wharfage*.

dock examination: U.S. Customs examination requiring that freight be opened for inspection rather than visually inspected.

dock receipt: proof given for a shipment received at a designated pier, quay, or wharf.

dock warrant: where merchandise is imported but immediate delivery is not required, and may be deposited in a warehouse, owned either by the dock authority or by the public warehouse people.

Doctrine of Sovereign Compliance: an international legal principle where those accused of behaving in ways contrary to their home-country laws have as their defense the argument that they acted as they did under compulsion by the foreign nation. Synonymous with *Sovereign Compulsion Doctrine*.

documentary collection: the means of export financing where specific documents are used to effect payment.

documentary credit:

(1) when a bank, on behalf of its customer, makes payment to (or to the order of) a third party (a beneficiary) or is to pay/accept/negotiate bills of exchange drawn by the beneficiary; or authorizes such payments to be made, or such drafts to be paid/accepted/negotiated by another bank.

(2) in financing foreign trade, a credit that may be confirmed or unconfirmed, revocable or irrevocable. This credit provides an exporter with immediate payment while providing the importer with credit.

documentary draft: synonymous with *bill of exchange; draft.*

documents against acceptance (DAA): domestic or foreign bills of exchange; notice that supporting statements will not be given to the drawee until acceptance of the bill. Cf. *documents on acceptance.*

documents against payment (DAP) (D/P draft): a method of payment for exports where the documents transferring title to the goods are released only after the importer has paid the value of the draft issued against him or her.

documents on acceptance (DOA): a payment method for exports where the documents transferring title to the items are released on the acceptance by an importer of the obligation to pay the time draft. Cf. *documents against acceptance.*

Doha Middle East/North Africa Economic Conference: held in Doha, Qatar, November 16–18, 1997. Its theme was Creating a new private/public partnership for trade and economic growth beyond the year 2000. Cf. *Amman Middle East/North Africa Economic Summit; Cairo Middle East/North Africa Economic Conference; Casablanca Middle East/North Africa Economic Summit.*

dollar:

(1) the monetary unit of the United States, which is shared by Guam, the Marshall Islands, Solomon Islands, and the Virgin Islands, U.S.

(2) the monetary unit of other nations, including Antigua, Australia, Bahamas, Barbados, Belize, British Honduras, Brunei, Canada, Dominica, Fiji, Grenada, Guiana, Guyana, Hong Kong, Jamaica, Kiribati, Liberia, Montserrat, Nauru, Nevis, New Guinea, New Zealand, Singapore, Somoa (British), St. Kitts, St. Lucia, St. Vincent, Taiwan, Trinidad and Tobago, Tuvalu, and Zimbabwe.

dollar acceptance: an acceptance of any bill of exchange drawn in a foreign nation or in the United States that is payable in dollars.

dollar bears: (slang) traders who believe that the dollar will drop in value against other foreign currencies.

dollar drain: the amount by which imports from the United States into a foreign country exceed that nation's exports to the United States.

dollar exchange: banker's acceptances and bills of exchange drawn overseas that are paid in the United States or around the world in dollars, or conversely drawn in the United States and paid overseas in dollars.

dollar gap: see *dollar drain.*

dollar glut: the excess supply of U.S. dollars in the hands of foreign monetary authorities outside the United States.

dollarize: to bring a foreign nation or its economy under the monetary power of the United States, as through conversion into U.S. dollars or investment in the United States.

dollar overhang: the significant amount of U.S. dollars retained by foreigners (mainly foreign financial institutions) as a result of past deficits in the balance of payments by the United States.

dollar premium: in Great Britain, the added premium or cost that investors are required to pay to purchase dollars for investment outside the country.

dollar shortage: a nation's lack of sufficient money to buy from the United States, caused by a steady favorable balance of payments for the United States.

dollar stabilization: acts by monetary authorities (i.e., the Federal Reserve Board, the International Monetary Fund), to reduce the fluctuation of the international exchange value of the dollar.

dollar standard: the system by which the U.S. dollar remains an international reserve currency without any gold backing.

domestic acceptance: any acceptance where the drawee and drawer are situated in the United States and consequently paid there.

domestic agent middleman: synonymous with *manufacturer's export agent.*

domestication: the slow transfer to foreign nationals, by overseas firms, of domestic capital assets and intellectual property.

domestic commerce: commercial market for a specific nation.

domestic content: see *North American Free Trade Agreement.*

Domestic Content Requirements (DCR): the demand that items must contain a certain percentage of national content by way of domestic factors of production, namely, land, labor, and capital. See *North American Free Trade Agreement; rules of origin.*

Domestic Credit Expansion (DCE): in Great Britain, the Public Sector Borrowing Requirement less the sales of public sector debt to the nonbank private sector, plus the increase in bank lending to the private and overseas sectors.

domestic debt: financial obligations owed by citizens of one country to other citizens of that same nation, payable in the currency of that nation.

domestic environment: all the uncontrollable forces originating in the home country that surround and influence the firm's life and development.

domestic exchange: any check, draft, or acceptance drawn in one location and paid in another within the United States. Cf. *foreign exchange.* Synonymous with *Inland Exchange.*

domestic exports: exports of domestic goods including commodities that are grown or manufactured in the U.S. and merchandise of overseas origin that has been substantially altered in the U.S., including in U.S. foreign trade zones, from the form in which they were imported.

Domestic International Sales Corporation (DISC): a special U.S. corporation authorized by the Tax Revenue Act to stimulate exports by lowering the effective tax rate on export income. Also allows exporters to borrow from the U.S. Treasury at reduced interest rates.

domestic offshore trade: areas subject to the jurisdiction of the United States, outside the contiguous 48 states, over which economic regulation of ocean shipping is exercised by the Federal Maritime Commission.

domestic value-added: the market price of a final item, less the cost of the imported inputs that were used in the production of the item. Cf. *value-added tax.*

Dominican peso: monetary currency of the Dominican Republic.

Donaulander: a regional cooperative group formed by Austria in May 1990. It includes the banks of the Danube, from Bavaria to Moldavia. It purports to upgrade the Danube as a cargo route and revive old Central European business and cultural links.

dong: the monetary unit of Vietnam.

DOP: the international standard code for the currency of the Dominican Republic—the Dominican peso.

douane: (French) *customs.*

double coincidence of wants: a situation in a barter of exchange when each party must possess precisely what the other wishes and must be able to trade at the exact amount and terms agreeable to both.

double-column tariff: two rates shown on a tariff schedule, one for preferred trading partners, the other for imports from nonpreferred trading nations.

double-disapproval principle: a liberalization of airline pricing where an airline's right to set a new cross-border fare can be challenged only if vetoed by the two governments involved. Although this principle does not itself pose an end to regulation, it makes interference by governments more difficult. See *cabotage*.

double taxation: a condition arising when a multinational firm is taxed on overseas income in both the source nation and the nation of the corporation's domicile. This problem is created because nations use varying systems of taxation; for example, a 1988 EC proposal for a Directive on the elimination of double taxation in connection with the adjustment of transfers of profits between associated enterprises (arbitration procedure). Some multinational firms currently suffer from double taxation because national tax authorities adjust transfer prices between subsidiaries in the group. The EC directive eliminated this source of double taxation within the Community. Effective January 1, 1992, double taxation or profits arising within a group of firms will be avoided by the setting up of a procedure designed to secure mutual agreement between tax authorities of member nations involved or the settlement of disputes by a commission in the absence of such an agreement.

downstream dumping: the condition that occurs when a foreign producer sells at below cost to a producer in its domestic market and the product is then further processed and shipped to another country. See *dumping*.

D/P draft: see *documents against payment*.

drachma: the monetary unit of Greece, divided into 100 lepta.

draft:

(1) an order in writing signed by one party (the drawer) requesting a second party (the drawee) to make payment in lawful money at a determinable future time to a third party (the payee).

(2) a financial instrument drawn on an importer's bank requiring payment to the bearer. See *bill of exchange*.

Draft Final Act (DFA): used in the early 1990s by GATT, now WTO, Director, with the tabling of a Draft Final Act. The DFA embodied all the rule-making agreements in the Uruguay Round as his compromise proposal to conclude that segment of the Round. In some cases, the texts were fully negotiated. In others, the Director-General proposed his own solution after extensive consultations with delegations. The Director General had hoped to have the DFA accepted quickly by all participants and the Round would be completed by mid–April 1992, which did not occur.

Drago Doctrine: named after Luis Maria Drago, the Foreign Minister of Argentina in 1902, who opposed intervention of any nation and the use of force to recover debts owed by a defaulting nation to foreign countries or to foreign nationals.

draught: European for *draft*.

drawback: synonymous with *duty drawback*.

draw-down: drawing funds made available under a *Eurocredit*.

drawee: any party expected to pay the sum listed on a check, draft, or bill of exchange. See *draft*.

drawer: any party who draws a check, draft, or bill or exchange for the payment of funds. See *draft*.

drayage: charge made for hauling freight, or trucks.

drop-off: delivery of a shipment by a shipper to a carrier for transport.

drop ship: shipment by exporter directly to an importer, with all shipping expenses to be included in the price.

dry dockage: a charge against a vessel that is placed in a dry dock for inspection or repair.

DTC: see *deposit-taking company*.

dual-currency bonds: bonds that are denominated in one currency, but pay interest in another currency at a fixed rate of exchange. Can also pay redemption proceeds in a different currency than the currency of denomination.

dual exchange rates: existence of two or more exchange rates for a single currency.

dual pricing: the selling of identical products in different markets for different prices, often reflecting dumping practices. See *dumping*.

dual-use: products and technologies that could be used for both military and civilian purposes. Controlling the export and granting of licenses for these items is a complex matter.

due bill:
(1) a bill rendered by a carrier for undercharges.
(2) a sight draft or time draft due for payment.

due from balance: (British) *nostro account*.

due from foreign exchange department: an asset account in the bank's financial statement showing the total funds within a foreign

n Newly Industrialized Countries (EANIC): major global
ers, composed of Hong Kong, Singapore, South Korea, and
a. See *Asian sector; Pacific Rim.*

ibbean dollar: monetary unit of Leeward and Windward

and Southern African Trade and Development Bank:
cial designation for the bank for the Preferential Trade Area
ern and Southern African States.

Caribbean Central Bank (ECCB): established in 1983; pro-
economic development, monetary stability and credit, and
ge for the eight participating countries in the Eastern
ean; headquartered in Basseterre, Saint Kitts.

Europe: see *Central European nations.*

l: prestigious award presented by the President of the
States for excellence in U.S. exporting.

e *European Bank for Reconstruction and Development.*

pean Community (Communities). See *European
nity.*

e *Eastern Caribbean Central Bank.*

uropean Community Chamber of Commerce): see
n-American Chamber of Commerce.

see *European Economic Area.*

e *Economic Community of Great Lake Countries.*

e *Export Credits Guarantee Department.*

e United Nations Latin American Economic Commission;
artered in Santiago, Chile; completes regional
nic-trade studies.

uropean Computer Manufacturers' Association): an
ation whose activity is in the field of standardization.

: unlike eco-labeling, which concerns goods, an eco-audit
ly to a company's production method and sites anywhere
le or regional community.

the European Union, any company that submits its pro-
facilities to an eco-audit by independent environmental
rs, covering areas such as energy efficiency, waste reduc-
d accident prevention, would receive an environmental
could use for public relations purposes. EU firms would
furnish a public statement explaining the verified audit
nd based on the audit, a firm's top management would

department for purposes of investment in foreign exchange activities.

due to balance: (British) *vostro account.*

dumping:
(1) the selling of goods abroad at prices below those that the
exporter charges for comparable sales in his or her own country,
often involving a subsidy. Subsidies include most financial benefits
granted to overseas corporations on the production or exports of
goods (but not rebates of custom duties, or internal sales taxes)
granted by governments when such items are exported.
(2) in the United States, selling imported items at prices less than
the cost of manufacture.
(3) selling items to other countries below cost for purposes of
eliminating surplus or to hurt foreign competition.
(4) See *boomerang; diversionary dumping; downstream dumping; dual
pricing; dumping margin; fair market value; non dumping certificate; persistent dumping; predatory dumping; sale at less than fair value; social
dumping; sporadic dumping; third-country dumping.*

dumping margin: a margin determined once a product is declared
to have been dumped. It represents the difference between the
home market price and the price at which the items are sold
abroad less incidental charges, such as export packaging, peculiar
to foreign sales. See *dumping.*

dumping, sporadic: see *sporadic dumping.*

dunnage: material used to prevent freight from coming into contact with the vessel's metal structure or with other freight.

dutiable list: a nation's tariff law giving those items that will be
subject to duty and the applicable rate.

duties: see *duty; tariff.*

duties collected: the amount of duties collected for a particular
commodity at a specified duty rate for a stated period of time.
Usually used as a guideline to assess the comparability or reciprocity of concessions between countries.

duty:
(1) an actual tax collected.
(2) a tax imposed on the importation, exportation, or consumption of goods; usually of foreign goods.

duty drawback: a tariff concession allowing a rebate of all or part
of the duty on goods imported for processing before being re-
exported. Synonymous with *drawback.*

duty-free: items that are not affected by any customs duty. See *free list*.

duty-free allowances: the allowance provided European Union visitors or returning residents to bring back certain goods duty- or tax-free, the amount depending on whether travel is within the Union or from third nations. Also, it is now possible to receive small parcels from abroad duty-free, including small quantities of tobacco and wine intended for private use. See *Customs Union; harmonization; value-added tax*.

duty-free port (DFP): see *free trade zone*.

duty-free shop: see *free trade zone*.

duty-free zone (DFZ): see *free trade zone*.

duty liability: the obligation of a government arising from the importation of dutiable items. Unpaid duties constitute a personal obligation to a nation and can be satisfied from any assets of the importer or estate. The government retains a lien on the imported items pending satisfaction of the debt.

duty-paid foreign goods: imported merchandise that has cleared customs with all appropriate duties and collected taxes.

duty remission: a refund of an import duty to an importer by a government that originally levied it contingent on the importer engaging in export production and thereby creating employment and tax revenue

DVP (delivery versus payment): synonymous with *cash on delivery*.

DWCC: deadweight cargo capacity.

DWT: deadweight tons/tonnes. See *deadweight*.

Dynamic Asian Economies: six Asian nations: Hong Kong, Korea, Malaysia, Singapore, Taiwan, and Thailand.

dynamic gains from trade: arising primarily from the economies of scale that freer trade makes possible.

DZD: the international standard code for the currency of Algeria—the Algerian dinar.

E

E: the European Union stamp placed on prod the item(s) has met with the standards establish Union.

EA: see *Edge Act*.

EAC: see *East African Community*.

EACC: see *European American Chamber of Comm*

EADB: see *East African Development Bank*.

EAEC: see *East African Economic Community*.

EAEG: see *East Asian Economic Grouping*.

EAI: see *Enterprise for the Americas Initiative*.

EANIC: see *East Asian Newly Industrialized Cou*

earned income: income derived from efforts participation in business.

Salaries, wages, bonuses, and commissions a

ease: the slow and/or minor drop in market

East African Community (EAC): an associat by Kenya, Uganda, and Tanzania in Arusha relates mainly to reciprocal rights and oblig contains provisions on the free movement freedom to supply services, and the right of panies from and in any of the signatory s population of 82 million people, new November 30, 1999 to reorganize EAC. T has been achieved. Synonymous with *Eas East African Economic Community*.

East African Customs Union: see *East Afri*

East African Development Bank (EADB): promote economic development amon Uganda; headquartered in Kampala, Uga

East African Economic Community (*Community*.

East Asian Economic Grouping (EAEG): of six members of the Association of S Brunei, Indonesia, Malaysia, the Phi Thailand—plus China, Taiwan, Hor Vietnam, and Myanmar, and ultimately trade bloc.

have to set targets for continued improvement in a plant's environmental performance. For each production site registered under the scheme, firms would have to establish internal environmental protection systems, including eco-audits every one to three years. Without an eco-audit system, there would be considerable risk that widely varying national standards would develop, leading to uneven environmental controls. Cf. *eco-label; Green Label.*

eco-label: use of this European Union label will help consumers identify environmentally sound products and protect them from choosing the often misleading "green labels" that businesses are increasingly using to market their products in response to green consumerism. Under an EU-approved system, only the best and most environmentally sound products in each category would be granted the eco-label. These products must also meet strict environmental criteria on production and packaging.

Products will be examined and graded for their impact on the environment throughout their life span by national competent officials using criteria agreed on at the EU level. Only products genuinely less damaging to the environment will receive the eco-label logo.

Although participation in the system will be voluntary, shifts in consumer preferences to environmentally friendly products could spur companies to use the logo for competitive reasons, cleaning up their images as well as their products.

The eco-label will signal consumers that the product with the EU sticker will be less damaging to the environment than others without such a label. This label is a sign that the EU is willing to use market forces as well as the law to protect the environment, and is intended to counter the plethora of dubious, unregulated advertisements of products claiming to be ecologically friendly.

These standards required for such labeling would be strict and based on an analysis of a product's impact throughout its life cycle, from the raw materials employed to produce it through distribution, packaging, use, and, ultimately, disposal. Cf. *eco-audit; Green Label.* See *genetically altered ingredients.*

e-commerce (E-commerce): use of the Internet to join together suppliers with companies and companies with customers.

Economic and Social Committee (EU): established by the European Economic Community Treaty to fulfill a role as an advisory institution. Based in Brussels, it consists of representatives of labor, employers, agriculture, consumers, and professional associations.

Economic Community of Great Lakes Countries (ECGC) (Communauté Économique des Pays des Grands Lac) (CEPGL): an international trade organization, established in 1976 and headquartered in Gisenyi, Rwanda. Burundi, Rwanda, and Zaire are members.

Economic Community of West Africa: synonymous with *Economic Community of West African States.*

Economic Community of West African States (ECOWAS): formed in 1975, with Benin, Burkina Faso, Cape Verde, Côte d'Ivoire, Gambia, Guinea, Guinea Bissau, Ghana, Liberia, Mail, Mauritania, Niger, Nigeria, Senegal, Togo, and Sierra Leone. Its goal is a common market among its members. Synonymous with *Economic Community of West Africa.*

Economic Cooperation Agreement: this European Union agreement established a financial and loan program with Costa Rica, El Salvador, Guatemala, Honduras, Nicaragua, and Panama. See *Caribbean Basin; Lomé Conventions.*

Economic Development Institute: see *International Bank for Reconstruction and Development.*

economic exposure: foreign exchange risk that international businesses face in the pricing of products, the source and cost of inputs, and the location of investments.

economic imperialism: efforts toward domination of the economies of developing nations by foreign business firms, which seek profits by controlling raw materials, labor, and markets in those nations.

economic integration: the harmonizing of different national commercial procedures and regulations and lowering, with the eventual hope to eliminate, trade barriers for nations forming the trade unit. See *harmonization.*

Economic Interest Grouping (EIG): see *European Economic Interest Grouping.*

Economic Partnership, Political Coordination, and Cooperation Agreement: between the EU and Mexico; entered into force October 1, 2000; institutionalizes a regular political dialogue at the highest level and extends bilateral cooperation. The centerpiece of the European Union–Mexico economic relationship is a free trade area in goods and services.

Economic Recovery Tax Act (ERTA): federal legislation of 1981, signed by President Reagan; introduced substantial income and corporation tax cuts, along with a switch to a system for increasing the tax benefits of depreciation.

economic sanctions: penalties, such as prohibiting trade, ceasing financial transactions, or barring economic assistance, etc., to achieve the goal of influencing a country.

Economic System of Latin America (SELA): see *Latin American Economic System.*

economic union: see *economic unity.*

economic unity: unification among partner nations in trade accords entails: (a) nations shall strengthen the coordination of their economic and monetary policies. An exchange rate system is needed with full participation by members. (b) A framework would be established to set key economic objectives and budget deficit limits for member nations. The community of members states would be responsible for monitoring performance if major deviations occur. A system of central banks would be created to form a common monetary policy. (c) Exchange rates would have to be irrevocably locked. Rules on macroeconomic and budgetary policy would become binding at this point. A central bank would be responsible for making the community's monetary policy, intervening in the currency markets, and holding reserves. At this time, a single currency could be adopted.

The community is tested in its coordination and press for economy unity. History does not readily aid in this process, for traditionally economic union necessitates keeping outsiders out, as this is the common thread that will bind the nations together. See *central bank.*

economic zones: regions in a nation that function under the rules that offer investment incentive, including duty-free treatment for imports and for manufacturing plants that re-export their merchandise.

ECOWAS: see *Economic Community of West African States.*

ecretement: a formula constituting a move toward tariff harmonization. It involves departing from the concept of a straight linear cut in tariffs by introducing the idea of target rates and reducing by 50 percent the difference between existing national rates and the target rates instead of the difference between existing tariff rates and nil.

ECS: the international standard code for the currency of Ecuador—the sucre.

ECSA: the East Coast of South America.

ECSC: see *European Coal and Steel Community.*

ECU: see *European Currency Unit.*

EDA: see *European Area of Development.*

EDC: see *Export Development Corporation.*

Edge Act (EA): an act that recreated a dual banking system for foreign banks by establishing a new class of federal charters for them. It also gives the U.S. Federal Reserve Board the right to impose reserve requirements on foreign banks. The 1978 International Banking Act restated the broad purpose of the Edge Act statute, in which Congress requires the Federal Reserve Bank to revise any of its regulations that unnecessarily disadvantage American banks in the conduct of business. The Act also allowed U.S. banks to open offices across state lines to assist in foreign trade financing. See *International Banking Act of 1978.* Synonymous with *Agreement Corporation.*

edge corporation: a foreign banking organization structured in compliance with the Federal Reserve Act.

EDM: see *European Domestic Market.*

EDR: see *European Depository Receipt.*

EEA: see *European Economic Area.*

EEC (E.E.C.): see *European Economic Community.*

EEIG: see *European Economic Interest Grouping.*

EES (European Economic Space): see *European Economic Area.*

EFF: see *Extended Fund Facility.*

effective access: see *reciprocity.*

effective exchange rate: any spot exchange rate actually paid or received by the public, including any taxes or subsidies on the exchange transaction as well as any applicable banking commissions; envisages that all effective exchange rates shall be situated within permitted margins around par value.

effective market access: see *reciprocity.*

effective rate of protection: the annual percentage of domestic prices of items which are attributed to tariffs that raise costs to consumers, in order to dissuade them from buying imported items. Cf. *nominal rate of protection.*

effective tariff: real tariff on the manufactured portion of developing countries' exports, which is higher than indicated by the published rates because the ad valorem tariff is based on the total value of the products, which includes raw materials that would have had duty-free entry.

effects doctrine: see *extraterritorial application of laws.*

efficiency of foreign exchange markets: when the future spot rate for foreign exchange has been accurately established by the forward rate.

EFTA: see *European Free Trade Association.*

EGP: the international standard code for the currency of Egypt—the Egyptian pound.

Egyptian pound: monetary unit of Egypt.

EIB:
(1) see *European Investment Bank.*
(2) see *Export-Import Bank of the United States.*

EIBJ: see *Export-Import Bank of Japan.*

EIG: see *Economic Interest Grouping.*

ejidos: in some Latin American nations, collective farms that have been a great symbol of revolutionary traditions. As trade agreements develop throughout Latin America, reforming agriculture may include attempts to allow private property rights on ejido land.

Ekuwele: the monetary unit of Equatorial Guinea.

elasticity: the ability of a bank to meet credit and currency demands during times of expansion and to reduce the availability of credit and currency during periods of overexpansion.

El Big Bang: deregulatory event in Spain in 1989, in which stock exchanges were no longer owned by the government, and government-appointed stockbrokers were replaced by private brokerage firms.

ELEC (European League for Economic Cooperation): an international nonparty organization that brings together experts in finance, economics, and industry to study economic and trade problems and to suggest solutions to them.

El Pacto Andino: see *Andean Pact.*

El Sistema de la Cuenca del Plata: see *RPBS.*

EMA (European Monetary Agreement): an agreement that

replaced the European Payments Union. Since 1958, EMA has provided a multilateral system of clearing foreign balances between the participating nations. See *European Monetary System*.

embargo:
(1) a governmental order prohibiting trade with a specific country or countries.
(2) the prohibition against the handling of transport of certain goods. Cf. *blockade*.

EMC: see *Export Management Company*.

EMCF: see *European Monetary Cooperation Fund*.

emergency rate: the rate established to meet some immediate and pressing need, and without due regard to the usual rate factors.

emerging economy: low- and middle-income country.

EMS: see *European Monetary System*.

EMUA (European Monetary Unit of Account): see *Units of Account*.

enabling clause: from the Tokyo Round Framework Agreement; legalized the extension of preferences by developed GATT contracting parties to developing countries.

end-use tariff: the duty rate for classifying an item, dependent on the intended use of the imported item.

enlargement: the process of adding any European nation to membership within the European Union. In spring 2004, 10 nations joined the EU, bringing the total population to 460 million. See *European Union—Treaty of Nice*.

en route: on the way.

enterprise: any entity constituted or organized under applicable law, whether or not for profit, and whether privately owned or governmentally owned, including any corporation, trust, partnership, sole proprietorship, joint venture, or other association.

Enterprise for the Americas Initiative (EAI): a plan proposed in a major policy address by President George H. W. Bush on June 27, 1990, that involved U.S. investments and government debt relief to Brazil, Argentina, Paraguay, and Uruguay. A tariff-free common market began in 1994 dismantling the barriers that long shielded them from competition. By setting sweeping proposals to lower trade and investment barriers, the Enterprise program is similar in tone to the creation of the European Common Market in 1957. The Latin American and Caribbean (LAC) region is of major economic significance to the United States. The EAI was inaugurated to advance the pace of reform in the region and follow the U.S. private sector to take advantage of new trade and investment opportunities. EAI focuses on stimulating economic growth in the entire western hemisphere through increased trade and investment and reduction of official debt owed by Latin American and Caribbean countries to the United States.

The three pillars of the program are: (a) Trade: a hemispheric free trade area, the long-term goal, will stimulate growth, jobs, and competitiveness for all countries in the region. After NAFTA, with the U.S., Canada, and Mexico, the President proposed negotiating framework agreements on trade and investment that establish councils and a consultation process to discuss trade and investment issues. (b) Investment: the EAI's investment goals are to stimulate investment reform and privatization under two programs administered by the Inter-American Development Bank (IDB), the Investment Sector Loan Program (ISLP), and the Multilateral Investment Fund (MIF). ISLP loans are designed to reinforce investment liberalization efforts on a sector-specific basis while the MIF is a five-year grant program to advance specific, market-oriented investment policy initiatives. (c) Debt: the United States, Latin American, and Caribbean countries are working to reduce debt obligation to the U.S. government. The reduction of official debt has an additional innovative component which complements the increasing environmental awareness movement. By providing seed money for environmental projects, the EAI aims to help preserve the environment. The EAI also make a provision for debt-for-nature swaps.

The EAI includes an environmental element in recognition of the important role of environmental protection and conservation in accomplishing sustainable economic development. By channeling interest payments on reduced debt in local currency to fund grass-roots projects, the EAI aims to build on the environmental awareness movement already taking place in the region. Additionally, by placing the emphasis on nongovernmental organizations, both in making decisions about the use of funds and in carrying out projects, the EAI complements other assistance programs already under way and provides a vehicle for institution building in the environmental area. For concessional debt, if certain conditions are met, the debtor country may make interest payments on the restructured and reduced concessional loans in local currency, and the local currency would be placed in a local fund to support environmental projects. To be eligible for these environmental programs, the debtor country would be required to first complete an Environmental Framework Agreement with the United States. These agreements provide for the creation of an environmental funds and a local environmental board to administer the fund. Each local board is comprised of representatives of the debtor country government, U.S. government, and local nongovernmental organizations. An Environment of the Americas Board has been established in Washington to oversee the process. This board includes representation from the U.S. government and key nongovernmental organizations.

When contrasted with the concepts for a New American Community, the EAI bears considerable overlap. While the EAI is primarily a strategy detailing efforts in trade, investment, and debt reduction, the NAC goes beyond this significant effort, and attempts to structure a full-fledged effort to upgrade the standard of living for more than 700 million people in 33 nations, with programs in health, education, and social welfare.

See *Free Trade Area of the Americas; New American Community; North American Free Trade Agreement.*

entireties doctrine: the principle of customs law permitting components, in some situations, to be entered for duty purposes under the tariff item applicable to the finished item.

entities: government ministries and departments; important to the Government Procurement Code, in which signatories agree not to discriminate against the products of other signatories in certain purchases of goods by code-covered government entities.

entrepot: an intermediary storage facility where merchandise is kept temporarily until distribution within a nation or for re-export.

entrepot trade: the re-export of imports from a warehouse. When the items are not sold from bonded warehouses, and duty has been paid, the re-exporter may be entitled to a refund of the duty.

entry (customs): a statement of the kinds, quantities, and values of goods imported, together with duties due, if any, declared before a customs officer or other designated officer. See *Informal Entry.*

entry documents: paperwork needed by an importer at the time merchandise is being cleared through customs.

entry papers: documents filed with customs officials describing merchandise imported.

entry strategies: ways of entering multinational business operations. They include exporting, licensing, franchising, foreign branch operations, joint ventures, and wholly owned subsidiaries.

entry summary system: minimum amount of documentation required to secure release of imported items.

entry value: defined by U.S Customs, the value reflected on the entry documentation presented by an importer.

environment: see *North American Secretariats.*

environmental climate: external conditions in host countries that could significantly affect the success of a foreign business enterprise.

Environment of the Americas Board: see *Enterprise for the Americas Initiative.*

EO Nomine: one of three methods for the classification of items for duty purposes; depends on finding the common name of the item within the tariff schedules. If not found, a customs examiner classifies the product according to its intended use, or according to the materials of which it is composed.

EOTC: see *European Organization for Testing and Certification.*

EPO (European Patents Office): see *European Patent Convention.*

EPZ (export processing zone): see *free trade zone.*

equalization: funds allotted to a customer should merchandise be picked up at a destination other than the one listed on the bill of lading.

equilibrium: the balance or near balance in a nation's external payments position, or in the payments balances of a group of major IMF countries.

equity:
(1) the value placed on the distribution of income.
(2) the ownership interest of common and preferred stockholders in a company.
(3) the remaining value of a futures trading account, if it is disposed of at current market prices.

equity capital: money raised by selling corporate stock that represents ownership of the corporation.

equivalent trade concessions: see *Trilateral Trade Commission.*

ERAS (export restraint agreements): see *voluntary restraint agreements.*

ERM (Exchange-Rate Mechanism): see *European Exchange Rate Mechanism*.

ERTA: see *Economic Recovery Tax Act*.

escape clause:

(1) a legal provision concerning products whose tariffs have been reduced. If, after reduction, imports increase and threaten the domestic producers of those products, this clause permits the tariff to be put back up. Cf. *tariff suspension*.

(2) with the World Trade Organization, formerly the General Agreement on Tariffs and Trade, a section allowing a signatory country to suspend tariffs when imports threaten to cause serious material injury to domestic makers of items competitive to those imported.

escrow: a written agreement or instrument set up for allocation funds or securities deposited by the giver or grantor to a third party for the eventual benefit of the second party (the grantee). The escrow agent holds the deposit until certain conditions have been met. The grantor can get the deposit back only if the grantee fails to comply with the terms of the contract, nor can the grantee receive the deposit until the conditions have been met.

escudo: the monetary unit of the Azores, Cape Verde Islands, Guinea Bissau, Madeira, Mozambique, Portugal, Portuguese East Africa, and Timor.

essential-industry argument: argument holding that certain domestic industries require protection for national security purposes.

estimated gross national product: an estimation of the GNP based on the combined estimates of its four main components: consumer spending; spending by business firms; spending by local, state, and federal governments; and net foreign spending.

estimated weight: the specific weight provided in a carrier tariff for application on a certain commodity regardless of the actual weight.

ETB: the international standard code for the currency of Ethiopia—the Ethiopian birr.

ETC: see *Export Trading Company*.

ETCA: see *Export Trading Company Act*.

ETSI (European Telecommunications Standards Institute): an organization that sets appropriate telecommunications standards, with considerable implications for the export of telecommunications equipment. It was established in Sophia Antipolis (near Nice), France.

EU: see *European Union.*

EUA (European Unit of Account): see *Units of Account.*

EUR: the Unit of Account of the EU used by the Statistical office of the European Union. See *Units of Account.*

EURI: customs form used to facilitate preferential rates of custom duty on EU-originating goods to be imported into EFTA countries plus a number of other Mediterranean, Central European, and some African Caribbean and Pacific (ACP) nations. See *ACP (states); European Free Trade Association; Lomé Conventions.*

EURCO: see *European Composite Unit.*

euro: a single currency of 12 nations replacing the currencies of these individual nations. There are seven euro-denominated notes and eight coins. As of January 2002, the euro was the official legal tender of 12 of the 15 EU nations. Represents the consolidation of European economic integration. The United Kingdom, Denmark, and Sweden remain independent and continue to utilize their national currencies. Since May 2004, with 10 new nations ascending into the EU, a gradual phase-in of the euro will be advanced over time. See *European Currency Unit.*

Euro-Arab dialogue: negotiations on economic, financial, trade, and other cooperation between the European Union and the Arab League, resulting from the Copenhagen summit of December 1973.

Eurobank: a Western European bank, especially one that receives deposits, makes loans, and extends credit in Eurocurrency.

Eurobill of Exchange: a bill of exchange drawn and accepted in the usual fashion but expressed in foreign currency and accepted as being payable outside the country whose currency is being used.

Eurobond: a bond released by a U.S. or other non-European company for sale in Europe. In this market, corporations and governments issue medium-term securities, typically 10 to 15 years in length. See *Eurocredit sector.*

Eurobonds: a long-term bond marketed internationally in countries other than the country of the currency in which it is denominated. This issue is not subject to national restrictions.

Eurobook: a portfolio of Euromarket assets and liabilities.

Euro-Canadian dollars: Canadian dollars dealt in the Euromarkets.

Eurocard: a European credit card developed by the German banking system that is accepted in most Western European countries.

Eurochecking (Eurochequing): an international payment system set up in 1968 by European financial institutions. In 1983, the European Community announced the waiving of antitrust rules to permit EC banks to continue applying a single set of terms for clearing international currency transactions made through the Eurocheque system. Members include banks and other credit institutions in some 40 European and Mediterranean countries, including the member states of the European Community. These checks may be cashed by bank customers at any of the system's member banks. They are often accepted as payment for hotel and restaurant bills and for purchases at shops and gas stations. Eurocheque customers are issued plastic "guarantee cards" assuring merchants and others who accept Eurocheques that the check will be honored by the bank it is drawn on. The primary advantage of the international use of Eurochequing is convenience to the check writer. Within the European Community, the rate of commission charged by Eurocheque clearing centers ranges from 1.25 percent in Luxembourg and the Netherlands to 2.25 percent in Belgium. There is no such clearing charge in some participating countries.

Eurocheque: see *Eurochecking*.

Eurocommercial paper:

(1) short-term, commercial paper issued in a Eurocurrency.

(2) a short-term, unsecured note issued or offered by a nonbank corporation in the Euromarkets. See *Eurocurrency*.

Euro-Control: the European Organization for the Safety of Air Navigation, created in 1963 to strengthen cooperation among member nations in matters of air navigation, and specifically to provide for the common organization of air traffic services in the upper airspace.

Eurocredit:

(1) any lending made using Eurocurrency. See *Eurocurrency*.

(2) medium-term international credits in a Eurocurrency, usually provided by a syndicate of banks.

Eurocredit sector: a sector of the Euromarket, where banks function as long-term lenders by constantly rolling over short- and medium-term loans at rates that fluctuate with the cost of funds. See *Eurobond*.

Eurocurrency:

(1) monies of various nations that are deposited in European banks and used in the European financial market. Synonymous with *Euromoney*. See *Eurodollars; Maastricht Treaty*.

(2) any currency being traded (i.e., bought and sold) outside the jurisdiction that issued the currency. Originally meant exclusively Eurodollars.

Eurocurrency deposit: an account where a currency denominated in a transferable West European currency is placed by an individual or a firm not resident in the country of the currency.

Eurocurrency swap: an exchange between two counterparties of either the currency of denomination or the form of interest (fixed versus floating rate) payable on debt instruments.

Eurodollar: see *Eurodollars.*

Eurodollar deposits: bank deposits, generally bearing interest and made for a specific time.

Eurodollars: dollar balances held by private people or firms in European banks. They provide a stock of international currency not appearing in governmental returns. Traffic is not confined to dollars. It is also a fund of international short-term capital that usually flows to those nations offering the highest interest rates. The system came into being during the Suez crisis of 1957. Other currencies have also filled this role, thus the term *Eurocurrency.* Cf. *Asian dollars.*

Euroequity: equity share denominated in a currency differing from that of the nation in which it is traded.

EuroFed: see *European Central Bank.*

Eurofrancs: Swiss, Belgian, or French francs traded on the Eurocurrency markets; now discontinued.

Euroguilder notes: notes denominated in Euroguilders; discontinued.

Euroguilders: Dutch guilders traded in the Eurocurrency market; discontinued.

Euro-Index: a Pan-European index found in Western European stock exchange, designed for the derivatives markets.

Euroland: 12 nations of the EU that participated in the launching of the Euro currency on January 1, 2002.

Euromarket: in general, international capital markets dealing in Eurobonds, Eurocredits, etc. See *Eurobond; Eurocredit.*

Euromoney: synonymous with *Eurocurrency.*

EURONORM: European standards accepted by the member nations of the European Union. See *standards.*

Europe: continent of the Eastern Hemisphere comprising 23 Eastern and Western European nations with a population of 520 million people and nearly $5 trillion gross national product, dwarfing the $4 trillion economy of the United States and Japan's $2 trillion. See *Eastern Europe; European Community; European Free Trade Association.*

European-American Chamber of Commerce (EACC): an organization formed in July 1990 by leaders of 11 bilateral European Community chambers of commerce in New York to promote trade and investment flows between the United States and the European Community. The only EC member state not represented is the Netherlands, which recently formed a similar organization, the European Community Chamber of Commerce (ECCC) in the United States.

European Area of Development (EDA): an industrial zone approved by the European Community in December 1986, with financial support from the EC authorities and a package of advantageous conditions ranging from direct grants and reimbursements to hire and train staff, to tax breaks. The European Area of Development is a cross-border industrial zone on 1,200 acres within one hour's drive of Luxembourg's international airport.

European Bank: synonymous with *European Bank for Reconstruction and Development.*

European Bank for Reconstruction and Development (BERD): created on January 15, 1990 by the 12 member nations of the European Community. The Bank's purpose is to make loans to help rebuild the former Soviet-bloc economies. The Bank commenced operations in April 1991 and is located in London. Synonymous with *European Bank; European Development Bank.*

European Central Bank: On November 13, 1990, the European Community's central-bank governors, meeting in Basle, completed their draft statutes for a future European Central Bank. The bank's statutory objective will be to maintain price stability. Members of the bank's council—the 12 governors of the existing national central banks plus six executive directors appointed by the European Council—are expressly forbidden to accept instructions from national governments or EC institutions.

Was inaugurated in Frankfurt on June 1, 1998, and became operational on January 1, 1999. The central bank of the European Union is based in Frankfurt, Germany. It sets interest rates along with the participation 12 national central bank chiefs in the Euro-zone. See *central bank; European System of Central Banks; Euro-zone.*

European Coal and Steel Community (ECSC): the first European Community created by the Treaty of Paris in April 1951. An agreement signed by the six founder members (Belgium, France, Germany, Italy, Luxembourg, and the Netherlands). Its goal was to transfer control of the basic materials of war (coal and steel) away from each national government to common institutions, and to plan the economic expansion, rational distribution and production, and safeguarding of employment within the industry. The Treaty sought to abolish duties and quantitative restrictions on trade in coal and steel between member nations and to eliminate restrictive practices such as cartels.

European Commission: The Commission, the driving force of EU policy, is the starting point for every Union action, presenting proposals and drafts for legislation. It is obliged to act in behalf of its members. The Commission has law-making powers, and is the guardian of its Treaties. It monitors applications for new members and institutes infringement proceedings in the event of any violations of its laws. It has 20 members, including one president and two vice presidents.

European Committee for Electrotechnical Standardization (CENELEC) (Comité Européen de Normalisation Electrotechnique): CENELEC has a membership composed of the standards institutions of the Community, the nations of the European Free Trade Association, and Spain. Standards are adopted by majority voting, and deal with inter-intra trade. See *European Committee for Standardization; harmonization.*

European Committee for Standardization (CEN) (Comite Europeen de Normalisation): a committee whose membership consists of the standards institutions of the Community, the nations of the European Free Trade Association. Standards are adopted by majority voting. See *European Committee for Electrotechnical Standardization; harmonization.*

European Common Market: synonymous with *European Community; European Economic Community.*

European Community (EC): the three European Communities, created by the Treaty of Paris and the Treaty of Rome—the European Coal and Steel Community, the European Atomic Energy Community, and the European Economic Community—

merged in 1965 to form the EC. In 1973, the six founding members (Belgium, France, Italy, Luxembourg, Germany, and the Netherlands) were joined by Denmark, the Irish Republic, and the United Kingdom. Greece became a full member on January 1, 1981, with Portugal and Spain joining in 1986.

Its aims are to break down trade barriers within a common market and create a political union among the peoples of Europe. It has its own budget raised from its own resources (e.g., customs duties, agricultural levies, a proportion of value added tax) and offers loans, subsidies, or grants through a variety of financial instruments.

The early 1990s were targeted by the E.C. as a "Europe for Europeans" when fiscal and trade barriers would fall, but it did not see the sunrise in sparkling fashion. More time will be needed before most or all planned goals are met, but the season is upon us when Europe flexes its muscle of recognition and independence. Should the domino theory apply, conflicts between industrial nations will abound. Europe may be, over time, on its way to becoming the world's single richest market. The New Europe is primarily the product of a continent-wide economic deregulatory movement where hundreds of rules that should have been discarded long ago are finally being swept away. The European Community today represents one of the greatest challenges to and reasons for the establishment of the New American Community.

The 1990s brought growing concern throughout the EC that the institution would no longer be able to deliver the combination commonly seen as a basic right throughout Western Europe: steadily rising living standards, along with the comforts of a cradle-to-grave welfare state. The problems went well beyond the widespread economic slowdown from which other parts of the developed world had begun to emerge. There was a growing consensus that the still deepening slump is not cyclical but structural, and that major economic re-engineering was needed.

Following reunification in 1992, Germany's economy began to falter. Other nation's economies drifted toward recession under tight-money economic policies that would hamper growth rather than spark it. Bankruptcies throughout the EC quickened, plant closings increased, and unemployment reached high levels.

Other economic threats are coming from former Soviet bloc

nations. Poland, Hungary, and the Czech and Slovak republics are making great economic strides. These nations do not have the welfare-state inflexibilities found in the EC nations. Their labor forces are cheap, but well educated.

At their June 1993 semi-annual Council of Ministers meeting in Copenhagen, the EC debated its lack of competitiveness in relation to the United States and Japan (at that time 17 million people were unemployed in the EC). An eight-part plan to spark their economic revival was presented, focusing on increased spending on research and development, enhanced transportation and telecommunications networks, educational reform, and job training or placement schemes designed to boost labor flexibility. At the same session, the EC faced its failure on Bosnia, failing their biggest foreign-policy test to date and thus frustrating the call for political unity. Responding to criticism that they had done little to aid emerging democracies of Eastern Europe, the EC formally invited six former Soviet-bloc nations to join the Community when their economic and political conditions permit.

In August 1993, finance ministers and central bankers of the European Community all but suspended the rules of the European Monetary System's ERM. Finance ministers allowed the French franc and most other EC currencies to fluctuate as much as 15 percent against the German mark.

With the signing of the February 7, 1992 Maastricht Treaty, the name was changed from the European Community to the European Union. See *European Free Trade Association; European Union.* Synonymous with *European Common Market.*

European Community Chamber of Commerce (ECCC): see *European-American Chamber of Commerce.*

European Composite Unit (EURCO): a nonofficial, private unit of account based on member currencies of the European Union; includes a quantity of each of the European Union's currencies, in a proportion that reflects the importance of the country's economy.

European Computer Manufacturer's Association: see *ECMA.*

European Convention on Contracts: a convention that governs contract disputes arising from the sales of goods (including exports and imports) and services between European Union member-state signatories. The Convention stipulates that the law of the nation where the consumer resides takes precedence over the law where the seller or supplier of services is based, in the event of a contract dispute (provided that both parties reside in signatory nations). Under the Convention, the seller's law can still be used, but only if it is explicitly stated in a written contract agreed to by both parties. Synonymous with *Rome Convention of 1980*.

European Cooperation Fund: see *European Currency Unit*.

European Council: brings together heads of state and government and the president of the Commission. It meets at least twice a year at the end of each EU member state's six-month presidency.

European Court of Auditors: see *Court of Auditors*.

European Court of First Instance: see *Court of First Instance; European Court of Justice*.

European Court of Justice: one of the European Union's four major institutions. The court has the responsibility of ensuring that the interpretation and application of Community law is observed. The court's judgments are final and cannot be referred to any other court. Based in Luxembourg, it has 15 judges, coming from 15 nations, and nine Advocates-General by common accord for a term of six years. For matters dealing with natural or legal persons, a *Court of First Instance* was added to relieve the Court of Justice. See *Court of First Instance*.

European Currency Unit (ECU): conceived on March 13, 1979, and linked with the European Monetary System. In January 1999, when the euro was introduced, the ECU was then replaced at par—that is, at a 1:1 ratio. See *euro*.

European Depository Receipt (EDR): a receipt patterned after the American depository receipt to facilitate investments by Americans in securities of foreign nations. The EDR was first issued in London in 1963, to facilitate international trading in Japanese securities. It is a negotiable receipt covering certain specified securities that have been deposited in a bank in a country of origin of the securities. Its use in trading eliminates the necessity of shipping the actual stock certificates, thus making transfer of ownership easier, faster, and less costly. See *Depository Receipt*.

European Development Pole: in November 1986, the European Community's Commission approved a bid by the Belgian, French, and Luxembourg governments to set up a three-frontiers European development pole that would give a boost to regional development and trade and contribute to European integration.

European Domestic Market (EDM): a plan to eliminate all nontariff barriers on trade within the European Union. It could have the effect of raising nontariff barriers against imports from outside the Union. See *voluntary export restraints.*

European Economic Area (EEA): a group formed by the European Union and the European Free Trade Association to deal with the implications of 1992 for the Continent's other trading bloc. All 18 nations unanimously declared their political support for cooperation between the groups.

On October 22, 1991, the EU nations and the seven-member EFTA concluded two years of negotiations and agreed to form a new common market of 380 million consumers and 46 percent of world trade. See *European Free Trade Association; European Free Trade Zone.* Synonymous with *European Economic Space.*

European Economic Community (EEC) (E.E.C.): one of the three European Communities established in 1958 under the Treaty of Rome by the six founder members (Belgium, France, Germany, Italy, Luxembourg, and the Netherlands), with goals to lay the foundations for a closer union among the peoples of Europe; to form a common market by eliminating trade barriers; and to work for the constant improvement of living and working conditions. It is coordinated by the European Commission, the Council of Ministers, the European Parliament, and the European Court of Justice. In 1965, the EEC merged with the European Coal and Steel Community and the European Atomic Energy Community, forming the European Community. Today, the EEC is the European Union. See *European Community; European Union.* Synonymous with *European Common Market.*

European Economic Interest Grouping (EEIG): after July 1989, a new instrument facilitating cross-frontier cooperation for firms within the European Community engaging in certain joint activities such as research and development; purchasing, production, and selling; operation of specialized services; quality control of substances; computerized data processing; and the formation of multidisciplinary consortia in the construction industry to tender for public or private contracts. EEIG lays down rules, applicable to all members, on the structure and method of operation, thus providing firms, particularly small and medium-size companies, with a framework that is more responsive to their needs and their potential, enabling them to group part of their economic activity, while still retaining their economic and legal independence within a structure that enjoys full legal capacity.

The first EEIGs were formed after July 1, 1989. EEIG encourages cross-border cooperation and benefits businesses that do not wish to merge or form joint subsidiaries, but wish to carry out certain activities in common. See *Company Law.*

European Economic Space (EES): synonymous with *European Economic Area.*

European Exchange Rate Mechanism (ERM): a system of fixed, though adjustable, exchange rates that underpins the European Monetary System. Ten of the 12 EU nations at one time were part of ERM, but in fall 1992, the United Kingdom and Italy withdrew. Each member of ERM has a central exchange rate relative to the ECU. The nation's central bank is obliged to intervene to stabilize its currency if needed, when it fluctuates by plus or minus 2.5 percent. See *currency band; European Currency Unit; European Monetary System.*

European Free Trade Agreement: see *European Free Trade Association.*

European Free Trade Association (EFTA): created in 1959 under the Stockholm Treaty as a counterinstitution to the European Economic Community. Its three goals are: (a) to achieve free trade among the member nations; (b) to assist in the creation of a single market embracing the nations of Western Europe; (c) to contribute to the expansion of world trade in general.

Presently EFTA members are Norway, Switzerland, Liechtenstein and Iceland. Since July 1, 1977, there has been an almost complete free trade area in industrial goods in 18 Western European nations. Tariff concessions apply to industrial items of EFTA origin; agricultural products to not come under the provisions of free trade.

Formal negotiations began on June 20, 1990, between EFTA and the EC to establish a common economic zone, the so-called European Economic Area of 380 million consumers and 46 percent of world trade. On October 22, 1991, the EC and EFTA concluded their negotiations and agreed to create the European Economic Area, thus forming a different economic rivalry and competition for the world. The 31 million people from EFTA nations with a per-capita income of $19,000 per year (twice that of the EC average) will add further resources in Europe's global struggle for market dominance. See *customs union; Eastern Europe; European Community; European Economic Area; European Free Trade Zone; External Trade.*

European Free Trade Zone: took effect January 1, 1984, which was the deadline for the dismantlement of the last of the industrial trade barriers between the European Community and the seven members of the European Free Trade Association (EFTA). It abolished the last of the tariffs that had existed between them on trade in industrial products and marked the culmination of a series of free-trade agreements signed between the European Community and the individual EFTA countries in the early 1970s. Initially, these agreements eliminated import quotas on industrial products traded between EC and EFTA countries. Import duties on the bulk of these products were eliminated by 1977. For a second group of industrial products—mainly textiles and nonferrous metals—tariffs were phased out gradually over a longer period. For the most economically sensitive products, such as paper, the timetable for dismantling EC-EFTA tariffs was extended until the beginning of 1984. On December 7, 1989, the Community reached a broad agreement to create an enlarged free-trade zone that would include the six members of EFTA. The pact was signed on December 19, thus creating a European Economic Area (Space).

European Investment Bank (EIB): set up by the Treaty of Rome in 1957; provides loans and guarantees in all economic sectors of the EU, especially to promote the development of less-developed regions, to modernize or convert undertakings or create new jobs, and to assist projects of common interest to several member states.

European League for Economic Cooperation: see *ELEC.*

European Monetary Agreement: see *EMA.*

European Monetary Cooperation Fund (EMCF): a fund established as the nucleus of a reserve system of the central banks. It has operational responsibility in the field of a Community currency exchange system. The Fund governors are from member states' central banks. It uses the Bank for International Settlements as its agent, and intervenes on the foreign exchange markets at the request of member nations. See *Bank for International Settlements (BIS).*

European Monetary Institute: created on January 1, 1994, by the EU Maastricht Treaty to manage the national currency reserves of the European Union and to encourage acceptance of the European Currency Unit.

European Monetary System (EMS): officially introduced on March 13, 1979; created a zone of monetary stability in Europe through the implementation of certain exchange rates, credit, and resource transfer policies to ensure that monetary instability does not interfere with the process of genuine integration with the Community. Assistance is conditional; a borrower nation must agree to certain economic and monetary conditions.

In June 1989, the 12 member nations, meeting in Madrid, agreed that by July 1, 1990, they would broaden the EMS to coincide with an end to exchange controls and obstacles to community-wide banking, securities, and insurance operations.

In October 1990, the United Kingdom joined the EMS, but then in 1992, along with Italy, withdrew, unwilling to fulfill EMS requirements for their currencies.

European Monetary Unit of Account (EMUA): see *Units of Account*.

European Organization for Testing and Certification (EOTC): in November 1990, European Community, European Free Trade Association, and other European standards agency representatives signed a memorandum of understanding on the creation of this organization. It will focus primarily on the proper functioning and coordinating of groups responsible for mutual recognition of testing and certification throughout the European Community and the European Free Trade Association.

European Parliament: comprises 626 members, directly elected in EU-wide elections for five-year terms. Although the Parliament cannot enact laws, it has co-decision procedure that empowers it to veto legislation in certain policy areas. It can question the Commission and the Council; amend or reject the EU budget; and dismiss the entire Commission through a vote of censure.

European Patent Convention: European agreement allowing firms to make a uniform patent search and application, which is then passed on to all signatory countries.

European Patents Office (EPO): see *European Patent Convention*.

European sector: this global area begins with the European Union, includes the nations of the European Free Trade Association, then Central and Eastern Europe. Combined, they have a total population in excess of 520 million people.

European Snake: in 1972, the six nations of the European Economic Community agreed to limit the fluctuation of their exchange rates against the U.S. dollar to plus or minus 2.25 percent; phased out in March 1973.

European System of Central Banks: defines Euro monetary policy and implements such policy; comprises the Central Banks of the Euro countries, and the independent European Central Bank. See *European Central Bank.*

European Telecommunications Standards Institute: see *ETSI.*

European terms: practice of using the indirect quote for exchange rates.

European Union (EU): the newest name (earlier it was known as the European Economic Community, then the European Community) of the 15 nations of western Europe (25 countries in the year 2004). The third group of European organizations comprises the European Union, which itself has grown out of the European Coal and Steel Community and the European Union.

The EU was created by means of the Treaty of Maastricht, signed on February 7, 1992. The EU is governed by five institutions: European Parliament, Council of the European Union, European Commission, European Court of Justice, and European Court of Auditors. See *genetically altered ingredients;* listings under *European.*

European Union—Amsterdam Treaty: signed by European Union political leaders on October 2, 1997; took effect in 1999, enabling the EU to meet the challenges of the future such as the rapid evolution of the international situation; the globalization of the economy and its impact on jobs; the fight against terrorism, international crime, and drug trafficking; ecological problems; and threats to public health.

European Union—genetically altered ingredients: see *genetically altered ingredients; traceability regulations.*

European Union—Mexico free trade agreement: see *Economic Partnership, Political Coordination, and Cooperation Agreement.*

European Union—Stability and Growth Pact: where all members of the EU are meant to aim for budgets that are "close to balance or in surplus." Governments that run fiscal deficits bigger than 3 percent of GDP must take swift corrective action. Should any of the 12 nations breach the 3 percent limit for more than three years in a row, they may be liable to fines of billions of euros. In 2002, France, Germany, and Portugal missed this goal.

European Union—Treaty of Nice: marks the completion of the Intergovernmental Conference, opened on February 14, 2000. The Treaty of Nice takes effect in 2005; the aim is to adapt the way in which European institutions operate in order to make it possible to take in new members states. See *enlargement.*

European Unit of Account (EUA): see *Units of Account.*

Europe Without Frontiers: a reference to the goal of eliminating trade barriers in the European Community, achieved in 1992. According to EU estimates, barriers that prevent the formation of a grand European area without internal frontiers costs Union citizens tens of billions of dollars each year. A White Paper endorsed by heads of state and government provided for the gradual dismantling, of all the physical, technical, and fiscal barriers still obstructing the free circulation of persons, goods, services, and capital between the nations of the Union. To abolish physical frontiers, a single document has replaced the 70 national forms previously used for bringing goods across frontiers. A system is in place to abolish technical frontiers that still inhibit the free circulation of persons, goods, services, and capital. To eliminate fiscal frontiers, although all member nations of the Union have the same system of value-added tax, there remain differences from country to country in the number and level of VAT rates. It requires the creation of mechanisms for compensation between member states, as well as substantial measures to approximate indirect taxes, so that the remaining disparities are insufficient to divert traffic or distort trade. See *Maastricht Treaty; nontariff barrier; White Paper.*

Euro-sterling (Euro-pounds): sterling deposits accepted and employed by banks outside the United Kingdom. Its market in such sterling is centered in Paris, and is smaller than the Eurodollar.

Eurosyndicated loans: large bank credits, usually with maturities of three to 10 years, granted by international bank syndicates put together on an ad hoc basis. Funds for the loans are drawn from the Euromarket.

Euro-zone (Eurozone): in 2003, the 12 European Union nations belonging to a cooperative single-currency effort; collective economy is second only to that of the U.S. Three member nations of the EU have chosen not to become participants. In 2004, Denmark, Sweden, and the United Kingdom remained outside the Euro-zone. See *European Central Bank.*

even-par swap: the sale of one block of bonds and the simultaneous purchase of the same nominal principal amount of another block of bonds, without concern for the net cash difference.

evergreen credit: a revolving credit free of a maturity date, but giving the bank the opportunity, once each year, to convert into a term loan.

evidence of origin: information presented in an exporter's certificate of origin certifying that the merchandise described are eligible for a preferential rate of duty under a trade program.

evidence of right to make entry: paperwork needed by an importer showing right to clear a shipment through customs.

ex-: the point from which an item is shipped, not necessarily its point of origin. For example, a machine made in New York and exported through the port of Elizabeth, New Jersey, is said to have been shipped "ex-Elizabeth."

Excel (Export Credit Enhanced Leverage): an export financing program agreed to by the World Bank and international export agencies of various governments in October 1989. To overcome the shortage of export credit, national credit insurers provide loans or guarantees in parallel with World Bank financing, which are channeled to the multilateral development banks.

exception rate: shipping rate set higher because the commodity requires special handling/care.

exceptions:
(1) transactions, either monetary or nonmonetary, that fail to meet the parameters of the system.
(2) special circumstances in trade accords that alter the relationship between the trading partners and their procedures and regulations for export and import. See *quantitative restrictions.*

excess freight: freight in excess of the quantity way-billed.

excess of loss treaty reinsurance: indemnifies a company for the excess loss over a sum that is specified on the policy in the event that there is a loss.

excess reserves: amount of reserves held by banks that exceeds that required by law.

exchange bill of lading: a bill of lading issued in exchange for another bill of lading.

exchange controls:
(1) governmental restraints limiting the right to exchange the

nation's currency into the currency of another country.

(2) the internal rationing of foreign currencies, bank drafts, and other financial paper to stabilize balance of payments problems. When this occurs, an importer must obtain permission from the government to expend foreign exchange. These measures can distort trade and are often viewed as a nontariff barrier.

exchange current: the current rate of exchange.

exchange depreciation: the decline experienced by a foreign currency or currencies. This is usually created by a reduction in the base, such as gold, of the currency, but can also be caused by other factors, such as monetary funds, stabilization, or government action.

exchange exposure: the risk occurring whenever an asset or a liability is expressed in a foreign currency.

exchange permit: a government permit sometimes required by the importer's government to enable the importer to convert his or her own country's currency into foreign currency with which to pay a seller in another country.

exchange rate: the price of one currency in relation to that of another, i.e., the number of units of one currency that may be exchanged for one unit of another currency.

exchange rate mechanism (ERM): see *European Exchange Rate Mechanism*.

exchange-rate risk: in activities involving two or more currencies, the risk that losses can occur as a result of changes in their relative value.

exchange-rate spread: the difference in the price of a currency between what it is bought and sold for.

exchanges: all checks, drafts, notes, and other instruments that are presented to a clearinghouse for collection. Synonymous with *clearinghouse exchanges*.

excise tax:

(1) taxes levied by a government on the manufacture, sales, or consumption of commodities.

(2) taxes levied on the right, privilege, or permission to engage in a certain business, trade, or occupation.

(3) a government levy imposed on the production and sale of some classes of items, whether produced or imported for domestic consumption.

(4) synonymous with *internal revenue tax*.

exclusionary tariff: synonymous with *prohibitive tariff.*

exclusive dealing agreements: agreements by which producers grant absolute territorial protection to specified distributors, by guaranteeing to the holder of the concession the exclusive right to secure supplies from the producer, and to be the only distributor to introduce the items into the territory allocated to him or her. This exclusive right is usually reinforced by prohibiting all resellers in other areas from exporting into the area allocated to the concession holder.

ex-coupon: without the coupon. A stock is sold ex-coupon when the coupon for the existing interest payment has been removed.

ex-dividend: identifying the period during which the quotes price of a security excludes the payment of any declared dividend to the buyer, and the dividend reverts to the seller.

ex-dock: from the (shipping) dock.

Eximbank (Ex-Im Bank): see *Export-Import Bank of the United States.*

exonerated cargo: dutiable merchandise that is now permitted duty-free entry into certain nations.

Exon-Florio Amendment: Section 5021 of the U.S. Trade Act of 1988 provides that the President or his nominee may investigate the effects on U.S. national security of any merger, acquisition, or takeover that could result in foreign control of legal persons engaged in interstate commerce in the United States. Should the President decide that any such transactions threaten national security, he may take action to suspend or prohibit them. This could include the forced divestment of assets. There are no provisions for judicial review or for compensation in the case of divestment. For some nations the Exon-Florio Amendment inhibits the free flow of foreign investment and hurts multilateral disciplines on trade-related investment measures with GATT, now WTO. See *Buy American Act; Trade Act of 1988.*

exotic: a currency in which a large international market does not exist. Synonymous with *exotics.*

exotics: synonymous with *exotic.*

expiration notice: a notice in a tariff that all or some part of it will expire at a stated time.

export:
(1) to ship an item away from a country for sale to another country (verb). See *exports.*

(2) (verb) to send an item or service out of one sovereign domain to another for purposes of sale.

(3) (noun) an item or service sent from one sovereign domain to another for purposes of sale.

Export Administration Act: see *Export Control Act.*

Export and Import Bank of Japan: see *Export-Import Bank of Japan.*

Export and Import Permits Act: see *Export-Import Permits Act.*

export bill of lading: a contract of carriage between a shipper and carrier.

export broker: a person or firm that brings together buyers and sellers for a fee but does not take part in actual sales transactions. See *export jobber.*

export buyer: an intermediary, nationally based, who purchases surplus production, distressed items, and discontinued lines at lowered prices, for resale to overseas buyers.

export carrier: the vessel on which a commodity is exported to another country.

export commission house: an organization that, for a commission, acts as a purchasing agent for a foreign buyer.

Export Control Act: U.S. legislation of 1949 requiring that all commercial exports from the United States be licensed. The Export Administration Act followed, which provides that all exports are under authority of license and subject to withdrawal by the government.

export controls: a reference to controls on military goods. In May 1991, the European Union's Commission called on the 12 member states to coordinate their export controls for products that have military as well as civilian uses. Efforts were limited to dual-use exports such as radar, chemicals, and industrial technology, because the European Union has no jurisdiction over military matters.

export credit:

(1) financing for domestic suppliers to generate goods and services that can be exported.

(2) deferred payment terms, loans, or other financial facilities provided to overseas buyers/importers of goods and services.

Export Credit Enhanced Leverage: see *Excel.*

Export Credit Insurance: insurance coverage against default in payment on overseas transactions; can cover both buyer and political risk. A European Union Directive was first proposed in 1977 for the adoption of uniform Union principles for medium- and long-term transactions with public and private buyers. It set minimum percentages for down payments, maximum repayment periods, and minimum interest rates. Guidelines on local costs were set and identified procedures for the working mechanism of the Arrangement.

Export Credits Guarantee Department (ECGD): an official U.K. government agency that provides support for bank financing of exports in the form of guarantees, foreign investment insurance, and interest rate subsidies aimed at lowering the rate from the U.K. market level to a level at which British firms can compete overseas.

Export Declaration: see *Shipper's Export Declaration*.

Export Development Corporation (EDC): the Canadian Government's official credit-granting agency that offers a wide range of services for Canadian exporters and importers. See *Allocations Under Lines of Credit*.

export disincentives: proposals made by the Competitiveness Policy Council to the President and to Congress: "[a] major effort is needed to eliminate, or at least sharply limit, our own export disincentives that block billions of dollars of foreign sales by American companies. All unilateral U.S. export controls would be sharply limited since only multilateral controls can be effective against a target country."

export diversification: the movement of a country away from the export of a single or limited number of items as the primary source of foreign exchange earnings.

export draft: an unconditional order drawn by the seller on the buyer to pay the draft's amount on presentation (sight draft) or at an agreed future date (time draft) that must be paid before the buyer receives shipping documents.

export duty: see *export levy*.

Export Enhancement Program: a U.S. program of 1985, permitting exporters to sell American products to foreign customers at world market prices. The U.S. Agriculture Department subsidizes the difference in the world price and the higher domestic price, which exporters have to pay for the product, in the form of commodities. See *subsidies*.

exporter: a person or firm who sells and/or transports items and/or merchandise to a foreign importer.

exporter participation: the share of the contract price lent by or arranged for by one or more exporters in transactions in which a bank (i.e., the Eximbank) is also a lender.

exporter retention: the percentage of the financed portion of a transaction on which the exporter retains the commercial risk.

export finance lease: a lease, the intent of which is to transfer the benefits and risks of ownership to the lessee, and title to the asset is expected to pass to the lessee at the end of the contract. Cf. *export operating lease.* Synonymous with *capital lease; conditional sale lease; full payment lease.*

Export-Financiering-Maatschappij: a Dutch export finance company set up by the large commercial banks in 1951.

export financing: any financial scheme to help exporters to capitalize the sale of their goods and services to a foreign importer.

export houses: trading houses specializing in selling virtually all categories of goods throughout the world. They can handle all aspects of international trade, including finance.

Export-Import Bank of Japan (EIBJ): a Japanese export credit financing institute established in 1950 that also administers government loans to developing countries within the framework of the official aid program; financed by capital issued by the government and by borrowing from a Trust Fund Bureau or by borrowing foreign exchange from commercial banks. It may not borrow from the Bank of Japan.

Export-Import Bank of the United States (EIB) (Eximbank) (Ex-Im Bank): an independent public federal banking corporation, established in 1934, that facilitates and aids in financing exports and imports and the exchange of commodities between the United States and foreign nations; it offers direct credit to borrowers outside the United States as well as export guarantees, export credit insurance, and discount loans.

Export-Import Permits Act: Canadian legislation providing the basis for government authority exercised in the areas of control of exports from and imports into Canada. See *Bureau of Export Administration.*

export incentives: subsidies or tax rebates paid by governments to firms to encourage them to export.

export instability: short-term shifts in export earnings and prices.

export insurance: insurance covering the risks of nonpayment by a foreign purchaser or institution that has extended credit to a foreign buyer or that has undertaken the payment obligation of the foreign buyer.

export jobber: a nationally based intermediary who purchases items domestically and resells them to foreign buyers, without ever taking physical possession of them. See *export broker.*

export-led development: industrialization policy emphasizing industries that will have export capabilities.

export levy: a tax added to exports from a country.

export license: a government document that permits the licensee to engage in the export of designated goods to certain destinations. In the United States, the export license will be either a *general export license* or a *Validated Export License*. Synonymous with *export permit*.

export license number: number assigned to an individually validated license authorizing exports of specific goods in specific amounts to stated destination.

Export Management Company (EMC): a private firm that serves as the export department for several manufacturers, soliciting and transacting export business on behalf of its clients in return for a commission, salary, or retainer plus commission. EMCs serve as the export arm of one or more U.S. manufacturers, helping to establish an overseas market for the firm's products, usually on an exclusive basis. The management firm, therefore, maintains close contact with its clients, and is supply driven. EMCs may take title to the goods they sell, making a profit on the markup, or they may charge a commission, depending on the type of products they are handling, the overseas market, and the manufacturer-client needs. Some EMCs also work on a retainer basis, especially if they are providing significant training and advice to their client or undertaking considerable up-front marketing. Cf. *Export Trading Company.*

export merchant: a domestically based firm that purchases on its own account and sells goods and services directly to foreign firms.

export netting: the open position held in two or more currencies reflecting the reality that the strengths and weaknesses of each currency are perceived to balance the other's.

export operating lease: a lease, the intent of which is to have the lessor retain the economic benefits of ownership. An export operating lease is essentially a rental contract. Cf. *export finance lease.*

export-oriented industrialization: policies and practices of developing nations of increasing the export of primary products and aggressively promoting the exporting of manufactured items, as a major part of the development strategy.

export packers: firms engaged in the preparation of export items for shipment.

export packing list: shipping document that itemizes the material in each individual package and indicates the type of package.

export performance requirements: obligations that host nations impose on foreign investors requiring them to export specified portions of goods produced as a result of the investments. An unhealthy practice.

export permit: synonymous with *export license*.

export pessimism: resulting when nations discourage trade rather than promote it, a concept that liberalizing trade will be self-defeating if too many developing nations try to do it simultaneously.

export privileges: the opportunity afforded by the U.S. government to engage in export transactions. See *Export Control Act*.

export processing zone (EPZ): see *free trade zone*.

export quotas: synonymous with *quantitative restrictions*.

export rate:
(1) a rate published on traffic moving from an interior point to a port for transhipment to a foreign nation.
(2) a freight rate specially established for application on export traffic and made lower than the domestic rate.

export refunds: see *restitution payments*.

export restitution payments: see *restitution payments*.

export restraint agreements (ERAs): see *voluntary restraint agreements*.

export restraints: a restriction by an exporting country of the quantity of exports to a specified importing country. Usually, this is a result of a request (formal or informal) of the importing country. See *voluntary export restraints*.

exports: items produced in one country and sold to another. See *export*.

export subsidies:
(1) payments made by a government to companies that export specific goods, to encourage them to compete in foreign markets.
(2) government benefits made available to domestic producers of

goods contingent on their exporting those items for which the benefits received apply. These include support prices, tax incentives, etc.

(3) any form of government payment or benefit to an exporter or manufacturing concern contingent on the export of goods. Under the GATT, now WTO, subsidies, especially export subsidies, are seen as a tool that distorts the normal behavior of the market. The Tokyo Round produced an agreement on subsidies and countervailing duties that prohibits export subsidies by developed countries on manufactured and semimanufactured goods.

export support efforts: program, usually maintained by governmental agencies, to assist domestic exporters, and usually located in the country where the import of goods will occur.

export targeting: a coordinated effort by a government to increase the export competitiveness of an industry or company.

export tariff: a tax or duty on goods exported from a country.

Export Trading Company (ETC): any company or firm engaged in international trade as established or invested, especially by banks. It is demand driven and transaction oriented. It acts as an independent distributor, linking buyers and sellers to arrange a transaction. ETCs identify what overseas customers want to buy and work with a variety of U.S. manufacturers to fulfill those requirements. Most ETCs take title to the products involved, but some work on a commission basis. They keep up with the markets they serve by continual travel, participating in trade shows, and working closely with distributors and customers. Cf. *Export Management Company.*

Export Trading Company Act (ETCA): U.S. legislation of 1982 in which Congress directed the U.S. government to provide assistance to export intermediaries. In 1988, the Omnibus Trade Act reiterated Congress's support for export intermediaries by modifying the Trading Company Act. See *Export Trading Company.*

export value: the price at which an overseas manufacturer offers for sale a given item for export to the United States in the usual wholesale quantities, less export discounts, packing, and costs of preparing the goods for export.

exposure:

(1) the condition of being open to loss from a specific hazard, event, or contingency.

(2) funds, or the insurable values, that are so exposed to loss.

(3) on foreign exchange markets, arising through the existence of an uncovered position, whether overall or for a single currency. The extent of exposure reflects the different maturity periods for the currencies in use.

expropriation: the taking over of ownership of private property by a country's government.

ex-quay: goods available at the quayside.

ex-rail: traffic handled by another agency of transportation delivered to it by a railroad.

ex-ship: price quotes for goods on arrival at port. It does not include costs of unloading and delivery to the premises of the purchaser.

Extended Fund Facility (EFF): assistance provided to IMF member nations with economies suffering from serious balance of payments difficulties due to structural imbalances in production, trade, and prices or economies characterized by slow growth and an inherently weak balance of payments position. Drawings are made over a period of three years under conditions similar to IMF standby drawings.

external account: an account in a national currency maintained for use by nonresidents.

external bill: a bill of exchange drawn in one country, but payable in another country. Cf. *foreign bill.*

external bond: a bond issued by a country or firm for purchase outside that country, usually denominated in the currency of the purchaser. Cf. *internal bond.*

external dimensions: the conditions that the European Union seeks to negotiate with its foreign trade partners for right of access to the single European market envisioned by the Union's 1992 legislative program. See *external trade.*

external public debt: that part of the public debt owed to nonresident foreign creditors, made payable in the currency of the nation of the creditors, as to both interest and principal.

external trade: in general, trade carried out by a nation with any other nation. For example, a European Union commercial trade policy is based on uniformly set principles dealing with tariff and trade agreements, liberalization, export policy, and protective measures, including cases of dumping and subsidies. Therefore, items imported into the Union are treated in the same fashion whichever nation they enter, and there are uniform regulations governing exports throughout the Union. Since January 1, 1975, all external trade negotiations are conducted by the Commission, subject to approval by the Council of Ministers, and not bilaterally by member nations. The Union has created a network of trading agreements with nations of all continents in the form of association agreements, free-trade agreements, trade or economic cooperation agreements, and the Lomé Conventions. External trade accounts, on average, for nearly 27 percent of the gross domestic product of the Union countries. See *dumping; General Agreement on Tariffs and Trade; Generalized System of Preferences.*

extinction pricing: a manipulation by producers to deliberately lower prices so as to eliminate weaker competitors from international markets.

extraterritorial application of laws: attempts by a government to apply its laws outside its territorial borders. In the United States, the Foreign Trade Antitrust Improvements Act of 1982 codified appropriate legal actions.

extraterritoriality: see *extraterritorial application of laws.*

F

FAC:

(1) see *fast as can*.

(2) a forwarding agent's commission.

face value: synonymous with *par value*.

facilitating agency:

(1) an organization that services other institutions but does not take title to goods.

(2) an agency that aids in the performance of some marketing functions but does not own the items and is not involved in buying or selling.

factor:

(1) an individual who carries on business transactions for another.

(2) an agent for the sale of goods who is authorized to sell and receive payment for the merchandise.

(3) rates, mileages, and amounts used in determining the proportion of a through rate due the carriers interested.

factorage: the commission collected by a factor.

factor endowment: endowment of a nation with one or more of the factors of production, capital, labor, and natural resources.

factoring:

(1) selling accounts before their due date, usually at a discount. Cf. *forfaiting*.

(2) a way of export financing where the financial institution buys the foreign trade debts owed by importers to an exporter. The financial institution (the factor) charges the exporter a fee to underwrite the real losses that will be incurred if the importers fail to pay.

factoring houses: firms that purchase export receivables at a discounted price.

factor mobility: free movement of factors of production, such as labor and capital, across national borders.

factor price equalization theorem: the tendency, under simplified conditions of trade between two countries that have different factor endowments, to equalize factor price ratios in the two countries.

fade-down: requiring a wholly foreign-owned company to transform itself into first a mixed, and later a completely nationally owned company. Found in the *North American Free Trade Agreement (NAFTA)*.

FAE: free alongside elevator.

fair market value: the value an imported item would command, under similar circumstances of sale, were the goods sold in the country of origin; often used when discussing dumping. See *dumping; less than fair value*.

fair-trader: see *free trade; protectionism*.

fair value: see *fair market value*.

Falkland Island Pound: monetary unit of Falkland Islands.

false billing: freight listed on shipping documents that misrepresents the actual contents or weight of the shipment.

Far East: the western coast of the Pacific Ocean in the vicinity of Japan, China, and the Philippine Islands.

farm subsidies: agricultural subsidies are intended to assure self-sufficiency in food in participating nations and prevent farmers from leaving the countryside, often for cities that are already overcrowded and lack jobs. However, such systems are anachronistic as farm productivity often rises and the risk of food shortages is lowered. Consumers and taxpayers pay twice for farm subsidies. Consumers pay inflated food prices because their market is insulated by levies from lower-priced imports. Taxpayers pay the subsidies needed to dump overpriced surpluses abroad.

FAS: see *free alongside ship*.

fast as can (FAC): a reference to the policy of loading or discharging a vessel as fast as she can take on board or unload. This implies a commitment on the part of the charterer to supply the cargo as rapidly as the vessel requires it. It is not an obligation to take cargo at a rate that is in excess of the customary daily discharging rate of the port.

fast freight line: two or more transportation lines jointly operating through fast freight schedules.

Fast Track Approval: see *Fast Track Negotiating Authority*.

fast track authority: procedures provide for extensive U.S. congressional consultation and formal notification in exchange for a simple up or down vote within 90 legislative days from the time implementing legislation is submitted by the President. The legislation is the result of collaboration between the Administration and Congress; therefore, amendments are not permitted.

Fast track approval from the U.S. Congress in May 1991 was followed with an announcement from the Bush administration that
it would pay for some retraining of U.S. workers displaced by a
free trade accord with Mexico. On the first of the month, the
President offered concessions to pick up support for the
Mexican–U.S. trade accord by pledging: (a) to work with
Congress to fashion an "adequately funded" program of assistance
for workers dislocated as a result of increased foreign competition;
(b) to exclude changes in immigration policy from the trade pact;
(c) to prevent Mexican products that do not meet U.S. health or
safety requirements from entering this country; (d) to put in place
an integrated environmental plan for the border between the
United States and Mexico and appoint representatives of environmental organizations to official trade advisory bodies.

President George H. W. Bush's action plan played a critical vote on
extending his trade-negotiating authority for two more years. The
House of Representatives, on May 23, backed the President's
authority 231 to 192, while the Senate vote, on May 24, was 59
to 36. Congress had given President Bush fast track authority to
negotiate with Mexico for a free trade agreement, subject to congressional approval without amendments.

Then, on September 18, 1992, the President notified Congress
under fast track procedures of his intent to enter into a North
American Free Trade Agreement (NAFTA). That act began a
90-calendar-day period for Congressional review of NAFTA. At
the end of those 90 days, the President signed the Agreement. No
action was required at that point by Congress.

At any time after the President signed the Agreement, he may
submit implementing legislation to Congress for approval.
Submission begins a 90-legislative day period during which
Congress will hold hearings, debate, and finally vote on the
Agreement.

On March 2, 1993, fast track authority lapsed. Then, on April 27,
1993, President Clinton requested from Congress a reinstatement
of fast track authority to December 15, 1993, giving him time to
finish up the NAFTA and GATT talks, enabling Congress to vote
on these treaties until April 15, 1994.

During the Administration of President George W. Bush, fast-track
authority, now renamed trade promotion authority, was again

approved by Congress. See *North American Free Trade Agreement; trade promotion authority.*

Fast Track Negotiating Authority: authority provided by the U.S. Congress to the President to seek congressional approval of trade agreements on an "up" or "down" vote without possibility of amendment and within a specified time period. See *fast track authority; trade promotion authority.*

favorable trade balance: the situation that exists when a nation's total value of exports is in excess of its total value of imports.

FCIA: see *Foreign Credit Insurance Association.*

FCL: see *full container load.*

FCN (friendship, commerce, and navigation): an international treaty specifying the rights and responsibilities of each nation toward the other regarding their trading relationship, and the use of each nation's roads, waterways, and territorial sea and airspace. See *most-favored nation.*

FCPA: see *Foreign Corrupt Practices Act of 1977.*

FD: see *free discharge.*

FDI: see *foreign direct investment.*

FE: see *foreign exchange.*

federal bond: the promissory note of a central government.

federalization: the process of combination between sovereign or independent nations for the purpose of establishing a common central government agency. Cf. *common market; federation.*

Federal Maritime Commission: see *FMC.*

federation: where the central power has law-making and executive authority in some areas, the members in others. Anti-federalists tend to stress the powers yielded to the center, pro-federalists those kept by states. Central decisions involve majority voting (no single state has a veto), and are automatically law throughout a federation. Cf. *common market; federalization.*

feeder vessel: a ship delivering cargo on a local basis to and from another vessel calling only at a major port.

fees and royalties from direct investments: income reported by companies with direct investments abroad. They represent income received by U.S. parent companies from their foreign affiliates for patent royalties, licensing fees, rentals, management services, other home office charges, and research and development.

FELABAN: the Latin American Banking Federation, based in

Bogota, Colombia. It groups the banking associations of Latin American nations.

FEMA: see *Foreign Extraterritorial Measures Act.*

FFF: see *foreign freight forwarder.*

FHEX: see *Fridays and holidays excluded.*

FI: see *free in.*

fiat money: money without precious metal backing, circulated by government decree.

FIBOR (Frankfurt Interbank Offered Rates): three- and six-month reference rates used as the basis for loan contracts, swaps, mark floating rate notes, etc.; calculated daily by Privat-Diskont AG, which takes the rates from 12 banks, discards the highest and the lowest, and averages the remaining 10 with a rounding to the nearest five basis points.

fictitious registration: a document issued by a country or state official to identify the exact ownership of a business, where the name of the business does not do so.

figure: (slang) meaning "00" and denoting an exchange-rate level.

FII: see *Foreign Investment Insurance.*

Fiji dollar: monetary unit of Fiji Islands.

FIM: the international standard code for the former currency of Finland—the markka. Now obsolete.

final commitment: an authorization by Eximbank setting forth the terms of financing offered by Eximbank under the direct loan, financial guarantees, and engineering multiplier programs. Final commitments are issued after the foreign buyer has decided to contract with a U.S. supplier(s). A final commitment is usually preceded by a preliminary commitment.

final list: a listing of items on which a unique standard of valuation was applied for duty purposes.

final sales: the total of net sales to consumers, governments, and foreigners. Final sales exclude sales made to producers, except sales of durable plant equipment and machinery.

final underwriting account: a complete and final list of participating underwriters drawn from written responses to underwriting invitations extended by a syndicate manager, and listed alphabetically within each bracket.

finance bill: any draft drawn by one bank on a foreign bank against securities retained by the overseas institution.

financial instruments: in the European Union, loans and guarantees granted by the European Investment Bank and Euratom, and those made under the New Community Instrument; European Coal and Steel Community operations (redeployment aid, loans, interest-rate subsidies and guarantees); Union budget expenditure on structural policy measures; and funds from the research budget.

financial integration: efforts to prepare for the single European market. The process of European Union financial integration was speeded up to allow the Union to play its full part in the internationalization and modernization of the financial system, and to create an open, competitive, and stable European financial area, a prerequisite for a frontier-free area. The Maastricht Treaty set up an appropriate timetable for financial monetary integration, with the creation of a single currency. By 2004, financial integration was achieved with the Euro. Twelve of the fifteen EU nations are participants. See *Maastricht Treaty; Single Europe Act; White Paper.*

financial markets: the money and capital markets of the economy. The money markets buy and sell short-term credit instruments. The capital markets buy and sell long-term credit and equity instruments.

financial services: financial services form an important element in the economy of all trading nations as a source of employment and of net exports. They are important both in their own right and because of their role in oiling the wheels of the competitive market economy. Financial services have not benefited to the same extent as manufactured goods in progress toward dismantling barriers to trade between nations, but it is clear that the benefits of a unified market might apply in the financial services sector as much as any other.

A general approach on financial services must be closely linked to the program of liberalization of capital movements, as a result of which residents of any nation will have access to the financial systems of other countries and all the financial products that are available there. Equally, there would be no restrictions on capital transfers and no discrimination in the form of fiscal measures.

A program in the financial services sector purports to break down national regulatory barriers that obstruct freedom of establishment and free trade in services that could continue even after exchange controls are fully removed.

financing transactions: movements of currency, gold, and gold equivalents used to settle a balance of payments deficit. See *balance-of-payments deficit*.

fine:

(1) a penalty charged a violator by government, court, or other authority for breaking a law or rule.

(2) a relatively low interest rate or margin, as when a loan is made at the finest rate.

(3) the purity of precious metals.

Finnish markka (mark): former monetary unit of Finland.

FIO: see *free in and out*.

FIRA: see *Foreign Investment Review Agency*.

firm price: an obligation to the maker of a stated price that must be met if accepted within a specified time period.

firm quote: in the foreign exchange market, a dealer is willing to trade at the rate just quoted.

firm surveillance: monitoring by the IMF of the exchange rate policies of member nations.

first flag carriage: the shipment of merchandise aboard a vessel flying the flag of the exporting nation.

first-mover advantage: cost reduction advantage due to economies of scale attained through moving into a foreign market ahead of competitors.

first notice day: the first day on which transferable notices can be issued for delivery in a specified delivery month.

fiscal agent: in the Eurobond market, a bank that is the appointed agent for an issue, including serving as principal paying agent.

fiscal controls: with reference to the European Community, the introduction over the years since 1967 of a common Value-Added Tax (VAT) system, in place of the widely varying national turnover taxes. It has been one of the European Union's success stories. As part of the "1992" agenda, the next major step was to align the number and level of VAT rates in the member states. Alignment of rates has removed all need for VAT controls at internal frontiers when taken in conjunction with the following measures: the treatment of VAT on intra-Union imports and exports in the same way as VAT on sales and purchases within a member state; and a clearinghouse mechanism for ensuring that VAT revenue is allocated to the member state of consumption. The 1985

White Paper also gave impetus to the process by programming proposals for harmonization of rates and for linkage of bonded warehouse system (which member states currently use for controlling movement of excise goods). See *value-added tax; White Paper.*

fiscal policy: the means by which a government influences the economy through its budget by changes in tax and welfare payments and/or government spending.

fishy-back: the transportation of truck trailers or containers on ships.

five dragons: synonymous with *five tigers.*

five tigers: Hong Kong, Singapore, South Korea, Taiwan, and Thailand. Synonymous with *five dragons.*

fix: setting the cost of an item or service.

fixed charges:
(1) charges that do not vary with an increase or decrease in traffic.
(2) items as interest, rent for leased roads and equipment, and amortization of discount on funded debt.

fixed credit line: synonymous with *irrevocable credit.*

fixed dates: fixed or standard periods for trading Eurocurrency deposits, which range from one to 12 months. See *Eurocurrency.*

fixed exchange rate: a concept within the European Monetary System where all members except Great Britain maintain fixed exchange rates between their currencies, promoting monetary stability in Europe and throughout the world. See *European Monetary System.*

fixed interest rate: an interest rate set when a loan is made that remains the same for the life of the loan regardless of whether other interest rates rise or fall.

fixed rate: see *fixed exchange rate.*

fixing a charter: the conclusion of a contract for the charter of a vessel.

fixing letter: the summary of an agreement between the ship's owner and the charterer pending signing of the actual charter party.

FJD: the international standard code for the currency of Fiji—the Fiji dollar.

FKP: the international standard code for the currency of the Falkland Island—the Falkland Islands pound.

flag: the nation of registration of a ship or aircraft.

flag discrimination: practices designed to secure preferential treatment for ships of a particular nationality, mainly in the assignment of cargo.

flag of convenience: the national flag flown by a ship that is registered in a country other than that of its owners (e.g., to avoid taxes and high domestic wages).

flat:

(1) with no interest.

(2) the price at which a bond is traded, including consideration for all unpaid accruals of interest. Bonds that are in default of interest or principal are traded flat. Income bonds, which pay interest only to the extent earned, are usually traded flat.

flat rack container: a standard shipping lines container, open with no sides or top.

flat rate: a uniformly charged rate for each unit of goods and services, irrespective of quantity, frequency of purchases, and so on.

fleet policy: a marine insurance policy covering vessels operated by a single ownership or management. Cf. *open insurance policy*.

flexible exchange rates: the condition that exists when exchange rates of varying world currencies freely change in reaction to supply-and-demand conditions, free from governmental maneuvers to hold a fixed rate in the exchange of one currency for another.

flexible tariff: in the United States, a tariff designed to even out differences between the cost of imported and domestically produced items.

flight of capital: the movement of capital, which usually has been converted into a liquid asset, from one place to another to avoid loss or to increase gain.

flight of the dollar: the purchasing of foreign securities with dollar exchange, to escape the adverse impact or inflation, deflation, or other economic condition.

float:

(1) the amount of funds in the process of collection represented by checks in the possession of one bank but drawn on other banks, either local or out of town.

(2) the portion of a new security that has not yet been bought by the public.

floater policy: synonymous with *all-risks insurance*.

floating currency: a currency whose value in terms of foreign currency is not kept stable (on the basis of the par value or a fixed relationship to some other currency) but instead is allowed, without a multiplicity of exchange rates, to be determined, (entirely or to some degree), by market forces. Even where a currency is floating, the authorities may influence its movements by official intervention; if such intervention is absent or minor, the expression "clean float" is sometimes used. See *clean float*.

floating exchange rates: see *floating rates*.

floating policies: marine insurance policies issued for a lump sum insured sufficient to cover all voyages expected by the insured over a period.

floating-rate bonds: the most commonly issued instrument, the interest coupons on which are adjusted regularly according to the level of some base interest rate plus a fixed spread.

floating-rate note (FRN): used by banks to raise dollars for their Euromarket operations, a mixture of the rollover credit market with the Eurosecurities market.

floating rates: the automatic determination of appropriate exchange rates by market forces, not by a nation's reserve holdings. Nations that do not follow these rates are pressured into line, otherwise they would see the value of their currency driven to unacceptably low levels or driven up to the point where no other nation would be able to purchase their goods.

florin: monetary unit of the Netherlands Antilles.

fluctuation exchange rates: see *floating rates*.

FMC (Federal Maritime Commission): a U.S. agency that regulates waterborne foreign and domestic offshore commerce to ensure that U.S. international trade is open to all countries on fair terms and that fair rates and conditions exist, permitting the commercial market for services to function without discrimination.

FO: see *free out*.

FOB: see *free on board*.

fonds de roulement: (French) working capital.

FOR: see *free on rail*.

forced billing: a means used to secure payments for freight delivery when no bill can be found.

force majeure: the title of a standard clause in marine contracts exempting the parties for nonfulfillment of their obligations as a result of conditions beyond their control, such as earthquakes, floods, or war. See *act of God*.

foreign accounts receivable financing: a means of export financing where (a) the exporter uses its lines of credit with a bank to borrow funds for terms of 30, 60, 90, or 180 days, or (b) the exporter sells its foreign accounts receivable to the bank, which can purchase them at a variable discount, depending on the degree of foreign commercial and political risk to payment involved.

foreign accounts receivable purchases: a means of export financing where the exporter sells its foreign invoice acceptance to a financial agency at a variable discount, depending on the degree of foreign commercial and political risk to payment involved.

foreign affiliate of a foreign parent: an affiliate of a major foreign corporation, which itself has an U.S. affiliate.

Foreign Assistance Act: U.S. legislation of 1961 providing authority to the executive branch of the government for the operation of the Trade and Development Program within the framework of the U.S. International Development Cooperation Agency.

foreign bill: a bill drawn in one state and payable in another state or nation. Cf. *external bill*.

foreign bond issue: a bond issue for a foreign borrower/guarantor underwritten by a bank or bank syndicate in a specific nation.

foreign carriers: a carrier, in making reference to all other carriers collectively.

foreign collections: bills of exchange that have either originated overseas and are import or incoming collections, or those that are export or outgoing collections payable in another country.

foreign commerce: trade between people or legal entities in differing nations.

foreign content: any portion or value added of the exported good or service that is manufactured, assembled, or supplied outside the United States.

Foreign Correspondent: a bank in another nation serving as agent for a U.S. bank maintaining sufficient balances.

Foreign Corrupt Practices Act (FCPA) of 1977: U.S. legislation that requires all companies registered with the Securities and Exchange Commission to keep accurate accounting records and to maintain an adequate system of internal control. See *bribery; Trade Bill of 1988*.

Foreign Credit Insurance Association (FCIA): an association formed by the Export-Import bank, a U.S. corporation owned by insurance firms providing export credit insurance.

foreign currency: the currency of any foreign country that is the authorized medium of circulation and the basis for record keeping in that country. Foreign currency is traded in by banks either by the actual handling of currency or checks, or by establishing balances in foreign currency with banks in those countries.

foreign currency account: an account maintained in a foreign bank in the currency of the country in which the bank is located. Foreign currency accounts are also maintained by banks in the United States for depositors. When such accounts are kept, they usually represent that portion of the carrying bank's foreign currency account that is in excess of its contractual requirements.

foreign department: a division of a company that carries out the needed functions for the company to engage in foreign operations of a business nature, such as exports, imports, and foreign exchange.

foreign deposits: those funds held in accounts in financial institutions outside the United States payable in the currency of the country in which the depository is located.

foreign direct investment (FDI): the flow of foreign capital into a business enterprise in which foreign residents have significant control.

foreign draft: a draft drawn by a bank on a foreign correspondent bank.

foreign drawings and remittances service: a service through which foreign exchange banks make their due from accounts available to their correspondents for use in arranging foreign exchange transfers.

foreign exchange (FE) (F/X) (forex): instruments used for international payments (i.e., currency, checks, drafts, and bills of exchange). Synonymous with *conversion (2)*.

foreign exchange broker: a person, company, or bank that engages in buying and selling foreign exchange, such as foreign currency or bills.

foreign exchange control: requirement that an importer of an item must apply to governmental authorities for permission to purchase foreign currencies to pay for the item.

foreign exchange markets: markets in which the monies of different countries are exchanged. Foreign exchange holdings of current or liquid claims denominated in the currency of another country.

foreign exchange position: see *FX position*.

foreign exchange rate: the price of one currency in terms of another.

foreign exchange reserves: gold, SDRs, U.S. dollars, and other convertible currencies held in a nation's treasury.

foreign exchange risk: the risk of suffering losses because of adverse movement in exchange rates.

foreign exchange speculation: the act of taking a net position in a foreign currency with the intention of making a profit from exchange rate changes.

foreign-exchange swap transaction: synonymous with *bank swap*.

foreign exchange trading: the buying and selling of foreign currencies in relation to either U.S. dollars or other foreign currencies.

foreign exchange transactions: the purchase or sale of one currency with another. Foreign exchange rates refer to the number of units of one currency needed to purchase one unit of another, or the value of one currency in terms of another.

Foreign Extraterritorial Measures Act (FEMA): Canadian legislation of 1984 permitting the government to prevent an individual or firm operating in Canada from complying with any U.S. regulation that prevents trade between Canada and any other nation. In 1996, FEMA added amendments (effective January 1, 1997) countering U.S. new legislation to minimize potential lawsuits by U.S. citizens against Canadians.

foreign financing: occurs when a foreign firm or other borrower comes to a nation's capital market and borrows in the local currency (e.g., when a Spanish company borrows U.S. dollars in New York or British sterling in London).

foreign freight forwarder (FFF): a firm, licensed by the Federal Maritime Commission (FMC), serving as the agent of a merchant in arranging the shipment of goods by water. The forwarder also obtains vessel space, prepares documents, and arranges delivery of merchandise to the pier. See *freight forwarder*.

foreign income: income earned by Americans from work performed in another country.

foreign investment: the purchase of assets from abroad.

Foreign Investment Insurance (FII): an insurance program of the Export Development Corporation that protects Canadians who invest in foreign nations.

Foreign Investment Review Agency (FIRA): FIRA was formed in 1974 by the Canadian Government to screen and monitor all direct investment into Canada, and assure that the nation would benefit from such activity.

Foreign Investors Tax Act: U.S. federal legislation of 1966 establishing a tax ceiling (30 percent) for overseas investors in U.S. securities, the purpose of which is to stimulate foreign investment in the United States and aid in lowering the deficit in the U.S. international account.

foreign invoice acceptance: a process of the importer acknowledging the receipt of, and agreeing to pay, the export invoice.

foreign market value: the selling price of merchandise, or price at which it is offered for sale, in the major markets of the nation from which is exported.

foreign money: see *foreign currency.*

foreign national pricing: local pricing in another nation.

foreign-owned subsidiary: a firm that is owned by another firm and is located in a country other than the home country of the parent organization.

foreign remittances: transfer of any monetary instrument across national borders.

foreign sales agent (FSA): an individual or firm that serves as the foreign representative of a domestic supplier and seeks sales abroad for the supplier.

Foreign Sales Corporation (FSC): an export incentive mechanism for U.S. firms, where such a company, formed under the U.S. Deficit Reduction Act of 1984, takes legal advantage of the U.S. Tax Reform Act of 1984. The firm chooses to be taxed as a U.S. corporation formed in one of more than 30 nations that have been approved by the Department of the Treasury and that have a satisfactory Tax Information Exchange Agreement with the United States.

foreign subsidiary: see *foreign-owned subsidiary.*

foreign tax credit: the credit an American taxpayer may take against American income tax for tax levied on the same income by a foreign government.

foreign trade financing: any of the payment methods used to settle transactions between individuals in different countries.

Foreign Trade Information System: a trade and investment computer databank service of the Organization of American States; provides databases with up-to-date import and export statistics and full text retrieval of all current U.S. federal regulations relevant to trade and business opportunities. Synonymous with *SICE*.

foreign trade multiplier: the concept that fluctuations in exports and/or imports may lead to significant variations in national income.

Foreign Trade Organization (FTO): a government agency, usually organized along product lines, that handles foreign sales and purchases.

Foreign Traders Index: a database of foreign importers and potential importers of American items; maintained by the U.S. Department of Commerce's International Trade Administration.

foreign trade zone (FTZ): synonymous with *free trade zone.*

foreign transaction: an interchange item or an international transaction either originating or routed to a point outside the United States or Canada.

forex: short for *foreign exchange.*

forfaiting:

(1) the purchase, without recourse, of receivables from the export sales of items.

(2) a procedure with the same purposes and procedures as factoring, which is the sale by an exporter of its accounts receivable for immediate cash. However, there are two important differences: (a) factoring involves credit terms of no more than 180 days, whereas forfaiting may involve years; (b) factoring does not usually cover political and transfer risks, whereas forfaiting does. See *factoring.*

forfeiture: the automatic loss of cash, property, or rights, as punishment for failure to comply with legal provisions and as compensation for the resulting losses or damages.

forint: the monetary unit of Hungary.

formula approach: a method of negotiating tariff reductions using an agreed-on formula applied to tariff rates (with limited exceptions being granted for very sensitive items) by all contracting parties. See *linear tariff cuts.*

forward book: the total of net forward positions in various currencies, indicating either current trading or a bank's view on a particular currency.

forward contract:
(1) a contract to exchange one currency for another currency at an agreed exchange rate at a future date, usually 30, 90, or 180 days.
(2) a contract for the settlement of a foreign exchange transaction at any date later than spot. See *forward rate*.

forward cover: an arrangement of a forward foreign exchange contract to protect a foreign currency buyer or seller from unexpected exchange rate fluctuations.

forward deal: an operation consisting of purchasing or selling foreign currencies with settlement to be made at a future date.

forward discount: an annual percentage by which the forward rate is below its spot rate.

forwarder's receipt: a document issued by a freight forwarder acknowledging receipt of goods into his or her custody for purposes of shipment to a given location. It is not a bill of lading.

forward exchange: a foreign bill of exchange purchased or sold at a stated price that is payable on a given date.

forward exchange rate: an exchange rate (price) agreed upon today that will be utilized on a specified date in the future.

forward exchange transaction: a purchase or sale of foreign currency for future delivery. Standard periods for forward contracts are one, three, and six months.

forward-forward: the simultaneous purchase and sale of one currency for different maturity dates in the forward market.

forward intervention: intervention by a central bank in forward markets aimed at influencing a currency's spot rate.

forward margin: the margin between today's price of a currency and the price at a future date.

forward market: the claim to sell or purchase securities, foreign currencies, and so on, at a fixed price at a given future date. This market deals in futures.

forward position: the situation of a trade of foreign exchange reflecting the net difference between outstanding commitments for forward purchase and the sale of a foreign currency at a given time.

forward premium: the annual percentage by which the forward rate is above its spot rate.

forward rate: the cost today for a commitment by one party to deliver to or take from another party an agreed amount of a currency at a fixed or future date. This rate is established by the forward contract. See *forward contract*.

FOT: see *free on truck*.

foul bill of lading: synonymous with *dirty bill of lading*.

fourchette: the higher and lower price levels between which member nations must operate their agricultural prices. It was first introduced for cereals.

four dragons: synonymous with *four tigers*.

Fourth World: a loosely defined term for the poorest of the globe's nations.

four tigers: Hong Kong, Singapore, South Korea, and Taiwan. Synonymous with *four dragons*.

FR: full range of ports.

framework agreement: the formal understandings and structure for developing trade goals and those arrangements set for reaching them.

Framework Agreements on Trade and Investment: by April 15, 1992, 16 such agreements were signed covering the United States and 31 countries: Colombia, Ecuador, Chile, Honduras, Costa Rica, Venezuela, El Salvador, Peru, Panama, Guatemala, Nicaragua, Dominican Republic, the South American Quadripartite Common Market (MERCOSUR)—Argentina, Brazil, Uruguay, Paraguay—and CARICOM (13 English-speaking nations)—Antigua and Barbuda, Bahamas, Barbados, Belize, Dominica, Grenada, Guyana, Jamaica, Montserrat, St. Kitts-Nevis, St. Lucia, St. Vincent and the Grenadines, and Trinidad and Tobago.

These accords open with a statement of agreed principles on the benefits of open trade and investment, increased importance of services to economies, the need for adequate intellectual property rights protection, the importance of observing and promoting internationally recognized worker rights, and the desirability of resolving trade and investment problems expeditiously.

franc: monetary unit of Benin, Burundi, Cameroons, Central African Republic, Chad, Comoros, Congo (Brazaville), Dahomey, Djibouti, French Somaliland, Gabon, Guadeloupe, Ivory Coast, Liechtenstein, Madagascar, Malagasy, Mail, Martinique, New Caledonia, New Hebrides Islands, Niger, Oceania, Reunion Island, Rwanda, Senegal, Switzerland, Tahiti, Togo, and Upper Volta.

franchise: in international trade, a provision in a marine cargo policy that partial losses can be adjusted if the loss exceeds a certain percentage of the total value of the shipment.

franco delivery: the full delivery of items to a consignee with all charges paid (e.g., a prepaid delivery).

franc zone: the currency zone grouping of most former French West African colonies and French dependencies in the Pacific, coordinated and assisted by the Banque de France.

franked dividend: in Australia, a dividend paid out of profits subject to tax at the company tax rate.

franked income: in the United Kingdom, income that has already suffered corporation tax.

franken: the former monetary unit of Liechtenstein.

Frankfurt Interbank Offered Rates: see *FIBOR*.

free alongside ship (FAS): shipping terms whereby an exporter pays all charges involved up to delivery on the quay. Cf. *free overside*.

free and open market: a market in which supply and demand are freely expressed in terms of price, as contrasted to a controlled market, in which supply, demand, and price may all be regulated. See *free trade*.

free astray: freight that is miscarried or delivered to the wrong location, then is billed and forwarded to the correct location without additional charge.

freeboard: the distance between the waterline and the vessel's main deck.

free carrier: similar to free on board, except that the seller fulfills his or her obligations when the merchandise is delivered into the custody of the carrier at the named point. Cf. *free on board*.

free discharge (FD): payment of the cost of unloading the ship by the charterer or receiver.

free domicile: a situation where the shipper pays all transportation charges and applicable duties.

Freedom Support Act (1992): a U.S. program to support free market and reform in Russia, Ukraine, Armenia, and other former Soviet Union states.

free enterprise: the condition under which a firm or individual is able to function competitively without excessive government restrictions.

free in (FI): a pricing term indicating that the charterer of a vessel is responsible for the cost of loading and unloading goods from the vessel.

free in and out (FIO): payment of the cost of loading and unloading by the charterer, shipper, or receiver, not by the ship owner.

free list: a statement, prepared by a customs department, of items that are not liable to the payment of duties.

freely convertible currency: a currency that may be used by citizens and foreigners without restriction.

freely offered: the concept that merchandise will be offered in the normal course of trade to all buyers on essentially the same basis.

free market: the unrestricted movement of items in and out of the market, unhampered by tariffs or other trade barriers.

free movement of goods: with reference to the European Union, a customs union that covers all trade in goods. It involves the prohibition between member nations of customs duties on imports and exports and of all charges having equivalent effect among member nations, and the adoption of a common customs tariff in their relations with countries that are not members.

free of capture and seizure: an insurance clause in the export insurance policy of private carriers providing that any loss of goods is not insured if the loss is due to certain specified political risks.

free of particular average: in the United States and the United Kingdom, denoting that no claim for partial loss or damage will be allowed by assurers unless the loss or damage is caused by the boat or vessel being in a collision, burned, stranded, or sunk. See *particular average.*

free on board (FOB): a pricing term indicating that the quoted price includes the cost of loading the goods into transport vessels at the specified place.

free-on-board airport:

(1) designates the place at which the seller's responsibility ends.

(2) where the seller must place the merchandise in the hands of the air carrier or his or her agent at the named airport of departure.

free on rail (FOR): the price of goods that includes the cost of moving them to a railhead for shipment and loading into a rail wagon.

free on truck (FOT): the price of goods that includes the cost of moving them to a truck for shipment and loading onto a truck.

free out (FO): a pricing term indicating that the charterer of a vessel is responsible for the cost of loading goods from the vessel.

free overside: in export price quotations, the seller paying all costs and accepting full responsibility for the goods until they have been safely unloaded at the place of importation in a foreign country. Thereafter, the buyer will pay all costs such as customs duty. Cf. *free alongside ship.*

free perimeter: a free-trade area similar ,to a free port, consisting of a defined geographical area, often in a nation's interior, where customary trade regulations are not imposed.

free port: synonymous with *free trade zone.*

free reserves: the margin by which excess reserves exceed the bank's borrowings.

free riders: with reference to the North American Free Trade Agreement (NAFTA), rules preventing free riders from benefiting through minor processing or transhipment of non-NAFTA goods. Mexico and Canada cannot be used as export platforms in the U.S. market. See *snap-back; worker protection.*

free time: the amount of time allowed by carriers for the loading or unloading of freight at the expiration of which demurrage or detention charges will accrue.

free trade: trade among countries in the absence of policy restrictions that may interfere with its flow.

Free trade will not benefit everyone; indeed objections can be raised as follows: (a) Trade diversion: Liberalization in trade, even if it is not accompanied by an increase in protectionism against imports from competing regions, can create perverse incentives that will lead to specialization in the wrong direction. The intent to have trade creation can deteriorate into trade diversion. (b) Beggar-thy-neighbor effects: The formation of a regional trade community can hurt nations outside of the Community, even without any overt increase in protectionism. (c) Trade warfare: The creation of a regional trading community, being larger than individual components, will evolve greater market power in world trade. This in turn may motivate member nations to engage in more aggressive trade policies, which can damage trade between competing blocs and result in everyone losing.

The theory necessitates that skilled workers win, while unskilled people lose, since the supply of unskilled laborers expands and that of skilled labor shrinks. The disparities in skill among the peoples of trading nations are great, and many may be disadvantaged during this period of adjustment.

In addition, the theory states that average incomes rise under free trade since unemployment can be expected not to be present. People terminated in any industry should easily find employment in new or expanding industries, so the theory continues. There is no certainty that average incomes throughout the nations participating in free-trade accords will increase by shifting to a system of free trade.

The theory also believes that the costs of making structural changes from one industry to another are zero. The recent experience with Eastern Europe suggests that these costs are usually great, with old facilities being torn down and new ones being built, infrastructures having to be constructed, and other costly projects needed.

Likewise, the theory assumes that people are paid salaries based on the demand for their services, not upon the industry in which they are employed. Jumping during this transition period from one industry to another will not guarantee equality of wages. The same task in a different industry will pay different salaries, let alone vary from nation to nation.

Consequently, free-trade accords between countries of dissimilar living standards, differing wage scales, varying cultures, and on and on, do not readily adapt in a short time period. See *laissez-faire; managed trade.*

free trade agreement (FTA): a comprehensive agreement designed to remove barriers to substantially expand all trade through eliminating tariffs and quotas, enhancing market access, improving standards for treatment of investors, strengthening enforcement of intellectual property rights, improving standards for health and safety, and restraining certain government actions, such as subsidies. Free trade agreements cover virtually every aspect of trade between signatories. They purport to remove all significant barriers to trade in goods and services and establish strong rules for investment and intellectual property rights, allowing participating economies to function according to market principles.

The benefits of free trade agreements are numerous. Firms will be able to make decisions based on their market advantage, rather than on arbitrary tariff and nontariff barriers. Expanded opportunities for economies of scale will improve global competitiveness. Increased exports in turn create new jobs, enhancing income and development in participating nations.

Therefore, free trade accords must cope with the primary issues of: (a) phased reduction and ultimate elimination of tariffs; (b) removing of nontariff barriers; (c) removal of barriers to the free flow of investment; (d) providing a greater number of services in foreign markets; (e) provision of adequate and effective protection of intellectual property rights; (f) removal of most custom restraints; and (g) definition of appropriate rules of origin.

By 2002 there were 120 free trade agreements in effect worldwide; four in the United States. By comparison, the EU had FTAs with 27 countries.

See *Canada Free Trade Agreement; comparative advantage; Fast Track Negotiating Authority; free trade; North American Free Trade Agreement; trade reform;* cf. *bilateral framework agreement; free trade zone.*

Free Trade Agreement (Area) for the Americas (FTAA): a proposed trade accord, combining all nations of North, Central, and South America and the countries of the Caribbean, except Cuba.

free trade areas: represents two or more customs territories in which duties and other restrictions on trade are eliminated on most of the trade between member nations. Unlike the Customs Union, however, free trade area territories do not pursue a common external trade policy and do not therefore have any common external tariff. Since there are no internal tariffs, its member are free to set their own tariffs on trade with the rest of the world. Cf. *common market; customs union; federation; free trade; Free Trade Agreement.*

Free Trade Areas of the Americas (FTAA): stretching from the Bering Strait to Cape Horn, with a population of 800 million and a combined gross domestic product of more than $11 trillion, the proposed FTAA would be the largest free-trade zone in the world. Talks in this area encompass 34 countries in North and South America and the Caribbean and would conclude by January 1, 2005, the accord taking effect within the year. Important tariffs on trade between member countries would fall to zero over the course of a decade or more. Nontariff barriers, such as quotas, would be gradually dismantled. Trade in services will also be liberalized. Investment rules will be harmonized. See *Enterprise for the Americas Initiative*.

Free Trade Commission: under the *North American Free Trade Agreement*, the Commission shall: (a) supervise the implementation of this Agreement; (b) oversee its further elaboration; (c) resolve disputes that may arise regarding its interpretation or application; (d) supervise the work of all committees and working groups established under this Agreement; and (e) consider any other matter that may effect the operation of this Agreement.

The Commission may: (a) establish and delegate responsibilities to ad hoc or standing committees, working groups, or expert groups; (b) seek the advice of nongovernmental persons or groups; and (c) take such other action in the exercise of its functions as the parties may agree.

The Commission shall establish its rules and procedures. All decisions of the Commission shall be taken by consensus, except as the Commission may otherwise agree.

The Commission shall convene at least once a year in regular session. Regular sessions of the Commission shall be chaired successively by each party. Cf. *North American Secretariats*.

free trade zone: a port designated by the government of a country for duty-free entry of any nonprohibited goods. Merchandise may be stored, displayed, used for manufacturing, and so on, within the zone and re-exported without duties being paid. Duties are imposed on the merchandise (or items manufactured from the merchandise) only when the goods pass from the zone into an area of the country subject to the customs authority. Synonymous with *bonded storage; bonded warehouse; foreign trade zone; free port*.

freeze:

(1) to fix prices at present levels, as with a price freeze. A freeze rarely takes place except during national crises or wartime.

(2) governmental seizure or impounding of property, goods, and so on. This action demands an executive order or the passage of a law, usually during emergencies.

free zone: see *free trade zone*.

freight:

(1) all merchandise, goods, products, or commodities shipped by rail, air, road, or water, other than baggage, express mail, or regular mail.

(2) the sum or fee paid for chartering a ship, or carrying its cargo.

freight absorption: a seller not charging a customer for freight out.

freight charge: the charge assessed for transporting freight.

freight claim: a demand on a carrier for the payment of overcharge or loss or damage sustained by shipper or consignee.

freight forwarder: an independent business that handles export shipments for compensation, or that acts as the shipper's appointed agent.

freight house: the station facility of a transportation line for receiving and delivering freight.

freight-in costs: expenses incurred by the purchaser in transporting purchased goods to its location for resale; included as part of the cost of goods sold.

freight inward: freight paid on shipments received.

freight outward: freight paid by a seller on outgoing customer shipments.

freight paid to: where a seller must forward the goods at his or her own expense to the agreed destination and is responsible for all risks of the goods until they are delivered to the first carrier.

freight release: when items are shipped with freight payable at their destination; a remittance for the amount of freight due is made to the vessel owner, who either endorses a freight release on the bill of lading, or retains the bill and issues a freight release as a separate document.

freight revenue: revenue from the transportation of freight and from transit, stop, diversion, and reconsignment arrangements, on the basis of tariffs.

French franc: former monetary unit of France.

French Pacific Community franc: see *CFP franc*.

FRF: the international standard code for the currency for Andorra, French Guiana, French Southern Territories, Guadeloupe, Martinique, Reunion, and St. Pierre and Miquelon—the French franc.

Fridays and holidays excluded (FHEX): in Islamic nations, unloading and loading that will not be carried out during official holidays nor on Fridays.

friendship, commerce, and navigation: see *FCN*.

FRN: see *floating-rate note*.

front-end fees: fees payable at the beginning of a loan.

front-end finance: finance for the initial part of a contract or project;

usually, as used in export finance referring to that part of a loan not covered by export credit insurance.

front-end loading: fees and other charges which are levied more heavily to begin with and then taper off.

frontier barriers: with reference to the European Union, the EU Commission's objectives, as required by the Single European Act, to coordinate policy and bring national legislation closer together. These efforts have eliminated completely the trade and fiscal barriers and controls in connection with crossing the Union's internal frontiers. Union citizens should not have to produce documents of identity and nationality and obtain customs clearance of goods in their baggage when passing from one member state to another. The single market envisages a two-stage process for removing frontier control of persons. In the first stage, frontier formalities were made more flexible and less systematic. In the second stage, when strengthening of the Union's external frontiers and cooperation between the relevant national authorities have reached appropriate levels, the frontier controls were eliminated. See *Single European Act*.

frustration: a condition that can lead to termination of a charter. A condition or occurrence during the time when a ship is under charter that precludes performance of the charter contract or has the effect of defeating the objective of the charter.

FSA: see *foreign sales agent*.

FSC: see *Foreign Sales Corporation*.

FTA: see *free trade agreement*.

FTAA: see *Free Trade Area of the Americas*.

FTA Commission: under the *Canada-U.S. Free Trade Agreement*, the top executives responsible for supervising the implementation of the Trade Agreement of 1989 between these two nations.

FTO: see *Foreign Trade Organization*.

FTZ: see *foreign trade zone, free trade zone*.

full container load (FCL):

(1) a fully loaded container, which may be defined in weight or cubic measurement terms.

(2) arrangement whereby a shipper utilizes all the space in a container that he or she packs.

full payment lease: synonymous with *export finance lease*.

full terms: a promise, in an offer to charter a vessel, that the owners must accept certain allowances or reductions in addition to normal commissions.

fully invested: a portfolio having only assets in the form of cash or cash equivalent.

functionalism: the step-by-step approach to economic integration, through agreements in economic sectors such as agriculture, tariffs, and transport.

functional standards: standards that provide needed selections from the range of options in the use of international standards, and do so in a harmonized way. See *standards.*

functional trade agreement: a trade accord limited to special measures used to manage trade between the trading partners.

Functioning of the GATT System (FOGS): an Uruguay Round negotiating group whose function is to strengthen the GATT, now WTO, process itself, with its major stated goals being to improve GATT surveillance of trade policies and practices, to encourage greater involvement of trade ministers in the GATT, and to strengthen the GATT's relationship with other international organizations such as the IMF.

fundamental disequilibrium:

(1) a situation of chronic balance-of-payments problems brought on by an unrealistic, protected foreign exchange rate.

(2) an International Monetary Fund expression indicating a substantial and persisting variation between the par exchange rate of a national currency and its purchasing-power parity with the currencies of other countries.

funded debt unmatured: unmatured debt (other than equipment obligations) maturing more than one year from date of issue.

fungible: goods or securities, any unit of which is the equal of any other like unit (e.g., wheat, corn).

further processing method: synonymous with *superdeductive.*

future exchange contract: a contract for the purchase or sale of foreign exchange to be delivered at a future date and at a rate determined in the present.

futures:

(1) foreign currencies bought or sold based on a rate that is quoted as of some future date.

(2) a contract under which the seller promises to sell the purchaser a given amount of foreign currency at a stated price sometime in

the future, regardless of the actual market price of the currency at that future date. A futures contract thereby protects a businessperson against an increase in the price of foreign currency between the time he or she places an order for a shipment of foreign goods and the future delivery date.

futures commission broker: a firm or party engaged in soliciting or accepting and handling orders for the purchase or sale of any commodity for future delivery on or the subject to the rules of any contract market and who, in or in connection with such solicitations or acceptance of orders, accepts any money, securities, or property (or extends credit in lieu thereof) to margin any trades or contracts that result there from.

futures contract: see *futures*.

FWAD: fresh water arrival draft.

F/X: see *foreign exchange*.

FX (foreign exchange) position: a bank's net holdings of any commitments in foreign exchange in any particular currency at any given point in time.

G

G-3: see *Group of Three.*

G-4: see *Group of Four.*

G-5: see *Group of Five.*

G-7: see *Group of Seven.*

G-8: see *Group of Eight.*

G-10: see *Group of Ten.*

G-11: see *Group of Eleven.*

G-13: see *Group of Thirteen.*

G-15: see *Group of Fifteen.*

G-24: see *Group of 24.*

G-77 (Group of 77): see *Generalized System of Preferences.*

GAB: see *General Agreement to Borrow.*

gaijin: non-Japanese investor who trades in Japan; a foreign competitor.

GAL: see *Guaranteed Access Level program.*

gap analysis: a technique to measure interest rate sensitivity.

garage: the transfer of liabilities or assets to a center that has little connection with the underlying transaction, usually to shift profits into a low-tax area.

gateway:

(1) a point at which freight moving from one territory to another is interchanged between transportation lines.

(2) a port or airport of entry into one territory from another.

GATS: see *General Agreement on Trade in Services.*

GATT: see *General Agreement on Tariffs and Trade.*

GATT Codes of Conduct: GATT, now WTO, instruments that prescribe standards of behavior by nations governing the use of non-tariff barriers to trade, which were negotiated during the Tokyo Round. Only signatories to each code are bound by its terms. Synonymous with *MTN Codes; Multinational Trade Negotiations Codes.*

GATT Customs Valuation Code: the multilaterally agreed formula of GATT, now WTO, for appraising imported items for the purpose of setting the amount of duty payable by the importer in the importing nation.

GATT Dispute-Settlement System: the formal arrangement of regulations and action to be carried out by participants in the GATT, now WTO, agreements for the reconciliation of their differences in matters involving mutual trade. See *Dispute-Settlement System.*

GATT Panel: a panel of neutral representatives established by the GATT, now WTO, Secretariat under the dispute settlement provisions of the GATT to review the facts of a dispute and render findings of GATT law and recommend action.

GATT Rounds: see *General Agreement on Tariffs and Trade.*

GBP: the international standard code for the currency of the United Kingdom—the pound sterling.

GCC: see *Gulf Cooperation Council.*

GCCI: see *Global Contracts Comprehensive Insurance.*

GDP: see *gross domestic product.*

geared: a vessel having heavy lifts and/or cranes.

gearing: in Great Britain, the relationship between equity capital and fixed interest capital. Synonymous with leverage in the United States.

General Agreement on Tariffs and Trade (GATT): on January 1, 1948, a multilateral trade treaty was signed embodying reciprocal commercial rights and obligations as a means of expanding and liberalizing world trade. It established common regulations and obligations concerning international trading arrangements and the framework for the negotiation of agreements to liberalize world trade. It was accepted by over 80 fully participating nations, with nearly 30 others signing under special arrangements. These nations accounted for almost 80 percent of world trade.

Thanks to GATT, after the end of World War II world trade expanded faster than global output did. With GATT, tariffs, worldwide, have been cut from an average of 40 percent in 1947 to less than 5 percent today, and consumers have reaped rich rewards in the form of lower prices and better merchandise. GATT has been remarkably successful and crucial to a strong world economy.

GATT rounds have been:

1947	Geneva Round creating GATT
1949	Annecy Round
1950–51	Torkay Round
1955–56	Geneva Round
1960–61	Dillon Round
1964–67	Kennedy Round
1973–79	Tokyo Round
1986–96	Uruguay Round

On December 7, 1990, the four-year-old GATT talks known as the Uruguay Round broke off in disarray, leading to passage of the deadline to reach an agreement to liberalize rules governing $4 trillion in annual world trade. The failure of this negotiation came at a particularly unfortunate moment. For the first time in the history of GATT, many developing nations—Mexico and Brazil, for example—were voluntarily trying to develop the competitiveness and efficiency of market economies and were moving away from state participation.

By early February 1991, they appeared to have been rescheduled, but were again put on hold until later in the year, when the European Community put off proposing major changes in their huge farm subsidy program.

Then, on April 16, 1991, a two-year review of GATT was published, pointing out that the European Community stood to gain from a strong multilateral trading system.

By the end of 1991, the Director General of the GATT talks placed a 500-page final document before the deadlocked negotiators, setting a mid-April 1992 as a final decision time. In 1993, President Clinton asked Congress to renew "fast track" authority giving GATT negotiators until December 15, 1993, to finish up the talks, and giving Congress until April 15, 1994, to vote on the treaty. This was extended to September 30, 1994.

Since 1995, GATT, was replaced by the WTO, the World Trade Organization, providing increased powers and legislative influence. It remains in Switzerland.

See *Dillion Round; external trade; fast track authority; GATT Customs Valuation Code; GATT Dispute-Settlement System; General Agreement on Trade in Services; Kennedy Round; Montreal Round; subsidies; Super 301; Tokyo Round; Uruguay Round; World Trade Organization.*

General Agreement on Trade in Services (GATS): tabled by the European Union June 18, 1990, an agreement that was intended to apply to all services. The proposal was aimed at promoting broad agreement among the various parties prior to the meeting of the Trade Negotiations Committee of GATT. See *General Agreement on Tariffs and Trade.*

General Agreement to Borrow (GAB): formed in 1962, involving the members of the Group of 10 plus Switzerland, under which nations concerned agreed to provide special credits to the IMF in their own currencies for G-10 member nations. See *Group of Ten.*

General Arrangement to Borrow: see *General Agreement to Borrow.*

general average (loss): a contribution by all the parties in a sea adventure to make good a loss sustained by one of their number because of voluntary sacrifices of part of the ship or cargo to save the remaining part, and the lives of those on board, from an impending peril.

general average loss: see *general average.*

general export license: any of various United States export licenses covering export commodities for which validated export licenses are not required. No formal application or written authorization is needed to ship exports under this license. See *export license; general license.* Cf. *Validated Export License.*

general imports: the measure of the total physical arrivals of items from foreign nations.

Generalized System of Preferences (GSP): GSP was adopted by the European Community on July 1, 1971. It involves a set of tariff preferences for developing countries to encourage diversification of their economies. Tariff preferences are either generalized—normally granted by the majority of industrialized nations (nondiscriminatory)—or unilateral—not the result of negotiations with the beneficiary nations. Preferences are not reciprocal in that the beneficiary nations are not required to grant corresponding duty exemption on imports. The Community submits its annual offer of reduced duty or duty-free imports on a large number of processed goods originating from developing nations, within the limits of certain quantities. Once that limit has been reached, the customs duties established in the common customs tariff can again be applied. In 1981, a different method was determined for calculating ceilings and quotas. By 1980, 13 nations, mainly from Asia and Latin America, accounted for 70 percent of preferential imports. The Community offered generalized preferences to all the member countries of the Group of 77 (G-77), to all those designated as developing countries by the United Nations, and to certain territories or countries dependent on Community nations, such as Hong Kong, Macao, and French Polynesia. In all, the Community scheme applies to 128 independent nations and more than 20 dependent territories. See *external trade; graduation; Lomé Conventions.*

general license: see *general export license.*

general order: a condition imposed on an item that is imported into the customs territory of the United States but that is not promptly cleared through customs.

general tariff: a tariff schedule in which a single rate of duty applies to a given commodity irrespective of the country of origin; makes no provision for preferential duties.

general trading companies: in existence throughout the world, including the United States. Well known in Japan as Sogo Shosha. See *sogo shosha*.

General Treaty of Central American Economic Integration: see *Central American Common Market*.

genetically altered ingredients: food containing more than 0.9 percent of a genetically modified organism. The European Union, in July 2003, approved legislation to require strict labels for food and feed made with such ingredients, requiring labeling indicating that the product contains a genetically modified organism, to take effect on January 1, 2004. Could become a barrier to trade, primarily with the U.S. See *traceability regulations*.

Geneva Round: see *General Agreement on Tariffs and Trade*.

gen-saki: a Japanese short-term money market; a market for conditional bond sales. A market where securities firms sell or buy bonds, usually for two or three months, while simultaneously including an agreement to repurchase them.

geographical hole: the absence of a global corporation from a place in one of the regional areas of the world that is considered important. Such an absence is harmful to the globalization of a firm's market offerings.

geographic indicators (GIs): a means of protecting traditional European products, such as that champagne must come from France; parma ham from Parma, Italy, etc.; a European Union form of protectionism, officials argue that it protect consumers and assures quality assurance.

German deutsche mark: former monetary unit of Germany.

GES: see *gold exchange standard*.

Gestion de l'Union Douaniere: see *GUD*.

GHC: the international standard code for the currency of Ghana—the cedi.

Gibraltar Pound: the monetary unit of Gilbraltar.

gilt-edge security: a security where the risk factor is at a minimum (i.e., a U.S. government bond).

GIP: the international standard code for the currency of Gibraltar—the Gibraltar pound.

GIs: see *geographic indicators.*

give-up: occurs when a member of a stock exchange on the floor acts for a second member by executing an order for him or her with a third member.

give-up order: securities not accepted for direct sale by a participating underwriter.

Glasnost: in Russian, openness. An official policy of the former Soviet Union relating to its people and its international trading partners.

global alliancing: an international marketing approach involving the formation of cooperative relationships between companies so as to lower overall operating costs, allowing these firms to have more profitable global marketing operations.

global bond: a Eurobond issue usually resulting in the printing of a number of pieces of paper indicating the debt incurred by the issuer to the bondholder.

Global Contracts Comprehensive Insurance (GCCI): an insurance program of the Export Development Corporation of Canada, which protects its exporters involved in continuous international trade by providing cover against nonpayment of a credit from an export sale because of commercial and political risks.

global firm: a firm that markets a standardized item worldwide and permits only minimal adaptations to local conditions and tastes. Its financial, marketing, and advertising strategies are global, with little differentiation among nations.

globalization:
deepening relationships and broadening interdependence among people from differing nations.
(2) becoming a global enterprise by expanding into global markets, using global production
facilities, forming alliances with global partners, and so on.

global marketing:
(1) where a multinational firm seeks to achieve long-run, large-scale production efficiencies by producing standardized products of sound value and long-term reliability in every segment of the market.
(2) the marketing of a standardized product worldwide with little allowance for, or acceptance of, regional or local differences.

global quotas: explicit limits set by one country on the value or quantity of goods that may be imported or exported through its borders during a given period on a global basis.

global safeguard: under NAFTA, a safeguard that will retain the United States's right to impose quotas or tariffs on Mexico and/or Canada as part of a multilateral safeguard action, when imports are a substantial cause of, or threaten, serious injury. See *free riders; North American Free Trade Agreement; snap-back; worker protection.*

global sourcing: the acquisition by a domestic firm of materials and supplies from overseas suppliers for domestic production or distribution.

Global System of Trade Preferences: see *Generalized System of Preferences.*

glut: (noun and verb) oversupply.

GmbH: Gesellschaft mit beschrankter Haftung (German limited liability company).

GMD: the international standard code for the currency of Gambia—the dalasi.

GNF: the international standard code for the currency of Guinea—the Guinea franc.

GNP: see *gross national product.*

GNP/capita: the gross national product of a nation divided by its population (an arithmetic mean).

godown: in the Far East, a commercial storage warehouse.

going global: entering the globalization arena. See *globalization.*

gold bullion standard: a monetary standard according to which: (a) the national unit of currency is defined in terms of a stated gold weight; (b) gold is retained by the government in bars rather than coin; (c) there is no circulation of gold within the economy; and (d) gold is made available for purposes of industry and for international transactions of banks and treasuries.

gold certificate:

(1) a document certifying the ownership of gold held at any authorized or recognized depository, primarily in the United States.

(2) in Germany, a certificate sold by a bank to residents that entitles the buyer to ownership of gold deposited in Luxembourg, thereby permitting the purchaser to escape German value-added tax on the purchases of the metal.

gold clause: a contract term for a money debt in terms of a U.S. dollar of a specified weight and quality of gold.

gold currency system: a monetary system that allows currency and gold to be freely converted one into the other at established rates.

gold exchange standard (GES): an international monetary agreement according to which money consists of fiat national currencies that can be converted into gold at fixed price ratios. See *Bretton Woods*.

gold export point: the mint parity plus transportation costs of shipping an amount of gold (equal to one unit of the foreign currency) between two nations.

gold fixing: method for setting the price of gold. In London, Paris, and Zurich, at 10:30 A.M. and again at 3:30 P.M., gold specialists or bank officials specializing in gold bullion activity determine the price for the metal.

gold franc: a form of currency. Different gold francs are still used under various international agreements as a means of calculating assets and liabilities under these accords (e.g., the Poincare franc for shipping, the balance sheet of the Bank for International Settlements (BIS)).

gold import point: the mint parity minus transportation costs of shipping an amount of gold (equal to one unit of the foreign currency) between two countries.

gold market: a foreign exchange market dealing in gold.

gold points: the range within which the foreign exchange rates of gold-standard countries will differ. Gold points are equal to the par rate of exchange plus and minus the cost of transporting gold. The cost of insurance is included.

gold pool: seven representatives of central banks of the United States, the United Kingdom, Belgium, Italy, Switzerland, the Netherlands, and Germany, who, operating through the Bank for International Settlements of Basle, seek to maintain equilibrium in the price of gold by purchasing and selling on the markets within certain minimum and maximum levels.

gold reserves: gold bullion content of a central bank's monetary reserves.

gold shares: shares in gold mining companies, mainly South African and Australian.

gold standard: a monetary agreement according to which all national currencies are backed 100 percent by gold and the gold is utilized for payments of foreign activity.

Gold Tranche Position in the International Monetary Fund: a position representing the amount that the United States can draw in foreign currencies virtually automatically from the International Monetary Fund if such borrowings are needed to finance a balance-of-payments deficit. The gold tranche itself is determined by the U.S. quota paid in gold minus the holdings of dollars by the fund in excess of the dollar portion of the U.S. quota. Transactions of the fund in a member country's currency are transactions in monetary reserves. When the fund sells dollars to other countries to enable them to finance their international payments, the net position of the United States in the fund is improved. An improvement in the net position in the gold tranche is similar to an increase in the reserve assets of the United States. On the other hand, when the United States buys other currencies from the fund, or when other countries use dollars to meet obligations to the fund, the net position of the United States in the fund is reduced. See *tranche*.

good: see *goods*.

goods:

(1) the result of industrial work, equaling the gross national product for one year.

(2) any tangible thing that people consider useful and which is a benefit within the meaning of that concept in our society. Synonymous with *merchandise; product*. See *originating goods*.

goods in free circulation: merchandise not subject to customs restrictions.

good till canceled (GTC): buy-or-sell order remaining in force until executed or canceled by a customer. Synonymous with *open order*.

gourde: the monetary unit of Haiti.

Government Account: synonymous with *Canada Account*.

Government Procurement Code: synonymous with *Agreement on Government Procurement*.

grace period: most contracts provide that the policy will remain in force if premiums are paid at any time within a period (the grace period) varying from 28 to 31 days following the premium due date.

gradualists: reformers of international trade who urge slow movement, which they claim is less costly economically and more feasible politically. They claim that hasty moves toward an open market will destroy most existing industry and unsettle too many people in the less-developed nations of the world, for example, Central Europe. Cf. *big bangers.*

graduation:

(1) the movement of a nation from eligibility on either the individual generalized system of preferences—eligible products—or on the entire schedule of them.

(2) some developing countries eventually (through rising living standards, increased production and export earnings, etc.) reach a point of greater economic competitiveness and independence. As developing countries increase their economic independence, they are removed from the list of Generalized System of Preference countries. Requiring that the graduated countries undertake the obligations of developed countries allows these developing countries to be more fully integrated into the trading system. See *Generalized System of Preferences.*

grain bill: a bill of exchange drawn against grain shipments.

grandfather clause:

(1) any condition that ties existing rights or privileges to previous or remote conditions or acts; more popularly used, when a new regulation goes into effect, to exempt people who are already engaged in the activity being regulated.

(2) a clause in an international trade accord providing that certain existing programs and practices are exempted from a specific obligation.

(3) a provision in the GATT, now WTO, that allows signatories to maintain certain domestic legislation (which was in effect when they joined the GATT) even though it may be inconsistent with GATT rules.

grants and loans: forms of financial assistance. The underlying purpose of all financial assistance geared to structural objectives is to improve living and working conditions. It is a manifestation of solidarity and is designed to bring about closer integration of member states' economies.

gray market:

(1) sources of supply from which scarce items are bought for quick delivery at a premium well above the usual market price.

(2) commodities that are either mimics or counterfeits of genuine items.

GRD: the international standard code for the currency of Greece—the drachma.

Greek drachma: former monetary unit of Greece.

green box: a category of farm subsidies that do not influence production or price decisions. According to the European Community, these would not have to be reduced, because they do not distort trade. See *subsidies.*

green currencies: money to support farm prices. Common support prices under the European Union's Common Agricultural Policy are fixed annually in Units of Accounts, but farmers actually receive money in their own currencies from the Farm Fund, calculated at special exchange rates called green currencies. See *Common Agricultural Policy.* Cf. *Green Pound.*

Green Label: a plan proposed by the European Community in November 1990 to establish a green label. Consumer products considered friendly to the environment would receive the award before export to other EC states or overseas in the hope that the initiative would increase the pressure on industry to develop products that reduce pollution levels. The plan calls for the label to be awarded by an independent jury set up at the EC level, although firms seeking the label would first apply to their national governments. The program would be taken over by the European Environment Agency. Approved in 1991, the European label is indicated by a yellow daisy on a green background.

Green Paper: a 1990s working document of the European Union that purports to upgrade the telecommunications industry and promote international trade of its evolving products and services. Legislation covers: (a) completing the phased opening up of the computer terminal equipment market to compensation; (b) opening up the telecommunications service market, excluding at this stage a number of basic services considered essential to meet current public service goals and objectives; (c) establishing the right for services to operate across member countries' national borders; (d) continuing the exclusivity or special rights for telecommunications administrations (public and private carriers) to supply and operate the network infrastructure, and a recognition of their central role in establishing future generations of infrastructures; (e) separating regulatory and operational functions of telecommunications administrations; (f) opening up of the market for satellite ground stations to the extent that the equipment is associated with telecommunications terminals rather than infrastructure; (g) recognizing that telecommunication tariffs should be responsive to cost trends; (h) developing a consensus from both sides of industry in order to smooth the transition and to maximize the opportunities presented by the new networks and services to create employment; (i) using telecommunications to accelerate economic development and reduce the isolation of outlying regions; (j) establishing common positions within the various international bodies; and (k) creation of a Standards Institute.

Green Pound: a monetary unit representing the rate at which the prices fixed under the European Community's Common Agricultural Policy translated into sterling. These prices are fixed in Units of Account originally based on the United States dollar. Cf. *green currencies.*

green taxes: at first proposed by the European Union, but now of global interest by other regional trading partners. These taxes would be imposed by member nations as an incentive to encourage consumers and industry to behave in ways that do little harm to the environment. For example, putting in place taxes to control pollution under a decree by allowing substantially higher taxes to be placed on car buyers who purchase leaded gasoline, rather than the more expensive but less taxed unleaded gasoline.

grey-area measures: trade actions, the legality of which are not clearly addressed by GATT, now WTO, rules. Examples of grey-area measures include voluntary export restraint agreements (VRAs) and orderly marketing agreements (OMAs). Grey-area measures are a subject of great interest to the negotiating group on safeguards. See *orderly marketing agreements; voluntary restraint agreements.*

gross charter: a vessel charter arrangement whereby all expenses (loading, unloading, etc.) are for the account of the vessel. Synonymous with *gross terms.*

gross domestic product (GDP):
(1) the total of goods and services produced in a nation over a given time period, usually a year. Cf. *gross national product.*
(2) the market value of a country's output attributable to factors of production located in the country's territory.

gross national debt: the total indebtedness of a government, including debts owed by one agency to another.

gross national product (GNP): the gross domestic product plus income from abroad less income paid abroad. It is equal to gross national income—the total of incomes of the residents of a nation from all sources. See *GNP/capita*. Cf. *gross domestic product*.

gross registered tonnage (GRT): total enclosed capacity in a ship, in units of 100 cubic feet, less certain exempted spaces.

gross terms: synonymous with *berth terms*.

gross ton: 2,240 pounds.

gross ton-mile: the movement of a ton of transportation equipment and contents a distance of one mile.

gross tonnage (vessel): applies to vessels, not cargo; determined by dividing by 100 the contents, in cubic feet, of the vessel's closed-in spaces. A vessel ton is 100 cubic feet. The register of a vessel states both gross and net tonnage. Cf. *cargo tonnage*.

gross weight:
(1) the weight of an article together with the weight of its container and the material used for packing.
(2) as applied to a carload, the weight of the car together with the weight of its entire contents. Cf. *tare weight*.

gross yield: the return obtained from an investment before the deduction of costs and losses involved in procuring and managing an investment.

gross yield to redemption: in Great Britain, the interest yield on a security plus the annual capital gain should the security be held to redemption.

ground storage: the storing of shipments on the ground.

Group of Three (G-3): organized in 1991 to promote energy cooperation. The G-3 (Venezuela and Colombia commenced an integration process with Mexico) pledged to implement a free trade zone through the signing of bilateral agreements by its members. The G-3 presidents announced the 1992 initiation of negotiations for a trilateral free trade agreement at their December 1991 meeting in Cartagena. Chile also expressed interest in participating. See *Andean Pact*.

Group of Four (G-4): the Latin American nations of the Southern Cone trading association: Argentina, Brazil, Paraguay, and Uruguay. Synonymous with *Mercosur*.

Group of Five (G-5): the more powerful members of the Group of Ten, the United States, Japan, Germany, France, and Great Britain. See *Group of Seven*.

Group of Seven (G-7): the group of industrialized nations that constitute the Group of Five, plus Canada and Italy. Russia is also a participant, making it a *Group of Eight (G-8)*. See *Group of Five; Group of Ten.*

Group of Eight (G-8): see *Group of Seven.*

Group of Ten (G-10): under the 1962 General Agreement to Borrow, 11 of the principal industrial nations—the United States, the Netherlands, the United Kingdom, Sweden, France, Japan, Germany, Italy, Belgium, and Canada—together with Switzerland (an unofficial member). This group makes available to the International Monetary Fund their currencies up to specified amounts to lend when supplementary funds are needed by the IMF. See *General Agreement to Borrow; General Agreement on Tariffs and Trade; Group of Five.* Synonymous with *Paris Club.*

Group of Eleven (G-11): formed in 1984; the largest debtor nations in Latin American.

Group of Thirteen (G-13): formed by the Group of Seven in September 1989 to rival the Organization of Economic Cooperation and Development. This group includes Algeria, Argentina, Egypt, India, Indonesia, Jamaica, Malaysia, Nigeria, Peru, Senegal, Venezuela, Yugoslavia, and Zimbabwe. See *Organization for Economic Cooperation and Development.*

Group of Fifteen (G-15): formed in 1990; consists of developed nations who meet to discuss the benefits of mutual cooperation in improving their international economic positions.

Group of 24 (G-24): an organization of the 24 industrialized nations of the world. It was formed at the Group of 77 meeting in Peru in 1972 and received quasi-official status by the IMF.

Group of 77 (G-77): see *Generalized System of Preferences.*

GRT: see *gross registered tonnage.*

GSP: see *Generalized System of Preferences.*

GST: goods and services tax.

GSTP (Generalized System of Tariff Preferences): see *Generalized System of Preferences.*

GTC: see *good till canceled.*

GTQ: the international standard code for the currency of Guatemala—the quetzal.

guarani: the monetary unit of Paraguay.

guarantee cards: see *Eurochecking.*

Guaranteed Access Level (GAL) program: a program allowing Caribbean Basin Initiative nations to negotiate with the United States to ensure access to the U.S. market for textile products, assembled from fabric formed and cut in the United States. See *Caribbean Basin Initiative.*

guaranteed fund: an International Monetary Fund program used as a means for reducing third-world debt. This fund requires the backing of governments. Its success depends on three conditions: that debtor nations agree on economic adjustment programs with the IMF; that commercial banks shoulder their share of the burden; and that creditor nations not belonging to any institutionalized community make an equivalent contribution. The fund aims to strengthen the multilateral approach to solving the debt problem.

guaranteed letters of credit: travelers' letters of credit or commercial letters of credit, whereby the party requesting the credit issuance does not pay the bank in cash for the equivalent amount of the credit upon its issuance. The bank substitutes its own credit for people or firms, to encourage more domestic and foreign trade.

guaranteed portion: the percentage of the finance portion of a transaction guaranteed by Eximbank once the exporter retention and commercial bank retention (if any) are deducted.

guaranteed price: this is the price determined as being the correct amount which farmers, as a whole, would receive for specified agricultural commodities. A risky business at best, as it perpetuates artificial prices and supports the use of subsidies. An obstacle within the European Union to reducing farm subsidies. In 2004, preparing for a WTO meeting in Doha, significant progress was made to reduce agricultural subsidies.

guarantor: an individual, financial institution, or government entity that guarantees the obligations of the foreign borrower or buyer.

GUD (Géstion de l'Union Douaniere): part of the European Union's Commission, with responsibility for administration of the Customs Union.

Guernsey pound: the monetary unit of Guernsey.

guide book: a tariff containing instructions for waybilling and routing shipments and bases for rates to certain points.

guide price: this is the equivalent of a target price for beef and veal.

It serves both as a target price and as the gauge for basing import control and intervention buying.

guilder: the former monetary unit of the Netherlands, Netherlands Antilles; also Surinam.

Guinea-Bissau peso: the monetary unit of Guinea-Bissau.

Guinean franc: the monetary unit of Guinea.

gulden: the former monetary unit of the Netherlands, divided into 100 cents.

Gulf Cooperation Council (GCC): Saudi Arabia, Kuwait, Qatar, the United Arab Emirates, Oman, and Bahrain are members of this economic, regional, and trade association; formed in 1981; headquartered in Riyadh, Saudi Arabia.

Guyana dollar: the monetary unit of Guyana.

GWP: the international standard code for the currency of Guinea-Bissau—the Guinea-Bissau peso.

GYD: the international standard code for the currency of Guyana—the Guyan dollar.

H

haircut finance: a borrowing made against securities as collateral.

half-life: the time that elapses until half the principal amount of a block of bonds has been redeemed.

Hamburg Rules: guidelines set in the 1960s by the United Nations Conference on Trade and Development, providing for an increase in the level of liability of sea carriers regarding loss and damage. The purpose is to set equitable terms regarding the rights and obligations of both shippers and ship owners.

hand off: see *North American Free Trade Agreement*.

handysize: in the United Kingdom, vessels around 15,000 to 25,000 tons deadweight.

Hang Seng Index: primary indicator of stock market activity in Hong Kong.

harbor: a port or haven where ships may anchor.

harbor dues: charges assessed for services at harbors.

hard currency: any internationally acceptable means of exchange that is not subject to government controls on its use and is not held up by artificially maintained exchange rates. A hard currency may, nevertheless, still be subject to weakness on world financial markets. It is in demand for transactions so that the party receiving payment can be confident of exchanging the funds into his or her own money, without fear of sudden massive devaluation or instability in the financial system of the nation issuing the currency. See *convertibility; unified exchange rates*.

hard ECU: see *European Currency Unit*.

hard loan: a foreign loan that must be paid in hard money.

hard money:
(1) currency of a nation that has stability in that country and abroad.
(2) a situation in which interest rates are high and loans are difficult to arrange.

hardship allowance: supplement to compensate expatriates for working in dangerous or adverse conditions.

harmonization (internal community trade): a reference to efforts to improve the common market in Europe. Customs duties (tariffs) were abolished among the six founder members of the European Community in 1968, later for all 15 member states. The

Council of Ministers periodically announced new Directives for the approximation (harmonization) of national laws or administrative regulations that affect the proper operations of the common market, expecting consumers to benefit from competition, and manufacturers to take advantage of a market of over 320 million people. For nontechnical barriers, applied in member nations sometimes for health or environmental reasons, the Commission sought harmonization by informal means rather than by Directive. The 1979 GATT Agreement on Technical Barriers to Trade is designed to check, at international levels, the proliferation of national divergent technical standards and regulations by signatory nations. Its activities are influenced by the judgment of the European Court of Justice.

Harmonization and its Directives take account of the objectives contained within the Single European Act, which commits the Commission to table proposals based on a high level of health, safety, consumer, and environmental protection. See *CE mark; Common Customs Tariff; Company Law; customs union; General Agreement on Tariffs and Trade; harmonize; ISO 9000; nontariff barrier; single customs document; standardization.*

harmonize:

(1) to bring into a state of mutual agreement those things that were not hitherto in such a state. See *harmonization.*

(2) among nations, to recognize in an agreement each other's laws as being equivalent and as having the same impact.

Harmonized Commodity Description and Coding System: synonymous with *Harmonized System.*

Harmonized System (HS): an internationally recognized goods classification system, adopted by the United States on January 1, 1989, that serves as the basis for the Canadian Free Trade Agreement's rules-of-origin and tariff elimination schedule. Prior to shipping to Canada, U.S. exporters must obtain a Harmonized System (HS) tariff number for their products. See *rules of origin.* Synonymous with *Harmonized Commodity Description and Coding System.*

Havana Charter: synonymous with *International Trade Organization.*

hazardous cargo certificate: a standard form used to declare the nature of any hazardous cargo being delivered to an airline.

heavy hold harmless assignment: a special U.S. form of assignment available to new-to-export and umbrella policies that ensures payment to the U.S. commercial bank assignee irrespective of most policy violations by the exporter, but only within the limits of coverage.

heavy lift: see *H/L.*

hedge clause: a disclaimer that disavows legal responsibility for the accuracy of information from outside sources.

hedger: an individual who is unwilling to risk a serious loss in his or her cash position and takes a counterbalancing position in order to avoid or lessen loss.

hedging: the practice of selling foreign currency forward into local currency, so that its value is not affected by subsequent exchange rate changes. Synonymous with *covering exchange risk.*

hegemony: the predominance of one nation over another.

HG: heavy grains.

HHDW: handy heavy deadweight, for highly compacted scrap metal.

Hickenlooper Amendment (1961): providing for the suspension of all foreign assistance to any country that nationalizes American-owned property in that nation or that has attempted to abrogate an existing contract without attempting to reach a settlement within a given time frame.

hidden damage: the condition of merchandise that has been damaged while in transit where the damage is not visible from a simple external examination.

hire: the revenue earned by a ship under charter.

historically planned economy: World Bank concept for second-world nations in transition to market economies. See *World Bank.*

hit list: a list of nations that systematically restrict access of American products to their markets. See *Super 301.*

HKD: the international standard code for the currency of Hong Kong—the Hong Kong dollar.

HKIBOR: see *Hong Kong Interbank Offered Rate.*

H/L (heavy lift): a unit of cargo that cannot be lifted by the normal ship's gear.

HNL: the international standard code for the currency of Honduras—the lempira.

home country: the domestic base of a national firm engaged in trade with an investment in foreign nations.

Hong Kong Interbank Offered Rate (HKIBOR): the Hong Kong equivalent of LIBOR—the rate at which deposits are offered to prime banks in Hong Kong. See *Singapore Interbank Offered Rate.*

horizontal expansion: any foreign direct investment where a firm produces the same product it produces at home.

horizontal export trading company: an export trading firm that exports a range of similar or identical items supplied by a number of producers.

host nation: the target nation of direct (foreign) investment and in which a business operates outside its domestic jurisdiction.

hot cargo: goods made or shipped by nonunion labor. Many unions refuse to handle such products, especially when they are produced or shipped by a truck company.

hot money:

(1) pertains to capital movements, usually of a short-term character, that take place either for speculative reasons or in response to interest-rate differentials.

(2) overseas funds placed in a nation at short term; they are liable to rapid withdrawal should confidence in a currency be shaken or if interest differentials swing against the nation where the funds are deposited.

hots: (slang) in Great Britain, Treasury bills on the day they are issued, with their full term to run.

housepaper: a commercial bill of exchange drawn and accepted by firms in the same group, as a subsidiary, and accepted by its parent firm.

HS: see *Harmonized System.*

HSS: heavy grains, sorghums, and soyas.

HTG: the international standard code for the currency of Haiti—the gourde.

HUF: the international standard code for the currency of Hungary—the forint.

hull insurance: insurance of a vessel together with liabilities arising from collision, etc.

Hume's species flow mechanism: the process whereby economies operating on the gold standard suffer inflation if exports exceed imports (and suffer deflation if imports exceed exports). The economy's competitiveness in international trade is altered as a result, and exports and imports ultimately are forced into balance.

hypothecation:

(1) in the United States, pledging of securities as collateral (e.g., to

secure the debit balance in a margin account).

(2) an agreement or contract that permits a bank or a creditor to utilize the collateral pledged to secure a loan in case the loan is unpaid at maturity.

(3) a letter of hypothecation permitting a shipper to borrow from a bank using the vessel as security, but without giving the bank ownership of the security.

I

IAC: see *Import Allocation Certificate.*

IACS: International Association of Classification Societies.

IADB: see *Inter-American Development Bank.*

IAIGC: see *Inter-Arab Investment Guarantee Corporation.*

IASC: see *International Accounting Standards Committee.*

IBA: see *International Banking Act of 1978.*

IBFs: see *International Banking Facilities.*

IBRD: see *International Bank for Reconstruction and Development.*

ICA:

(1) see *International Commodity Agreement.*

(2) see *International Coffee Agreement.*

ICC: see *International Chamber of Commerce.*

ICD: see *Islamic Corporation for the Development of the Private Sector.*

Icelandic krone: monetary unit of Iceland.

ICS: International Chamber of Shipping.

ICSID: see *International Center for the Settlement of Investment Disputes.*

IDA: see *International Development Association of the United Nations.*

IDB:

(1) see *Inter-American Development Bank.*

(2) see *Islamic Development Bank.*

identical treatment: the position taken by some European Union officials who want firms operating abroad to receive the identical treatment and rights that the European Union would extend to foreign firms. In banking, for instance, the European Union might seek an exemption from U.S. restrictions on bank activities. The United States would argue strongly that nations have differing regulatory views on how best to serve and protect the public and that U.S. firms should not be excluded from other markets because of such differences. See *reciprocity.* Cf. *national treatment.*

identity of shipment: preservation of the original character of shipments stopped in transit, so that no substitution occurs outbound from the transit point.

IDR: the international standard code for the currency of Indonesia—the rupiah.

IELAR (Institute for European-Latin American Relations): see *Latin America.*

IEP: the international standard code for the former currency of Ireland—the Irish pound.

IET: see *Interest Equalization Tax*.

IFC: see *International Finance Corporation*.

IGA: see *International Grain Agreement*.

IGC: see *Interagency Group on Countertrade*.

IITSSA: see *International Investment and Trade in Services Act*.

ILS: the international standard code for the currency of Israel—the Israeli shekel.

IMCO (Intergovernmental Maritime Consultative Organization): a specialized agency of the United Nations that was established in 1959 to facilitate cooperation between governments on technical issues affecting international shipping, such as navigation, safety, and pollution control.

IMF: see *International Monetary Fund*.

imitation lag: strategy for exploiting temporary monopoly advantages by moving first to those nations most likely to develop local production.

IMM: see *international money management*.

immediate delivery: the means for immediate release of a shipment being imported to the U.S.; requires a special permit from the U.S. Customs office.

immediate transportation entry: customs form listing items for transport by a bonded carrier from a port of entry to a bonded warehouse at an inland port or another entry port.

impairment: when a country's trade interests are negatively affected by changes in the trade regime of another country or another country's failure to carry out its WTO, formerly GATT, obligations.

implementation: the process of carrying out a measure, a law, a policy, a plan, etc., usually as laid down in a treaty or agreement.

import:
(1) (verb) to receive goods and services from abroad.
(2) (verb) to bring goods and services from abroad.
(3) (noun) an imported item.

Import Allocation Certificate (IAC): a document that Japan's Ministry of International Trade and Industry requires Japanese importers to complete and submit to a foreign exchange bank as a prerequisite to obtaining an import permit.

import broker: person who secures various governmental permissions and other clearances before forwarding necessary paperwork to the carrier that will deliver the goods from the dock to the importer.

import certificate: the way that the government of the nation of ultimate destination exercises legal control over the internal channeling of the goods covered by an import document.

import cover: the number of months of gross imports whose cost would be covered by a nation's monetary reserves.

import credit: commercial letter of credit issued for the purpose of financing the importation of merchandise.

import deposits: a means for restricting imports by requiring importers to deposit a percentage of the value of their imports for a set time before it is repaid.

import duty: any tax on imported items.

imported substitution: see *import substitution*.

importer: individual liable for payment of duties on items bought from an exporter, or an authorized agent acting on the importer's behalf.

importer distributor: merchant who imports merchandise, often on an exclusive territory arrangement, maintains inventory, and, usually with a staff for sales, sells to retailers.

import license: a document required and issued by some national governments authorizing the importation of goods into their individual nations. See *North American Free Trade Agreement*.

Import Licensing Code: synonymous with *Agreement on Import Licensing*.

import merchant: merchant buying overseas for own account for the purpose of later resale, and handling all details of import documentation and transport.

import policy: the course of action of a domestic government to create a favorable environment to both attract foreign imports and sound direct investment.

import quota auctioning: the process of allocating the right to import a good that is subject to an import quota by auctioning the quota, in whole or part, to future importers.

import quotas: synonymous with *quantitative restrictions*.

import rate: a rate established specifically for application on import traffic and generally less, when so published, than the domestic rate.

import relief: see *import restrictions.*

import restrictions: a government scheme for reducing or controlling imports through a variety of measures, including import deposits, licenses, and quotas.

import substitution: reducing imports through local manufacture of the item; a common policy in developing nations, where foreign exchange is very scarce and where importers have developed the local market.

import surcharge: a charge on imports over and above regular tariffs or customs fees. See *side agreements.*

import surges: see *North American Free Trade Agreement.*

import tariff: tax on merchandise entering a country.

Import Trade Control over Notices: directives issued by the Ministry of International Trade and Industry of Japan specifying which imported goods are subject to import quotas.

impost: a tax, usually an import duty.

in bond: shipments under the control of U.S. Customs until all charges and regulations have been satisfied.

in bond industry: a business based on the importation of parts into a free trade area without payment of duties; parts are processed and then re-exported.

inchoate: newly begun or incomplete.

INCOTERMS: a publication of the International Chamber of Commerce containing international rules for the interpretation of terms used in foreign trade contracts.

indent: the request from a purchaser to an importer to import specific items at a stated price (i.e., a purchase order). The importer has a given time period in which to accept or refuse the offer.

indenture: a written agreement under which debentures are issued, setting forth maturity date, interest rate, and other terms.

independence: an extreme situation where a nation would not rely on other nations at all.

index linking: relating wages, prices, interest rates, or loan values to an index, usually of prices. See *indicator.*

indicator: any quantity (average, composite, or index) that is correlated to the performance of the stock market or to general economic conditions. Indicators are observed in an attempt to predict market conditions. See *index linking.*

indicator price system: an arrangement whereby the deficiency payment to the U.K. producers is based on the difference between the guaranteed price and an indicator price. It represents a price that producers might reasonably be expected to secure should the market not be overloaded.

indirect exchange: a strategy employed in arbitrage of foreign exchange in purchasing foreign exchange in one market and quickly selling it in another market at a rate that produces a profit over the purchase price plus the expenses of the transaction.

indirect exporting: export sales by a domestic firm to a foreign purchaser via a domestically based intermediary.

indirect quotation: a quotation of fixed units of domestic currency in variable units of foreign currency.

indirect selling: a sale of goods by an exporter through another domestic firm as an intermediary.

indirect standard: a monetary system that does not directly convert its currency into a standard metal such as gold or silver but allows, as a right of ownership, the exchange of the domestic currency into the currency of a nation that is on a metal standard. The ratio of exchange is credited and held with only occasional changes.

indirect tax: a tax that is levied on expenditures (i.e., a sales tax, excise tax, or value-added tax).

indirect taxation: synonymous with *double taxation*.

individual tariff: a tariff issued by a transportation line individually.

inducement: in shipping, the tender by a shipper to a carrier of a sufficient amount of cargo so as to warrant a vessel calling at a port not ordinarily scheduled during its voyage.

industrial country: high-income country.

industrial espionage: spying by a utilizing operative to secure secret information about a business competitor. At times referred to as *competitive intelligence*.

industrial property: a generic classification for patents, trademarks, copyright, "know-how," and agreements relating to these.

industrial standards: see *harmonization; standards*.

industrial targeting: government strategy of assisting specific industries.

infant industry: a concept derived from the idea that temporary protection in the form of tariffs or nontariff barriers can help establish an industry and ensure its eventual competitiveness in world markets. Although a case may be made for restricting trade due to the infant industry argument under the WTO, the country may be required to compensate adversely affected signatories.

inflation: the increase in the price level creating a decrease in the purchasing power of the monetary unit. The inflation rate is the rate of change in prices, determined on an annual, monthly, or other basis.

informal economy: these businesses often pay no taxes, have no licenses, offer no social security or medical benefits, and sometimes deal in smuggled goods and even illegal drugs. The informal economy is represented by companies that are involved in legal activities but are not registered with the government because of excessive red tape, which in some countries takes up to one year to complete.

Informal Entry: an abbreviated entry procedure allowed by U.S. Customs for shipments of merchandise under $250 and certain household effects.

infrastructure: a nation's internal structure to support an effective market economy, such as roads and telephones.

infrequent exporter: a firm with limited exporting activity, traditionally between one and 50 export shipments in a year. Nevertheless, the U.S. Department of Commerce believes that such companies should be assisted to increase their export shipments.

initial carrier: the transportation line to which a shipment is delivered by the shipper.

initial margin: the amount a buyer is requested to deposit with a broker before commencing trading.

Initial Negotiating Right (INR): a right held by one WTO country to seek compensation for an impairment of a given bound tariff rate by another WTO country. INRs stem from past negotiating concessions and allow the INR holder to seek compensation for an impairment of tariff concessions regardless of its status as a supplier of the product in question.

initial point: the point at which a shipment originates.

injury: in U.S. law, a finding by the U.S. International Trade Commission that imports are causing harm to a U.S. industry. It is a requirement in all antidumping and most countervailing duty cases. The ITC determines whether there is serious injury to U.S. industry in a Section 201 case, while in antidumping and countervailing duty cases, it investigates whether there is material injury. See *Section 201 of the Trade Act of 1974.*

inland bill of lading: a bill of lading used in transporting goods overland to the exporter's international carrier. Cf. *air waybill*.

inland carrier: see *inland transport*.

inland exchange: synonymous with *domestic exchange*.

inland marine insurance: insurance developed originally by marine underwriters to cover goods while in transit by other than ocean vessels. It now covers any goods in transit (except transoceanic) and also includes numerous floater policies. Cf. *ocean marine insurance*.

inland transport: a transportation line that hauls export or import traffic between ports and inland points. See *transport*.

Inmarsat: see *International Maritime Satellite Organization*.

Inner Six: the first six nations of the European Community: Belgium, France, Germany, Italy, Luxembourg, and the Netherlands.

INR: the international standard code for the currency of Bhutan and India—the Indian rupee.

See *Initial Negotiating Right*.

insider trading: the practice of participating in transactions based on privileged information gained by one's position and not available to the public. When such transactions affect the price, giving an unfair advantage to a trader, they are illegal in the United States.

inspection certificate: a document issued by regulatory agencies in either the exporting country or the importing country providing evidence that the goods have been inspected and meet the prescribed standards for goods of that type.

Institute Warranty Limits: see *IWL*.

institutional pot: the percentage, usually 20 percent, of an offering of a security that has been set aside by managers for large institutional orders.

insurable interest: any interest in or relation to property of such nature that the occurrence of an event insured against it would cause financial loss to the insured.

insurance certificate: evidence that marine insurance has been obtained to cover stipulated risks during transit.

Integrated Border Plan: a strategy for cleaning up the polluted 1,600-mile border with Mexico under the North American Free Trade Agreement; unveiled by the President of the United States on February 25, 1992. Under the plan, the United States provided

$380 million over two years for cleaning the frontier environment. Additional funds are released by the U.S. every two years following review of progress made in pollution efforts within Mexico.

integrated cargo service: all portions of the cargo system providing combined services of carrier, freight forwarder, handler, and agent.

integration: the procedure of bringing about much closer relations between states. See *harmonization; internal market.*

intellectual property: an intangible creation that is possessed; examples include patents, trademarks, copyrights, computer software, industrial designs, and trade secrets. See *intellectual property rights.*

intellectual property rights (IPRs): international trade accords are seeking to find adequate and effective protections for intellectual property rights, for patents, trademarks, copyrights, computer software, industrial designs, and trade secrets. For the United States in particular, the competitiveness of many industries relies on effective protection of these rights and the ability to receive compensation for development costs. Adequate intellectual property rights protection encourages firms to invest in ongoing research and development, aiding the development of national economies.

Differences between member nations' trademark, copyright, and patent laws have an adverse impact on international trade and on the ability of firms to treat a common market as a single environment for their activities.

With trademarks, the existence of the distinct national systems creates obstacles to international trade marketing, in addition to cumbersome and costly administrative and legal burdens.

Protection rights are needed for intellectual property such as patents, copyrights, and trademarks. Patents should be protected for 20 years, copyrights for 75 years, and the initial registration of a trademark would be valid for 10 years.

The confusion in dealing with intellectual property is further complicated by the need to provide protection to inventions in new technologies such as computer software, microcircuits, and biotechnology. These technologies were not in existence when the present intellectual property laws were originally drafted, and so methods for legal protection are obscure. Needs of intellectual property include: (a) to create a trademark applicable throughout a regional trading area. (This will remove the current requirement to make separate applications for trademarks in each country.); (b) to ensure that registered trademarks enjoy the same protection under the legal system of all trading countries; (c) to specify the fees payable to a trademark office and its methods of payment; (d) to standardize national legislation regarding the protection of topographies (design) of semiconductor products and to provide protection for the creator of the design, thereby allowing for the free movement of semiconductors within participating nations; (e) to standardize national legislation regarding the innovations with the biotechnology field; (f) to standardize national legislation regarding the innovations within the computer field.

The North American Free Trade Agreement (NAFTA) assures a strong overall level of protection for patents, copyrights, trademarks, and trade secrets. Each country is required to provide adequate and effective protection and enforcement of intellectual property rights. The agreement provides for specific commitments on: copyrights, including sound recordings; product and process patents; trademarks; plant breeders' rights; industrial designs; trade secrets; integrated circuits (semiconductors); and geographical indications. In addition, the agreement sets out stringent procedures for the enforcement of intellectual property rights. See *intellectual property.*

Interagency Group on Countertrade (IGC): an organization chaired by the U.S. Secretary of Commerce, or appointed representative. Its purpose is to review and evaluate U.S. policy on countertrade and offsets; the uses of such practices by the U.S. government in U.S. exports and foreign economic assistance programs; and the need to reach agreements through international negotiations on the use of countertrade and offsets. The IGC makes recommendations to the President and Congress on the basis of the review and evaluation. IGC held its first meeting in Washington, D.C., on October 2, 1990.

inter alia: an allowable adjustment when calculating the value for merchandise being imported.

Inter-American Development Bank (IADB) (IDB): a bank established in 1959 to encourage economic development of 21 member nations in Latin America. Twenty representatives from Latin American countries and the United States initiated this effort. See

Enterprise for the Americas Initiative; Organization of American States.

Inter-American Investment Corporation: see *Alliance for Progress.*

Inter-American Treaty of Reciprocal Assistance: see *Organization of American States.*

Inter-Arab Investment Guarantee Corporation (IAIGC): established in 1972, with headquarters in Kuwait; goals are to promote the transfer of capital within the Arab area, in particular by providing insurance coverage for investments with substantial Arab equity against loss resulting from noncommercial risks.

interbank: the market between banks for foreign exchange, Eurodeposits, or domestic funds.

interbank offered rate: rate of interest where banks lend to other prime banks. See *London Interbank Offered Rate (LIBOR); Singapore Interbank Offered Rate (SIBOR).*

interbank placements: short-term (often overnight) interbank loans of Eurocurrency time deposits.

interbank rate: see *interbank offered rate.*

interchange point: a station at which freight in the course of transportation is delivered by one transportation line to another.

intercompany market: a market for borrowing and lending of funds between nonbanking firms, without any involvement of banks.

interest arbitrage: transfer of short-term funds from one market to another in a different country so as to profit from a higher interest rate.

Interest Equalization Tax (IET): a form of foreign-exchange control established by the U.S. government in the early 1960s whereby any U.S. resident has to pay a special tax on any purchase of overseas securities.

interest period: a rollover credit made available to a borrower on the understanding that he or she may select to borrow for periods, varying typically between one month and one year.

interest rate arbitrage: the movement of funds from one money-market center to another through the foreign exchange market in order to obtain higher rates of interest. See *arbitrage.*

interest rate swap: a transaction in which two parties exchange interest payment streams of differing character based on an underlying principal amount. The three main types are coupon swaps (fixed rate to floating rate in the same currency); basis swaps (one floating rate index to another floating rate index in the same currency); and cross-currency interest rate swaps (fixed or floating rate in one currency or fixed or floating rate in another currency). See *swap contract.*

interest yield: the uniform rate of interest on investments computed on the basis of the price at which the investment was purchased, giving effect to the periodic amortization of any premiums paid or to the periodic accrual of discounts received.

interest yield equivalent: the measurement of the rate of return on a security sold on a discount basis, which assumes actual days to maturity and a 360-day year.

Intergovernmental Conference (of the European Union): see *European Union—Amsterdam Treaty; European Union—Treaty of Nice.*

Intergovernmental Maritime Consultative Organization: see *IMCO.*

interline: between two or more transportation lines.

interline freight:
(1) freight moving from its point of origin to its destination over the lines of two or more transportation lines.
(2) freight moving from its point of origin to its destination by means of two or more transport operators.

interline waybill:
(1) a waybill covering the movement of freight over two or more transportation lines.
(2) a waybill showing freight movement by two or more transport operators.

intermediate carrier: a transportation line over which a shipment moves but on which neither the point of origin nor the destination is located.

intermediate clause: a clause or basis contained in a tariff to provide for rates to a point not named therein, but which is intermediate to points that are named.

intermediate consignee: the bank or other intermediary that acts in a foreign nation as agent for an exporter so as to effect the delivery of the export to the ultimate consignee.

intermediate goods: merchandise sent into an export processing or free-trade area that has already had some processing and will undergo further processing as it becomes a part of another product.

intermediate traffic: synonymous with *overhead traffic.*

intermediation: the investment process in which savers and investors place funds in financial institutions in the form of savings accounts and the financial institutions in turn use the funds to make loans and other investments.

intermodal: carriage by differing modes of transport. Cf. *multimodal.*

internal bond: a bond issued by a country that is payable in its own currency. Cf. *external bond.*

internal community trade: see *harmonization; standardization.*

internal debt: the debt of a nation.

internal market: activities within the European Union's member states. Its Commission's White Paper urged the completion of the internal market as a prerequisite for an efficient, modern Europe that can provide industry and commerce with a structural framework in which they can be fully competitive. Directives, decisions, and recommendations are required for dealing with three primary barriers: physical barriers; technical barriers—for example, on public contracts; and the free movement of workers and tax barriers. In all, 282 directives were debated, down from the 300 original proposals because some were no longer required and others were grouped together. See *Europe Without Frontiers; Single European Act; White Paper.*

Internal Reserve: in Japan, reserves after dividend payments, including contingency funds such as those for planned research and development spending in the coming year.

internal revenue tax: synonymous with *excise tax.*

International Accounting Standards Committee (IASC): international private-sector organization that sets financial accounting standards for worldwide use.

international agreement: an official instrument whereby nations (at times international organizations) formalize some understanding between or among themselves.

International Bank for Reconstruction and Development (IBRD): an organization that commenced operation in June 1946 to provide funds and technical assistance to facilitate economic development in its poorer member countries. Funds come from capital subscribed by member nations, sales of its own securities, sales of parts of its loans, repayments, and net earnings. See *Bretton Woods; International Development Association of the United Nations;*

International Finance Corporation; World Bank Group. Synonymous with *World Bank.*

international banking: bank operations dealing with foreign exchange, making foreign loans or serving as investment bankers for foreign nations, provinces, municipalities, and companies.

International Banking Act of 1978 (IBA): U.S. federal legislation designed to remove many of the competitive advantages that foreign banks had over their domestic counterparts. The Federal Reserve bank is now authorized to impose reserve requirements on foreign banks, for example, and for the first time there are restrictions on their ability to take deposits nationwide.
See *Edge Act.*

International Banking Facilities (IBFs): specially designated offices in the United States, identified by the Federal Reserve Board, permitting banks to take deposits from and make loans to nonresidents, including overseas subsidiaries of U.S. firms.

International Carriage of Dangerous Goods by Road: see *ADR.*

International Center for the Settlement of Investment Disputes (ICSID): established in 1966 by the World Bank's treaty and headquartered with the World Bank. The Center mediates between foreign investors and governments as an independent forum for settling disputes.

International Chamber of Commerce (ICC): created in Paris in 1919; provides an arbitration court for settling international business disputes, with more than 7,500 members in over 80 nations.

International Coffee Agreement (ICA): coffee is an important commodity in the world economy, accounting for trade worth approximately US $5.6 billion in 2000/01. ICA entered into force for six years on October 1, 2001; has no provisions for price regulation. As of 2001, there are 40 exporting members, and 18 importing members.

International Commodity Agreement (ICA): a formal agreement among producers of a commodity to control the export output of an item to stabilize prices and export earnings for it.

international competitive bidding: procurement forms completed by a World Bank borrower to assure that proper procedures are followed.

International Confederation of Free Trade Unions: established in 1949; headquartered in Brussels; represents nearly 100 nations; a confederation of more than 140 unions to promote the trade union movement by recognizing workers' institutions and the rights of employees to bargain collectively.

international corporation: a corporation with business interests in different countries. It often focuses on the import or export of goods and services.

international countertrade: see *countertrade (2)*.

International Dairy Arrangement: signed by 16 nations at the Tokyo Round of the Multilateral Trade Negotiations, to promote the growth of dairy products worldwide through the lowering of trade barriers.

international debt issue: a debt issue underwritten and sold outside the country of the borrower/guarantor. It can be a foreign bond or a Eurobond.

International Development Association of the United Nations (IDA): established in 1960; has the status of a United Nations Specialized Agency. It is an affiliate of the IBRD, having the same management and staff, but is a separate legal entity with separate funds. It was established to meet the problem of a growing number of less-developed nations whose need for outside capital is greater than their ability to service conventional loans. Cf. *International Bank for Reconstruction and Development.*

international direct investment: see *foreign direct investment.*

international division: a division in the organization that is at the same level as the domestic division in the firm and is responsible for all non–domestic country activities.

international exchange: see *foreign exchange.*

international finance center: a multinational's or global's office that handles the great majority of international money transactions for all the firm's units.

International Finance Corporation (IFC): an affiliate of the World Bank, established in July 1956. It supplements the activities of the World Bank by encouraging the growth of productive private enterprises in less-developed member nations. IFC has been involved with Eastern European states since the late 1980s. The IFC assists nations in privatizing, banking, and attracting foreign investors to export-oriented firms, cooperatives, and larger industries, all designed to reap precious foreign exchange. See *International Bank for Reconstruction and Development; World Bank Group.*

international financing: occurs when a borrower raises capital in the Eurocurrency or Eurobond markets, outside the restrictions that are applied to domestic or foreign offerings.

international Fisher effect: a relationship implying that interest rate differentials on similar instruments between two countries will be offset by exchange rate differentials between their currencies.

International Grain Agreement (IGA): replaced the International Wheat Agreement in 1995. Administered as an intergovernmental forum for cooperation on wheat and coarse-grain matters. Donor countries pledge to provide annually large quantities of food aid to developing countries in the form that is grain suitable for human consumption or cash to buy suitable grains. See *International Wheat Agreement.*

International Importation License: a license covering import of restricted goods from one country when the goods are to be re-exported to a third country.

International Investment and Trade in Services Act (IITSSA): federal legislation dealing with reporting requirements for foreign investment; all foreign investments in U.S. business enterprises in which a foreign person owns a 10 percent or more voting interest (or the equivalent) are subject to reporting.

international investment position: the balance of the amount and distribution of a nation's assets in a foreign country relative to the foreign country's investment in the home nation.

internationalization: the strategy of a parent company to retain control over its foreign operations, primarily because it is found to be less costly.

internationalization of currency: the situation when a currency is used widely to denominate trade and credit transactions by non-residents of the country of issue.

international lease: a lease in which the lessor and the lessee are in the same country other than the United States.

international liquidity: the total liquidity for all internationally acceptable currencies in the monetary system of the world. See *national liquidity.*

International Maritime Satellite Organization (Inmarsat): an organization that operates satellites to provide telephone, data, and facsimile, as well as distress and safety communication services for shipping and offshore industries.

international marketing channel: the path through which a company's merchandise reach the final consumer or user in the export process.

International Monetary Fund (IMF): a fund established on December 27, 1945, as an independent international organization of the United Nations. It is authorized to supplement its resources by borrowing; its purposes include promoting international monetary cooperation; expanding international trade and exchange stability; assisting in the removal of exchange restrictions and the establishment of a multilateral system of payments; and alleviating any serious disequilibrium in members' international balance of payments by making the resources of the Fund available to them under adequate safeguards. See *Bretton Woods; conditionality; Special Drawing Rights.*

international monetary system: agreements, practices, laws, customs, and institutions that deal with money (debt, payments, investments) internationally.

international money management (IMM): strategies used by firms with multinational cash flows to maximize earnings from interest and exchange rate movements while reducing exposure to risk.

international mutual fund: a mutual fund that invests in stocks from around the world so that should one market be in a slump, money can still be made in others.

International Organization for Standardization: see *International Standards Organization.*

international payments mechanism: the organization of markets whereby the monies of different nations are exchanged. See *swap.*

international product life-cycle: a product life-cycle theory that aids in the explanation of trade flows and foreign direct investment on the basis of a product's position in the four stages of (a) exports of an industrialized country; (b) beginning of foreign production, (c) foreign competition in export markets; and (d) import competition in the nation where the product was introduced originally.

international reserves: a means of payment generally acceptable in settlement of balances among countries (e.g., gold, dollars, pounds, SDRs).

International Standard Industrial Classification (ISIC): a categorization of economic activity used in compiling and presenting official statistics issued by the United Nations. Cf. *NACE*. See *Standard Industrial Classification*.

International Standards Organization (ISO): created in 1947, with 90 member nations; covers standardization in all fields except electrical and electronic engineering standards.

International Sugar Agreement (ISA): Updated and revised in 1992. Provisions include: (a) to insure enhanced international cooperation in world sugar matters and related issues; (b) to provide a forum to international consultations on sugar and on ways to improve world sugar economy; (c) to facilitate trade by collecting and providing information in the world sugar market and other sweeteners; and (d) to encourage increased demand for sugar, particularly for nontraditional uses.

international takeover: the bid by a foreign firm to seize control in the open market of a domestic company.

international trade: foreign trade measured by merchandise exports and imports of a country for a stated period, often one year.

International Trade Administration (ITA): see *U.S. International Trade Administration*.

International Trade Commission (ITC): see *U.S. International Trade Commission*.

International Trade Organization (ITO): an organization drawn up in March 1948, but replaced in its functions by GATT, now WTO. Synonymous with *Havana Charter*.

International Transport Workers Federation: see *ITF*.

international unit: a statistical device used to put data from a number of nations on a uniform base so that the different economies can be compared.

International Wheat Agreement (IWA): in 1995 reorganized and renamed as the International Grain Agreement. See *International Grain Agreement*.

Intertanko: the International Association of Independent Tanker Owners.

intervention: a monetary agency's transaction to maneuver the exchange rate for its currency or the level of its foreign exchange reserves.

intervention currency: the foreign currency a country uses to ensure by means of official exchange transactions that the permitted exchange rate margins are observed. Intervention usually takes the form of purchases and sales of foreign currency by the central bank or exchange equalization fund in domestic dealings with commercial banks.

interventionists: people who want an overt industrial policy and trade protection. Some countries will urge continuing subsidies for primary industries. These interventionists surface when the nation's economy is weak and in recession.

intervention price: a method for retaining a target price. The intervention agency of each member nation of the European Union has the responsibility of buying in produce when market prices fall below a certain established intervention price (e.g., cereals between 12 and 30 percent below the target price). See *Common Agricultural Policy.*

inti: monetary unit of Peru.

intraregional trade: see *export.*

Intrastat: a system for collecting statistics on the trade in goods between EC countries. Introduced on January 1, 1993, the information is collected by means of companies' VAT.

intrinsic value:

(1) the market value of the material in a thing (e.g., the value of the metal in a gold tooth filling).

(2) the excess of the market value of the underlying stock over the striking price of the option for a call, or the excess of the striking price of the option over the market value of the underlying stock for a put.

Investment Bank, European: see *European Investment Bank.*

Investment Canada Act: Canadian legislation that governs the review of foreign investment in Canada. The *Canada Free Trade Agreement* with the United States required revisions of this Act. Canada eliminated review of U.S. new and indirect investments and increased the threshold for review of U.S. direct investments to Canadian $150 million. Under the CFTA, investment decisions are to be based on business-trade factors, not on artificial barriers.

investment company: a company or trust that uses its capital to invest in other companies.

investment performance requirements: conditions imposed on foreign investors seeking authorization to make direct investments in a country.

Investment Sector Loan Program (ISLP): see *Enterprise for the Americas Initiative.*

investment trust: any firm, company, or trust that takes its capital and invests it in other companies.

invisible charge: see *balance on goods and services.*

invisible economy: see *informal economy.*

invisible imports: services, financial or personal, rendered by foreigners to the natives of a given country. These may consist of freight and passenger charges, insurance and banking services, and so on.

invisible items of trade: items, such as freight and insurance charges, that, though not shown as exports or imports, are considered along with exports and imports in determining the balance of payments between two or more nations. Cf. *visible items of trade.*

invisibles: see *invisible items of trade.*

invisible trade balance: as contrasted with the import and export of goods, the trade balance created by the import and export of services (i.e., consulting and advisory services).

inward collection: in Great Britain, the collection of payment on a bill from a British firm.

IPRs: see *intellectual property rights.*

IQD: the international standard code for the currency of Iraq and the Neutral Zone (between Saudi Arabia and Iraq)—the Iraqi dinar.

Iran-Libya Sanctions Act: U.S. legislation that imposes sanctions on foreign companies that do business in those two countries.

Iraq Trade Bank: see *Trade Bank of Iraq.*

Irish pound: former monetary unit of the Irish Republic.

IRR: the international standard code for the currency of Iran—the Iranian rial.

irrevocable credit: a credit that cannot, before the date it expires, be canceled, revoked, or withdrawn without the consent of the person in whose favor the credit is given. Used mostly in foreign travel and trade. Synonymous with *fixed credit line.*

irrevocable letter of credit: a letter of credit that cannot be canceled. See *irrevocable credit.* Cf. *revocable letter of credit.*

ISA: See *International Sugar Agreement.*

ISBN: International Standard Book Number.

ISF: International Shipping Federation.

ISIC: see *International Standard Industrial Classification.*

ISK: the international standard code for the currency of Iceland—the Iceland krona.

Islamic banking: banking based on the adherence to Islamic principle that forbids usury. This is usually meant to exclude the receipt or payment of interest.

Islamic Common Market: synonymous with *Arab Common Market*.

Islamic Corporation for the Development of the Private Sector (ICD): a full-fledged internationally independent institution in Jedda, Saudi Arabia; with authorized capital of U.S. $1 billion and paid-up capital is U.S. $500 million; its mission to be a multilateral finance institution for the promotion and development of the private sector in member countries.

Islamic Development Bank (IDB): founded in 1974, headquartered in Jeddah; assists in financing the development of countries with substantial Islamic populations. See *Islamic banking*.

Islamic dinar: equals one special drawing right.

ISLP (Investment Sector Loan Program): see *Enterprise for the Americas Initiative*.

ISO: see *International Standards Organization; ISO 9000*.

ISO 9000: a series of five international industrial standards for quality assurance. There is a growing global demand that suppliers be registered or certified according to these standards, developed by the International Organization of Standards. ISO 9000 will not regulate industry-specific criteria, such as the dimensions of audio cassettes. Instead it will aid a trading firm to devise a step-by-step guide on quality standards for each core process in almost every department. Development of a system that complies with the external standards leads to registration or certification and uniform standards that are acceptable universally.

Although there is no legal requirement that a firm adopt the standards, many European and American firms are pushing their suppliers to become registered under the ISO guidelines so that there is a documented quality system in place to insure that the products they purchase will be of acceptable quality. A company without an ISO 9000 registration risks being effectively barred from bidding on new business.

While ISO 9000 standards are the rules set by the ISO for setting quality system procedures in any industry, there is considerable overlap, and standards are cross-referenced.

The five standards cover: (a) ISO 9000: an overview and introduction to the other standards in the series, including definitions of terms and concepts related to quality that are used in the other standards. (b) ISO 9001: comprehensive general standard for quality assurance in the design, development, manufacturing, installation, and servicing of products. (c)ISO 9002: less-comprehensive standard focusing specifically on the manufacturing and installation of products. (d) ISO 9003: the least-comprehensive standard, covering final inspection and testing of completed products. (e) ISO 9004: guidelines for managing a quality-control system; more details on managing the quality systems that are called for in the other standards; not intended for use in auditing quality systems, but designed to aid auditors in better understanding the intent of 9001. See *harmonization; ISO; standardization; standards.*

Israel: see *U.S.-Israel Free Trade Agreement.*

ISSN: International Standard Serial Number. Used to number periodical publications.

issuing bank: the bank that issues a documentary credit, on behalf of the buyer, in favor of the beneficiary. Synonymous with *opening bank.*

issuing carrier: the carrier by which a tariff is published or a bill of lading or other documents are issued.

Istituto Centrale per il Credito a Medio Termine: Italian government agency that pays interest rebates on or refinances export credits granted by Italian banks.

ITA (International Trade Administration): see *U.S. International Trade Administration.*

Italian lira: former monetary unit of Italy.

Italian Stock Market: based in Milan; merger of 10 national exchanges in 1991.

ITC (International Trade Commission): see *U.S. International Trade Commission.*

ITF (International Transport Workers Federation): an organization of transport workers. The crew of a vessel must be members of this federation if the vessel is destined for specified nations, including Finland, Sweden, Australia, and France,

ITO: see *International Trade Organization.*

IWL (Institute Warranty Limits): areas where ships sail free of hazards such as icebergs, etc.

J

Jamaica Accord: see *Jamaica Agreement*.

Jamaica Agreement: a 1976 IMF meeting that abolished the official gold price. The Agreement set up new rules and guidelines for the exchange rate regime, moving from a system of fixed rates, on which IMF rules were based, to one permitting greater flexibility.

Jamaica dollar: monetary unit of Jamaica.

Japan Corporate Program: established in 1991, an effort of the U.S. Department of Commerce to help increase exports to Japan.

Japan Development Bank: established in 1951; owned by the Japanese government. Created to aid in developing and diversifying the Japanese economy.

Japanese Long-Term Prime Rate (JLTPR): the rate charged by Japanese banks to their most-creditworthy customers for loans of over one year.

JapaNIEs: a word reflecting Japan's deepening trade relations with Asia's newly industrialized economies (NIEs). Most Japanese firms have transferred much of their production to Asia. See *Asian sector; East Asian Newly Industrialized Countries; Pacific Rim*.

Japan Special Fund (JSF): a Japanese government financial scheme to make grants available to cofinance operations of the multilateral development banks for pre-investment and feasibility studies, small projects, and so on.

Jason clause: in marine insurance, risks that could not be discovered even by exercising considerable care.

J-curve:
(1) a curve describing the expected impact of a devaluation on a nation's trade balance.
(2) a graphic description of the initially perverse and then benign reaction of the trade balance after devaluation. The trade balance deteriorates when import costs climb, then recovers to surplus as exports increase in volume because of cheaper exchange costs.

jebble: synonymous with *blue finger*.

jeopardy clause: a Eurocurrency agreement clause stating that should certain events curtail a lender's activity or the operation of the Euromarkets, other designated actions (e.g., the substitution of another agreed rate of interest) will come into effect.

jerquer: a customs official assigned to examine vessels to ensure that all cargo has been offloaded for examination.

JETRO: Japan's External Trade Organization.

jettison: to unload or throw overboard at sea a part of a ship's paraphernalia or cargo to relieve the ship when in danger.

J-list: a list issued by the U.S. Secretary of the Treasury excepting certain classes of items from country of origin marking requirements.

JLTPR: see *Japanese Long-Term Prime Rate.*

JMD: the international standard code for the currency of Jamaica—the Jamaican dollar.

job: in foreign exchange, a bank dealing on its own behalf with other banks.

Jobs and Growth Tax Relief Reconciliation Act of 2003: third-largest tax reduction in U.S. history. Major features include:

Dividend and Capital Gains Tax Reduction: qualifying dividends will now be added to net capital gain, and therefore taxed at the same rate as long-term capital gains.

Acceleration of Tax Rate Reductions: accelerates 2006 marginal tax bracket mounts; retroactive to January 2003; effective until December 31, 2010.

Acceleration of Marriage Tax Penalty Phase-Outs: beginning in 2005, the standard deduction for married taxpayers filing a joint return will gradually increase to two times the standard deduction for single taxpayers by 2005.

Increase in AMT exemption amount: effective 2003 and 2004, the AMT exemption amount for joint filers increases from $49,000 to $58,000, and from $35,770 to $40,250 for single filers.

Acceleration of Child Tax Credit Increase: accelerates the increase to $1,000 for tax years 2003-4 before reverting to the earlier schedule.

JOD: the international standard code for the currency of Jordan—the Jordanian dinar.

Johannesburg Stock Exchange (JSE): established in 1886; largest stock exchange in Africa. Opened its trading to foreign and corporate members in 1995.

joint account: a record kept by a firm operating a joint facility showing the debit and credit transactions with each of the carriers participating in the joint use of transport facilities.

joint agent: a person having authority to transact business for two or more transportation lines.

Joint Committee for Investment and Trade: established in 1990, a U.S.-Mexico joint committee to promote closer economic cooperation.

joint rate: a rate applicable from a point located on one transportation line to a point located on another transportation line, made by agreement or arrangement between them, and published in a single tariff under proper concurrence of all transportation lines over which the rate applies. See *joint tariff; joint through rate.*

Joint Stock Banks: in England, the name for all commercial banks; does not apply to the Bank of England, private banks, and so on.

joint tariff: a tariff containing joint rates. See *joint rate.*

joint through rate: a joint rate published as a unit to apply from a point on the line of one transportation line to a point on another.

joint traffic: traffic moving between stations located on one transportation line and stations located on another transportation line.

joint venture: the cooperation between two or more firms or nations to produce mutually agreeable results from a particular project.

Jordan: See *U.S.-Jordan Free Trade Agreement.*

Jordanian dinar: monetary unit of Jordan.

JPY: the international standard code for the currency of Japan—the Japanese yen.

JSE: see *Johannesburg Stock Exchange.*

JSF: see *Japan Special Fund.*

judgment currency clause: a clause found in a Eurocurrency credit agreement protecting lenders against any loss arising because the loan is made in one currency and judgment is given by the courts in another.

junction point:
(1) any point where two carriers interchange freight.
(2) a point at which a branch-line rail track connects with a main-line track.

jurisdictional clause: a clause in an international contract between the exporter and the importer that specifies the law under which the agreement will operate. Its objective is to anticipate, and hopefully avoid, potential disputes by agreeing that the parties involved will be bound by the laws the an agreed-on jurisdiction. Cf. *jurisdictional rule of reason.*

jurisdictional rule of reason: the legal principle that balances the vital interests of one nation against those of a foreign nation. Cf. *jurisdictional clause.*

K

Kabutocho: Tokyo's equivalent of Wall Street.

Kaffirs: term used by European investors when describing mining shares from South Africa.

Kampo: Japan's Post Office Insurance Fund, one of the world's largest investors.

Kangaroos: (slang) Australian stocks.

Kapeik: monetary unit of Belarus.

Karbovanetz: monetary unit of Ukraine.

Kassenobligation: a medium-term note issued at auction by the German government or state-owned entities such as the railway and postal authorities.

KD:

(1) see *knocked down*.

(2) Kuwaiti dinar.

keelage: the charge levied on a ship for the privilege of entering into, or anchoring in, a harbor.

keidanren: in Japan, a national association of associations—the Federation of Economic Organizations—that includes all firms in major keiretsu. See *keiretsu*.

keiretsu: groups of linked Japanese companies, considered to be Japan's most important contribution to modern capitalism. In the marketplace, the members of one keiretsu battle their rivals in other groups. For suppliers, the benefits of belonging to a keiretsu-favored status include facilitating centers of technological excellence and economies of scale that last only as long as the company demonstrates its continued responsiveness to market forces. Such companies enjoy a safety net that encourages long-term investments and high-tech risk taking. See *keidanren*. Cf. *chaebol*.

kengen: in Japan, the privilege or legitimacy of a manager to use authority by issuing orders within a well-defined work situation.

keni: in Japan, the ability of a manager to influence employees based on his or her strength of character, not social status or position.

Kennedy Round: covered three elements, which were agreed to at the GATT, now WTO, ministers meeting in May 1963 and put into effect on May 4, 1964. The program was completed on June 30, 1967. The elements were a reduction, by an average of 35 to 40 percent, in tariffs and other barriers to trade; improvement in access to world markets for agricultural products; and expansion of outlets for the exports of less developed nations. See *Dillon Round; General Agreement on Tariffs and Trade; Montreal Round; Tokyo Round; Uruguay Round.*

Kenya shilling: monetary unit of Kenya.

kerb:

(1) trading outside official market hours.

(2) on the London Metal Exchange, a 15-to-20-minute period at the end of every morning and afternoon session when all metals are traded simultaneously.

KES: the international standard code for the currency of Kenya—the Kenyan shilling.

key currencies: those held extensively as foreign exchange reserves.

key industry: an industry that by virtue of size or influence exerted over other industry sectors, affects a nation's economy.

KHR: the international standard code for the currency of Kampuchea, Democratic—the riel.

kina: monetary unit of Papua New Guinea.

kip: monetary unit of Laos.

KMF: the international standard code for the currency of Comoros—the Comoros franc.

knocked down (KD): description of sales or shipments of equipment that are to be assembled by the receiver.

know-how licensing: these are agreements through which one firm possessing technical information not covered by patents authorizes another to use it to produce goods or services. Like patent licenses, know-how agreements are pro-competitive in that they facilitate the transfer of technology and boost innovation, but they may, in particular circumstances, inhibit competition within the trading nations by imposing territorial restrictions. Given that the transfer of know-how is frequently irreversible, trading partners need to provide greater legal certainty for undertakings as regards the compatibility of such agreements with the competition rules.

known damage: a damage discovered before or at the time of delivery of a shipment.

known loss: a loss discovered before or at the time of delivery of a shipment.

kobo: monetary unit of Nigeria.

koruna: the monetary unit of Czech Republic.

KOTRA: Korea Trade Promotion Corporation.

krona: monetary unit of Iceland.

krone: monetary unit of Denmark and Norway, divided into 100 ore.

kroon: monetary unit of Estonia.

krugerrand: the gold bullion coin minted by the Republic of South Africa, having one troy ounce of gold. Krugerrands traditionally sell for 4 to 5 percent more than the current value of their gold content.

KRW: the international standard code for the currency of the Republic of Korea—the won.

Kuala Lumpur Stock Exchange: established in 1989, the largest securities exchange in Malaysia.

Kuwait dinar: monetary unit of Kuwait.

kwacha: monetary unit of Malawi and Zambia.

kwanza: monetary unit of Angola.

KWD: the international standard code for the currency of Kuwait, Neutral Zone (between Saudi Arabia and Iraq)—the Kuwaiti dinar.

kyat: monetary unit of Burma.

KYD: the international standard code for the currency of the Cayman Islands—the Cayman Islands dollar.

L

LAAI: see *Latin American Integration Association*.

LAAITC: see *Latin American Association of International Trading Companies*.

LAARI: monetary unit of the Republic of Maldives.

Labor Advisory Committee: a committee of private advisors, consisting of trade union representatives and other experts, which advised the U.S. Labor Department and the United States Trade Representative on U.S. trade policy matters.

LAC (LA/C): see *Latin American and Caribbean*.

LACP: see *Latin American Capital Markets Institute*.

ladder: used in the control of money market and foreign exchange positions; consists of a listing, day by day, or month by month, of the outstanding maturity of money market deposits or forward exchange contracts.

lading: that which constitutes a load. The freight is in a railcar or vessel. See *bill of lading*.

LAES: see *Latin American Economic System*.

LAFTA (Latin American Free Trade Association): formed in 1961 by Argentina, Brazil, Chile, Mexico, Paraguay, Peru, and Uruguay. Colombia, Ecuador and Venezuela joined later. Replaced by LAIA (Latin American Integration Association).

lag: see *leads and lags*.

lag strategy: operational strategy involving delaying collection of foreign currency receivables if the currency is expected to strengthen, or delaying payment of foreign currency payables when the currency is expected to weaken.

LAIA: see *Latin American Integration Association*.

laissez-faire: a doctrine that government should refrain from any form of trade regulation, leaving productivity and wealth distribution purely to market forces and individual industry.

LAK: the international standard code for the currency of Lao People's Democratic Republic—the kip.

Lake Chad Basin Commission (LCBC): formed in 1964 to coordinate economic-trade programs and activities of the Chad Basin among nations of the area. Members are Chad, Cameroon, Niger, and Nigeria, with headquarters in N'jamena, Chad. Synonymous with *Commission du Bassin du Lac Chad (CBLC)*.

landbridge (land-bridge):
(1) transporting items by both land and water as a substitute for an all-water movement.
(2) the overland movement of freight in containers having a prior or subsequent movement by ship.
landed weight: the weight at the point of landing.
landesbanken: state savings banks of Germany.
landeszentralbank: German regional central bank, part of the Bundesbank.
Large Exposures: a European Union directive approved by finance ministers in March 1992. Legislation limits how much banks can lend to a single creditor, thus protecting banks from overextending themselves. The directive, phased in over eight years beginning in 1994, prevents banks from lending more than 25 percent of their equity to one party or group. Banks have to report to national regulators any loan exceeding 10 percent of equity. Bank loans or credit lines after 1994 to individuals are limited to 40 percent of equity. After 1999, new loans were kept at 25 percent, though loans outstanding at as much as 40 percent of equity could run three more years. Less-restrictive rules apply to interbank lending.
LASH (lighter aboard ship): an oceangoing vessel designed to carry barges that are particularly effective in shallow ports where deep-water ships are unable to berth.
latent defect: a deficiency in merchandise offered for shipment not discernible by careful inspection.
Latin America: the region's economy has turned around from the debt crisis of the 1980s to growth in the 1990s, and has become a major trading area. The attraction of this market, of 27 countries, has always been its considerable size, its large resource base, and its proximity to the United States. By 2000, the total population in the region was approaching 500 million. More than 50 percent of the region's trade is with the United States.
With inflation rates declining, her trade with the world continues to rise dramatically. Trade climbed from $140 billion in 1986 to $285 billion in 2002. During that same period, merchandise trade with the United States grew from $84 billion to a record high of more than $160 billion.
At the turn of this century, Latin America has become the fastest-growing regional market for U.S. exports, with U.S. manufactured

goods accounting for 83 percent of the exports. Leaders were motor vehicle parts, aircraft, electrical switching gear, telecommunications, construction and mining equipment, and electrical machinery.

Latin America is the most U.S.-oriented market in the world. It is the natural area for the United States to seek product-sharing operations and other kinds of strategic alliance. The reverse is also true: the United States is the most important market for Latin America. See *Andean Pact*; *Mercosur*.

Latin American and Caribbean (LAC) (LA/C): a large region, with nearly 500 million people.

Latin American Association for Integration (LAAI): synonymous with *Latin American Integration Association*.

Latin American Association of International Trading Companies (LAAITC): established in September 1988 in Brazil, with 10 Latin American and Caribbean nations, to provide a forum for uniting ALAT nations in the export of goods from the region. Synonymous with *Asociación Latino-Americano de Traficantes (ALAT)*.

Latin American Capital Markets Institute (LACP): headquartered in Caracas, Venezuela, to coordinate information on regional capital market development.

Latin American Economic System (LAES): established in 1975; comprises all the Latin American countries and a number of the Caribbean countries. It has a two-fold objective: to promote regional cooperation and integration, and to encourage consultation between its member countries in order to coordinate their position in international forums and other countries; Permanent Secretariat is in Caracas. Synonymous with *Sistema Económico Latinoamericano (SELA)*.

Latin American Free Trade Association: see *LAFTA*.

Latin American Integration Association (LAIA): formed in 1980 to replace LAFTA, with Chile, Columbia, Ecuador, Mexico, Paraguay, Peru, Uruguay, and Venezuela. Purports to support progressive trade and economic integration among nations. Synonymous with *Latin American Association for Integration (LAAI)*. In Spanish, *Asociación Latino-Americana de Integración*.

Latin American think tank: first proposed in mid-summer 1991 by Latin American economists and U.S. free trade supporters calling for increased leadership on inter-American trade issues. Specifically, there was a growing demand to create a U.S.-based organization working closely with Latin American nations to promote unrestricted hemispheric commerce, to serve as: (a) a clearinghouse, to collect, systematize, and disseminate trade statistics and information on national trade policies; (b) a think tank, to analyze trade and trade-related issues; (c) a trade monitor, to review and evaluate proposed trade arrangements among nations; (d) a source of technical assistance, to provide expertise to countries formulating trade policies and negotiating trade agreements.

It was suggested that, in time, such a hemispheric trade organization would be entrusted with the more sensitive tasks of defining rules to guide hemispheric trade negotiations, mediating them, investigating alleged violations of trade accords, and settling disputes.

latticework structure: (slang) the structure of vertical and horizontal relationships found in many large Japanese corporations.

lay day:
(1) the period of time in which a ship is to be loaded or unloaded
(2) specific period in days during which a vessel must have arrived and be prepared for loading operations under a charter party.

lay time: the maximum period during which a charterer can use a ship for the purpose of loading and unloading freight without incurring financial liability known as demurrage. See *demurrage.*

lay up: to withdraw a ship from trading and moor it semipermanently at a given location.

LBP: the international standard code for Lebanon—the Lebanese pound.

L/C: see *letter of credit.*

LCBC: see *Lake Chad Basin Commission.*

LCL:
(1) see *less-than-carload lot.*
(2) see *less-than-container load.*

L/D: load/discharge.

LDCs: see *less-developed countries.*

lead country strategy: approach of introducing a product on a test basis in a small-country market that is considered representative of a region, before investing to serve larger-country markets.

leading: the quick conversion of all soft foreign currencies into the stronger dollar to be sent home.

leads and lags: changes in the pattern of international payments terms. Should a devaluation of a nation's currency be feared; its importers with overseas currency obligations will rush to pay to avoid their debts becoming greater following devaluation; they lead payments. Conversely, exporters will benefit by not rushing to convert export receipts in foreign currency; they lag payments.

lead subsidiary organization: foreign subsidiary having global responsibility (serving as corporate headquarters) for one of a nation's items or functions.

League of Arab States, The: see *Arab League.*

lease insurance policy: provides insurance coverage to banks and other firms that lease U.S.-manufactured equipment to foreign entities.

Lebanese pound: monetary unit of Lebanon.

ledger value: synonymous with *book investment.*

left-hand side: the rate at which a bank offers a foreign currency.

legal list: a list of investments selected by various states in which certain institutions and fiduciaries, such as insurance companies and banks, may invest.

legal weight: used in foreign trade; the weight of the goods and the interior packing but not the container.

lei: monetary unit of Moldava.

lek: monetary unit of Albania.

lempira: monetary unit of Honduras.

lending institution: a finance company, bank, loan company, or other organization that lends money and makes money by advancing funds to others.

lending margins: the fixed spread that borrowers agree to pay above an agreed base rate, often LIBOR, to banks providing a Eurocredit. The full rate of interest paid by the borrower is adjusted, usually every six months, to reflect changes in LIBOR.

leone: monetary unit of Sierra Leone.

Leontief Paradox: derived from a study of Wassily Leontief of U.S. trade statistics in 1947 covering 25 years. He found that the capital/labor ratios of U.S. exports were lower than those of imports during the same time period. These findings contradict conventional views that a country exports products in which it enjoys a relative factor advantage.

less-developed countries (LDCs):
(1) poor nations with low per-capita income, little industrial development, and limited economic and social infrastructure. See *third world*.

(2) a country showing (a) a poverty level of income; (b) a high rate of population increase; (c) a substantial portion of its workers employed in agriculture; (d) a low proportion of adult literacy; (e) high unemployment; and (f) significant reliance on a few items for export. See *underdeveloped countries*.

lessor company: a transport company whose property is leased to and operated by another company. It maintains a separate legal existence and keeps financial but not operating accounts.

less-than-carload lot (LCL): goods requiring less space when shipped than that available in a single freight car; the rate applied to such a shipment. Cf. *less-than-container load*.

less-than-container load (LCL): a consignment of cargo that does not fill a shipping container, and is grouped with other consignments for the same destination. Cf. *less-than-carload lot*.

less than fair value (LTFV): a claim by the U.S. International Trade Commission that foreign goods have been imported into the United States and sold there at a dumped price. Antidumping actions may follow. See *dumping; fair market value*.

letter of credit (L/C): a document, issued by a bank per instructions by a buyer of goods, authorizing the seller to draw a specified sum of money under specified terms, usually the receipt by the bank of certain documents within a given time. The acceptance by the bank of drafts drawn under the letter of credit satisfies the seller and the seller's bank in the handling of the transaction. Synonymous with *banker's credit*.

letter of indemnity: a document issued by a merchandise shipper to a steamship company as an inducement for the carrier to issue a clean bill of lading, where it might not otherwise do so. This letter of indemnity serves as a form of guarantee whereby the shipper agrees to settle a claim against the line by a holder of the bill of lading arising from issuance of a clean bill. See *bill of lading*.

letter of moral intent: an undertaking by a firm usually short of a legal guarantee, usually given by a parent firm in respect of a subsidiary.

leu: monetary unit of Romania.

lev: monetary unit of Bulgaria.

level playing field: synonymous with *reciprocity*.

levies: varying duties applied to imports from another nation.

levy subsidy: a subsidy to producers or suppliers of a commodity financed by a levy on sales of that commodity. The subsidy can be payable to domestic producers or to specific overseas suppliers. The levy can be raised on all sales or simply on imports.

liability of foreignness: overseas companies' lower survival rate than local firms for many years after they began operations.

LIBO: see *London Interbank Offered Rate*.

LIBOR: see *London Interbank Offered Rate*.

Libyan dinar: monetary unit of Libya.

license:

(1) general: formal or legal permission to do some specified action.

(2) international: governmental means of fixing the exchange rate by requiring all recipients, exporters, and others that receive foreign exchange to sell it to the central bank at the official buying rate.

licensed production: the component of a type of countertrade transaction where the exporter agrees to allow all or a part of the total export contract to be manufactured offshore, based on the acceptance by the importer of technology transfer.

licensee: see *licensing agreement*.

licensing: a business arrangement in which the manufacturer of a product (or a firm with proprietary rights over technology or trademarks) grants permission to a group or an individual to manufacture that product in return for specified royalties or other payments. See *licensing agreement*.

licensing agreement: the contracts between the exporter (a licensor) and an importer (a licensee) to make available to an importer some property of the exporter for a charge.

licensor: see *licensing agreement*.

lien: a legal claim upon goods for the satisfaction of some debt or duty.

LIFFE: see *London International Financial Futures and Options Exchange*.

light displacement tonnes: the weight of a vessel's hull, machinery, equipment, and spares. Usually used when such vessels are bought for purposes of scrapping them.

lighter aboard ship: see *LASH*.

lighterage:

(1) a service, or charge for the service, involved in the movement of freight in a lighter or barge between points in a harbor.

(2) in railroads, the lightering between points of a harbor of freight loaded from, or to be loaded into, cars.

lighterage limits: the limits of the area within which freight is handled by lighters or barges under certain lightering charges, rules, and regulations.

lighterage to shipside: the charge made for lightering freight to alongside a vessel.

lightering: the hauling of freight on lighters or barges.

lightering to shipside: the lightering of freight to alongside a vessel.

lilangeni: monetary unit of Swaziland.

limit:

(1) the maximum allowed price fluctuation of a commodity in any day before trading is suspended.

(2) the restriction on the number of futures contracts any one individual or firm may hold.

limited company (Ltd.): a British business corporation. Use of the abbreviation "Ltd." indicates registration under the Companies Act and formally establishes the limited liability of stockholders.

limited order: an order in which the customer has set restrictions with respect to price.

limit order: see *limited order*.

line:

(1) in the United Kingdom, a large quantity of stock or shares.

(2) in the United Kingdom, an acceptance of a risk by an insurance underwriter and, should there be more than one underwriter, each underwriter's proportion of the sum assured.

linear reduction of tariffs: see *linear tariff cuts*.

linear tariff cuts: a uniform reduction in tariffs, determined by its relation to the different sectors of a national tariff. See *formula approach*.

line haul: direct movement of freight between two major ports by a single ship.

liner service: the service provided by a shipping firm whereby cargo-carrying vessels are operated between ports on a regular basis. The freight rate charges are based on the shipping company's tariff or, if the firm is a member of a liner conference, on the tariff of that conference.

liner shipping: a cargo-carrying ocean shipping service between ports in different nations on a regular basis.

liner terms: where the owner of a vessel is responsible for arranging and paying for the loading and discharging of the vessel.

link:

(1) the relationship between trade and currency reform.

(2) the relationship between SDR allocations and development finance.

linkage (linking): the pressure an industry can exert on the rest of the economy.

liquidity:

(1) the solvency of a business, which has special reference to the speed with which assets can be converted into cash without loss.

(2) the ability of the market in a particular security to absorb a reasonable amount of buying or selling at reasonable price changes.

liquidity, international: see *international liquidity.*

liquidity, national: see *national liquidity.*

liquidity preference: theory that helps explain capital budgeting; when applied to international operations, means that investors are willing to take less return in order to be able to shift resources to alternative uses.

lira: the currency of Turkey.

Lisbon Stock Exchange: founded in January 1969; Portugal's largest exchange trading stocks, bonds, and unit trusts.

little dragons: nickname for developing nations, including Malaysia, Singapore, and Taiwan, that pose a challenge to Japan— the big dragon.

LKR: the international standard code for the currency of Sri Lanka—the Sri Lanka rupee.

Lloyds: an association of English insurance underwriters, the oldest of its kind in the world. The Corporation of Lloyds also provides a daily newspaper (LLOYDS LIST AND SHIPPING GAZETTE), a classification of ships (LLOYDS REGISTER OF SHIPPING), and other publications.

LME: see *London Metal Exchange.*

LOA: the overall length of a ship (length, overall).

load:

(1) a package or group of packages included in a shipping unit (e.g., a carload, an airplane load, etc.).

(2) an item or group of items included in a single outer shipping container.

loans and other long-term assets: a part of total transaction in U.S. government assets, this account includes the flow of capital abroad resulting from all loans and credits with an original maturity of more than one year made by the federal government to foreign countries. Most of these credits finance U.S. exports of goods and services.

local authorities: U.K. municipal governing authorities, whose deposits and loans constitute an important secondary money market in London.

local concern: costs incurred within a given country, usually as a percentage of total costs.

local content: the proportion of an item manufactured in a European Union nation to a non-EU nation. For example, in the production of cars, the Treaty of Rome states that member states may not impose quotas against each other's goods. However, should a significant proportion of the item be manufactured in a non-EU state, quotas may still be fixed. See *North American Free Trade Agreement.*

local costs: expenses incurred for goods or services purchased from suppliers in the buyer's country. The goods or services purchased must be needed to execute the exporter's contract or to complete the project of which the exporter's contract is a part.

local rate: a rate applicable between stations located on the same transportation line.

locals: citizens of the country in which they work.

local tariff: a tariff containing rates applicable only between stations located on the same transportation line.

local waybill: a waybill covering the movement of freight over a single transportation line.

location advantages: factors that affect the desirability of host country production relative to home country production.

locked market: a market in which the trader is willing to bid for and after a particular security at a single price.

Lombard loan: a central bank loan supported by collateral such as stock and bonds. Terms used primarily in England and parts of Europe.

Lombard rate: (German) the rate of interest charged for a loan against the security of pledged paper.

Lombard Street: the financial area in London.

Lomé Conventions: a reference to two conventions held at Lomé, Togo. The first Convention (Lomé I) was signed on February 28, 1975. It became effective on April 1, 1976, and expired on February 28, 1980. Lomé II, a renegotiated Convention, came into force on March 1, 1980, and expired on March 1, 1985. It was designed to provide a "balanced response" to the varying needs of developing nations that are signatories to the Convention. Under Lomé I, 99.5 percent of African, Caribbean, and Pacific (ACP) agricultural exports entered the Community market duty-free and Community Funds were authorized to help finance projects. Lomé II, signed by 58 ACP nations, since extended to 60, set up duty-free arrangements affecting agricultural items such as the exports of tomatoes, carrots, onions, and asparagus, and preferential arrangements for beef and veal were consolidated.

In December 1984, 66 African, Caribbean, and Pacific countries signed a new convention with the Community, to run to 1990. It freed the signatories from all customs duties on 99.5 percent of their exports to the Community, with no reciprocal concessions required on their part.

In July 1989, the European Community agreed on a revised offer to a new five-year trade and aid pact, including a plan to compensate ACP nations for losses in earnings from commodity exports because of world market fluctuations. The Lomé Agreement was ratified in December 1989. The Lomé IV ran from 1990 to the year 2000, and then was reapproved. See *ACP (states); Caribbean Basin; external trade; Generalized System of Preferences; Stabilization of Export Earnings; third world*.

London Commodity Exchange: merged with the London International Financial Futures and Options Exchange in September 1996.

London Interbank Offered Rate (LIBOR): a measure the major international banks charge each other for large-volume loans of Eurodollars, or dollars on deposit outside the United States. See *LUXIBOR; Singapore Interbank Offered Rate*.

London International Financial Futures and Options Exchange: trades futures and options contracts on short- and long-term interest rates, denominated in world currencies, with links to all major global exchange. See *London Commodity Exchange.*

London Metal Exchange (LME): members, approximately 110, dealing in copper, lead, zinc, and tin.

London options: contracts on commodities, such as cocoa and gold, traded in London.

London Stock Exchange: stock exchange located in London; deals with Euroequities.

long of exchange: when a trader in foreign currency holds foreign bills in an amount exceeding the bills of his or her own that have been sold and remain outstanding, the trader is long of exchange.

long-position: purchase of foreign currency for delivery in the future.

long-term capital account: a balance-of-payments term differentiating investment and government expenditure and receipts overseas from short-term capital or hot-money flows.

long-term national financial markets: capital markets in different countries; that is, markets for long-term financial instruments such as stocks and bonds in different countries.

long-term sales: sales of goods and services on terms of five years or more.

long ton: 2,240 pounds. Cf. *short ton.*

Louvre Accord: an agreement reached in Paris, France, in 1987 by the Group of Five, plus Canada. The group agreed to cooperate more actively to increase stability of the rates of exchange of their respective currencies. This followed a unanimous call to halt the U.S. dollar's decline. Often called *Paris Pact.*

low interest: an account on which the rate has been reduced to 12 percent per annum simple interest or less.

loyalty agreement: a contract between the shipper and a conference where the shipper pledges to move all or a specified portion of the cargo aboard conference vessels in return for certain economic inducements.

LRD: the international standard code for the currency of Liberia—the Liberian dollar.

LSL: the international standard code for the currency of Lesotho—the loti.

Ltd.: see *limited company.*

LTFV: see *less than fair value.*

Lugano Convention: an agreement signed by the six EFTA nations in September 1988, so that they could play a part in the consolidation of the Single European Market. It improves legal security and simplifies business and trade between the European Community and EFTA-based firms by unifying certain judicial processes. See *European Free Trade Association; Luxembourg Declaration.*

lump-sum charter: a flat fee payable by charterer to the ship owner, irrespective of whether the stipulated cargo, or any portion thereof, is actually shipped.

Luxembourg Declaration: the European Community and EFTA agreed during 1988 to modify the Stockholm Convention, which established the European Free Trade Association in 1960, and other agreements in order to simplify rules of origin, exchange notifications on draft technical regulations, and ensure mutual recognition of test results and certifications. The groups also abolished existing export restrictions and prohibited new ones.

Luxembourg franc: former monetary unit of Luxembourg.

LUXIBOR: the Luxembourg Interbank Offered Rate.

LYD: the international standard code for the currency of Libyan Arab Jamahiriya—the Libyan dinar.

M

Maastricht Treaty: the Maastricht Treaty of the European Union was signed by the 12 European Union ministers in Maastricht, the Netherlands, on February 7, 1992. The Treaty, a 189-page document, provides for the creation of a single currency—the Euro—gives new powers to the European Parliament, and allows the European Union to forge common foreign and defense policies for the first time. The Pact had to be ratified by the national parliaments of all member nations in order for it to come into effect. On June 2, 1992, Denmark voters rejected the Maastricht Treaty in the first of many referenda. Meeting in Lisbon, at their June 1992 semiannual summit conference, EU leaders voted limits to a United Europe, emphasizing their support for the principle of subsidiarity, and determination to have the Maastricht Treaty ratified. Then on September 20, in a French referendum, by a 51 percent vote, the people chose to support the Treaty.

Since January 1999, the Euro has been the single currency for all members of the EMU.

See *central bank; Euro; single currency; subsidiarity.* Synonymous with *Treaty on European Union; Treaty on Monetary and Political Union.*

macro-political risk: negative political actions affecting a broad spectrum of foreign investors. Cf. *micro-political risk.*

MAD: the international standard code for the currency of Moroccos and Western Sahara—the Moroccan dirham.

Madrid Agreement: a multilateral treaty signed by 22 member nations (the Madrid Union), agreeing to automatic trademark protection for all members. The United States is a participant only to the extent that a subsidiary of a U.S. company located in one of the member nations can effect protection for its firm in all member nations. See *Madrid Union.* Synonymous with *Madrid Agreement Concerning the International Registration of Marks.*

Madrid Agreement Concerning the International Registration of Marks: see *Madrid Agreement.*

Madrid Agreement for the Repression of False or Deceptive Indications of Source on Goods: see *Madrid Union.*

Madrid Interbank Offered Rate: see *MIBOR.*

Madrid Stock Exchange: largest stock exchange in Spain, linking others in Barcelona, Bilbao, and Valencia with Madrid.

Madrid Union: established in 1891 and revised several times (Stockholm in 1967); its objective is to suppress the false or misleading origin markings on goods sold in international trade. See *Madrid Agreement.* Synonymous with *Madrid Agreement for the Repression of False or Deceptive Indications of Source on Goods.*

Mahgreb Agreement (Union): a trade agreement signed with Algeria, Morocco, and Tunisia in April 1976. Libya and Mauritania would join later.

Mahgreb Common Market: see *MCM.*

make bulk: the process of placing together large shipments from multiple or smaller shipments to take advantage of large-volume discounts from carriers. Synonymous with *consolidation.*

make-versus-buy decision: choice for a firm to either produce a product or input for itself or buy it from an outside supplier. By producing it within the firm, internationalization of that input's production takes place.

Malagasy franc: monetary unit of Madagascar.

maloti: monetary unit of Lesotho.

Maltese lira: monetary unit of Malta.

managed currency: a currency whose quantity is increased or decreased according to changes in the general price level or other objectives. The management is by the government of a country or its central bank. The management may be designed to influence the internal price level of a nation or the ratio of that price level to the price levels of other nations, or both, or to pursue other objectives.

managed exchange rates: aggressive efforts by a government to dictate the rate of exchange through economic policies rather than permitting market forces to determine the value of the nation's currency.

managed float: the practice of a government administering its exchange rate to achieve goals other than those normally associated with monetary policy. See *floating rates.*

managed floating-exchange rate system: a government's policy of administering short-term fluctuations in its exchange rates by intervention.

managed money: a monetary system in which government tries to control the circulation of money to achieve a specific goal, such as the stabilization of prices.

managed trade:
(1) where goods entering borders are primarily determined by the

political and economic weight of more dominant economic nations, with others left very much on the margins.

(2) any international commercial transactions that are impacted by nonmarket factors such as nontrade measures and quantitative restrictions. Cf. *free trade.*

management fee: the charge made to an investment company for supervision of its portfolio. Frequently includes various other services, and is usually a fixed percentage of average assets at market.

manager: in international trade and commerce, a bank involved in managing a Eurocredit or an issue of a security.

managing agent: foreign-based intermediary hired by firms to exclusively represent companies in business dealings with overseas governments; possesses authority to make commitments on behalf of the firms it represents.

manifest: a document that describes a ship's cargo or the contents of a car or truck.

manufacturer's export agent: a domestic-based intermediary who serves as an export sales agent for several noncompeting manufacturers who, in turn, pay commissions for services provided.

manufacturer's representatives: salespeople who sell items of an exporting manufacturer from a foreign base of operations, usually within the target-market territory itself. Synonymous with *manufacturer's reps.*

manufacturer's reps: synonymous with *manufacturer's representatives.*

Maple Leaf: bullion coin of Canada; 99.99 percent pure gold or silver, and 99.95 percent pure platinum.

maquila: see *maquiladoras.*

maquiladoras: since the 1970s, U.S. firms, along with other nations from around the world, have opened more than 2,000 assembly plants in Mexico that are close to the U.S. border. The maquiladoras, grew at a 15 percent annual clip, employed half a million Mexicans, paying them an average, in the early 1990s, of $5 to $6 a day, with a free lunch. (The Mexican government makes the maquiladora an exception to nationalistic restrictions on 100 percent foreign ownership and also offers duty-free imports of high-quality components and machinery.)

U.S. firms and other foreign firms sent $12 billion in parts to these so-called screwdriver assembly plants, which are mostly foreign operations on Mexican soil where plants purchase 97 percent of their parts from the United States and sell almost none of their products within Mexico. Duty to the United States is paid only on components that are not of U.S. origin, and on the value added in assembly or manufacture in Mexico.

The industry in the 1990s generated more than $12 billion in products and over $3 billion of value-added income for Mexico. It ranks second only to petroleum as a generator of foreign exchange.

A free trade accord would rapidly alter this activity, changing such plants to regional firms that buy and sell on both sides of the border. Within a decade, continued changes led to free trade promoters, making parts in regional areas that are among Mexico's poorest and trucking these items closer to the U.S. border for assembly. Since early 1990s, new maquiladoras are sweeping throughout Mexico, and as wages continue to climb, some U.S. firms are beginning to plan to transfer or add new subsidiaries across the border into Guatemala.

Maquiladoras, and the more efficient bi-national, shared-production operations that they represent, have saved hundreds of U.S. firms from succumbing to Asian competition, thereby preserving U.S. jobs. If the U.S. firms had not shifted the labor-intensive aspect of manufacturing to Mexico, their products would no longer have been competitively priced on world markets.

A study investigating the benefits and costs of having maquiladoras found: (a) in most cases, the U.S. firms not only survived but grew, increasing their sales as their cost position strengthened. (b) After an initial job loss in the United States, between one and two new jobs were created as the production-sharing firm for every job originally eliminated. (c) As sales grew in the product lines subject to production-sharing, procurement volumes from U.S. suppliers to maquiladoras increased as well. (d) In the aggregate, the combined employment gained in the U.S. firms and their supplier totaled two or more new jobs created for each job initially established in Mexico. (e) Most U.S. firms that resorted to production-sharing with Mexico did so under intense and competitive attack, typically from Asian firms. They contemplated Mexico, in spite of the special regulations governing maquiladoras, as a desperate and defensive move. As they recover, they can be expected to bring back to the United States much of the off-shore sourcing that they moved away to non-American locations.

The average dollar wage rate, fully fringed, in maquiladoras had risen from 90 cents in 1987 to $2.50 in 2002. In central Mexico, the minimum wage with legally prescribed benefits is about 90 cents. Furthermore, Mexican workers belong to a nationwide social security system and share, by law, 10 percent of the profits of the firms that employ them. In fact, maquiladoras represent the segment of the Mexican economy in which wage rates are rising fastest.

Since the beginning of the new century, many plants in the maquiladoras have closed and shifted operations to China, where labor costs remain lower.

Synonymous with *screwdriver assembly plants*.

margin:
(1) the difference between the cost of sold items and the total net sales income.
(2) the incremental percentage referring to deposits, collateral, or permissible exchange rate fluctuations.

marginal propensity to import: tendency to purchase imports with incremental income.

marginal risk: the risk that a customer goes bankrupt following entry into a forward contract when the bank must close its commitment in the market, thereby running the risk that the exchange rate has shifted unfavorably in the interim. The risk is confined to the marginal amount of such a movement.

margin call: a demand upon a customer to put up money or securities with a broker. The call is made when a purchase is made or when a customer's equity in a margin account declines below a minimum standard set by the exchange or firm.

margin of preference: the difference between the duty that would be paid under a system of preferences and the duty payable on a most-favored-nation basis.

margins: the limits around the par value within which a spot exchange rate of a member nation's currency is allowed to move in actual exchange market dealings and public transactions.

marine bill of lading: see *bill of lading*.

marine insurance: insurance that compensates the owners of goods transported overseas in the event of loss that cannot be legally recovered from the carrier. Also covers air shipments. Cf. *credit risk insurance*.

marine protection and indemnity insurance: insurance against legal liability of the insured for loss, damage, or expense arising out of or incident to the ownership, operation, chartering, maintenance, use, repair, or construction of any vessel, craft, or instrumentality in use in ocean or inland waterways, including liability of the insured for personal injury or death and for loss of or damage to the property of another person.

maritime: business pertaining to commerce or navigation transacted on the sea or in seaports in such matters as the court of admiralty have jurisdiction over, concurrently with the courts of common law.

maritime lien: a claim on a ship arising from a maritime operation.

mark: former monetary unit of Germany.

market:
(1) any group possessing or potentially possessing the ability and desire to purchase products or services.
(2) a geographical area that includes a significant number of potential customers.

market access:
(1) the degree of difficulty of admittance to an overseas market by an exporting nation.
(2) the ability of a domestic industry to penetrate a related market in a foreign country. The extent to which the foreign market is accessible generally depends on the existence and extent of trade barriers.

market amount: the amount usually considered the minimum for dealings in a market, especially foreign exchange.

market disruption: difficulties in a domestic market as a result of a sudden increase in imports into that market. See *dumping*.

market economies: economies that are characterized by a relatively large, free (nongovernmental) market sector. There is no such thing as a totally free market; all governments regulate, tax, and intervene in various ways. Cf. *nonmarket economy*.

market-if-touched order (MIT): an order to buy or sell at the market immediately if an execution takes place at a certain price stated in the order.

market indicators: economic data used to measure relative market strengths of nations or geographical areas.

market maker: a broker or bank that is prepared to make a two-way price to purchase or sell, for a security or a currency on a continuous basis.

market order: an order to buy or sell something at the price prevailing when the order reaches the market.

marking duties: a special duty, in addition to ordinary duties, imposed on merchandise not properly marked so as to indicate to the ultimate purchaser the country of origin.

marking goods: a reference to the EU procedure increasingly relied on by exporters and importers. The European Union's mark of approval indicates a product's compliance with a government's technical regulations. In the European Union, a mark of approval indicates a product's compliance with EU technical regulations, where (a) the mark shall signify a product's conformity to rules on technical standardization; (b) national certifying bodies shall receive from the EU Commission an identification number to place next to a product's mark once they notify the Commission of a product's conformity; (c) as a general rule, the year in which the product was certified should not have to appear next to the mark; (d) products carrying the mark could also have marks demonstrating compliance with national standards or other EU regulations; (e) the mark shall, whenever possible, appear on the product itself or on its identification plate; and (f) penalties for violating the rules should be progressive, with withdrawing products from the market as the ultimate penalty.

markka: former monetary unit of Finland.

marks: letters, numbers, and/or characters placed on a package for purposes of identification.

Mark Sheet: in Japan, a report of import required for submission by a Japanese importer to a Japanese foreign exchange bank to secure foreign exchange for imports valued at more than 1 million yen, even when the items are not subject to import quotas.

marks of origin: the physical markings on a product that indicate where the article was produced. Most countries have customs rules requiring marks of origin. See *Madrid Agreement*.

marpol: a convention whose objective was to reduce marine pollution from ships. It was adopted by the International Maritime Organization.

MAS: see *Monetary Authority of Singapore*.

Mashrag states: Egypt, Jordan, Lebanon, and Syria. These nations signed trade and cooperative agreements in January and February 1977 and thus completed the European Community Mediterranean Policy.

matched sales method: strategy used by firms to circumvent foreign government–imposed price controls.

matching: the process of equating assets and liabilities, either by time or currency.

Matchmaker Program: a U.S. Department of Commerce's effort to help U.S. firms realize the opportunities created by the 1993 EU single internal market. The Program, which is designed exclusively for new-to-export and new-to-market firms, locates overseas representatives, distributors, joint-venture, or licensee partners for U.S. businesses. Prescreened one-on-one meetings, arranged by the American embassies and consulates, provide U.S. firms with the opportunity to develop overseas contacts, to promote market awareness for their products and services, and to achieve export sales.

mate's receipt: a document issued by a vessel's officer acknowledging receipt of a specific quantity of cargo; usually issued only in conjunction with a vessel charter.

mature economy: the condition of a nation's economy with a declining rate of population growth and a decrease in the proportion of national income utilized for new capital investment, accompanied by a relative increase of national income used in purchasing consumer goods.

maturity: the date on which a note, time draft, bill of exchange, bond, or other negotiable instrument becomes due and payable. Presentation and request for payment of the instrument are made on the maturity date.

maturity gap exposure: the risk created by having an asset and liability of the same size and in the same currency but of different maturity.

Mauritius rupee: monetary unit of Mauritius.

maximum rate: the highest rate that may be charged.

May 1, 2004: see *New Europe, the; Nice Treaty.*

MCA: see *Millennium Challenge Account.*

MCC (Mercado Común Centroamericano): see *Central American Common Market.*

MCF: see *Monetary Cooperation Fund*.

MCM (Mahgreb Common Market): a multilateral agreement signed in Marakesh, Morocco, in 1989 for the economic-trade integration of the Arab nations of the region of North Africa. Member nations are Algeria, Libya, Mauritania, Morocco, and Tunisia. Synonymous with *Arab Mahgreb Union (AMU)*.

measurement cargo: cargo where the transportation charge is assessed on the basis of measurement.

MEC: see *Middle East Community*.

Mediterranean global approach: see *Mediterranean Policy*.

Mediterranean Noncandidates: see *MNCs*.

Mediterranean Policy: an EC policy purporting to create a global relationship with the nations of the Mediterranean basin (Algeria, Morocco, Tunisia, Egypt, Jordan, Libya, Syria, and Israel). In 1972, the Community announced a "Mediterranean global approach" that gave them a common framework. Agreements implementing free entry for industrial goods were drawn up with all the Mediterranean nations, except Albania and Libya. The Mediterranean countries are granted duty-free access to the Community for their industrial products, various customs concessions for agricultural produce, and European Investment Bank loans. The Mediterranean countries constitute the European Union's third-largest customer and its fourth-largest supplier. See *Mashrag states; MNCs, third world*.

medium of exchange: any commodity that is widely accepted in payment for merchandise and services, and in the settlement of debts.

medium-term sales: sales of goods and services on terms of 181 days to five years.

Memorandum of Understanding (MOU): an agreement signed by representatives from two or more nations calling for closer cooperation and joint action on a topic. For example, on May 3, 1991, the U.S.-Mexico Labor MOU was signed calling for such action on significant labor issues, including occupational safety and health, child labor, and labor statistics.

memorandum tariff: an abstract of a freight tariff; its objective is to highlight information of wide interest.

Mercado Común Centroamericano (MCC): see *Central American Common Market*.

Mercado Común del Sur: synonymous with *Mercosur*.

mercantilism: an economic philosophy based on the beliefs that a country's wealth is dependent on its holding of treasure, usually in the form of gold, and that countries should export more than they import in order to increase wealth.

Mercator: a European Union project designed to link European ports and test the feasibility of exchanges of data between parties involved in international trade.

merchandise: synonymous with *goods.*

merchandise car: a railcar containing several less-than-carload shipments.

merchandise exports: goods sent out of the country.

merchandise imports: goods brought into the country.

merchandise processing fee: a customs user fee levied by the U.S. government on all imported merchandise, except for products from the least-developed countries, from eligible countries under the Caribbean Basin and the Andean Trade Preference Act, or from U.S. insular possession. The fee was fixed at 0.17 percent of the value of the imported goods for 1988 and 1989. The Omnibus Budget Reconciliation Act of October 1990 extended the fee. See *Omnibus Budget Reconciliation Act of 1990.*

merchandise trade balance: part of a country's current account that measures the trade deficit or surplus; its balance is the net of merchandise imports and exports.

merchanting: the process whereby an operator in country A purchases items in country B and ships them direct from B to C without bringing them to A; a third-country trade.

merchantman: a vessel engaged in the business of carrying merchandise.

Mercosul: synonymous with *Mercosur* (Spanish).

Mercosur: the Southern Cone Common Market Treaty or the Treaty of Asuncion (Paraguay), modeled on the European Community's 1957 Treaty of Rome. With headquarters in Montevideo, Uruguay, it will dismantle trade barriers and encourage cross-border investment and joint projects over the coming years.

The four-nation Southern Common Market is now South America's richest market. Its aim is to accelerate economic growth by linking Argentina, Brazil, Paraguay, and Uruguay in a market of nearly 190 million people, with a $427 billion total gross regional product and Latin America's biggest industrial base. U.S. exports to the region rose to $12 billion in 2003, up from $6.7 billion in 1990. Argentina and Brazil will supply the bulk of the trade and investment opportunities for U.S. businesses. The four nations have agreed to reduce import duties to zero for trade among themselves. Mercosur nations are negotiating implementation of the Treaty of Asuncion provisions which all for the establishment of a common external tariff (targeted at 35 percent) and coordination of exchange rate and macroeconomic policy. And in the future, provisions exist for other neighboring nations to join.

In September 2003, Peru became an associate member, along with Chile and Bolivia.

In Portuguese *Mercosul.* See *Andean Pact; Buenos Aires Consensus; Community of Andean Nations; Free Trade Agreement for the Americas.* Synonymous with *Mercado Común del Sur; Mercosul* (Portuguese).

merger:
   (1) the combining of two or more entities through the direct acquisition by one of the net assets of the other. A merger differs from a consolidation in that no new entity is created by a merger.
   (2) any business combination.

MERM: see *Multilateral Exchange Rate Model.*

method of entry: the way that a company enters into a foreign country with merchandise, technology, etc.

metical (meticais): monetary unit of Mozambique.

metric system: a system of weights and measures introduced in France in 1799 and widely used by most countries of the world. The U.S. government has been promoting a metric transition program for the use of metric units in its business-related activities. For purposes of international trade, the metric system is essential, for it includes product standards and preferred sizes that are accepted by industries and governments worldwide.

metric transition program: see *metric system.*

Mexican peso: monetary unit of Mexico.

Mexican Stock Exchange: only stock exchange in Mexico; owned by 33 stock brokerage firms, of which five are foreign; formerly called *Bolsa Mexicana de Valores.*

MFA: see *MultiFibre (Multifiber) (Multi-Fibre) Arrangement (Agreement)*

MFN: see *most-favored nation.*

MGF: the international standard code for the currency of

Madagascar—the Malagasy franc.

MIBOR: Madrid Interbank Offered Rate; the Spanish equivalent of *LIBOR*.

micro-political risk: negative political actions aimed at specific, rather than most, foreign investors. Cf. *macro-political risk*.

Middle East Community (MEC): proposed in the 1990s; a regional economic integration organization for effective cross-border activities and an institutional form of governance throughout the Middle East region. Based on earlier Middle East/North Africa meetings. See *Amman Middle East/North Africa Economic Summit; Cairo Middle East/North Africa Economic Conference; Casablanca Middle East/North Africa Economic Summit; Doha Middle East/North Africa Economic Conference.*

Middle East Economic Community: see *Middle East Community.*

MIF: see *Multilateral Investment Fund.*

MIGA (Multilateral Investment Guarantee Agency): an affiliate of the International Bank for Reconstruction and Development that became operational in June 1988. It encourages private investment in developing nations through the provision of insurance against noncommercial risks.

Milan Stock Exchange: largest regional stock exchange in Italy, with more than 90 percent of that nation's trading volume.

mileage allowance: an allowance, based on distance, made by carriers to owners of privately owned freight cars.

mileage pro-rate: the process of dividing through rates, using mileage as factor.

mileage rate: rates applicable according to distance.

mileage tariff: a tariff containing rates applicable according to distance.

Millennium Action Plan: a 2001 African initiative for African recovery; presented at the Organization of African Unity meeting in Zambia.

Millennium Challenge Account of 2003: U.S. grants for economic trade in developing nations; expected to total $5 billion by 2008. Sixty three countries are eligible because their per capita income levels are below $1,415 (U.S.).

milliard: European, for 1,000 million. Often superseded by the use of billion.

milling-in-transit rate: a through rate (plus an additional charge, if any, for transit service) applied to a shipment stopped at some point between its origin and its destination for the purpose of milling.

minibridge: movement of cargo from a port over water, then over land to a port on an opposite coast.

minimum bill of lading: an ocean bill of lading that incurs the minimum charge provided in the carrier's tariff, usually $40 to $75, which is imposed to prevent inundation with small, unprofitable shipments. See *bill of lading*.

minimum carload weight: the lowest weight specified in the tariff or classification upon which a carload rate is applicable.

minimum charge: the least charge for which a shipment will be handled.

minimum rate: the lowest rate that may be charged.

minimum truckload weight: the least weight at which a shipment is handled at a truckload rate.

minimum yield: the lesser of yield to call and yield to maturity.

ministerial declaration: decisions of trade ministers prior to negotiations. Before launching a round of multilateral trade negotiations, trade ministers of WTO, formerly GATT, countries meet in special session to discuss whether to begin negotiations and the topic to be negotiated. Their decisions are set out in a ministerial declaration.

Ministry of International Trade and Industry: see *MITI*.

mint: where metallic money is coined or manufactured.

mintage: the charge made by a government for converting bullion into coins.

mirror-image reciprocity: the denying of equivalent treatment to one nation by another nation unless its institutions gain reciprocal treatment. No nation should accept anything less than national treatment and should reject any request for mirror-image reciprocity. See *national treatment*.

mismatch: the imbalance of assets and liabilities in a foreign currency, the failure to balance being either in maturity or size.

misrouted freight:

(1) freight that, through the carrier's error, is forwarded to the correct destination via a route taking a higher rate than is applicable via the route specified by the shipper.

(2) freight for which the route is not specified by the shipper but

which is forwarded via a route taking a rate higher than is applicable via the cheapest available route.

missionary rate: a freight rate established at a particularly low level as an impetus to an infant industry.

MIT: see *market-if-touched order.*

MITI: Japan's *Ministry of International Trade and Industry.* MITI spends 0.26 percent of Japan's gross national product in basic research, nearly as much as the United States. MITI can decide that a specific branch of industry—for example, steel, computers, or bicycles—should be developed and initiate appropriate strategies to accomplish that goal. It then selects those projects and firms, searches for proper financing, and makes recommendations.

To enhance Japanese industry, a primary objective of MITI has been to encourage growth and concentration of companies. MITI is one of the major sponsors of official Japanese cartels, to promote production or prevent an economic downturn.

New MITI strategies for Japan in the new centry include: the contribution of the structures to the international economy and community; changes in domestic economic factors; and new lifestyles.

MITI encouraged the government to shift from export-led to domestic demand–led growth as a key element of the internationalization of Japan. MITI had become Japan's primary industrial goal-setter and influenced significantly the country's economic growth. It carefully supervised the acquisition of foreign technology via licensing agreements with other nations, established foreign exchange controls, and arranged for the best of technology to be secured under the most advantageous terms by those individuals and/or firms best positioned to use it.

MITI became the omnipotent regulator of production and distribution of goods and services in Japan.

Every three or four years MITI presents its "visions," which are sweeping examinations of major world trends and how they impact on Japan. These reports are legitimized by recommendations fed back to them by an industrial council. And MITI, shrouded in mystery, continues to send shivers down the back of world executives and government officials also responsible for industry, research, and development within their own nations, forever trying to figure out why and how Japan has been so successful with MITI.

mixed car: commodities shipped in the same railway car to which, otherwise, a variety of rates would apply.

mixed-carload rate: a rate applicable to a carload of different articles in a single consignment.

mixed credit: financial terms extended by developed nations to developing nations, traditionally for development activities.

mixed currency: a currency consisting of (a) precious metals and notes, or (b) various kinds of precious metals.

Mixed-Enterprise Corporation: in Canada, a business company that is owned or controlled jointly by private interests and a government agency, chiefly for the purpose of promoting national objectives.

mixed tariff: synonymous with *compound duty.*

mixing rates: in the foreign exchange rate system, the use of varying rates of exchange for specific categories of overseas trade goods.

MMK: the international standard code for the currency of Myanmar—the kyat.

MNC: see *multinational corporation.*

MNCs (Mediterranean Noncandidates): countries with which the European Union has preferential trade agreements. They are Algeria, Cyprus, Egypt, Israel, Jordan, Lebanon, Malta, Morocco, Syria, Tunisia, Turkey, and Yugoslavia. Albania and Libya have no agreements with the European Union, while Portugal and Spain are new EU members. By 1984, the situation was broadly that all MNCs had free entry to Union markets for their manufacturers, without limits of the kind that exist in the Generalized System of Preferences. See *General Agreement on Tariffs and Trade; Mediterranean Policy.*

MNE: see *multinational enterprise.*

MNT: the international standard code for the currency of Mongolia—the tugrik.

modifications: the altering and withdrawal of tariff concessions within the GATT, now WTO. Article XXVIII deals specifically with the modification of concession schedules.

MOL: more or less.

monetary: a country's currency and/or coinage.

Monetary Authority of Singapore (MAS): supervises much of the Asian dollar market with the Central Bank of Singapore.

Monetary Cooperation Fund (MCF): this fund would be established as the nucleus of a reserve system of a NAC central bank, and could have operational responsibility in the field of a community currency exchange system. The Fund governors would come from member nation's central banks.

monetary policy: the management by a central bank of a nation's money supply to ensure the availability of credit in quantities and at prices consistent with specified national objectives.

monetary reform: the process of negotiating and drafting a revised international currency system.

monetary sovereignty: a nation's right to safeguard its fiscal system against severe deflation, unemployment, or imbalance of its foreign payments, despite pledges of cooperation that may have been given to such organizations as the International Monetary Fund.

monetary system: the goal of a monetary system is to create a zone of monetary stability through the implementation of certain exchange rates, credit, and resource transfer policies to ensure that monetary instability does not interfere with the process of genuine integration with the trading community. Assistance is conditional; a borrower nation must agree to certain economic and monetary conditions.

Monetary fluctuations require the creation of an exchange rate scheme to limit the margins of fluctuation between national currencies to a permissible margin of fluctuation against.

Different stages are needed. The emphasis during the first stage will be on enhancing economic and monetary coherence among member states of a trading partnership, strengthening policy coordination within the existing institutional framework, implementing the internal market program, and reforming structural funds.

monetary unit: the unit of money of a nation. It may or may not be defined in terms of a commodity into which it is convertible.

monetize: to convert assets into money.

money broker: a person or institution serving as a go-between for borrowers and lenders of money.

money markets: places where currencies are traded or capital is raised.

money supply: the total sum of currencies circulating in a country.

monopolistic advantage theory: the idea that foreign direct investment is made by firms in oligopolistic industries that possess technical and other advantages over indigenous companies.

monopoly: ownership of the source of a commodity or domination of its distribution; often acquired by a franchise or government patent.

Montant de Soutien (Amount of Support): one of the Mansholt proposals for dealing with agriculture in the Kennedy Round of GATT. It involved the binding of the amount of support. For any given commodity, it means agreeing to a world price or reference price that is taken as the norm for international commercial transactions. Each country concerned with that commodity would then submit for international confrontation the total remuneration received by its producers for that item. The world or reference price would then be subtracted from the total remuneration, and this difference would constitute the amount of support that would be bound for three years.

Montant Forfaitaire: sums by which the levy on imports from one member nation to another is reduced, giving European Union suppliers a preference over outside suppliers. This sum is to be increased by stages so that at the end of the transitional period the levies on trade between member states will be eliminated. Synonymous with *Abattement Forfaitaire.*

Montreal Exchange: oldest in Canada, with second-largest dollar value of trading.

Montreal Round: a meeting in December 1988. This 96-nation trade meeting was called to give political momentum to the four-year round of world trade talks that began in 1986. The following were resolved: efforts to liberalize trade in services; swifter settlement of trade disputes; freer trade in tropical products; reduction of tariffs by 30 percent; easing of nontariff barriers; easing of some investment restrictions; and monitoring of countries' trade policies. The meeting agreed on immediate steps to bring down import barriers for tropical products such as coffee, rubber, and bananas. A central objective was to give strong impetus particularly to the process of writing multilateral rules for trade in services. Four issues were deadlocked: liberalizing trade in agriculture; new protections for intellectual property; textile trade reforms; and rules for safeguards against imports. In February 1989, the United States decided to abandon its insistence that Europe commit itself in advance to seeking the elimination of all trade-distorting farm subsidies by some specified date after the year 2000.

The United States urged a "ratchet down" approach to farm subsidies over many years. See *Dillon Round; General Agreement on Tariffs and Trade; Kennedy Round; Tokyo Round; Uruguay Round.*

moorage: synonymous with *wharfage.*

MOP: the international standard code for the currency of Macasi—the pataca.

moratorium : the arrangement whereby a borrower states his or her inability to repay some or all of his or her outstanding debts. See *most-favored nation agreements and arrangements.*

more-than-one-consignment waybill: a waybill used for more than one consignment of freight.

Moroccan dirham: monetary unit of Morocco.

Morocco: see *U.S.-Morocco Free Trade Agreement.*

Moscow Interbank Currency Exchange: created in 1992; best financial exchange system in Russia, with the Central Bank owning 6 percent of the exchange.

most-favored nation (MFN):

(1) in international trade, a provision against tariff discrimination between two or more nations. It provides that each participant will automatically extend to other signatories all tariff reductions that are offered to nonmember nations. See *retaliatory duty.*

(2) a concept, embodied in the GATT, now WTO, of granting to other nations any advantage, favor, privilege, or immunity that is granted to the trade of a nation receiving the most-favorable treatment. An exception to this is made in the WTO for preferential tariff margins existing at the inception of the WTO. See *conditional most-favored-nation treatment.*

most-favored nation agreements and arrangements: the seven nontariff barrier agreements negotiated during the Tokyo Round of Multilateral Trade Negotiations. These include agreements on aircraft, antidumping, customs valuation, government procurement, import licensing, standards, and subsidies. See *most-favored nation.*

MOU: see *Memorandum of Understanding.*

MRAs: see *Mutual Recognition Agreements.*

MRO: the international standard code for the currency of Mauritania and Western Sahara—the ouguiya.

MTL: the international standard code for the currency of Malta—the Maltese lira.

MTN Codes: synonymous with *GATT Codes of Conduct.*

MTNs: see *multilateral trade negotiations.*

multicurrency issue: a loan or bond involving several currencies. The bond issue can be made in a given currency and be repayable in several. A rollover credit can be available in differing currencies to suit the borrower.

multicurrency loan: a loan in which several currencies are involved. See *multicurrency issue.*

multidomestic company: firm with international operations that allows operations in one country to be relatively independent of those in other countries.

MultiFibre (Multifiber) (Multi-Fibre) Arrangement (Agreement) (MFA): a system of limits, under GATT, now WTO, on imports of textiles and clothing from less costly countries. The MFAs generally do not affect MNCs, whose exports of textiles and clothing are subject to voluntary export restrictions. See *General Agreement on Tariffs and Trade.*

multifocal strategy: strategy aimed at achieving the advantages of worldwide integration whenever possible, while still attempting to be responsive to important national needs.

multilateral agreement: a consent agreed to by at least several nations, coordinated by an international agency, that is commercial, political, military, or humanitarian, or some combination thereof.

multilateral cumulation: see *European Free Trade Association.*

Multilateral Exchange Rate Model (MERM): developed by the International Monetary Fund, a model for measuring changes in the effective exchange rates of some nations. Use to develop sophisticated weights based on bilateral trade in indices for inclusion in the calculation of trade-weighted exchange rates.

Multilateral Investment Fund (MIF): established in 1993. Designed as a technical assistance mechanism to stimulate innovation and extend beyond existing bilateral and international instruments for Latin America and the Caribbean. In 2003, $900 million was approved for 600 projects. In 2004, 32 countries from Latin America, the Caribbean, Europe, and North America participated in the functioning of the MIF.

Multilateral Investment Guarantee Agency: see *MIGA.*

multilateralism:

(1) the practice or system of freedom of trade and convertibility of currencies among many nations.

(2) an international policy having as its object the freeing of international trade from the restrictions involved in bilateralism, in an effort to permit nations to specialize in production and exchange in accordance with the principle of comparative advantage. See *comparative advantage.*

multilateral trade: any trade among more than four nations (sometimes refers to only three nations). See *General Agreement on Tariffs and Trade; protectionism.* Cf. *plurilateral.*

multilateral trade negotiations (MTNs): the negotiations, usually over multiple sessions, conducted among many nations with respect to the conditions and rules of international trade (e.g., the Uruguay Round of GATT). Eight rounds of multilateral trade negotiations have been held under GATT, now WTO, auspices since 1947. Each negotiation has had the goal of reducing or eliminating tariffs among signatory countries. The Tokyo and Uruguay Rounds have focused on nontariff measures as well. Synonymous with *round of trade negotiations.*

multilateral trade negotiations codes: synonymous with *GATT Codes of Conduct.*

multilingual notes: paper money issued with a legend in two or more languages, as in India or Cyprus.

multimodal: a transport service offering more than a single mode. See *intermodal.*

multinational corporation (MNC): a corporation that participates in international business activities; a firm that produces, markets, and finances its operations throughout the various nations of the world.

multinational disclosure rules: when multinational firms situated within a regional trading community or trading partnership publish comparable information drawn up on uniform lines to provide a minimum degree of protection for shareholders, employees, and third parties. To ensure proper comparisons, items incorporated in group accounts might be valued using identical methods, although a degree of flexibility would be permitted in applying these principles, as there may be practical difficulties in exceptional cases. A special valuation method for group accounts is needed with respect to the holdings of group undertakings in the capital of other firms not belonging to the group but where, by virtue of the holdings, a substantial influence is exerted on the running of the firms, as in a joint venture. Certain information would be given in the notes to group accounts, to disclose the structure of the group, the identity of the group undertakings, and the relationship between them.

multinational economic union: a group of nations that have reduced barriers to intergroup trade and are cooperating in economic matters.

multinational enterprise (MNE): an organization that operates subsidiaries, branches, or other controlled affiliates in countries other than its home country.

multinational marketing: selling the product in several different country markets.

multinational reciprocity: mutual exchange of benefits between a host country and a multinational corporation.

Multinational Trade Negotiations Codes: synonymous with *GATT Codes of Conduct.*

multiple currency practice: a practice that arises when two or more effective exchange rates exist simultaneously, at least one of which, as the result of official action, is more than 1 percent higher or lower than the par value. Such practices are usually to be found where a dual exchange market exists or where the monetary authorities set different exchange rates for imports, exports, current invisibles, and capital. They often result from taxes or subsidies on specified exchange transactions.

multiple currency system: a means of controlling foreign exchange where domestic currency can be exchanged for foreign currency only through a governmental unit or controlled bank.

multiple exchange rate: used by a nation of several exchange rates for differing operations. For example, foreign investment and specific imports can be given a lower rate, while imports of a different nature can be charged with a higher rate of foreign exchange.

MUR: the international standard code for the currency of the British Indian Ocean Territory and Mauritius—the Mauritius rupee.

mushroom line: a transportation line operating mushroom steamers. See *mushroom steamers.*

mushroom steamers: a vessel that has no established operating policy and whose service is inaugurated on short notice to and from advantageous ports.

mutual acceptance of test data: a reference to the acceptance of test data in trading. Under the Standards Code, signatories are not obligated to recognize foreign-generated test data or certification marks from other signatories, though acceptance is encouraged. The Code recognizes that "prior consultations" may be needed to arrive at a mutually acceptable understanding of test methods and results. Negotiating reciprocal acceptance agreements represents a new mechanism for reducing barriers to trade in the area of testing and certification. See *Standards Code.*

mutuality of benefits: see *reciprocity.*

mutual recognition: a principle developed by the European Union Court of Justice in its case law, notably in the Cassis de Dijon judgment. It signifies acceptance by all member states of products lawfully and fairly manufactured and sold in any other member state, even if such products are manufactured on the basis of technical specifications different from those laid down by national laws in force insofar as the products in question protect in an equivalent fashion, the legitimate interests involved. See *Cassis de Dijon Case; excise tax; standards.*

Mutual Recognition Agreements (MRAs): agreements with trading nations on conformity assessment for regulated products that cover testing, certification, accreditation, and quality assurance; saves money by not having such procedures conducted in both nations.

MVR: the international standard code for the currency of the Maldives—the rufiyaa.

MWK: the international standard code for the currency of Malawi—the Malawi kwacha.

MXP: the international standard code for the currency of Mexico—the Mexican peso.

MYR: the international standard code for the currency of Malaysia—the Malaysian ringgit.

MZM: the international standard code for the currency of Mozambique—the metical.

N

NAC: see *New American Community.*

NACE (Nomenclature Générale des Activités Economiques des Communautés): used by the original European Community nations for the classification of economic-trade activities. It is an alternative to the International Standard Industrial Classification. See *International Standard Industrial Classification.*

NAFTA:

see *North American Free Trade Agreement.*

see *New Zealand Australia Free Trade Agreement.*

see *North Atlantic Free Trade Area.*

NAFTA-plus: see *side agreements.*

NAFTZ (North American Free Trade Zone): synonymous with *North American Free Trade Agreement.*

N.A. gulden: monetary unit of the Netherlands Antilles.

naira: monetary unit of Nigeria.

name:

(1) shorthand in foreign exchange markets referring to other participants (e.g., "I can't do the name," meaning "I am not allowed to trade with that institution").

(2) in Great Britain, a marking name. Synonymous with *street name.*

narrower bands: the tighter exchange rate fluctuation margins applied as a matter of standard international practice.

National Bank of Poland: Poland's central bank; responsible for issuing currency, holding foreign reserves, serving as the government's bank and clearing house.

national competition: the ability of a nation's producers to compete successfully in the world markets and with imports in their own domestic markets.

national debt: the total indebtedness of a national government resulting from cumulative net budget deficits.

national defense argument: argument in favor of governmental intervention in trade holding that a nation should be self-sufficient in critical raw materials, machinery, and technology.

National Economic Council (NEC): created by President Clinton soon after his inauguration in 1993, the NEC is the final tier of the interagency trade policy mechanism. Chaired by the President, the

NEC is composed of the Vice President, the Secretaries of State, the Treasury, Agriculture, Commerce, Labor, Housing and Urban Development, Transportation, and Energy, the Administrator of the Environmental Protection Agency, the Chair of the Council of Economic Advisors, the Director of the Office of Management and Budget, the U.S. Trade Representative, the National Security Advisor, and the Assistants to the President for Economic Policy, Domestic Policy, and Science and Technology Policy. All executive departments and agencies, whether or not represented on the Council, coordinate economic policy through the Council.

national economic plan: a plan developed by any government stating its economic goals and means for achieving them for periods of usually up to five years.

national exports: exports consisting of goods domestically produced or items produced within customs-bonded facilities.

nationalism: feeling of pride and/or ethnocentrism focused on an individual's home country or nation.

nationalism (of currency): the condition that occurs when a central bank imposes restrictions on the borrowing and lending of its currency by nonresidents of the nation. See *nonresident account.*

nationality principle: jurisdictional principle of international law which holds that every country has jurisdiction over its citizens no matter where they are located.

nationalization: the government takeover of private property; the process of transferring ownership of foreign-owned private property from a private firm to a foreign government, with compensation provided by the government to the firm's foreign owners.

nationalized exports: merchandise previously imported and cleared through customs that is exported without having changed in form or substance.

national liquidity: a nation's monetary situation as determined by its rates of interest on all loans and deposits. See *international liquidity.*

national representative: readiness to implement operating adjustments in foreign countries in order to reach a satisfactory level of performance.

national responsiveness: readiness to implement operating adjustments in foreign countries to reach a satisfactory level of performance.

national salary: host nation compensation provided to expatriates.

national tax jurisdiction: taxation on the basis of nationality regardless of where in the world the taxpayer's income is earned or where the activities of the taxpayer take place.

National Trade Data Bank: see *NTDB*.

National Trade Estimate Report on Foreign Trade Barriers (NTE): the Office of the USTR is required by the Trade Act of 1974, as amended by section 303 of the Trade and Tariff Act of 1984 and section 1304 of the Omnibus Trade and Competitiveness Act of 1988, to submit to the President, the Senate Finance Committee, and appropriate committees in the House of Representatives an annual report on significant foreign trade barriers.

The statute requires an inventory of the most important foreign barriers affecting U.S. exports of goods and services, foreign direct investment by U.S. persons, and protection of intellectual property rights. Such an inventory may facilitate negotiations aimed at reducing or eliminating these barriers.

The report is required to provide, if feasible, quantitative estimates of the impact of these foreign practices upon the value of U.S. exports. Information also is included on actions being taken to eliminate any act, policy, or practice identified in the report. See *Special 301.*

national trademark: see *trademark.*

national treatment: a form of friendship where laws governing the marketing of domestic items in nations that have signed treaties are extended to items designated as "foreign" or "imported." The United States accords national treatment in virtually every sector and believes that it should be granted unconditionally. However, the European Union may make national treatment and the right to do business conditional on receiving the same treatment for EU firms in the foreign country. Cf. *identical treatment.* See *mirror-image reciprocity; reciprocity.*

national wealth: the combined monetary value of all the material economic products owned by all the people in a country.

natural advantage: international concept; an advantage a country has in the manufacture of a specific item due to conditions such as climate or access to certain natural resources.

natural resource–based products: one of the 14 negotiating groups in the Uruguay Round. Traditionally, these include forestry products, fishery products, and nonferrous metals and minerals. Delegations to the GATT, now WTO, have emphasized the need for improving market access for these products.

NBA (Niger Basin Authority): created in 1964 to promote economic-trade resources of nations within the Niger Basin. Headquartered in Niamy, Niger, it includes Benin, Burkina Faso, Cameroon, Chad, Guinea, Côte d'Ivoire, Mali, Niger, and Nigeria. Synonymous with *Authorité du Basin du Niger (ABN).*

NCI: see *New Community Instrument.*

NCM: see *New Community Medium.*

NCTA (Northern Corridor Transit Agreement): served by the Port of Mombasa, Kenya, a multilateral agreement of 1985 by Kenya, Uganda, Burundi, Rwanda, and Tanzania. Zaire joined in 1987. Objectives include free movement of traffic among the nations, the reduction of administrative activities, etc.

near concessional financing: export credits of governments that are more complex and market-driven than the terms of repayment for concessional financing. Cf. *concessional financing.*

near money: highly liquid assets (e.g., government securities) other than official currency.

NEC: see *National Economic Council.*

negative pledge clause: a covenant in an indenture to the effect that the corporation will not pledge any of its assets unless the notes or debentures outstanding under the particular indenture are at least equally secured by such pledge.

negative premium: synonymous with *discount margin.*

negotiable:
(1) anything that can be sold or transferred to another for money or as a payment of a debt.
(2) a security, title to which is transferable by delivery.

negotiable bill of lading: bill of lading transferred by endorsement.

negotiable instrument: the Uniform Negotiable Instruments Act states: "An instrument, to be negotiable, must conform to the following requirements: (a) it must be in writing and signed by the maker or drawer; (b) it must contain an unconditional promise or order to pay a certain sum in money; (c) it must be payable on demand, or at a fixed or determinable future time; (d) it must be payable to order or to bearer; and (e) where the instrument is addressed to a drawee, he or she must be named or otherwise indicated therein with reasonable certainty."

negotiating group: a forum in which contracting parties plan and manage the multilateral negotiations dealing with a particular issue.

nemawashi: Japanese practice of arriving at a decision via consensus, thus allowing people to participate in the process and to state their opinions.

nenko system: the general pattern of human resource management commonly used in large-scale Japanese organizations.

neo-mercantilism: means of nations that apparently attempt to run a favorable balance of trade in an attempt to achieve some social or political goal.

Nepalese rupee: monetary currency of Nepal.

nested: packed one within another.

net barter terms of trade: synonymous with *commodity terms of trade.*

net capital flow: capital inflow minus capital outflow, for other than import and export payment.

net charter: in the United States, where all charges beyond delivery of a vessel to the first port of call are for the account of the charterer.

net currency exposure: the sum of all the long and short foreign currency positions in the portfolio.

net export of goods and services: the excess of exports of goods and services (domestic output sold abroad and production abroad credited to U.S.-owned resources) over imports (U.S. purchases of foreign output, domestic production credit to foreign-owned resources, and net private cash remittances to creditors abroad).

net foreign investment: the net change in a nation's foreign assets and liabilities, including monetary gold stocks, arising out of current trade, income on foreign investment, and cash gifts and contributions. It measures the excess of (a) exports over imports; (b) income on public and private investment abroad over payments on foreign investment abroad over payments on foreign investment in the nation; and (c) cash gifts and contributions of the United States (public and private) to foreigners over cash gifts and contributions received from abroad.

net import change: import displacement minus import stimulus.

net liquidity balance: the U.S. Department of Commerce's description for the overall balance of payments.

net negative international investment position: the situation when residents of a nation have less investments abroad than nonresidents have in the country.

net price trading: in the United Kingdom, when a deal is done at the selling (bid) price or the buying (offer) price, with no commission payable.

net registered tonnage: see *NRT*

netting: employed by multinational companies, enabling them to lower the amount of cash flow. This is done by moving cash between subsidiaries quickly and efficiently.

net ton: 2,000 pounds.

net ton–mile: the movement of a ton of freight one mile.

net tonnage (vessel): a vessel's gross tonnage minus deductions for space occupied by accommodations for crew, machinery for navigation, the engine room, and fuel. It represents the space available for the accommodation of passengers and the stowage of cargo. A ton of cargo, in most instances, occupies less than 100 cubic feet. The tonnage of cargo carried is usually greater than the gross tonnage. See *NRT*

net weight:

(1) the weight of an article clear of packing and container.

(2) as applied to a carload, the weight of the entire contents of the railcar.

network alliance: interdependence of countries; each firm is a customer of and a supplier to other firms.

neutralizing the balance sheet: having the assets in a given currency approximate the liabilities in that currency.

New American Community (NAC): a projected unification, first proposed by J. M. Rosenberg in *The New American Community* (Praeger, 1991), of the social, economic, and political policies of participating Western Hemispheric countries purporting to upgrade the standard of living for all, and to enrich the world from its interactions. Heavily engaged in international and regional trade, this complex structure will have numerous components, a commission, a council of ministers, a court of justice, an economic and social committee, a central bank, an investment bank, a social charter, and so on. All these units will be an outgrowth of an agreed-upon treaty The NAC will prove to be the primary tool to raise hopes and aspirations to a point of economic, social, and political reality. Frequently, experiments with institutions can improve the lives of more people than efforts of individual ambition, which can fray when faced with organizational obstacles. The chance the New

American Community will have for success involves a significant degree of mutual trust and influence among NAC nations.

First in place is a free trade accord between the United States, Canada, and Mexico, the North American Free Trade Agreement (NAFTA). This will, with mounting success across borders, lead to further social and political overtures and agreements. As these phases move forward, concurrent attempts at diplomacy and negotiation should introduce prospects for independent free trade agreements between any of the three founding members of the NAC with other Latin American neighbors, or pursued in a parallel effort by the central administration of the NAC. In any case, all sides should encourage and support those nations interested in joining the partnership of the New American Community.

The NAC shall not be perceived as having the legal character of a federal government, as is true with any of its participating member nations. Sovereign powers are to be provided on its institutions only, and these organizations shall not have the authority to upgrade or increase their control merely by flexing their own will. The NAC shall be limited by not possessing the universal jurisdictional characteristics of a member nation, nor the power to establish new fields of competence.

On the other hand, although the NAC will not be perceived or able to function as a nation, it is to evolve as a sophisticated unit established under traditional international law. Its only given similarity with traditional international units is the fact that it also was formed by a treaty that evolves from international law. The treaty is at the same time the foundation document forming an independent community provided with its own sovereign rights and competence.

By necessity and will, all member nations will pool certain parts of their own legislative powers in favor of the NAC, giving them over to Community institutions in which, however, they are given in return substantial rights of participation.

The New American Community must evolve as a comingler with member nations, endowing it with an independence and possessing its own sovereign rights and a legal system independent of member nations. Its evolution shall always rest primarily with the will of its responsible member nations. Once in place, a 33-nation economic, trade, political, and social bloc, of 700 million people, will emerge in full strength from Anchorage, Alaska, to Patagonia, Chile. See *Objectives of the New American Community.* Cf. *Enterprise for the Americas Initiative.*

new cedi: monetary unit of Ghana.

New Community Instrument (NCI): NCI was launched in 1978 as a European Community borrowing and lending scheme. It is administered jointly by the European Commission and the European Investment Bank. Loans go toward projects that are in line with Community objectives primarily to help finance investments in energy, industry (especially small businesses), and infrastructure.

New Community Medium (NCM): NCM complements the same sources as the European Investment Bank but constitutes an inflexible medium, to the extent that its sources are distributed among specific regional priorities. The NCM was created in 1978 and finances small to medium-size enterprise investments and industrial programs as well as programs for the integration of advanced technology into production activity. Loans are provided based on a "basket" of currencies, or in a single currency (ecus included); and through conditions similar to those of the EIB. See *European Investment Bank.*

New Europe, the: as of May 1, 2004 composed of 25 Eastern and Western European nations, with a population of 520 million and a gross national product of nearly $5 trillion, compared with the $4 trillion economy of the United States and Japan's $2 trillion. The term implies post–Cold War Europe. See *Nice Treaty.*

New International Economic Order: an idea created in the U.S. in the early 1970s that intended to develop mechanisms for redistribution of income between rich and poor countries. The effort was essentially dropped after the oil crisis of 1973–74, though the concept remains in discussion.

newly independent states: twelve nations of the former Soviet Union.

newly industrializing economy: see *NIE.*

New Middle East: a vision for the Middle East region proposed in 1993 by Shimon Peres, while Minister of Foreign Affairs for Israel. His model calls for regional economic integration as the key to peace and security, to promote stability and economic development, national growth, and individual prosperity.

new money: in international debt financing, further monies made available to the government of a debtor nation by members of the Paris Club. See *Group of Ten*.

new world order: the new world order was initially perceived by President George H. W. Bush as the acceptance of the growing trend of nations toward democracy, the observance of the rule of law, and the respect for human rights. Its mechanism will demand institutions with the authority to proclaim international law and the tools to impose it effectively, and, if need be, forcefully, on those violating it.

New Zealand Australia Free Trade Agreement (NAFTA): a free trade accord established in 1965 to remove tariffs and trade barriers between the two nations.

New Zealand dollar: monetary unit of New Zealand.

Ngultrum: monetary unit of Bhutan.

NHF: the international standard code for the currency of New Herbrides—the New Hebrides franc.

NIBOR: the New York Interbank Official Rate.

Nice Agreement: synonymous with *Nice Agreement Concerning the International Classification of Goods and Services for the Purposes of the Registration of Marks*.

Nice Agreement Concerning the International Classification of Goods and Services for the Purposes of the Registration of Marks: a 1977 multilateral treaty signed by countries providing protection of intellectual properties. The treaty is administered by the *World Intellectual Property Organization*. Synonymous with *Nice Agreement*.

Nice Treaty: European Union summit meeting of December 2000, in Nice, France, which established the framework for the EU enlarging from 15 nations to 27, by 2004. Romania and Bulgaria's timetable for entry was postponed, and only 10 new nations would join the E.U. on May 1, 2004. See *New Europe, the*.

NICs: newly industrializing (industrialized) countries; for example, Mexico, South Korea, Brazil, Taiwan.

NIE (newly industrializing economies): nations that are no longer poor.

NIFs: see *note issuance facilities*.

Niger Basin Authority: see *NBA*.

Nikkei: the Tokyo Stock Exchange. Its Index is a measure of the performance of 225 importantly listed stocks.

NIMEXE: the Nomenclature for the External Trade Statistics of the European Union, and statistics of trade between member nations. See *BTN.*

NIO: the international standard code for the currency of Nicaragua—the Cordoba oro.

Nippon Kaiji Kyokai: see *NKK.*

NIST: National Institute of Standards and Technology (U.S. Department of Commerce).

NKK (Nippon Kaiji Kyokai): the Japanese Ship Classification Society.

NME: see *nonmarket economy.*

NOK: the international standard code for the currencies of Antarctica, Bouvet Island, Dronning Maud Land, Norway, and Svalbard and Jan Mayen Islands—the Norwegian krone.

Nomenclature Générale des Activités Economiques des Communautés: see *NACE.*

nominal:

(1) the face value of a bond.

(2) the probable level of a market, but that level is not based on actual transactions.

nominal rate of exchange: the post rate of exchange, which allows a person to have a sound idea of the foreign exchange rate and which is used for small foreign exchange transactions.

nominal rate of protection: the tariff rate as applied to less costly foreign imports to protect domestic manufacturers against injury from them. Cf. *effective rate of protection.*

nominal tariff: taxes or duties charged on items being imported into a country.

noncompetitive traffic: traffic in the movement of which there is no competition between transportation lines.

nonconference carrier: a steamship line that is not a member of the conference over a given trade route.

noncontract rate: the freight rate applicable to commodities shipped by a firm that has not executed an exclusive patronage contract.

nondumping certificate: a seller's certificate indicating that the items described are being sold at a price no lower than that applicable to like sales in the country of origin. See *dumping.*

nonincoterms: terms of sales used in international transactions that are common and acceptable between and among those using them.

nonmarket economy (NME): an economy where commercial activity is centrally planned. While the GATT, now WTO, has some NME members, it is difficult to enforce the rules, since the GATT system is based on market principles. See *command economy*.

nonmarket measures: the use of currency controls, tariffs, or quotas to correct a balance-of-payments deficit.

nonperforming loans: loans that are in trouble; loans where the lender's management judges that the borrower fails to have the ability to fulfill the original contractual terms of the loan or where payments of interest or principal are overdue by 90 days or more.

nonreciprocal trade partners: nations that sell (export) goods to other nations but do not buy (import) from them.

nonrecourse financing: the process of making available monies to capitalize a trade transaction where the provider of capital can look to no one for repayment except the issuer of the instrument that has been tendered. See *forfaiting*.

nonresident account: an account owned by an individual who is not a resident of the nation where the account is held.

nonresident-owned (NRO) funds: open-end investment companies, notably in Canada, the shares of which are sold to U.S. investors.

nonrevenue freight: company materials and supplies transported without charges in freight trains of a particular railroad, for its own use.

nonsovereign public buyer:
(1) a government-owned or -controlled entity—such as a development bank, province, or municipality—that does not carry the full faith and credit of its government.
(2) an entity whose obligations are not guaranteed by a sovereign public agency. Eximbank usually requires that the obligation of the buyers be guaranteed by the ministry of finance, the central bank, or an acceptable commercial bank.

nonsterilized intervention: intervention in the foreign exchange market without adjusting for the change in money supply.

nontariff barrier (NTB): any law, regulation, or requirement that prevents or impedes the importation of goods without good cause. The most direct of these barriers are import licensing requirements and quotas. Other examples are subsidies that distort trade and injure competing firms, and requirements that specify a certain level of domestic content in a product being manufactured or sold. Some legal and regulatory protections for consumers or the environment can operate as nontariff barriers. See *Europe without Frontiers; harmonization; quota; subsidies.* Cf. *nontariff measure.*

nontariff measure (NTM): differing from NTB only in that it is an action by a government that may eventually have restrictive implications on goods traded in the world market. Though it cannot always be proven as such, an NTM is perceived as having a restrictive effect. Cf. *nontariff barrier.*

nontraded goods and services: items and services for which there exist supply and demand for import and export, but that are not traded.

nonvessel operating common carrier: see *NVOCC*.

norazi agent: an export/import middleman who trades in illicit merchandise and/or is engaged in trade of otherwise legitimate cargoes to nations ordinarily closed to normal commercial channels.

Nordek Treaty: a treaty approved by the Norwegian, Swedish, Danish, and Finish governments on February 4, 1970. It strengthens economic and trade cooperation between their nations and provides for a Customs Union and Common External Tariff with alignments in two steps; the first was on January 1, 1972, and the other on January 1, 1974. The *Common External Tariff* was based on the four countries' average current tariffs and became the same general level as the EC's tariff.

Nordic Council: a treaty between the Nordic nations signed in Helsinki in 1953, going into effect in 1962. It purports to develop cooperation in the fields of legislation; of cultural, social, and economic policies; and of transport and communications. The Treaty was revised in 1971.

normal price:

(1) the value basis for assessing ad valorem duties on imports.

(2) the price the goods would command in an open-market sale between buyer and seller for delivery at the time and place of actual importation. When the purchase price does not reflect all consideration given by the buyer to the seller, the value of the goods will be adjusted for customs purposes.

North America: a unit of the Northern Hemisphere of three nations, the United States, Canada, and Mexico, with a total population of more than 400 million.

North American Commission: see *North American Secretariats.*

North American Community: the three nations—the United States, Canada, and Mexico—that form the area described by President George H. W. Bush in his North American Free Trade Agreement.

North American Free Trade Agreement (NAFTA): the name given to economic links formed by the United States, Canada, and Mexico by President George H. W. Bush. NAFTA has also been referred to as the trilateral FTA with Mexico and Canada. On February 5, 1991, the Presidents of the United States and Mexico and the Prime Minister of Canada announced their intention to begin negotiations on a North American Free Trade Agreement. (The concepts for the New American Community were first introduced at the University of Yucatan, Merida, Mexico, one month earlier.)

The gross national product of the United States (population 250 million) in 1991 was $5.2 trillion, that of Canada (population 26 million) $463 billion, and of Mexico (population 86 million) $201 billion. This agreement creates a free trade area comprising over 400 million people with a combined output in excess of $6 trillion. Negotiations were on such topics as market access, trade rules, services, investment, intellectual property rights, and dispute settlement.

NAFTA's major provisions include: (a) Tariffs: approximately 65 percent of U.S. industrial and agricultural exports to Mexico were eligible for duty-free treatment either immediately or within five years. Mexico's tariffs average 10 percent, which is two-and-a-half times the average U.S. tariff. (b) Financial services: Mexico's closed financial service markets were opened, and U.S. banks and securities firms are allowed to establish wholly owned subsidiaries. Existing restrictions, including limits on foreign market share, were eliminated on January 1, 2000, giving U.S. banks and securities firms the opportunity to compete with local firms. (c) Insurance: U.S. insurance firms gained major new opportunities in the Mexican market: firms with existing joint ventures were permitted to obtain 100 percent ownership in 1996, and new entrants to the market were able to obtain a majority stake in Mexican firms in 1998. In the year 2000, all equity and market share restrictions were eliminated, which opened up completely a

$3.5 billion market. (d) Telecommunications: NAFTA opens Mexico's $6 billion telecommunications services and equipment market. It gives U.S. providers of voice mail or packet-switched services nondiscriminatory access to the Mexican public telephone network and eliminated all investment restrictions in July 1995. (e) Trucking: More than 90 percent of U.S. trade with Mexico is shipped by land, yet U.S. truckers had been denied the right to carry cargo in Mexico or to own warehouses. With NAFTA, U.S. truckers are no longer be forced to "hand off" trailers to Mexican drivers and return home empty. NAFTA permits U.S. trucking companies to carry international cargo to the Mexican states contiguous to the United States and gave them cross-border access to all of Mexico in 1990. (f) Motor vehicles and auto parts tariffs: U.S. autos and light trucks enjoy greater access to Mexico, which has the fastest-growing auto market in the world. With NAFTA, Mexican tariffs on vehicles and light trucks are cut in half. Within five years, duties on three quarters of U.S. parts exports to Mexico were eliminated, and Mexican "trade balancing" and "local content requirements" were phased out over 10 years. (g) Auto rule of origin: Only vehicles with substantial North American parts and labor content benefit from tariff cuts under NAFTA's strict rule of origin. NAFTA requires that autos contain 62.5 percent North American content, considerably more than the 50 percent content requirement of the United States Canada Free Trade Agreement. NAFTA contains tracing requirements so that individual parts can be identified to determine the content of major components and subassemblies; for example, engines. (h) Textiles and apparel: Barriers to trade on $250 million of U.S. exports of textiles and apparel to Mexico were eliminated and another $700 million were freed from restriction within six years under NAFTA. All North American trade restrictions were eliminated within 10 years, and tough rules of origin ensure that benefits of trade liberalization accrue to North American producers. (i) Agriculture: Eliminates import licenses, which were required on 25 percent of U.S. agricultural exports, and phases out Mexican tariffs. (j) Energy: provides increased access for U.S. firms to Mexico's electricity, petrochemical, gas, and energy services and equipment markets. (k) Intellectual property rights: provides a higher level of protection than that in any other bilateral or multilateral agreement. U.S. high technology, entertainment, and consumer goods producers that rely on protection for their patents, copyrights, and trade markets all realize substantial gains under NAFTA. For example, NAFTA limits compulsory licensing, resolving a major concern with Canada. (l) Investment: Mexican "domestic content" rules were eliminated, permitting additional sourcing of U.S. inputs, and for the first time, U.S. companies operating in Mexico received the same treatment as Mexican-owned firms. Mexico agreed to drop its export performance requirements, which forced firms to export as a condition of being allowed to invest.

On December 17, 1992, the leaders of Mexico, Canada, and the United States signed the North American Free Trade Agreement. In 1993, President Clinton moved forward with the NAFTA, by not reopening the agreement. The Administration negotiated a series of supplemental treaties governing worker rights, environment safeguards, and protection against import surges.

In May 1993, Canada's House of Commons approved the NAFTA with the Senate following with its approval on June 23, 1993.

On August 13, 1993, the United States struck deals with Canada and Mexico resolving issues that stalled approval of the NAFTA. The nations agreed to establish two North American Commissions (secretariats) that would try to insure the enforcement of labor and environmental laws. The agreement on side issues do not require the nations to enact new laws, only to enforce those already on the books. The new labor and environment agreements call for fines of up to $20 million on national governments and limited trade sanctions on countries that allow their companies to gain a competitive advantage by breaking domestic labor and environmental laws. A third pact calls for annual consultations on any import increases that appear to be devastating an industry.

On August 24, 1993, the U.S. Court of Appeals heard the Justice Department's appeal of a District Court ruling requiring an environmental impact statement on the effect of the trade accord.

Congress debated the NAFTA in the fall of 1993, where approval by a simple majority of both houses was needed for passage. The trade accord passed and took effect on January 1, 1994.

By 2004, NAFTA achieved its U.S. objective of increasing trade, especially doubling American agricultural exports to Mexico. Though the United States's trade deficit with Canada and Mexico grew nine-fold to nearly $90 billion, total trade among the three nations grew by 109 percent.

See *Enterprise for the Americas Initiative; fast track authority; Latin America; New Zealand Australia Free Trade Agreement; North American Secretariats; objectives of the North American Free Trade Agreement; Preamble (North American Free Trade Agreement); side agreements.* Cf. *New American Community; North Atlantic Free Trade Area.* Synonymous with *North American Free Trade Zone (NAFTZ).*

North American Free Trade Secretariats: see *North American Secretariats.*

North American Free Trade Zone (NAFTZ): synonymous with *North American Free Trade Agreement.*

North American Secretariats: to address most labor and environmental issues arising under the NAFTA, the three nations agreed on August 1, 1993, to establish a mechanism to assure that all participating countries will enforce labor and environmental laws and regulations. The agreement calls for the establishment of two secretariats, one in Canada, to handle environmental complaints, and the other in Washington, to deal with labor issues. A five-stage process would be followed: (a) people or groups in each country would be allowed to file complaints that one of the other countries has failed to enforce its own laws. Complaints would go to the environmental secretariat or national labor offices in each country; (b) representatives from the three countries would try to negotiate settlements. In the United States, the Labor Secretary would handle labor issues and the Administrator of the Environmental Protection Agency would handle environmental issues; (c) if representatives cannot agree, and if the complaint asserts that the failure is persistent and has had a demonstrable effect on trade, a panel of experts would be formed. If the panel rules against a country, it has 60 days to develop a plan that enforces the law and satisfies the complaining country; (d) if no settlement is reached in 60 days, the panel reconvenes and can impose a fine on the offending country of up to $20 million and require that an enforcement plan be drafted within 60 days; (e) if Mexico or the United States refuses to pay the fine and correct the problem, the injured country can raise tariffs or cancel other trade concessions. If Canada refuses to obey, the panel will ask a Canadian court to order the Government to do so. The court must comply with such requests and no appeal is allowed. Cf. *Free Trade Commission*. See *North American Free Trade Agreement; side agreements*.

North Atlantic Free Trade Area (NAFTA): with GATT stalled in early 1993, the *Masstricht Treaty* facing an uncertain future, Margaret Thatcher, former Prime Minister of England, along with other leaders, called for a North Atlantic Free Trade Agreement linking the United States and the E.C., to form a common European American market.

Such an agreement served to overcome the current gridlock in trade talks. Business would benefit from barrier-free trade between Europe and North America for the same reasons that prompted the creation of the common market in Europe and NAFTA. If a similar agreement between the E.C. and the United States were to be made, an increase in the flow of trade between the various regions of such an expanded area would be an immediate result. Easier access to market would allow for greater movement of goods and would increase sales.

By establishing a North Atlantic Free Trade Area, they claim, we would no longer have to waste precious time worrying about trade wars between the United States and the E.C. and how they would affect business. The concept of a North Atlantic Free Trade Area failed to capture the imagination of the general public and by 2004 no longer appeared feasible. Cf. *European Community; New American Community; North American Free Trade Agreement*.

Northern Corridor: the transport infrastructure located in East Africa and served by the Port of Mombasa, Kenya.

Northern Corridor Transit Agreement: see *NCTA*.

Norwegian krone: monetary unit of Norway.

NOS: see *not otherwise specified*.

no show: freight scheduled to be on a ship, but has not physically arrived in time for loading.

nostro account: an account maintained by a bank with a bank in a foreign country. Nostro accounts are kept in foreign currencies of the country in which the monies are held, with the equivalent dollar value listed in another column. Cf. *vostro account*. See *due from balance*.

nostro overdraft: part of a bank's statement indicating that it has sold more foreign bills of exchange than it has bought, resulting in the domestic bank's owing currencies to foreign banks in the amount of the nostro overdraft.

note: an instrument, such as a promissory note, which is the recognized legal evidence of a debt. A note is signed by the maker, called the borrower, promising to pay a certain sum of money on a specified date at a certain place of business, to a certain business, individual, or bank, called the lender.

note issuance facilities (NIFs): spawned issues similar to Euro-commercial paper.

notification: the principle within the European Union to prevent the creation of new technical barriers to trade. Its Council requires member states and national standardization boards to submit draft regulations and standards for industrial products to its Commission for review to ensure compliance with EU directives prior to adoption. During the review period, member states must suspend implementation (standstill obligation), and the Commission may make information on the proposals available to other members for their evaluation and comment. Any technical regulations enacted by member states without complying with this procedure are considered invalid.

not otherwise specified (NOS): relates to commodities not specifically named in tariffs or freight commodity classes.

NPR: the international standard code for the currency of Nepal—the Nepalese rupee.

NRO: see *nonresident-owned funds.*

NRT (net registered tonnage): that portion of a ship's gross registered tonnage considered for cargo. It is the gross tonnage less the machinery, boiler and bunker, crew, and stores space.

NTB: see *nontariff barrier.*

NTDB (National Trade Data Bank): provides useful information for U.S. exporters with a compact disk–based information system, in part produced by the U.S. Department of Commerce.

NT dollar: the monetary unit of Taiwan.

NTE: see *National Trade Estimate Report on Foreign Trade Barriers.*

NTM: see *nontariff measure.*

nuevos pesos: monetary unit of Peru.

nullification or impairment: adverse economic effect stemming from another GATT, now WTO, party's trade action, nullification, or impairment of GATT rights and obligations that gives rise to a formal action under GATT dispute settlement procedures.

numeraire: (French) a standard by which values are measured, such as exchange rates in the international monetary system.

NV: Naamloze Vennootschap (a Dutch corporation).

NVOCC (nonvessel operating common carrier): a physical distribution/logistical domestically based intermediary that is not an international forwarder; it offers to transport items across water, but does not operate any vessels itself.

NYBOR: New York Interbank Offered Rate.

NZD: the international standard code for the currencies of the Cook Islands and Niue Islands, New Zealand, Pitcairn Islands, and Tokelauk—the New Zealand dollar.

O

OAB: see *African Timber Organization.*

OAPEC: see *Organization of Arab Petroleum Exporting Countries.*

OAS: see *Organization of American States.*

OATS: (French) government bonds.

OAU: see *Organization of African Unity.*

objectives of the New American Community: the Community shall have as its task, a common market, to progressively bring together the economic policies of member nations, to promote throughout the NAC a harmonious development of economic activities, a continuous and balanced expansion, an increase in stability, an accelerated raising of the standard of living, and closer relations among countries belonging to it.

The following objectives can become the rational for the creation of the New American Community: (a) to establish the basis for a closer union among Western Hemisphere nations; (b) to further the economic and social progress of member nations by jointly eliminating barriers dividing them; (c) to further the improvement of working and living conditions with the Community; (d) to act together to promote steady expansion, balanced trade, and fair competition; (e) to strengthen the unit of member countries' economies by bringing the various regions into line with each other, and assisting developing areas; (f) to abolish restrictions on international trade by means of a common commercial policy; (g) to strengthen the bonds between Western Hemispheric nations and nations overseas; (h) to combine resources to promote peace and freedom. A series of measures to achieve these goals include: (i) the elimination of customs duties and trade restrictions between member countries; (ii) the establishment of a uniform external customs tariff and a common commercial policy toward nonmember nations; (iii) the removal of restrictions on the freedom of movement of labor, capital, and services; (iv) the establishment of a common transport policy; (v) the establishment of a common agricultural policy; (vi) the setting up of a system to prevent distortion of competition within the Community; (vii) the coordination of member countries' economic policies; (viii) the modification of national laws to bring them into line with each other, in cases where such laws have an effect on the establishment or functioning of the common market; (ix) the establishment of a Social Fund to improve employment possibilities for workers and to help raise the standard of living; (x) the creation of an Investment Bank to further economic expansion of the Community; (xi) the association of nonmember countries with the Community in order to expand trade and assist economic and social development, both within the Community and abroad. Cf. *objectives of the North American Free Trade Agreement.*

objectives of the North American Free Trade Agreement: Article 101: Establishment of the Free Trade Area

The Parties to this Agreement, consistent with Article XXIV of the General Agreement on Tariffs and Trade, hereby establish a free trade area.

Article 102: Objectives

1. The objectives of this Agreement, as elaborated more specifically through its principles and rules, including national treatment, most-favored-nation treatment and transparency, are to: (a) eliminate barriers to trade in, and facilitate the cross-border movement of, goods and services between the territories of the Parties; (b) promote conditions of fair competition in the free trade area; (c) increase substantially investment opportunities in the territories of the Parties; (d) provide adequate and effective protection and enforcement of intellectual property rights in each Party's territory; (e) create effective procedures for the implementation and application of this Agreement, for its joint administration and for the resolution of disputes; and (f) establish a framework for further trilateral, regional and multilateral cooperation to expand and enhance the benefits of this Agreement.

2. The Parties shall interpret and apply to provisions of this Agreement in the light of its objectives set out in paragraph 1 and in accordance with applicable rules of international law.

Article 103: Relation to Other Agreements

1. The Parties affirm their existing rights and obligations with respect to each other under the General Agreement on Tariffs and Trade and other agreements to which such Parties are party.

2. In the event of any inconsistency between this Agreement and such other agreements, this Agreement shall prevail to the extent of the inconsistency, except as otherwise provided in this Agreement.

Article 104: Relation to Environmental and Conservation Agreements

1. In the event of any inconsistency between this Agreement and the specific trade obligations set out in: (a) the Convention of International Trade in Endangered Species of Wild Fauna and Flora, done at Washington, March 3, 1973, as amended June 22, 1979; (b) the Montreal Protocol on Substances that Deplete the Ozone Layer, done at Montreal, September 16, 1987, as amended June 29, 1990; (c) the Basel Convention on the Control of Transboundary Movements of Hazardous Wastes and Their Disposal, done at Basel, March 22, 1989, on its entry into force for Canada, Mexico and the United States, or; (d) the agreements set out in Annex 104.1. Such obligations shall prevail to the extent of the inconsistency, provided that where a Party has a choice among equally effective and reasonably available means of complying with such obligations, the Party choose the alternative that is the least inconsistent with the other provisions of this Agreement.

2. The Parties may agree in writing to modify Annex 104.1 to include any amendment to an agreement referred to in paragraph 1, and any other environmental or conservation agreement.

Article 105: Extent of Obligations

The Parties shall ensure that all necessary measures are taken in order to give effect to the provisions of this Agreement, including their observance, except as otherwise provided in this Agreement, by state and provincial governments.

(Annex 104.1) Bilateral and Other Environmental and Conservation Agreements

1. The agreement between the government of Canada and the government of the United States of America concerning the transboundary movement of hazardous waste, signed at Ottawa, October 28, 1986.

2. The agreement between the United States of America and the United Mexican states on cooperation for the protection and improvement of the environment in the border area, signed at La Paz, Baja California Sur, August 14, 1983.

Cf. *objectives of the New American Community.*

OBO: ore/bulk/oil carrier.

observer: a country or international/regional organization officially approved to observe GATT, now the WTO, but not participate in the WTO, its committees, and its negotiating groups.

obsolescing bargain theory: concept that a firm's bargaining strength with a host government diminishes after the firm transfers assets to the host country.

OBU: see *offshore banking unit*.

OCAM (Organisation Commune Africaine et Mauricienne): a common market agreement formed in 1965 in Mauritania; strengthens and promotes economic and trade unity among members (Benin, Burkina Faso, Central African Republic, Côte d'Ivoire, Gabon, Mauritius, Niger, Rwanda, Senegal, and Togo) dealing with economic and social programs, sponsored by the Organization for African Unity. Synonymous with *African and Mauritian Common Organization (AMCO)*.

OCAS (Organization of Central American States): formed in 1962 in Panama to deal with economic-trade and social issues of Central America. OCAS is headquartered in El Salvador. See *Central American Common Market*.

OCDE (Organisation de Coopération et de Développement Économiques): see *Organization for Economic Cooperation and Development*.

ocean bill of lading (B/L): a bill of lading indicating that the exporter consigns a shipment to an international carrier for transportation to a specified foreign market. Unlike an inland B/L, the ocean B/L also serves as a collection document. If it is a straight B/L, the foreign buyer can obtain the shipment from the carrier by simply showing proof of identity. If a negotiable B/L is used, the buyer must first pay for the goods, post a bond, or meet other conditions agreeable to the seller. Cf. *air waybill; inland bill of lading; through bill of lading*.

ocean freight differential: the sum representing the difference in freight costs associated with moving subsidized agricultural exports on American instead of cheaper foreign ships.

ocean marine insurance: coverage on vessels of all types, including liabilities connected with them, and on their cargoes. Cf. *inland marine insurance; marine protection and indemnity insurance*.

Ockrent Report: the European Economic Community's statement on the establishment of a Free Trade Area running parallel with the EEC. It was denounced by the French government in 1958 when negotiations terminated.

ODA: see *official development assistance.*

odd dates: dealings in foreign exchange and money markets for periods other than the regular market periods.

OECD: formerly OEEC. See *Organization for Economic Cooperation and Development.*

OECD Arrangement: a 1978 agreement by OECD members to limit competition among the member governments in officially supported export credits. The guidelines cover cash payment requirements, minimum interest rates, maximum repayment periods, local costs, and procedures for negotiating derogations from the Agreement. The guidelines apply to all Eximbank programs except the Working Capital Guarantee Program. Participating nations include Austria, Australia, Belgium, Canada, Denmark, Finland, France, Germany, Greece, Ireland, Italy, Japan, Luxembourg, the Netherlands, Norway, Portugal, Spain, Sweden, Switzerland, the United Kingdom, the United States, and New Zealand. Synonymous with *OECD Arrangement on Guidelines for Officially Supported Export Credits.*

OECD Arrangement on Guidelines for Officially Supported Export Credits: synonymous with *OECD Arrangement.*

OECE (Organisation Européenne de Coopération Économique): see *Organization for European Economic Cooperation.*

OECF: see *Overseas Economic Cooperation Fund.*

OEEC: see *Organization for European Economic Cooperation.*

OEMs: see *original equipment manufacturers.*

OF: see *offshore funds.*

off-balance-sheet financing: financing that is not clearly displayed on the balance sheet (i.e., some leasing).

offer list: the list of items, usually prepared in conjunction with multilateral trade negotiations, on which a country is prepared to negotiate trade liberalization; may also identify merchandise that will be exempted from discussion.

offer price: either that price at which a foreign-exchange trader will sell a currency (asked or asking price) or the rate at which a lender will lend money.

offer rate: the amount for which a foreign exchange trader is willing to sell a currency.

off-hire: the time period when a chartered vessel is not earning income for its owner.

official development assistance (ODA): government monies of developed nations provided to developing nations to assist in their economic and social development.

official exchange rate: the ratio that is applied by the monetary authority of one nation in exchanging its money for that of another nation.

official reserves: total of a nation's holdings of gold, special drawing rights, and foreign currencies.

official reserve transactions balance: the account on the balance-of-payments statement that records the total of the balance on the goods-and-services account, the balance on the unilateral transfers account, and the balance on the capital account, plus the allocation of special drawing rights and net errors and omissions. See *Special Drawing Rights.*

Official Settlement Account: a U.S. balance-of-payments measure based on movements of dollars in foreign official holdings and in U.S. reserves. Synonymous with *Reserves Transactions Account.*

official value: the value, for duty purposes, officially assigned by a country to certain imported items. It is usually compared with the invoice value, and ad valorem duties are levied upon the higher value.

offset deals: countertrade transactions between exporter and importer. They can be indirect offsets, where the exporter receives payment by either receiving part in cash and undertaking to counter-purchase nonrelated items, or by receiving part in cash and agreeing to assist in the export marketing of unrelated items. They can be direct offsets, where the exporter receives payment by agreeing to activities directly related to the goods or services being imported. See *countertrade.*

offshore assembly: overseas production of goods whose inputs are fabricated in another country, typically done to reduce labor costs. That is, basic materials are made in one country, they are shipped abroad for assembly or processing, and then the products are shipped to the target market for sale.

offshore banking: locations, often found on an island, such as the Caymans or the Bahamas, where liberal banking laws seek funds in Eurocurrency.

offshore banking unit (OBU): a bank in Bahrain or any other center with similar organizations. It is not allowed to conduct business in the domestic market, only with other OBUs or with foreign institutions.

offshore financial centers: cities or nations that provide large amounts of funds in currencies other than their own and are used as locations in which to raise and accumulate cash.

offshore funds (OF): as they affect U.S. citizens, mutual funds that have their headquarters outside the United States or off its shores. Usually, such funds are not available to Americans but are sold to investors in other parts of the world.

offshore manufacturing: overseas production of items by a domestic firm primarily for import into its home country.

offshore profit centers: branches of major international banks and multinational corporations in Nassau, Bermuda, the Cayman Islands, and other low-tax banking centers, used as a way of lessening taxes.

offshore trusts: a personal trust that is foreign, not domestic. Its situs is usually in a country that does not have significant taxes on these trusts.

Old Lady of Threadneedle Street: a popular name for the Bank of England.

old-to-market: large companies, where a major part of their production capability is foreign-sourced, usually more than 15 percent of total sales.

OMAs: see *orderly marketing agreements*.

Omnibus Budget Reconciliation Act of 1990: the United States imposes user fees with respect to the arrival of merchandise, vessels, trucks, trains, private boats and planes, as well as passengers. This act increases the levels of the fees and demonstrates a tendency to seek to use fees, rather than taxes as a source of revenue. Excessive fees levied for customs, harbor, and other arrival facilities (that is, for facilities particularly used by importers) place foreign products at an unfair competitive disadvantage, according to some foreign governments.

It also further extended the report requirements and related provisions not only to subsidiaries of foreign firms, but also to all other foreign entities such as branches, which will primarily affect foreign banks, which could discourage foreign investment in the United States.

Omnibus Trade (Trading) and Competitiveness Act: U.S. legislation of 1988 to improve the comparative advantage of U.S. firms in international trade by permitting the President's office in the enforcement of existing laws. See *Export Trading Company Act; Interagency Group on Countertrade*. Synonymous with *Title VII of the Trade Act of 1988*.

OMR: the international standard code for the currency of Oman— the rial omani.

on-board bill of lading: a bill of lading in which a carrier certifies that goods have been placed on board a certain vessel.

on-deck bill of lading: a bill of lading bearing the specific endorsement "on deck" (or similar words); indicates cargo that is to be stowed on deck because its size does not permit stowage below decks, or where the hazardous character of the merchandise obliges that it be kept on deck for easy jettison in the event of danger.

on-lend: (British) to lend (borrowed funds) to others.

onus of good faith: the foundation for cargo insurance. People who have their cargo insured do not have a right to abandon the cargo or to fail to take any action that might lead to averting or reducing loss or damage.

O/O: ore/oil carrier.

OPEC: see *Organization of Petroleum Exporting Countries*.

open account: a trade arrangement in which goods are shipped to a foreign buyer without guarantee of payment. The obvious risk that this method poses to the supplier makes it essential that the buyer's integrity be unquestionable.

open charter: a charter party that specifies neither the port(s) of destination nor the cargo to be carried.

open-door policy: a policy whereby citizens and products of foreign countries receive the same treatment as domestic citizens and products. Cf. *most-favored nation; peril point*.

open economy: an economy that is free of trade restrictions.

opening bank: synonymous with *issuing bank*.

open insurance policy:
(1) an insurance policy that applies to all shipments made by an exporter over a period of time rather than to one shipment only.
(2) an insurance concept for a continuous, open-term contract designed to insure automatically all cargo moving at the insured's risk. Cf. *fleet policy*.

open order: synonymous with *good till canceled*.

open position: the state of a trader in foreign exchange who has not yet made or received payment in a foreign currency contracted for at some future date. The trader (and the currency) are open to risk (i.e., exposed to the possibility of some fluctuation in the exchange rate between the time the original contract was made and the settlement date).

open rate: the freight rate that is not set by a conference and is therefore to be negotiated.

open-top container: a standard shipping lines container with a removable canvas top.

operating company: a company whose officers direct the business of transportation and whose books contain operating as well as financial accounts.

operating differential subsidy: payment of the U.S. government to vessels carrying the U.S. flag, to offset the difference in operating costs between U.S. and overseas carriers.

operating expenses:
(1) actual expenses incurred in the maintenance of property (e.g., management, repairs, taxes, insurance). Not included as operating expenses are mortgage payments, depreciation, and interest paid out.
(2) expenses of furnishing transportation services, including the expense of maintenance and depreciation of the plant used in the service.

operating lease: where the asset is not wholly amortized during the obligatory period of the lease, and where the lessor does not rely for his or her profit on the rentals in the obligatory period.

operating ratio: the ratio of the operating expenses to the operating revenues.

operating revenue: the amount of money that a carrier becomes entitled to receive from transportation and from operations incident thereto.

OPIC: see *Overseas Private Investment Corporation*.

optimum tariff: the best duty rate for merchandise being imported into a country. It is the rate that maximizes the net national economic gain accruing from any improvement in trading terms of a nation.

optimum tariff theory: where an exporter lowers the price of merchandise when an import tax is placed on items.

option: foreign-exchange instrument that gives the purchaser the right, but not the obligation, to buy or sell a certain amount of foreign currency at a set exchange rate within a specified amount of time.

optional bill of lading: an ocean bill of lading giving the carrier the prerogative of stowing cargo anywhere aboard the ship at his or her convenience, thus permitting suitable cargoes to travel on deck. See *ocean bill of lading*.

optional origin contracts: transaction involving an export-sales contract between an exporter and an overseas buyer where the exporter retains the option of exporting the commodity from the U.S. or one or more other exporting nations.

order bill of lading: a negotiable bill of lading made out to the order of the shipper.

orderly marketing agreements (OMAs): bilateral agreements limiting imports from one

country to another; generally undertaken to avoid the imposition of unilateral import restrictions.

This is an example of a grey-area measure. Cf. *voluntary restraint agreements*.

order notify: providing for the surrender of the original bill of lading before the freight is surrendered.

ordinary course of trade: a principle that places the dutiable value of merchandise at the price at which it would normally sell if customary channels of distribution were observed.

Organisation Commune Africaine et Mauricienne: see *OCAM*.

Organisation de Coopération et de Développement Économiques (OCDE): see *Organization for Economic Cooperation and Development*.

Organisation Européenne de Coopération Économique (OECE): see *Organization for Economic Cooperation and Development*.

Organizacion de Estados Centro-Americanos (OCAS): see *Organization of Central American States*.

Organization for Economic Cooperation and Development (OECD) (Organisation de Coopération et de Développement Économiques) (OCDE): an organization created by the Paris Convention of 1960 by 20 founder states (Austria, Belgium, Denmark, France, Germany, Greece, Iceland, Ireland, Italy, Luxembourg, the Netherlands, Norway, Portugal, Spain, Sweden, Switzerland, Turkey, the United Kingdom, the United States, and Canada). It was later joined by Japan, Finland, Australia, and New Zealand. Its objective is promoting economic and social welfare throughout the OECD area by assisting member governments in the formulation and coordination of policies; stimulating and harmonizing members' aid efforts in favor of developing nations; and contributing to the expansion of world trade. It supplanted the Organization for European Economic Cooperation. See *European Community; OECD Arrangement; Organization for European Economic Cooperation.*

Organization for European Economic Cooperation (OEEC): an organization created to assist European nations in their recovery from World War II. On June 5, 1947, U.S. Secretary of State George Marshall suggested American assistance in Europe's economic recovery, on the understanding that the European nations would reach some agreement about their requirements and the part they themselves would take in giving proper effect to the action of the United States. In July, 16 nations met in Paris and created the Committee of European Economic Cooperation (CEEC). They signed a report formulating an economic recovery program. On March 15, 1948, a report recommended the need for a permanent coordinating body. Its functions were to develop economic cooperation between member nations and to assist the United States government in carrying out its program of aid to Europe. The primary activities of the OEEC included the following: the European Payments Union (EPU) from July 1, 1950, superseded the previous Intra European Payments Agreements; it provided an automatic multilateral system for offsetting monthly surpluses and deficits of each member nation with all other members and the determination of a resulting single balance owed to or by the Union; the automatic granting of credits, coupled with gold and dollar payments that increased when the country's indebtedness rose, facilitated the overbridging of short-run fluctuations in the balance of payments; the position of each nation included that of its monetary area (e.g., in the case of the United Kingdom, the net position determined each month was that of the whole of the sterling area vis-a-vis all other member nations). It was replaced by the Organization for Economic Cooperation and Development in 1961. See *Organization for Economic Cooperation and Development.*

Organization for International Economic Cooperation: see *Council for Mutual Economic Assistance.*

Organization of African Unity (OAU): created in Ethiopia in 1963 of all African nations, except South Africa. Replaced by the African Union in 2002. See *OCAM*.

Organization of American States (OAS): on April 14, 1890, in Washington, D.C., the First International Conference of American States founded the International Union of American Republics, the world's oldest regional organization. In 1945, President Truman organized a hemispheric foreign ministers' meeting in Mexico City, where it was agreed to redesign the Pan-American system. The Rio Pact (Treaty) of 1947 was the beginning, with a Treaty (the Inter-American Treaty of Reciprocal Assistance) defining an attack on any American country, from inside or outside the hemisphere, as an attack on all.

Thus, at the March 1948 meeting in Bogota, Colombia, the OAS was established. Its structure included a legal charter creating a council to deal with day-to-day commerce, inter-American conferences every five years, and foreign ministers' meetings to handle hemispheric threats. Today, the OAS has 35 member states and has granted permanent observer status to 28 nations in Europe, Africa, and Asia, as well as to the Holy See and the European Community.

The basic purposes of the OAS are: to strengthen the peace and security of the continent; to promote and consolidate representative democracy, with due respect for the principle of nonintervention; to prevent possible causes of difficulties and to ensure the pacific settlement of disputes that may arise among the member states; to provide for common action on the part of those States in the event of aggression; to seek the solution of political, judicial, and economic problems that may arise among them; to promote, by cooperate action, their economic, social, and cultural development; and to achieve an effective limitation of conventional weapons that will make it possible to devote the largest amount of resources to the economic and social development of the member states.

The *Inter-American Development Bank (IDB)* was created by the OAS in 1959 to help accelerate economic and social development in the hemisphere, and is the largest regional multilateral development financial institution. Cf. OCAS. See *Foreign Trade Information System*.

Organization of Arab Petroleum Exporting Countries (OAPEC): includes members of OPEC less Ecuador, Gabon, Indonesia, Iran, Nigeria, and Venezuela, plus Bahrain, Egypt, and Syria; aids in setting international oil prices and acts as liaison between the Arab oil states and other Arab nations. See *Organization of Petroleum Exporting Countries*.

Organization of Central American States: see *OCAS*.

Organization of Petroleum Exporting Countries (OPEC): the group's 13 members are concentrated in the Middle East but also include countries in Africa, South America, and the Far East. By virtue of their large exports, Saudi Arabia and Iran have been the most powerful influences. See also *Organization of Arab Petroleum Exporting Countries; petrodollars*.

original equipment manufacturers (OEMs): used in reference to the right to appeal. In 1990, the European Community's Court of Justice ruled that OEMs may have the right to appeal from regulations of the Commission and the Council imposing antidumping duties. Previously, this had been limited to complaining parties, producers/ exporters, and related importers.

original SITC: see *Standard International Trade Classification*.

originating goods (North American Free Trade Agreement): Article 401: A good shall originate in the territory of a Party where: (a) the good is wholly obtained or produced entirely in the territory of one or more of the Parties; (b) each of the non-originating materials used in the production of the good undergoes an applicable change in tariff classification set out in Annex 401 as a result of production occurring entirely in the territory of one or more of the Parties, or the good otherwise satisfies the applicable requirements of that Annex where no change in tariff classification is required, and the good satisfies all other applicable requirements; (c) the good is produced entirely in the territory of one or more of the Parties exclusively from originating materials; or (d) (with exception of certain listed goods) the good is produced entirely in the territory of one or more of the Parties but one or more of the non-originating materials provided for as parts under the Harmonized System that are used in the production of the good does not undergo a change in tariff classification because (i) the good was imported into the territory of a Party in an unassembled or a disassembled form but was classified as an assembled good pursuant to General Rule of Interpretation 2(a) of the Harmonized System, or (ii) the heading for the good provides for and specifically describes both the good itself and its parts and is not further subdivided into subheadings, or the subheading for the good provides for and specifically describes both the good itself and its parts, provided that the regional value content of the good, determined in accordance with Article 402, is not less than 60 percent where the transaction value method is used, or is not less than 50 percent where the next cost method is used, and that the good satisfies all other applicable requirements.

origin, point of: see *point of origin*.

origin, rules of: see *rules of origin*.

OS&D: see *over, short, and damaged*.

Oslo Stock Exchange: founded in 1819 in Oslo, Norway, as a commodity exchange. In 1881 securities were added.

OTC: Organization for Trade Cooperation (of GATT).

ouguiya: monetary unit of Mauritania.

Outer Seven: the members of the European Free Trade Association.

out-of-pocket costs: the expense directly occasioned by or attributable to the movement of traffic.

outsider: a carrier not a member of a given steamship conference.

outsourcing: when a firm uses foreign suppliers to purchase supplies or parts to achieve low costs and improve quality.

outturn report: the document issued by a ship on arrival in port specifying the cargo off-load.

outward processing: synonymous with *production sharing*.

overage:
(1) items additional to those shown on a bill of lading.
(2) the situation created by a spending program that exceeds a specified budget target during a specified time period.

Overall Balance of Concessions: a European Union measure of overall reciprocity based on the degree of market access provided EC firms in specific foreign markets or the magnitude of the concessions offered by individual foreign countries in the current multilateral trade negotiations under the GATT, now WTO. See *reciprocity*.

overbase compensation: additional payments to workers who are compensated for their hardships.

overcarriage: the transportation of goods beyond the initially intended destination, usually resulting from the goods being refused at the destination.

overcharge: to charge more than the applicable rate as published in the carriers' tariff.

overfreight:
(1) freight separated from its waybill and bearing no identifying marks.
(2) freight bearing identifying marks and loaded in a wrong railcar at origin or transfer point. See *astray freight*.

overhang: involuntary foreign official holdings of a currency, usually a generalized condition relating to a significant number of nations and involving historically large amounts of the currency concerned, net of working balances; represents temporary inconvertibility due to the inability of the reserve currency nation to convert the overhang into other forms of acceptable reserve asset.

overhead traffic: revenue traffic, moving in line haul, received from and delivered to a connecting carrier. Synonymous with *bridge; intermediate traffic*.

over on bill: additional freight described on the bill of lading.

overseas business reports: publications that evaluate various foreign markets by discussing pertinent marketing factors, presenting economic and commercial policies, issuing semi-annual outlooks for U.S. firms in the respective country, and publishing selected statistical reports on the direction, volume, and nature of U.S. foreign trade.

Overseas Economic Cooperation Fund (OECF): a Japanese financial institution purporting to provide new funds via cofinancing with Japanese private-sector financial agencies.

overseas investment:
(1) direct investment in a host nation by a foreign investor for the purpose of commercial profit. See *direct investments*.
(2) a component of a type of countertrade transaction called direct offsets where the exporter agrees to direct capital investment in the overseas nation that is the import customer. See *countertrade*.

Overseas Private Investment Corporation (OPIC): a U.S. agency that insures its companies against seizure of their overseas property by foreign governments, damage to property from acts of war, or conditions under which they are unable to take their profits out of the foreign country.

overshooting: the failure of an exchange rate to find its true level but to move beyond it, owing to temporary pressures, which then are reversed as the excessive movement of the exchange rate is perceived.

over, short, and damaged (OS&D): the discrepancy between the amount and/or condition of cargo on hand and that shown on the bill. See *clean bill of lading*.

overside delivery clause: a provision in some charter parties permitting the consignee to take delivery in his or her own lighters, providing that the discharged parcels reach a specified minimum quantity. Synonymous with *tackle clause*.

overtrading: the activity of a firm that even with high profitability cannot pay its own way for lack of working capital and finds itself in a liquidity crisis.

overvalued currency: a situation where the market and economic conditions and pressures indicate that a currency should be devalued. Opposite of *undervalued currency*.

owner's account: the expense, during the course of a vessel charter, that is borne by the ship owner.

owner's broker: a broker representing the ship owner in ship chartering.

ownership advantage theory: theory stating that foreign direct investment occurs because of ownership of valuable assets that confer monopolistic advantages in foreign markets.

P

pa'anga: the monetary unit of the Tonga Islands.

PAB: the international standard code for the currency of Panama—the balboa.

Pacific Economic Cooperation Conference (PECC): synonymous with *Pacific Economic Cooperation Group.*

Pacific Economic Cooperation Group (PECG): established in 1989, an organization representing nations with international trade interests in the Pacific Rim arena. Representatives from Brunei, Indonesia, Malaysia, the Philippines, Singapore, Thailand, Australia, Canada, Hong Kong, Japan, New Zealand, South Korea, Taiwan, and the United States, first met in Canberra, Australia in 1989 to form a subregional organization.

In November 1993, a Pan-Pacific summit meeting was held in Seattle, Washington, bringing the heads of state together to strengthen relationships throughout Asia. Synonymous with *Asia-Pacific Economic Cooperation Group (APEC); Pacific Economic Cooperation Conference.* See *APEC.*

Pacific Rim: an inadequate term, as the western hemisphere also has a Pacific Rim. However, when used by most people, it is the extensive area that extends from Japan and South Korea through the South China Sea, including Taiwan, China, Hong Kong, the Philippines, Malaysia, Singapore, Thailand, and Indonesia, then on to Australia and New Zealand, an area twice as vast as Europe and the United States combined. See *Asian Sector; Association of South-East Asian Nations; East Asian Newly Industrialized Countries.* Cf. *parallel imports.*

package car: a railcar loaded with several less-than-carload shipments destined for distant points and moving in fast freight trains.

package freight: merchandise shipped in less-than-carload quantities.

packing list: a list showing the number and kinds of items being shipped, as well as other information needed for transportation purposes.

paipu: in Japan, the access a person has to another who is important or possesses power.

Pakistan rupee: monetary unit of Pakistan.

Pakistan-Trade and Investment Framework Agreement: see *Trade and Investment Framework Agreement.*

PANLIBHON Group: an acronym for a group of nations where for-eign ships are registered under flags of convenience. Derived from first three letters of Panama, Liberia, and Honduras.

paper basis: indicating that a nation does not employ a metallic basis for its currency.

paper rate: a published rate; no traffic moves at rates lower than these.

paper standard: a monetary system, based on paper money, that is not convertible into gold or any other item of intrinsic value.

parallel exporting: a situation where, in addition to the official route by which the goods are exported by the exclusive distribu-tor into a given territory, there is also a second parallel route, by which another trader in the territory exports the goods, which he or she has obtained from a third party outside the territory. The parallel exporter is a source of competition for the exclusive dis-tributor. Cf. *parallel importing*.

parallel importer: a wholesaler who imports products independently of manufacturer-authorized importers, or buys items for export and diverts them to the domestic market. See *parallel importing*.

parallel importing: the importing of goods by an independent operator that is not part of the manufacturer's channel of distri-bution. The parallel importer may compete with the authorized importer or with a subsidiary of the foreign manufacturer that produces the item in the local market. See *parallel importer*. Cf. *par-allel exporting*.

parallel imports: exists where, in addition to the official route by which goods are imported by an exclusive distributor into a given territory, there is also a second parallel route, used by another trade in the territory who has obtained the goods from a third party outside the territory. The parallel importer is a source of compe-tition for the exclusive distributor.

Under parallel import exclusion, a U.S. firm, for example, could block the imports of its product in Venezuela, where it holds patent, from a licensed manufacturer in a third nation. Cf. *parallel exporting*.

parallel trading: see *parallel exporting*.

parastatal: agencies with a quasi-government standing, such as high-way authorities, nationalized industries, and so on. Usually is appli-cable to agencies with more than 50 percent government control.

parcel receipt: a receipt given by a steamship company for a parcel shipment.

parcel shipment: in international trade, a small package restricted as to value; generally samples of goods or advertising matter.

parent bank: bank found in an industrial nation that establishes a subsidiary in a developing country.

parent company:

(1) a controlling organization that owns or manages business properties.

(2) a firm engaged in trade with and investment in foreign nations and that owns at least one commercial business located there.

parent-country nationals: employees who are citizens of an international business's home country and are transferred to one of its foreign operations.

Parent/Subsidiary Directive: approved by the European Community's Council on July 23, 1990; to prevent the triple taxation of the profits of foreign subsidiaries in the Community. It does so by requiring the State of the parent company either to refrain from taxing profits distributed by the foreign subsidiary or to deduct tax already paid abroad up to the limit of the amount of the corresponding domestic tax; neither the State of the subsidiary nor the State of the parent is to levy withholding tax.

par exchange rate: the free market price of one country's money in terms of another country's currency.

pari delicto: fault or blame that is equally shared.

Paris Club: synonymous with *Group of Ten*.

Paris Convention (for the Protection of Industrial Property): an international accord of 96 nations signed in 1883, to recognize minimum standards for the protection of identified intellectual properties.

Paris Pact: see *Louvre Accord*.

parity:

(1) the state or quality of being equal or equivalent; equivalence of a commodity price expressed in one currency to its price expressed in another.

(2) equality of purchasing power established by law between different kinds of money at a given ratio.

parity value for currency: the official exchange rate of a currency. When exchange rates are fixed, monetary authorities are required to purchase and sell other currencies in money markets as necessary to preserve parity. See *parity*.

par of exchange: the market price of money in one national currency that is exchanged at the official rate for a specific amount in another national currency or for another commodity of value (gold, silver, etc.).

part cargo: see *PC*.

partial shipment: when the merchandise being shipped does not represent the full order as requested by the purchaser.

participating carrier (tariff): a transportation line that is a party, under concurrence, to a tariff issued by another transportation line or by a tariff publishing agent.

participation certificate:

(1) a formal credit instrument carrying a contractual interest obligation on a specified principal.

(2) a document showing participation in a syndicated Eurocredit; usually in negotiable form so that it can legally be sold to another bank.

(3) in Switzerland, a nonvoting form of equity issued by Swiss firms.

participation fee: in the Euromarket, a bank's fee for participating in a loan.

particular average: the liability attaching to a marine insurance policy in respect to damage or partial loss accidentally and immediately caused by some of the perils insured against. See *Free of Particular Average*.

partner: the "other" nation signatory of a trade agreement. Cf. *ROW*.

par value (of currency): the value of a currency in terms of gold as formally proposed to the International Monetary Fund, normally subject to fund concurrence. The Fund's Articles of Agreement envisage that each member country shall have an effective par value, i.e., a unitary, fixed exchange rate for spot transactions that is established and maintained in accordance with the provisions of the Articles. Synonymous with *face value*. See *margins; spot exchange transaction*.

passing report: a report of waybills received from or delivered to another railroad at junction point.

passive income: income from a firm's activities in a tax haven nation which is the result of investments in other nations, including income from sales and services involving purchasers and sellers located elsewhere. Either the purchaser or the seller is required to be part of the same organizational structure as the corporation earning the passive income.

pass-through: a foreign country's use of one nation in a trading bloc as a way of gaining preferential treatment from other nations within the bloc.

pasta war: a reference to a longstanding dispute between the European Community and the United States. On October 27, 1986, the two parties endorsed an agreement to end a long-running argument over pasta and citrus fruit. The agreement marks U.S. recognition for the first time of the European Community's right to grant special and unreciprocated trade concessions to third world countries. The United States had challenged preferential trade agreements with non-EC Mediterranean states, which it said discriminated against its own exports of citrus fruit to Europe. The agreement also traded greater access for American citrus exports to the European Community for greater access for EC exports of olives, olive oil, and cheese to the United States. It also ended U.S. restrictions on pasta imports, mainly Italian, imposed in retaliation for the complaints on citrus.

pataca: the monetary unit of Macao.

patent: a right granted by a sovereign power or state for the protection of an invention or discovery against infringement. See *Paris Convention; Patent Law.*

Patent-Cooperation Treaty: see *Patent Law.*

Patent Law: the Community Patent Convention (CPC) signed in December 1975 in Luxembourg, together with the European Patent Convention (EPC), offers a complete body of European Patent Law and procedure. It provides a choice between acquiring a national patent governed by national law, and a Community patent. The Patent-Cooperation Treaty became effective in 1978. See *European Patent Convention; harmonization.*

payable in exchange: requirement that a negotiable instrument be paid in the currency of the place from which it was originally issued.

payee: the person or organization to whom a check or draft or note is made payable. The payee's name follows the expression "pay to the order of."

payer: the person or company responsible for honoring a draft on its maturity date; usually an importer.

paying agent: an agent to receive funds from an obligor to pay maturing bonds and coupons, or from a corporation for the payment of dividends.

payment document: a document ensuring that the exporter receives payment for the goods. The most common form of payment is a letter of credit.

payment guarantee: a guarantee to the supplier of merchandise that if he or she performs his or her obligations, payment will follow.

payment in advance: a means of export financing where the importer sends full payment to the exporter prior to the receipt of the items. See *CBD*.

payments deficit: the excess of the value of a nation's imports over its exports. Cf. *payments surplus*.

payments surplus: the excess of the value of a nation's exports over its imports. Cf. *payments deficit*.

payments union: a regional, multilateral payment system to encourage multilateral trade and payments among nations. It can lead to a monetary agreement.

Pays et Territoires d'Outre-Mer: see *PTOM*.

PC (part cargo): acceptance by a ship owner of a charter under which the vessel will not be fully loaded and the unused space is not paid for.

PEC (President's Export Council): the premier U.S. advisory committee on international trade.

PECC: Pacific Economic Cooperation Conference. Synonymous with *Pacific Economic Cooperation Group*.

PECG: see *Pacific Economic Cooperation Group*.

pecuniary exchange: any trade that uses money.

peddler car: a railcar handled by carriers for less-than-carload shipments from only one consignor over a specified route, the shipments being delivered at points along the route direct from the car to the various consignees.

PEFCO (Private Export Funding Corporation): an organization that lends to foreign buyers to finance exports from the United States.

peg (pegging): to fix or stabilize the price of something (e.g., stock, currency, commodity) by manipulating or regulating the market. For example, the government may peg the price of gold by purchasing all that is available at a stated price. See *pegged exchange rate.*

pegged exchange rate: an exchange rate in which a nation's currency is fixed in terms of another nation's currency. Frequently, the other nation is a major trading partner or a country with which there was a colonial relationship.

PEMEX: see *Petroleos Mexicano.*

PEN: the international standard code for the currency of Peru—the neuvo sol.

per capita output: the gross national product of a nation divided by its population. This is often used to identify a country's standard of living.

per diem charge: a charge made by a transportation line against another for the use of its railcars. The charge is based on a fixed rate per day.

per diem reclaim: an amount paid by the line haul carrier to the switching company to reimburse the latter for the per diem or railcar rental the switching company has to pay the car-owning company for the time the car is in possession of the switching company performing the switching operation. The per diem reclaim rate per railcar is established for each company in every terminal by study of each company's terminal operations for an annual period.

Perestroika: (Russian) used by former Soviet Union President Gorbachev to define the modernization of its economy; substituting a command economy with more market-driven initiatives and decentralizing the decision-making power from government.

per hatch (PH): a means for measurement of loading or discharging; often given as so many tons per hatch day (PHD).

periphery: that segment of a country's population that is least advantaged economically.

peril point: under U.S. Customs law, the greatest reduction in U.S. import duty that could be made for a stated item without creating a major hardship to domestic manufacturers or to makers of a closely related item.

perils of the sea: in marine insurance, used to designate heavy weather, stranding, lightning, collision, and seawater damage.

period of investigation: the time span, often six months, beginning at least 150 days before and continuing 30 days after the first day of the month when an antidumping petition is filed, during which an exporter's home market (or third country) and U.S. prices and other appropriate facts are investigated to determine if sales to the U.S. have been at less than fair value.

perishable freight:
(1) freight subject to decay or depreciation.
(2) commodities subject to rapid deterioration or decay, including fresh fruits and vegetables, dairy products, and meats, and which require special protective services in transit, such as refrigeration, heating, and ventilation.

persistent dumping: the continuing trend of profit-seeking enterprises resident in one nation to export items for sale in another nation at below the normal market price of the goods in the domestic market of the exporter. See *dumping.*

peseta: the monetary unit of Andorra, Balearic Island, Canary Islands, and Spain.

peso: the monetary unit Argentina, Chile, Colombia, Cuba, Dominican Republic, Mexico, the Philippines, and Uruguay.

petrobonds: instruments that are backed by a specific number of barrels of oil. Since 1977, the Mexican government has been raising money by selling these bonds, which trade in direct relation to the rapidly rising official price of Mexico's crude oil.

petrodollars: huge sums of money from oil-producing nations other than the United States or Great Britain. These funds are initially converted into Eurocurrency and deposited with international banks to be used for future investment and for paying debts. These banks traditionally set limits on the sums they will accept from any one country. See *Organization of Petroleum Exporting Countries.*

Petroleos Mexicano (PEMEX): the state-owned oil monopoly of Mexico.

Pfandbrief: paper issued by German mortgage banks and traded on the Euromarkets. Secured by lendings of at least equal amount and yielding at least equal interest.

PFP: see *policy framework paper.*

PG: Persian Gulf.

PGK: the international standard code for the currency of Papua New Guinea—the kina.

PH: see *per hatch.*

phantom freight: freight charges paid by the purchaser that were never absorbed by the seller.

Phare Program: additional funding provided in early 1991 by the European Community to help Community firms wishing to develop joint ventures with trading partners in East and Central Europe, particularly small to medium-size enterprises. Additional monies were set aside for technical assistance programs.

PHD: see *per hatch.*

PHP: the international standard code for the currency of the Philippines—the Philippine peso.

physical distribution:
(1) the movement of merchandise from manufacturer to consumer.
(2) activities, exclusive of production, involved in moving merchandise from its point of origin to a point of destination.

Phytosanitary Inspection Certificate: a certificate, issued by the U.S. Department of Agriculture to satisfy import regulations for foreign countries, indicating that a U.S. shipment has been inspected and is free from harmful pests and plant diseases. See *sanitary and phytosanitary regulations.*

PIC: see *prior informed consent.*

pickup allowance: an allowance made by a carrier to the consignor or consignee for delivery of freight to a pickup-from-carriers terminal in lieu of such service being performed by the carrier.

pick-up and delivery: a service involving the collection of freight from the door of the consignor and delivery to the door of the consignee.

P&I Club (protection and indemnity club): the various associations of shipping firms that were formed to provide protection against risks not covered by ordinary marine insurance.

piggyback exporting: a foreign distribution operation where another company's merchandise is sold along with that of another producer. This form of exporting is used by firms that have similar or complimentary but noncompetitive items.

pilferage: taking of another's property while such goods are in transit or being stored.

pilotage:
(1) the duty or office of a pilot.
(2) the charges for navigating a vessel in and out of a harbor and/or through a channel.

PKR: the international standard code for the currency of Pakistan—the Pakistan rupee.

placement memorandum: a document prepared by the lead manager of a syndicate in the Eurocredit market; seeks to provide information to other potential leaders to assist them in deciding whether to participate in the credit.

placing power: the ability of a bank or broker to sell securities to investors.

planned market economy: see *nonmarket economy.*

Plaza Agreement: a meeting of leaders of the major industrial nations held at the Plaza Hotel in New York City in September 1985. At this meeting, the United States decided that the dollar was too strong, and the other major economic powers agreed. The central banks then intervened, helping to push the dollar down rapidly and bring the Japanese yen and the German mark up.

plurilateral: a select few countries involved with negotiations among themselves. This differs slightly from multilateral, which involves a larger number of participating parties. Cf. *multilateral trade.*

PLZ: the international standard code for the currency of Poland— the zloty.

point of origin: the location at which goods are received for transportation.

polarization: see *retaliation.*

policy framework paper (PFP): paper describing steps a nation takes while receiving structural adjustment aid from the International Monetary Fund; outlines the nation's difficulties and problems.

political risk: in export financing, the risk of loss due to such causes as currency inconvertibility, government action preventing entry of goods, expropriation or confiscation, or war.

polycentric stage: the development of a company's overseas production capacity, when management thinks of its business as based on regions or multiple nations, each becoming an integral part of the firm, although domestic activities and sales remain the most central.

polycentrism: characteristic of a person or organization that feels that differences in a foreign country, real and imaginary, great and small, need to be accounted for in management decisions.

pool:

(1) any combination of resources of funds, and so on, for some common purpose or benefit.

(2) an agreement between two or more companies to curtail output, divide sales areas, or in any other way avoid competition.

(3) firms joined to share business over a fixed time.

port:
(1) the left side of a ship, barge, or airplane.
(2) a ship's place of entry; any destination of a ship where federal customs officials are able to inspect cargo and levy duties.

port charge: a charge made for services performed at ports.

port congestion surcharge: a charge imposed by a steamship to offset the loss of revenue sustained by vessel calls at ports lacking adequate discharging facilities or adequate labor.

Port Data Processing Association: an association jointly financed by the ports of the European Union. It involves a computer system aimed at lowering costs, reducing the risk of pollution, and increasing safety and efficiency in the shipping sector.

port differential: the difference between through rates on the same class or commodity to or from competing ports, from or to the same point.

port mark: in foreign shipping, the final destination, not the port of entry, except when such port is the final destination.

port of discharge: port where a shipment is unloaded.

port of entry: a port, officially designated by the government, at which foreign goods are admitted into the receiving country.

port of export: customs point, airport, or port from which an export shipment leave a country for another nation.

port shopping: when both exporters and importers select a specific port on the basis of their assessment of customs' treatment, rather than on the quality of facilities and efficiency; at times a questionable practice.

port-to-port: from one port to another port.

Portuguese escudo: monetary unit of Portugal.

positive concept of valuation: an application of ad valorem duties holding that duties should be applied on the actual value of the transaction as defined by the buyer and seller.

postshipment verification: verification to conclude whether a commodity is being used for purposes for which its export was licensed.

post-trade financing: credit extended to the exporter or importer after shipment but before the
firm receives its payment for the goods.

pound (pound sterling): the currency of the United Kingdom and its dependencies.

pound note: British currency that ceased to be legal tender at the end of 1985.

PP: picked (selected) ports.

PPA: see *protocol of provisional application.*

PPPs: see *Public and Private Programs.*

Preamble (North American Free Trade Agreement): the Government of the United States of America, the Government of Canada, and the Government of the United Mexican States, resolved to:

STRENGTHEN the special bonds of friendship and cooperation among their nations;

CONTRIBUTE to the harmonious development and expansion of world trade and provide a catalyst to broader international cooperation;

CREATE an expanded and secure market for the goods and services produced in their territories;

REDUCE distortions to trade;

ESTABLISH clear and mutually advantageous rules governing their trade;

ENSURE a predictable commercial framework for business planning and investment;

BUILD on their respective rights and obligations under the General Agreement on Tariffs and Trade and other multilateral and bilateral instruments of cooperation;

ENHANCE the competitiveness of their firms in global markets;

FOSTER creativity and innovation, and promote trade in goods and services that are subject of intellectual property rights;

CREATE new employment opportunities and improve working conditions and living standards in their respective territories;

UNDERTAKE each of the preceding in a manner consistent with environmental protection and conservation;

PRESERVE their flexibility to safeguard the public welfare;

PROMOTE sustainable development;

STRENGTHEN the development and enforcement of environmental laws and regulations; and

PROTECT, enhance and enforce basic workers' rights. See *North American Free Trade Agreement.*

predatory dumping: the strategy of temporarily selling exported items in another nation below the normal market price of the goods in the exporter's market, with the goal of driving local producers or foreign competitors out of the market. Should the objective be achieved, prices of the items are then increased by the export-predator, who hopes to take maximum advantage of its newly acquired monopoly status. See *dumping*.

predatory rate: an ocean freight rate set intentionally low so as to drive out the competition.

preemption: the prerogative of customs authorities to seize and sell items that an importer has deliberately undervalued to avoid the payment of duties.

preferences: special trade advantages (e.g., tariff preferences) given by governments to trading partners in order to promote export growth and development. These are often granted by developed countries to less-developed countries. Licensing practices, quotas, or preferential application of other measures, including taxes, can also be granted in the nontariff areas.

preferential tariff: a tariff that grants lower rates of duty on goods imported from certain "preferred" countries than on the same goods from other nations.

preferential trade: favor granted to the trade of a nation or group of nations. It may be in terms of preferential tariff treatment or other charges, or other trade rules or formalities (e.g., import or export licensing).

preferential trade area: see *PTA*.

Preferential Trade Area for Eastern and Southern African States: successor to the East African Economic Community, which was discontinued in 1978. It reformed in 1982, with 15 member nations in East and Southern Africa, to increase trade among members. In October 1988, this PTA lowered tariffs by 10 percent, having a goal of zero percent over a 10-to-15-year time span.

preferential treatment: special tariff reductions provided by treaty members of a preferential trade area.

pre-license checks: inquiries to determine that dual-use items on a specific export licence application are destined for a proper and legitimate end use by a reliable and approved end user.

preliminary commitment: an authorization by Eximbank detailing in advance of a particular transaction the terms and conditions under which Eximbank will provide assistance in its direct loan, financial guarantee, and engineering multiplier programs.

Preliminary commitments are usually issued in the early stage of a transaction to help the U.S. supplier market its goods or services more effectively. Ultimate authorization of Eximbank funding is contained in a final commitment.

preliminary determination: a dumping determination by the U.S. Government (International Trade Administration (ITA)) stating the results of its inquiry carried out in the past 160 days following a petition that has been filed or initiated by the ITA.

premium:

(1) the amount by which one form of funds exceeds another in buying power.

(2) a charge sometimes made when a stock is borrowed to make delivery on a short sale.

(3) the redemption price of a bond or preferred stock, if this price is higher than face value.

prepaid charges: the amount of transportation and other charges paid at point of origin or en route.

prepaid shipment: a statement indicating that freight charges have been or are to be collected by the originating carrier at the point of origin.

Preparatory Committee: a group of contracting parties, organized under the auspices of the GATT, now WTO, and representing all GATT countries. This committee was responsible for determining the agenda for the Uruguay Round. Synonymous with *Prep Com*.

prepay: to pay before or in advance of receipt of goods or services.

prepay station: a station to which the transportation charges on shipments must be prepaid.

Prep Com: synonymous with *Preparatory Committee*.

preshipment finance: loans taken out to cover an exporter's costs prior to the shipment of goods.

President's Export Council: see *PEC*.

pretrade financing: credit extended to an exporter to enable that firm to produce the goods that will be exported; a form of working capital financing.

price actually paid (payable): the full payment made or to be made by a buyer to, or for the profit of, the seller for imported items.

price discrimination: the practice of charging different prices to different buyers for the same quality and quantity of merchandise. Should this practice result in reducing competition, it is illegal under U.S. antitrust laws. International trade agreements make some types of price discrimination illegal.

price repression: the deliberate reduction of domestic prices when imported items that are competitors are sold at significantly lower prices than the domestically produced items. Synonymous with *price suppression*.

price-specie flow theory: a theory stating that imports of precious metals increase the supply of funds and therefore advance the price level of items that use these metals.

price support: financial assistance, perhaps in the form of a subsidy, offered to farmers, distributors, manufactures, etc., in accordance with government policy to prevent market prices from dropping below a certain minimum level. Today, this is a major issue, as reflected in major subsidies to farmers in the EU.

price suppression: synonymous with *price repression*.

primacy: within the European Union, EU law overrides national laws of member states. The European Court of Justice concluded that EU law prevailed over the laws of member nations whose acceptance of the founding Treaty "carries with it a permanent limitation of their sovereign rights." Cf. *subsidiarity*.

primage: a gratuity formally paid to a vessel's captain and crew by a shipper of merchandise to ensure safe handling of the items.

primary commodity: a commodity that has not undergone any significant amount of processing (i.e., raw wool, crude oil).

primary producer: a nation producing a primary commodity.

primary product: any product of a farm, forest, or fishery, or any mineral, in its natural form or that has undergone only such processing as is customarily needed to prepare it for marketing in substantial volume in international trade.

principal:

(1) one of the major parties to a transaction; either the seller or purchaser.

(2) the original amount of a deposit, loan, or other amount of money on which interest is earned or paid.

(3) the face value of an instrument, which becomes the obligation of the maker or drawee to pay to a holder in due course. Interest is charged on the principal amount.

(4) the person for whom a broker executes an order, or a dealer buying or selling for his or her own account.

principal markets: in customs, the chief places in the nation of exportation where the items are freely sold or offered for sale, not necessarily the place where they are manufactured or delivered.

principal supplier: the country that has the largest portion of total WTO trade in a product imported into a given country. The principal supplier has first rights to negotiate compensation should a country assess a duty in excess of its bound rate. Any tariff concessions granted to the principal supplier are granted automatically to all other countries accorded most-favored-nation status.

prior deposits: a government requirement that an importer deposit in a commercial bank or central bank a specified sum of money (usually a percentage of the value of the imports) for a specified length of time as a condition of importing. These deposits are often held without interest and thus represent a real cost. They are recognized as barriers to trade.

prior import deposits: import deposits that must be paid before an import license can be granted.

prior informed consent (PIC): concept of requiring an exporter of a banned or restricted chemical to obtain, through the home country government, the expressed consent of the importing country to receive the banned or restricted substance.

priority foreign countries: the nations determined by the office of the U.S. Trade Representative to have engaged in "unfair trading acts, policies, and practices." See *snap-back; Super 301.*

priority practices: unfair trading acts that are or will become trade barriers to an exporting nation.

priority watch list: see *Special 301.*

private carrier: a transportation line that is not a common carrier.

Private Export Funding Corporation: see *PEFCO.*

Private Sector Development Program: see *PSDP.*

privatization: in practice, public companies are both servant and client to the government. They are by definition anticompetitive and likely to be a magnet for a host of explicit and implicit subsidies. In a truly open single market, the question of government ownership cannot be left to each nation. Nations that push for privatization at the same time must realize that privatization is by no means the perfect solution to all the ills of an economy or nation.

When a nation privatizes, it must proceed gradually, with tries and reevaluations each step of the way. Attempts with smaller firms are to be encouraged before privatizing the giant firms of the nation, for once the process begins it is virtually impossible to reverse it. Although reducing the net proceeds to a government that once controlled the company, the firm would be sold outright for cash. Workers, at all levels, must be brought into the privatizing process and they must be told what role they will have in any transition. Firms must also enter into negotiations with their union(s), specifically concerning mobility clauses, in order to increase the firm's productivity.

Privatization of large firms should be carried out in two phases. First, there is the screening of potential buyers, which leads to an elimination of inappropriate bidders (i.e., an individual or syndicate must be able to demonstrate that they can run the firm better than the government). Second is the selling price, determined via negotiations. Accompanying this is a need to provide investors in nations that privatize with a secure environment, assuring them of the existing programs for economic stabilization.

proclamation authority: "up-front" authority from U.S. Congress (the Trade Act of 1974) to the President of the United States to negotiate and implement tariff reductions with certain guidelines.

procurement and lead time: time needed by a purchaser to choose a supplier and to place and obtain a commitment for specific quantities of materials at stated times.

producer commodity cartel: an organization of producers of a key raw material commodity in world trade (e.g., the Organization of Petroleum Exporting Countries).

product: synonymous with *goods*.

product cycle theory: suggests that firms initially establish themselves locally and expand into foreign markets in response to foreign demand for the product; overtime, the *MNC* will grow in foreign markets; after some point, its foreign business may decline unless it can differentiate its product from competitors.

production division: organizational structure where differing foreign operations report to different product groups at headquarters.

production effect (of a tariff): the increase in domestic production of an item as a result of its increase in price resulting from a protective tariff.

production sharing: a situation in which a product is manufactured in one country, assembled in another, and marketed in a third. See *duty drawback*. Cf. *re-export*. In the European Union, synonymous with *outward processing*.

production switching: shifting of production from one nation to another as a result of changing costs and/or location benefits.

product liability: an effort to free the consumer from the burden of proving fault. In 1990, the European Community's Commission placed liability on the manufacturer or importer of defective items, irrespective of fault. See *consumer protection*.

product payback: trade financing where an import is financed with some of the exports it helps to produce.

product shifting: the switch from the manufacture and export of one item to the manufacture and export of another.

product testing: a system for testing and certifying products, calling for the mutual recognition of testing and certification so that a product approved by authorities in one country would be marketed anywhere else in the European Union or trading zone.

profit: value utilized for the purposes of a constructed value in an antidumping duty investigation. The profit is the profit normally earned by a manufacturer, from the nation of export, of the same or similar item as that under inquiry.

pro forma: an informal document submitted in advance of the arrival of merchandise or in the preparation of the needed documents.

pro forma invoice: an invoice provided by a supplier prior to the shipment of merchandise, informing the buyer of the kinds and quantities of goods to be sent, their value, and important specifications (weight, size, etc.).

prohibited articles: in shipping, articles that will not be handled.

prohibitive tariff:

(1) a tax on items imported into a nation, where its volume exceeds a permitted level of imports.

(2) a duty that is sufficiently high so as to reduce and eventually halt all international trade in the imported item subject to the duty.

(3) synonymous with *exclusionary tariff*.

project line: a line of credit made available to finance a specific project; used in export credits financing.

project link: economic model tying all the economies in the world and forecasting impact of changes in each on the other.

prompt: a vessel able to arrive at a required loading port within a few days.

proof of delivery: evidence that one party has turned over merchandise to another; a signed and dated acknowledgment of receipt.

propensity to import: the relationship between income and the value of imports, expressed in terms of money.

proportional rate: a rate specifically published to be used only as a factor in making a combination through rate. Cf. *basing rate.*

pro-rata basis: the procedure when imported items under absolute quota are released when the total quantity of entries filed at the beginning of the quota period exceeds the quota; the ratio between the quota amount and the total quantity being offered for entry.

protected markets: buyers and sellers who are kept from market fluctuations and disruptions by the use of voluntary export restraints (VERB) imposed on them by exporters of items to these markets. See *restrained exporters; voluntary restraint agreements.*

protection: the imposition of high (protective) tariffs on imports that are presumed to compete with domestic items, with the objective of giving the domestic manufacturer an advantage.

protection and indemnity club: see *P&I Club.*

protection cost (of a tariff): the financial loss of productive efficiency accompanied by distortions in consumptions resulting from the effects of any tariff protection of inefficient firms. Synonymous with *deadweight loss (of a tariff).*

protectionism:
(1) the imposition of border taxes and/or customs duties on imports to protect a domestic industry from cheaper competitive goods. See *General Agreement on Tariffs and Trade; pyramid of privilege.*
(2) a central bank system to protect currency with restrictions in order to move the exchange rate in a direction consistent with the economic policies of the concerned government.

protectionist business practices: synonymous with *PTPs.*

protectionists: people who favor high tariffs and other import restrictions to enable domestic items to compete more favorably with foreign items.

protectionist trading practices: see *PTPs.*

protective measures: measures that may be taken by a trading partner nation when a sudden balance of payments crisis occurs and where no immediate assistance has been given. See *protectionism; standards.*

protective tariff: a tax on imported goods, designed to give domestic manufacturers an economic shield against price competition from abroad.

protest: a written statement by a notary public, or other authorized person, under seal, for the purpose of giving formal notice to parties secondarily liable that an instrument has been dishonored, either by refusal to accept or by refusal to make payment.

protocol of accession: the legal document that recognizes the rights and obligations agreed to as a consequence of signing an international agreement or joining an organization.

protocol of provisional application (PPA): a legal device that enabled the original contracting parties of the GATT, now WTO, to grandfather existing domestic practices that would otherwise be inconsistent with GATT obligations.

PSDP (Private Sector Development Program): a program of the Inter-American Development Bank purporting to provide Latin American nations with financial incentives to privatize their economies, thereby lowering government involvement in daily activities of the national and regional economies.

PTA (preferential trade area): a form of economic integration where lower tariffs are created among members of the international accord.

PTOM (Pays et Territoires d'Outre-Mer): the Overseas Countries and Territories.

PTPs (protectionist trading practices): a nation's actions that attempt to alter its trade. Synonymous with *protectionist business practices.*

Public and Private Programs (PPPs): organization that works with District Export Councils and other agencies to promote U.S. exports; provides crucial information and support for small to medium-size firms looking to promote their services abroad. See *District Export Councils.*

public-private ventures: joint ventures involving a partnership between a privately owned foreign firm and a government.

public procurement: using public monies for government projects (i.e., building water reservoirs, industrial ports, airports, highways). Any procurement program would require: broadening of the scope of the obligations that already supposedly exist and blocking any loopholes in them; equipping itself with greater powers to enforce those obligations; improving the redress that disappointed or disenfranchised bidders will have if they feel themselves unfairly excluded; and extending open procurement to businesses that have remained exempt from it until now. The opening of public procurement practices is a keystone to the successful completion of an internal trade market.

Public procurement objectives contain: (a) transparency, which can be assured by a centralized system of publication of contract notices in an official journal. Publication could cover annual indicative plans where the authority sets out a list of contracts likely to be awarded in the coming year, notices of individual contracts, and notices of awards. In this way, private enterprises are given the information to enable them to plan for and tender for contracts, and to know who ultimately was awarded a particular contract. (b) Objectivity, which can be assured by common rules on technical specifications, qualification of candidates, and criteria for the award of the contract. These rules can be designed to eliminate all possibility of undue preference being given to national champions. (c) National judicial remedies, where, by way of remedies, national courts would be required to provide injunctive relief and/or damages to a tenderer who has not been treated fairly in accordance with the trade agreement rules. (d) Policing, where national remedies are reinforced by a power of the trading partners to intervene, of its own motion or as the result of a complaint by an aggrieved tenderer, and require a participating country to correct an irregularity in an award procedure.

public stores: a warehouse or other structure operated by the U.S. government for the storage of contraband, seized items, or goods not released from federal custody.

publishing agent: a person authorized by transportation lines to publish tariffs of rates, rules, and regulations for their accounts.

pula: the monetary unit of Botswana.

punitive duty: synonymous with *countervailing duty*.

Punta del Este: a city in Uruguay where a declaration (which included a statement of objectives and an agenda for the negotiations to follow) was written by contracting parties in September 1986 to launch a round of multilateral trade negotiations called the Uruguay Round. See *Alliance for Progress; Uruguay Round*.

purchase commitment: in the medium-term credit and small-business credit programs, an Eximbank commitment to purchase the foreign buyer's note or draft from the bank at a discounted interest rate. Eximbank retains full recourse to the bank.

purchase from foreign seller: transaction of the purchase of a commodity from a seller whose business location is outside of the U.S.

purchase of drawings under a documentary credit: the type of export financing where the exporter sells a draft drawn against a term documentary credit of which it is the ultimate beneficiary. The exporter draws a draft on the issuing bank under a term credit, and his or her bank buys the draft, usually at a discount. The exporter can also use the term draft for establishing a line of credit with his or her bank, against which the exporter can draw, using the term drafts as collateral.

purchase price: statutory rule used in dumping inquiries to refer to the U.S. sales price of goods that are sold or likely to be sold prior to the date of importation, by the producer or the reseller of the items for exportation to the U.S.

purchaser: in the export process, the person overseas who has entered into the export transaction with the applicant to buy the commodities or technical data for shipment to the ultimate consignee.

purchasing agent: an agent who purchases goods in his or her own country on behalf of foreign importers such as government agencies and large private concerns.

purchasing power parity: an explanation of exchange rate changes based on keeping prices of goods in different countries fairly similar by offsetting inflation differentials with changes in the currency exchange rates.

purpose clause: a clause in a Euromarket borrowing stating the purpose for which the borrowing is made.

put: an option contract that entitles the holder to sell a number of shares of the underlying stock at a stated price on or before a fixed expiration date.

PYG: the international standard code for the currency of Paraguay—the guarani.

pyramid of privilege: amid increased complaints of protectionism, increased barriers to international trade, and the negative impact of various policies, the perception of nations of the globe, especially third world countries, that they are at the bottom of this pyramid. See *protectionism*.

Q

QAR: the international standard code for the currency of Qatar—the Qatari rial.

Qatar riyal: monetary unit of Qatar.

QERs (quantitative export restraints): see *quantitative restrictions.*

QRs: see *quantitative restrictions.*

Quad: see *Quadrilaterals.*

Quadrilaterals (Quad): meetings of trade officials from the European Union with the United States, Canada, and Japan to discuss trade problems. They have been held each year since 1981. Usually, these representatives are the U.S. Trade Representative, the Canadian Minister of International Trade, the Minister of International Trade and Industry from Japan, and the Commission for External Relations of the European Union.

quadrilateral trade: those trade activities among the nations of the European Union, Japan, Canada, and the United States. See *Quadrilaterals.*

quadrilateral trade agreement: a trade accord among the nations of the European Union, Japan, Canada, and the United States. See *Quadrilaterals.*

quantitative export restrictions (QERs): see *exceptions; voluntary restraint agreements.* Cf. *quantitative restrictions.*

quantitative restrictions (QRs): specific limits on the quantity or value of goods that can be imported or exported during a specific time period. GATT, now WTO, generally prohibits the use of quantitative restrictions except under specified exceptional conditions. Cf. *quantitative export restrictions (QERs).* Synonymous with *export quotas; import quotas; quantity restrictions.*

quantity: actual contract quantity stated in the agreement between an exporter and a overseas purchaser or seller.

quantity controls: government limitations on the amount of foreign currency that can be used for specific purposes.

quantity restrictions: synonymous with *quantitative restrictions.*

quarantine: time period during which an arriving shipment, including passengers, crew, and cargo, suspected of carrying a contagious disease, is retained to prevent the potential spread of the disease.

quasi international law: regulations pertaining to the relationships among countries and private legal entities, such as corporations.

Queen's Warehouse: a warehouse operated by Canadian customs for the safe storage of imported items that have been abandoned, seized, or left unclaimed. Such items can be sold or disposed of after two months within the warehouse.

quetzal: the monetary unit of Guatemala.

quintal: a unit of weight equal to 100 kilos.

quota:

(1) the restricted volume of imports or exports, or of imports admitted at a particular tariff rate.

(2) assigned to each member of the International Monetary Fund; determines the voting power and subscription of that member and the normal quantitative limitations on its use of the Fund's reserves. See *quantitative restrictions; tariff quota.*

quota auctioning: see *import quota auctioning.*

quota cartel: an agreement among firms to a specific industry by which each participant is assigned a portion of market demand.

quota system: commodity agreement whereby producing and/or consuming countries divide total output and sales in order to stabilize the price of a particular item.

quotation: an offer to sell goods at a stated price and under specified conditions.

R

rail and water: shipment partly by rail and partly by water transport.

rail line transportation revenue: the revenue that the carrier becomes entitled to receive or that accrues to its benefit from service rendered in transporting property or persons by rail line.

rail waybill: freight statement showing merchandise was received for shipment by rail.

railway operating income: net revenue from railway operations less railway tax accruals.

rand: the monetary unit of Lesotho, Republic of South Africa, and South-West Africa.

ratchet down: see *Montreal Round*.

rate:
(1) as applied to transportation, or the movement and handling of goods or persons, the determining factor used in arriving at the charge or fare for services rendered.
(2) as applied to tariffs, the determining factor used to assess duties.

rate, blanket: see *blanket rate*.

rate breaking point: the point on which rates are made or at which the rate is divided.

rate, combination: see *combination rate*.

rate, commodity: see *commodity rate*.

rate, conference: see *conference rate*.

rate, continental: see *continental rate*.

rate, conversion: see *conversion rate*.

rate, directional: see *directional rate*.

rate, exchange: see *exchange rate*.

rate, forward: see *forward rate*.

rate, interbank: see *interbank rate*.

rate-making lines: the transportation lines that control the making of rates from one point to another point by reason of their geographical location.

rate, mileage: see *mileage rate*.

rate, missionary: see *missionary rate*.

rate, multiple exchange: see *multiple exchange rate*.

rate of exchange (ROE): the amount of funds of one nation that can be bought on a specific date for a sum of currency of another country. Rates fluctuate often because of economic, political, and other forces.

rate of return: the ratio of net operating income to the value of the property in common carrier use, including allowances for working capital.

rate, open: see *open rate.*

rate, paper: see *paper rate.*

rate prorate: a division of revenue on interline shipments on the percentage basis that each carrier's local rate to or from the interchange point is to the total of such local rates from origin to destination.

rate, released: see *released rate.*

rate scale: a table of rates graduated according to distances or zones.

rate, standard: see *standard rate.*

rate, tariff: see *tariff rate.*

rate, through: see *through rate.*

rate, transit: see *transit rate.*

rate, transportation: see *transportation rate.*

rating:

(1) the evaluation of the moral or other risk of an individual or company.

(2) a system of rating that provides the investor with a simple system of gradation by which the relative investment qualities of stock and bonds are indicated.

rationalized production: companies manufacturing differing parts of their product lines in differing locations globally, enabling them to take advantage of lower costs for labor, capital, and, often, raw materials.

rationing of exchange: governmental control of foreign exchange through the forced surrender of exchange by exporters for domestic currency at the government rate, and the subsequent allocation of such exchange to importers according to a government ration schedule.

RBPs: see *restrictive business practices.*

RCD (Regional Cooperation for Development): a regional international institution, formed in 1964 by Iran, Pakistan, and Turkey, with headquarters in Tehran, Iran. Purports to develop and promote technical cooperation and economic progress to further integrate members' economies and trade.

readily marketable staples: items suitable for warehouse financing under eligible banker's acceptances.

real: monetary currency of Brazil.

real effective exchange rate: an effective exchange rate adjusted for inflation differentials between the nation whose exchange rate is being measured and other nations making up the group against which the exchange rate is calculated.

realignment: simultaneous and mutually coordinated revaluation and devaluation of the currencies of several nations.

real income: the sum total of the purchasing power of a nation or individual.

real value of money: the price of money measured in terms of goods,

reasonable dispatch: the duty of a common carrier to convey merchandise from shipper to consignee with all reasonable speed, with no obligation on the part of the carrier for loss of market or other losses resulting from delays in transit.

rebate of duties: a government rebate of customs duties assessed on imported items that are subsequently exported. See *value-added tax*.

rebilling: issuing an additional waybill to extend or complete the haul of freight.

receipt-of-goods dating: see *ROG dating*.

receivership: the status of a carrier's property while in charge of a receiver appointed by a court of equity.

reciprocal switching: a mutual interchange of inbound and outbound carload freight that is switched to or from a siding of another carrier under a regular switching charge. The charge is usually absorbed by the carrier receiving the line haul.

reciprocal trade agreement: an international agreement between two or more countries to establish mutual trade concessions that are expected to be of equal value. See *Reciprocal Trade Agreements Program*.

Reciprocal Trade Agreements Program: largely superseded by the *Trade Expansion Act of 1962* and *WTO*. Federal legislation of 1934, which amended the Smoot-Hawley Act, and authorized reductions up to 50 percent in tariff rates under bilateral agreements.

reciprocity:
(1) provision of a guarantee of similar or at least nondiscriminatory opportunities for enterprises to operate in foreign markets on the same basis as local firms. See *Government Procurement Code.*
(2) the principle governing WTO negotiations under which governments extend comparable concessions to each other. In past rounds, developing countries have not been obliged to offer fully reciprocal concessions.
(3) the position expounded by the European Community. When the European Community's Commission on October 19, 1988, announced that they had failed to include a statement on external trade policy in their 1985 White Paper, they concluded that firms benefiting from a single Europe should give matching market access to European companies, with bilateral negotiations with other countries or groups of countries, and then spread these concessions multilaterally through the GATT, now WTO. The intent is to provide a guarantee of similar or at least nondiscriminatory opportunities for EC enterprises to operate in foreign markets on the same basis as local firms. The United States, Japan, and other nations question whether the European Community will respect its international obligations. In general terms, the Commission is not asking for mandatory reciprocity, just the power to seek it where appropriate. Not all EC trading partners, according to the Commission, would be asked to make the same concessions, nor would the Community insist on concessions from all its partners. Many developing countries would be let off the reciprocity threat totally. The European Community will seek reciprocity in testing and certification procedures. There will also be bilateral accords for transport, telecommunications, and information database services. Should the 15 states agree on common rules for takeover bids, the Commission negotiates reciprocity for foreign states. Before allowing foreign firms to take over an EU company, the Commission wants to be assured of the right of an EU company to do the reverse in that foreign company's home territory. See *General Agreement on Tariffs and Trade; Government Procurement Code; Identical Treatment; mirror-image reciprocity; national treatment; Overall Balance of Concessions; sectorial reciprocity.* Synonymous with *level playing field.*

reconsignment:
(1) relinquishment of shipment at the point of origin.
(2) change in the place of delivery.

reconsignment and diversion:
(1) privileges provided by transportation carriers allowing shipping instructions to be changed as to consignee, destination, and routing.
(2) changes in consignee or destination before or after arrival of a shipment at original destination; diversion includes changes in destination or routing while the shipment is in transit.

recourse: the rights of a holder in due course of a negotiable instrument to force prior endorsers on the instrument to meet their legal obligations by making good the payment of the instrument if dishonored by the maker or acceptor. The holder in due course must have met the legal requirements of presentation and delivery of the instrument to the maker of a note or acceptor of a draft, and must have found that this legal entity has refused to pay for or defaulted in payment of the instrument.

rectifications: changes made to a country's schedule of WTO concessions, usually involving only correction of errors but occasionally involving limited duty changes or withdrawal of items from a schedule as a result of the negotiated settlement of a dispute.

red clause: a clause, printed in red, on a letter of credit, authorizing a negotiating banker to make advances to a beneficiary so that he or she can buy the items and deliver them for shipment.

redelivery: the point in time at which a charterer returns operational control of the ship to the owner.

redemption: the liquidation of an indebtedness on or before maturity, such as the retirement of a bond issue prior to its maturity date.

red label: a label required on shipments of articles of an inflammable character.

reduced debt servicing: where unwilling banks and financial institutions do not want to provide further funds to indebted credited nations. Banks are then given the change to convert current claims to a repayment of financial obligations by issuing new bonds from future debt reduction measures.

reefer: a refrigerated cargo vessel or container.

re-export:
(1) (verb) to export already imported items, without duty charges,

in basically similar form to a third country. Cf. *production sharing.*
(2) (noun) the export of imported items or commodities without substantial processing or transformation.

refund: money returned to the consignor or consignee as a result of the carrier having collected charges in excess of the legally applicable amount.

regiocentrism: business relationship created to support regional market needs, acknowledging and accepting similarities between regions.

Regional Cooperation for Development: see *RCD.*

regional development bank: bank whose mission is to promote economic development of poorer nations within the region it serves.

regional economic integration: expansion of commercial and financial ties among countries in a regional group, leaving the rest of the world outside of the group; ranges from free trade agreements to full economic and political union.

regional International: an organization of trade unions from a specific region of the world, for example, Western Europe.

regionalization of trade: a means for members of regional groups to concentrate and liberalize international trade among each other, to move from customs and economic integration to monetary integration and a single market, and to move away from liberalized trade on an open, global basis.

regional trading arrangements: multilateral trade carried out within a formal geographic area.

Reichsbank:
(1) (German) imperial bank;
(2) the Central bank of Germany, which receives and disburses state funds.

reimbursement arrangement: an arrangement by which a foreign correspondent bank is reimbursed for payments made according to the instructions of the bank issuing credit.

reinvoicing: a strategy employed by international firms where one of its national companies imports commodities through an offshore firm and dumps the profits made on the transaction in the offshore tax haven, thus lifting its apparent costs in order to lower taxes on the mainland firm.

Related Company: synonymous with *Associated Company*

related specificity: a rule of customs law that, when two or more tariff provisions might be applied to an item, the one that most specifically describes the article shall be applied.

relationship enterprises: networks of strategic alliances among big companies, spanning different industries and countries.

relative factory endowments: theory stating that a country will have a comparative advantage in producing goods that intensively use factories of production it has in abundance.

relative price: the price of an item as it relates to the price of another item.

released rate: a rate based on a limitation of the carrier's liability for loss and damage, and therefore less than a rate applying without such limitation.

relet: a vessel already on period commitment that is made available for a single trip or period to a further charterer.

relief claim: a request made by an agent of a transportation line to clear his or her accounts of outstanding bills.

Rembrandt: a domestic Dutch Guilder issue by a foreign borrower.

remitting bank: a bank that sends a draft to an overseas bank for collection.

remote delivery: sending goods from a central warehouse to customers by truck or via area delivery stations located in the outer city.

renegotiation: process by which international firms and governments decide on a change in terms for operations.

reparation: a payment made by a carrier to a shipper in satisfaction of improper charges levied.

repatriation: the liquidation of overseas investments and the return of the proceeds to the country of the investor.

reply time: the time period during which an offer to charter a ship remains valid.

reporting day: the day on which a vessel under charter advises it is available to begin loading.

representative: see *foreign sales agent.*

representative office: an office of an out-of-state or foreign bank that is not allowed to carry out direct banking functions. The purpose of such an office is to solicit business for its parent bank, where it can conduct such functions.

repudiation: a government's refusal to acknowledge a contract.

request/offer: a negotiating approach whereby requests are submitted by a country to a trading partner identifying the concessions it seeks through negotiations. Compensating offers are similarly tabled and negotiated by delegates of the countries involved.

resale price maintenance: the practice by a supplier of prescribing, and taking action to enforce, retail or wholesale prices for the resale of items.

rescheduling: the renegotiation of the terms of existing debt.

reserve: a portion of the profits allocated to various reserve accounts to protect any depreciation in asset values. The reserves are taken from profits before any declaration of dividends by the board of directors.

reserve account: that portion of the balance of payments which reflects changes in the government's international reserves.

reserve clause: a Eurocurrency credit clause allowing a lender to pass on to a borrower any further costs resulting from the imposition on the lender of new reserve requirements.

reserve currency:

(1) foreign funds retained by a nation's central bank as a vehicle for settling international financial obligations.

(2) currency that is internationally acceptable and is used by central banks to meet their financial commitments abroad.

reserves (official): official foreign exchange reserves kept to ensure a government is able to meet current and near term claims. They are an asset in a nation's balance of payments.

Reserves Transactions Account: synonymous with *Official Settlement Account.*

reserve tranche: a position where a member nation of the *International Monetary Fund* exceeds its quotas of the IMF's holding of its currency, excluding holdings arising out of the purchases made by the member under all policies on the use of the IMF's general resources.

reshipment: goods reshipped under conditions that do not make the act subject to the reconsignment rules and charges of the carrier.

residual restrictions: quantitative restrictions that existed prior to a nation's membership into the General Agreement on Tariffs and Trade, now the World Trade Organizaton, and are consequently allowed under a grandfather clause.

resolution panel: a means for dealing with discord by nations involved in international trade. When arguments or disagreements arise, a nation goes to a resolution panel to deal with such issues, with fair representation from all sides. Should a nation lose a dispute before the resolution panel, that country shall have three choices: it can repeal its law, rework it, or retain the law and in some fashion compensate the exporting nation; for instance, by reducing tariffs on other products. See *North American Secretariats.*

resource: anything a country uses to produce goods and services (manpower, minerals, oil, etc.).

resource-oriented production: production of raw materials, minerals, or components in a foreign country for shipment to a multinational corporation's home country or other component unit.

respondentia: the pledge of cargo by a vessel master as collateral for a loan permitting the vessel to continue on its journey or to make arrangement to forward items.

restitution payments: payments on exports by EU member nations to make up the difference between the world price and the higher domestic price in the exporting nation. Payments are gradually charged to the EU's Agriculture Guidance and Guarantee Fund, so that by the end of the transitional period all exports of agricultural produce from the Union will be financed out of this central fund. Synonymous with *compensation payments; export refunds.*

restrained exporters: nations that use voluntary export restraints to slow down the export of particular items to identified markets. See *protected markets.*

restraint of trade: see *conspiracy in restraint of trade.*

restricted articles: articles that are handled only under certain conditions.

restrictive business practices (RBPs): acts of enterprises, public or private, that limit access to markets or indirectly restrain competition.

restrictive practices: the European Union's version of American antitrust laws.

restrictive trading practices: see *restrictive practices.*

retaliation:

(1) legal actions, approved by the General Agreement on Tariffs and Trade, now WTO, where an "injured party" can take against an "offending party" with new tariffs or increased rates of existing

tariffs on the imported items of a nation against whom a panel has judged appropriate.

(2) counterclaims taken by a nation in response to what are considered inappropriate behaviors of a trading partner. See *Super 301.* Cf. *retortion.*

Retaliation List: see *Super 301.*

retaliatory duty: a differential duty designed to penalize foreign nations for alleged discriminatory commerce activity or to force them into making trade concessions. See *tariff war.* Cf. *most-favored nation.*

retortion: a lawful but unfriendly act of retaliation. Cf. *retaliation.*

returned without action: for export control purposes, the return of a license application without action; for example, when the application fails to be properly completed.

revalorization: synonymous with *revaluation.*

revaluation: restoration of the value of a depreciated national currency that has previously been devalued by lowering the request for or raising the supply of foreign currencies through restriction of imports and promotion of exports. Cf. *devaluation.* Synonymous with *revalorization.*

revenue cars loaded: the number of cars loaded with revenue freight, both carload and less–than–carload. See *revenue freight originated on respondent's road.*

revenue effect of a tariff: the income derived by a government from levying a duty.

revenue freight: a local or interline shipment from which earnings accrue to the carrier on the basis of tariff rates.

revenue freight carried: shipment of revenue freight originated on the line or received from connecting carriers.

revenue freight originated on respondent's road:

(1) shipments that originated directly on respondent's road.

(2) shipments received from water lines and highway motor truck lines, except when identified as having had previous rail transportation.

(3) shipments that received first-line haul on respondent's road but originated on switching lines connecting directly or indirectly with respondent's road.

(4) import traffic received from water carriers, and traffic from outlying possessions of the United States.

(5) outbound freight that has been accorded transit privileges.

revenue freight received from connecting rail carriers:
(1) all shipments received directly from connecting rail carriers.
(2) shipments received from water lines and highway motor truck lines, when identified from information on waybills or abstracts as having received previous rail transportation.

revenue freight revenue tariffs: duties placed on imports with the goal of increasing revenues rather than protecting domestic industries.

revenue freight terminated on line:
(1) shipments terminated directly on respondent's road.
(2) shipments delivered to water lines and highway motor truck lines.
(3) shipments that receive last-line haul on respondent's road but are delivered to switching roads connecting directly or indirectly with respondent's road.
(4) export traffic delivered to water carriers and shipments to outlying possessions of the United States.

revenue per ton-mile: synonymous with *ton-mile revenue.*

revenue ton–mile: the movement of a ton of 2,000 pounds of revenue freight a distance of one mile.

revenue waybill: a written description showing a shipment's charges and goods.

reverse imports: products made by a nation's overseas subsidiary that are exported back to the home nation.

reverse preferences: trade concessions granted by developing nations to developed countries.

reversible laydays: within a charter party, permitting the charterer to combine the laytime for loading and discharging into a single unit, applying the time as required.

revocable letter of credit: a letter of credit that can be canceled or altered by the drawee after it has been issued by the drawee's bank. Cf. *irrevocable letter of credit.*

revolving account: a line of credit that may be used repeatedly up to a certain specified limit.

Rhine waterway: a system of rivers and canals that is the main water transportation artery of Western Europe.

rial: the monetary unit of Iran, Oman, and Yemen.

rider: a producer employing piggyback exporting with the foreign distribution operatons of another firm's products to sell its own items. Usually employed by small companies with limited export experience.

riel: the monetary unit of Cambodia and Kampuchea.

right-hand side: the rate at which a bank will buy foreign currencies.

right of establishment: rights of foreign direct investors to establish and operate a business in a foreign nation under the same rights given to businesses operated by citizens of the foreign nation.

ringgit: the monetary unit of Malaysia.

ringisei: (Japanese) decision making by consensus.

Rio Declaration (Earth Summit): result of the Rio Earth Summit, which sets out fundamental principles of major environmental issues.

Rio Pact (Treaty): see *Organization of American States.*

risk position: the situation of a trader of foreign exchange reflecting the net amounts of spot and forward locations of a foreign currency that is traded.

River Plate Basin System: see *RPBS.*

riyal: the monetary unit of Oman, Saudi Arabia, and Yemen.

RNR: rate not reported.

ROE: see *rate of exchange.*

ROG dating (receipt-of-goods dating): under this condition of sales, the date for payment and the discount period are determined from the date the buyer obtains the shipment, rather than from the invoice date. This procedure is primarily employed when great shipping distances are involved.

ROL: the international standard code for the currency of Romania—the leu.

rollback: under the Uruguay Round rollback commitment, all participants agreed to phase out or bring into conformity with the GATT, now WTO, all trade-restrictive or distorting measures.

roll on/roll off: see *RO/RO.*

roll-up fund: an investment fund outside Great Britain, investing in world currencies on which no dividend is paid; the return is taxed as a capital gain instead of income.

Rome Convention of 1980: synonymous with *European Convention on Contracts.*

Rome Treaty: see *Treaty of Rome.*

RO/RO: *roll on/roll off* ships, allowing containers, trucks, and other vehicles to be driven on and off without the use of cranes.

round: a multilateral trade negotiation under the auspices of the GATT, now WTO, culminating in trade agreements to reduce tariffs or nontariff barriers among participating countries.

round of trade negotiations (RTN): synonymous with *multilateral trade negotiations.*

round table: the traditional name given to any organization composed of key industrialists. They often are involved in international trade recommendations, prepare strategies for improved competitiveness, and make views known to political decision makers.

route:

(1) (noun) the course or direction that a shipment moves.

(2) (verb) to designate the course or direction a shipment shall move.

routing order: a document, usually a printed form, signed by a foreign buyer, instructing the supplier to effect shipments through a named freight forwarder.

ROW: rest of the world. Cf. *partner.*

royalties: payments for the use of intangible assets abroad.

RPBS (River Plate Basin System): established in 1969 in Brasilia, Brazil, by Argentina, Bolivia, Brazil, Paraguay, and Uruguay, with headquarters in Buenos Aires, Argentina. Its objective is to set trade policies and to encourage the development of natural resources along the River Plate Basin.

RTN (round of trade negotiations): synonymous with *multilateral trade negotiations.*

rubel: monetary unit of the Republic of Belarus.

ruble: the monetary unit of nations of the former Soviet Union, such as Georgia, Kazakhstan, Republic of Kyrgyz, Russia, Tajikistan, Turkmenistan, and Uzbekistan.

rufiyaa: monetary unit of the Republic of Maldives.

rules of competition: these rules are contained in the E.U.'s Treaty of Rome and its implementing regulations. It encompasses the wide field of restrictive trade practices, types of trade agreement prohibited and permitted, monopolies and the dominant position, merger. Laws, traditions, and procedures include:

(1) the following shall be prohibited an incompatible with the E.C. common market: all agreements among undertakings, deci-

sions by associations of undertakings, and concerted practices which may affect trade among member nations and which have as their object the prevention, restriction, or distortion of competition within the common market, and in particular those which: (a) directly or indirectly fix purchase or selling prices or any other trading conditions; (b) limit or control production markets, technical development or investment; (c) share markets or sources of supply; (d) apply dissimilar conditions to equivalent transactions with other trading parties, thereby placing them at a competitive disadvantage; (e) making the conclusion of contracts subject to acceptance by the other parties of supplementary obligations which, by their nature or according to commercial usage, have no connection with the subject of such contracts.

(2) any agreements or decision prohibited pursuant to this article shall be automatically void.

(3) the provision of paragraph 1 may, however, be declared inapplicable in the case of: (a) any agreement or category of agreements between undertakings; (b) any decision or category of decisions by associations of undertakings; (c) any concerted practice or category of concerted practices, which contributes to improving the production or distribution of goods or to promoting technical or economic progress, while allowing consumers a fair share of the resulting benefit which does not: (I) impose on the undertakings concerned restrictions which are not indispensable to the attainment of these objectives; (II) afford such undertakings the possibility of eliminating competition in respect of a substantial part of the products in question.

rules of content: see *rules of origin*.

rules of navigation: a set of formalized regulations, adopted by the United States in 1889, which today are administered by the International Maritime Organization.

rules of origin: used by nations to assign a nationality to products that are treated differently in international commerce according to their country of origin. Shifting percentages-of-content rules inevitably stirs criticism. The United States and Canadian accord of 1989 set 50 percent as a minimum of parts coming from North American nations.

The rules of origin between the United States and Canada include: (a) Goods wholly obtained in the United States or

Canada or made from goods wholly produced in either country qualify for free trade agreement duty benefits. The term "obtained" would not be construed as "purchased." Products in this category refer to goods extracted from the soil or the sea. (b) Goods composed of imported materials which have been changed in ways that are physically and commercially significant are eligible for Canadian Free Trade Agreement tariff treatment. The exporter must ensure that the goods have been sufficiently altered, using the changes in Harmonized System nomenclature. (c) In addition to a change in the Harmonized System tariff classification, some goods require that a percentage (generally 50 percent) of the direct cost of processing be American, Canadian, or a combination of the two. (d) For certain limited cases where no change in tariff classification occurs between the end product and the imported components materials, a value-added criterion only (50 percent or more) may be applied.

Setting excessive rules of origin conditions should not be based on political considerations, which usually create a crude form of restrictive industrial policy. Nations must be on guard that rules of origin remain a set of criteria by which to determine what country a given product is made in; that a product's country of origin is to be the last country where assembly or processing operations "substantially transformed" the inputs or components into a new product. Trade policy considerations of one nation should not determine these rules.

Strong rules-of-origin provisions assist customs inspectors to make determinations of what passes free of tariffs or duty, while not unduly inhibiting and impeding trade. See *dumping*.

rupee: the monetary unit of India, Mauritius, Nepal, Pakistan, Seychelles, and Sri Lanka.

rupiah: the monetary unit of Indonesia.

Russian Trading System: electronic system created in 1995; a Russian form of NASDAQ, where the majority of Russian equities are traded.

R/V: round voyage.

Rwanda franc: monetary unit of Rwanda.

S

SAD: see *Single Administrative Document.*

SADC: see *Southern Africa(n) Development Community.*

SADCC: see *South African Development Coordination Conference.*

safeguards: temporary restrictions to trade levied unilaterally by a government on an emergency basis against imported items that are seen as causing significant injury to a domestic industry. As long as they remain temporary, the General Agreement on Tariffs and Trade finds such measures legitimate. Cf. *snap-back.* See *World Trade Organization.*

safe-haven currency: the currency of a nation that is politically secure.

safe port: a port into which a ship can enter, remain in, and depart from without abnormal dangers that are avoidable through the exercise of normal care and seamanship.

SAFTA: see *South American Free Trade Agreement.*

sailing day: used by transportation lines to designate schedules for receiving freight destined for certain points.

sale at less than fair value: the sale of items to a foreign purchaser at a price below the price that would be charged for a like sale in the home market. Such sales can serve as the basis for an allegation of dumping. See *dumping.*

sales company: a corporate entity established in a foreign country by the parent firm to sell goods or services imported from the parent firm and other foreign affiliates.

sales representative: an agent responsible for distributing, representing, servicing, or selling merchandise on behalf of foreign sellers.

salvage: compensation for the rescue of a ship, often its cargo, or its passengers from loss at sea.

Samurai Bond: bond issued on the Japanese market in Yen outside Japan.

sanction:

(1) a penalty for the breach of a rule of law.

(2) a coercive measure, usually undertaken by several nations, to force another country to cease violation of a treaty or an international agreement.

(3) see *side agreements; North American Secretariats.*

sanitary and phytosanitary regulations: government standards imposed to protect human, animal, and plant life and health. These may apply to animals and plants and their products to help ensure that they are safe for consumption and do not damage the environment. Phytosanitary regulations apply only to plants and plant products. See *Phytosanitary Inspection Certificate.*

SAR: the international standard code for the currency of Saudi Arabia—the Saudi riyal.

SASO: see *Saudi Arabian Standards Organization.*

Saudi Arabian Standards of Organization (SASO): created in 1972; the only Saudi Arabian government institution to promote and monitor standards and measurements with the kingdom.

Saudi riyal: monetary currency of Saudi Arabia.

SBD: the international standard code for the currency of the Solomon Islands—the Solomon Islands dollar.

scale economies in distribution: cost reductions achieved by shipping large quantities of products, thus lowering the unit shipping cost relative to competitors that ship lower quantities.

scarce currency: in international finance, a situation where the demand for a particular nation's currency threatens to exhaust the available supply at the usual rates of exchange. When a currency becomes scarce in the International Monetary Fund, members of the Fund are authorized to introduce exchange restrictions against that nation.

Schatzwechsel: a German Treasury bill. The rate on the Schatzwechsel bill is usually higher than the official discount rate but below the rate currently allocated to repurchase agreements.

Schedule B: a reference to "Schedule B, Statistical Classification of Domestic and Foreign Commodities Exported from the United States." All commodities exported from the United States must be assigned a seven-digit Schedule B number.

schedule of concessions: a schedule maintained by most GATT signatories, as a condition of their accession to GATT, now the WTO. This schedule of concessions consists, usually, of a list of goods and the import duties applicable to those goods that the country has agreed to reduce and bind or bind at current rates.

Schengen Accord: initially ratified by Belgium, Germany, France, Luxembourg, and the Netherlands on June 19, 1990; agreement that their citizens will not be subject to customs inspection when entering or leaving any of the Schengen nations. Other EU countries have since joined the Agreement.

schilling: the former monetary unit of Austria.

schuldschein: private loan agreements in Germany, where the borrower draws up an agreement with a large investor, usually a bank, that makes the loan. With the borrower's authorization, the bank can resell the loan to another investor or divide it among several of them. The loans are traded on an interbank market.

scientific tariff: when a tariff is placed on an imported item as a form of protection providing the domestic producers with needed relief to meet competition. See *tariff.*

SCM (Southern Common Market): synonymous with *Mercosur.*

SCR: the international standard code for the currencies of the British Indian Ocean Territory and Seychelles—the Seychelles rupee.

screwdriver assembly plants: synonymous with *maquiladoras.*

screwdriver duties: where imported components of foreign products made within a national country or member of an international trade agreement might be vulnerable to antidumping duties unless an adequate proportion of the final unit is made outside the foreign nation. See *dumping; World Trade Organization.*

script sheet:
(1) a form of statement, carried by a truck driver, showing essential details of all shipments loaded in his or her truck.
(2) a transcript of the lading.

SD: see *sight draft.*

S&D: see *special and differential treatment.*

SDP: the international standard code for the currency of Sudan—the Sudanese pound.

SDRs: see *Special Drawing Rights.*

SEA: see *Single European Act.*

seabridge: a service offered by some ocean carriers where cargo moving between East Asia and Europe is taken by one ship from the exporting nation to a U.S. port for relay, from the same port, to destination. The merchandise moves under a single through bill of lading.

sec: (French) in foreign exchange, outright.

secondary boycott: the boycotting of a company because of its business dealing with a firm in a boycotted country.

second flag carriage: the shipment of merchandise aboard a vessel that flies the flag of the importing nation.

second of exchange: a duplicate copy of a draft.

second-tier subsidiaries: subsidiaries that report to a tax-haven subsidiary.

Secretariats: see *North American Secretariats.*

sectional tariff: a tariff containing two or more sections that, in accordance with the rules of the tariff, may or may not be used alternately. See *alternative tariff.*

Section 15: a provision of the U.S. Shipping Act of 1916 permitting ocean carriers to enter into agreements to eliminate rate and service competition between them.

Section 201 of the Trade Act of 1974: a provision requiring the U.S. International Trade Commission to investigate petitions filed by domestic industries or workers claiming injury or threat of injury due to expanding imports. Investigations must be completed within six months. If such injury is found, restrictive measures may be implemented. Action under Section 201 is allowed under the escape clause, GATT Article XIX. See *escape clause; Section 301 of the Trade Act of 1974.*

Section 203 of the Trade Act of 1974: provides that should the ensuing inquiry establish that an import complaint is valid, relief can be granted in the form of adjustment assistance, or temporary import restrictions in the form of tariffs, quotas, or other nontariff barriers. May last not longer than five years except if extended by the President for another three years.

Section 232 of the Trade Act of 1974: authorizes the Department of Commerce to determine whether items imported into the U.S. threatens national security. Allows the President to adjust imports; the President must inform Congress within 30 days of administration's decision.

Section 301 of the Trade Act of 1974: legislation whose purpose is to eliminate unfair foreign government trade practices that adversely affect U.S. trade and investment. Its scope includes U.S. trade in both goods and services. Under Section 301, the President must determine whether the alleged practices are unjustifiable, unreasonable, or discriminatory and burden or restrict U.S. commerce. The law directs that, if the President determines the action is appropriate, he shall take all appropriate and feasible action within his power to secure the elimination of the practice. Amended in 1988, Section 301 of the U.S. Omnibus Trade Act of 1988. See *Super 301.*

Section 337 of the Trade Act of 1974: requires investigation of unfair practices in import trade; prohibits unfair competition and unfair importing practices and sales of products in the U.S. that threaten a domestic industry, prevent the creation of such an industry, or restrain U.S. trade and commerce; also prohibits infringement on intellectual property.

sectoral reciprocity: where governments share mutual concessions with each other in the trade of items in particular industrial areas. See *reciprocity*.

sectoral trade agreement: a bilateral or multilateral agreement limited to trade exchange relations for a specific industry.

sector specific: pertains to a particular industry sector.

seignorage: a government's profit from issuing coins at a face value higher than the metal's intrinsic worth. It is the difference between the bullion price and the face value of the coins made from it. A principle of the Bretton Woods conference of the 1940s.

SEK: the international standard code for the currency of Sweden—the Swedish krona.

SELA: see *Latin American Economic System*.

selectivity: trade actions that countries take against a certain nation or select groups of countries—as opposed to taking actions on a nondiscriminatory, most-favored-nation (MFN) basis affecting all nations.

selling period: the period allotted to a selling group of an issue to complete its goal.

selling rate: the rate at which a bank or financial institution is willing to sell foreign exchange, or to lend funds.

semi-privatization: a portion of a particular industry owned and operated as government-owned business transferred to private hands.

senior: a debt ranking ahead of other debts.

senior-commercial officer: the senior person, assigned to a U.S. Embassy, responsible for economic and business matters within a specific nation.

sensitive products: products in sectors that are deemed highly vulnerable to injurious import competition.

September 11, 2001: terrorists destroy the World Trade Towers in New York City, and a portion of the U.S. Pentagon in Washington, D.C., with a significant loss of lives and negative impact on U.S. and world trade.

series: options of the same class having the same exercise price and expiration time.

service exports: international received earnings other than those derived from the exporting of tangible items. Cf. *service imports.*

service imports: international paid earnings other than those derived from the importing of tangible items. Cf. *service exports.*

service operations management: international operations management decisions and processes involving the creation of intangible services.

services: there are currently no international rules governing services, making it difficult and sometimes impossible for companies to provide a host of services in other nations. Services are a critical and complex issue when negotiating free trade accords between nations. Targets for negotiations will be laws or regulations that impede the provision of services, including licensing and registration requirements that effectively exclude foreign providers, or that bar individuals from providing professional services. Negotiations must seek to remove these barriers and create strong and transparent rules for the provision of services.

Any unified market necessitates the free movement of goods, persons, services, and capital. The continued maintenance of barriers perpetuates the costs and disadvantages of separate national markets for services. There is a need for substantial action, for being free to establish a branch in another nation has little meaning if local regulations that prevent the branch from operating on an equal footing with local competitors.

Some nations maintain requirements that foreign firms establish a local commercial presence before they can conduct business in that nation. Such requirements protect local firms from foreign competition across the border. Under free trade accords, companies from either nation could be exempt from this requirement, except where licensing regulations would require some form of commercial presence.

The list of services goes beyond the above to include cultural, historic, language, artistic, religious, and so on. The complexities are considerable as additional countries participate in international trade accords. Each nation, possessing differing expressions of service for its population, will be forced to reexamine and often surrender traditional schemes in favor of those regulated by any trade accord. See *services (North American Free Trade Agreement)*.

services (North American Free Trade Agreement): under the NAFTA, all three countries must provide to services companies of other NAFTA countries the better of national treatment or most-favored-nation (MFN) treatment. NAFTA specifies each country's obligations regarding movement of business persons to allow service professionals equal access to all three markets. Citizenship requirements to do business are eliminated in the professional services sector. In addition, professional licensing bodies in the three countries will work to eliminate burdensome and discriminatory licensing requirements. Exceptions (or reservations) to these obligations can be temporary or permanent, but must be explicitly stated in the Annexes to the agreement.

NAFTA covers service sectors such as: banking, securities, insurance, enhanced telecommunications, advertising, road and rail transportation, tourism, bus services, professional services (such as legal service, accounting, and engineering), educational service, environmental services, management consulting, computer services, construction, specialty air services, and publishing firms (except in Canada). Civil aviation is completely excluded from the agreement.

NAFTA ensures U.S. firms nondiscriminatory access to virtually all service sectors, vastly improving accessibility to the Canadian and Mexican service market, eliminating existing federal barriers and removing citizenship or permanent residency requirements for licensing of professional service providers. See *services*.

services account: part of a country's current account that measures travel and transportation, tourism, and fees and royalties.

Service Supply License: a validated export license issued by the U.S. government to a U.S. or foreign company, authorizing the export of spare and replacement parts to controlled purchasers abroad who originally purchased U.S. equipment under license.

settlement: actual payment of currency in a foreign exchange transaction.

settlement day: the deadline by which a purchaser of stock must pay for what has been bought and the seller must deliver the certificates for the securities that have been sold. The settlement day is usually the fifth business day following the execution of an order.

settlements bank: see *Bank for International Settlements.*
Seychelle ruppee: monetary unit of Seychelles.
SFSC: see *shared foreign sales corporation.*
SGD: the international standard code for the currency of Singapore—the Singapore Dollar.
shadow economy: an underground economy that has similar features to a black market. Cf. *gray market; informal economy.*
shared foreign sales corporation (SFSC): a foreign sales firm consisting of more than one and fewer than 25 unrelated exporters.
shekel: the official currency of Israel, resurrected from Biblical times, that replaced the pound in 1980. Sometimes spelled Shequel, Shequalim.
shequel (Shequalim): see *shekel.*
Sherman Act: 1890 U.S. legislation barring contracts, combinations, or conspiracies in restraint of trade, making it a violation of law to monopolize, attempt to monopolize, or to conspire to monopolize any trade in interstate or foreign commerce.
shield: in the U.S., an interagency export control unit that reviews licenses involving chemical or biological weapons.
shilling: the monetary unit of Kenya, Somalia, Tanzania, and Uganda.
shipbroker: an agent for the ship owner or shipping firm handling cargo space, insurance, freight, passengers, ship chartering, etc.
ship demurrage: a charge for a delay to a steamer beyond a stipulated period. See *demurrage.*
shipment:
(1) delivery and transport of items by a carrier.
(2) a collection of items that are transported as a unit.
(3) merchandise sent to a manufacturer to be processed, or items sent from the manufacturer to a wholesaler or retailer.
shipment consolidation: a type of consolidation. See *make bulk.*
shipper: the consignor of cargo, usually an exporter.
shipper's agent: an international service facilitating intermediary who buys cargo capacity on transport modes and then resells this to shippers.
shipper's cooperative: an incorporated firm, owned by shippers of goods and run on a not-for-profit basis, that performs the functions of a foreign freight forwarder.
shipper's credit agreement: the arrangement by which specified

conferences grant terms, usually 14 to 30 days, for freight services performed by member carriers.

Shipper's Declaration of Canadian Origin: a document completed by a shipper, indicating that the items described originated in Canada, and as exported items to the United States, are Canadian articles according to the Free Trade Agreement's rules of origin. See *rules of origin*.

Shipper's Export Declaration: a form required by the U.S. Treasury Department and filled out by a shipper, showing the value, weight, consignee, destination, etc., of shipments to be exported.

shipper's load and count: a statement denoting that the contents of a car were loaded and counted by the shipper and not checked or verified by the transportation line.

Shipping Act of 1916: see *Section 15*.

shipping conference: synonymous with *conference*.

shipping order: instructions of shippers to carrier for forwarding all goods; usually the duplicate copy of the bill of lading.

shipping permit: authority issued by a transportation line permitting the acceptance and forwarding of goods against the movement of which an embargo has been placed.

shipping tolerances: a means of exporting additional quantities or dollar values that are listed on the individually valid export license, without amending the license or applying for a new one. Should the commodity be reported in dollar value, there is no tolerance.

shipside: alongside a vessel.

ship's manifest: see *manifest*.

shogun bond: a bond not denominated in yen but issued in Japan by foreign concerns.

shogun lease: an international lease denominated in Japanese yen, which offers a very attractive long-term financing.

shogun security: security issued and distributed in Japan by a non-Japanese firm and denominated in a currency other than the yen.

shortage: a deficiency in quantity shipped.

short dates: standard Euro-deposit periods from overnight up to three weeks.

short-form bill of lading: a bill of lading that, unlike the conventional, or long-form, document, does not include the full terms and conditions of transport but refers to them.

short of destination: before reaching the final destination.

short of exchange: the position of a foreign exchange trader who has sold more foreign bills than the quantity of bills he or she has in possession to cover the sales.

short selling: selling a stock and purchasing it at a lower price to receive a profit. Cf. *bear squeeze.*

short supply: commodities that are subject to export controls to protect a domestic economy from the excessive drain of scarce materials and to lower the serious inflationary impact of satisfying overseas demand. Often used in the petroleum industry.

short-term sales: sales on terms of up to one year for capital equipment and machinery, up to 180 days for all other products.

short ton: 2,000 pounds. Cf. *long ton.*

SHP: the international standard code for the currency of St. Helena—the St. Helena pound.

shrink wrapping: a method, used by export packers, of enclosing an entire palletized load of crates or boxes with strong, flexible, plastic film to immobilize the items, thereby facilitating handling and movement as well as minimizing the risk of damage.

shut-out: leaving behind certain cargoes when too much cargo arrives for a given ship sailing. Usually the cargo is not turned away on delivery to the pier but is accepted by the carrier and dispatched aboard a subsequent ship.

SIBOR: see *Singapore Interbank Offered Rate.*

SIC: see *Standard Industrial Classification.*

SICE: synonymous with *Foreign Trade Information System.*

side agreements (North American Free Trade Agreement): to get NAFTA successfully voted upon in Congress in the fall 1993, President Clinton promised to add two or three side agreements to the accord, covering workers' rights, environmental standards, and import surges. Side agreements (or supplemental agreements) can serve a host of purposes, including helping to ensure: (a) that the enforcement of domestic environmental laws and workplace standards and requirements will be strengthened; (b) that no nation will lower labor or environmental standards, only to raise them. All states or provinces can enact more stringent measures; (c) that the process of consultation, evaluation, and dispute settlement will be open to the public; (d) that the safeguards protecting against import surges will be upgraded; (e) that due process rights will be extended to environmental and labor matters, and that administrative remedies, or court procedures, will be available to the parties involved. This provision helps to ensure that labor and environmental standards will be enforced; (f) that commissions on labor and the environment will be established to evaluate and settle disputes; (g) that enforcement proceedings will have strength to ensure compliance; (h) that Mexico and the United States will undertake joint measures to address and fund border cleanup and infrastructure development; and (i) that cooperation on the environment and labor will be established, allowing for the continual upgrading of standards throughout North America signed in Mexico, Canada, and the United States on Sept. 14, 1993. Synonymous with *supplemental agreements*. See *NAFTA-plus; North American Free Trade Agreement; North American Secretariats; snap-back*.

sight draft (SD): a draft that is payable on presentation to the drawee. Cf. *time draft*.

signature service: provides continuous responsibility for the custody of merchandise in transit; a signature is needed from each person handling the shipment.

SII: see *Structural Impediments Initiative*.

silent partner: an individual who gives funds for a business partnership but takes no part in the management of the firm.

similitude: a practice of customs authorities when an imported article does not conveniently fit into any existing classification within the customs tariff. Articles are compared with similar articles listed in the tariff for justification.

Singapore: See *U.S.-Singapore Free Trade Agreement*.

Singapore Declaration: see *Association of South-East Asian Nations*.

Singapore dollar: monetary unit of currency in Singapore.

Singapore Interbank Offered Rate (SIBOR): the rate of interest at which Asian currency units in Singapore are prepared to lend funds to first-class banks.

Single Act: synonymous with *Single European Act*.

Single Administrative Document (SAD): one of the measures implemented by the European Community's Commission on January 1, 1988, that affects trade. It is a new trading form, replacing an array of others, to be used for the export, import, and transit of goods over Community frontiers. The 12 member states of the European Community agreed to abolish SAD from January 1, 1993. After this date, therefore, moving goods across the European

Community requires no customs documentation. Although third-country exporters will still have to file the SAD on shipments to the European Community, once shipments enter the Community, no additional customs documentation is required en route to other EC member states. The SAD is still used for the declaration of exports from EC states to third countries. See *Europe Without Frontiers; Single Customs Document; TARIC.*

single buyer policy: Export-Import Bank of U.S. policy providing insurance coverage to the U.S. exporter for short- and medium-term credit sales to a single buyer.

single consignment waybill: a waybill used for a single shipment.

single-country mutual funds: mutual funds investing in the securities of a single nation.

single currency: a reference to efforts to establish a uniform currency throughout the European Union. It was projected that a single currency throughout the Union and the elimination of the cost of changing currencies while traveling or conducting business within the Union would save from $18 to $26 billion a year. The use of a single currency would spur an accumulated gain of 5 percent in the Union's gross domestic product.

Over the longer term, by reducing the uncertainty associated with currency fluctuations, investors would accept a lower rate of return on their funds. That, in turn, would boost investment and growth. The main costs of a single currency would be the loss by member states of the ability to devalue their currency or guide national interest rates.

By 2004, 12 of the 15 EU nations had adopted the Euro—a single currency. The United Kingdom, Denmark, and Sweden chose to remain outside the Euro-zone. See *European Monetary Institute; Euro-zone; Maastricht Treaty.*

single customs document: a replacement for the sheaf of some 70 different forms once used in trade across the European Union's internal borders. The single customs document, effective 1988, attempts to harmonize and simplify trade procedures and alleviate the long delays at Europe's border crossings. Less data has to be reported than was required in the past. The document has been adapted to the planned computerization of customs administration and, with some modifications, is used in trade with third countries. See *CACTUS; CADDIA; Harmonized System; Single Administrative Document.*

single declaration form: statement where the importer reports import shipments scheduled to arrive, in order to request insurance coverage.

Single European Act (SEA): a major amendment to the European Union's Treaty of Rome. It was designed to facilitate the adoption of the White Paper measures within its time frame. It adapted the then Community's procedures for decision making and increased the scope for a type of majority (as opposed to unanimous) voting in the Council of Ministers. Effective July 1, 1987, it was ratified by the Parliaments of all member states to improve significantly the institutional system and set new objectives for the Community, notably the completion of the internal market, "an area without internal frontiers in which the free movement of goods, persons, services and capital is ensured in accordance with provisions of this Treaty" by 1992 and the strengthening of economic and social cohesion, without internal frontiers. On January 1, 1993, the SEA went into effect, with the majority of the 285 original European Community directives having been approved, although not all implemented by individual countries. Fiscal and trade barriers for the most part were eliminated between the 12 nations of the European Community. See *internal market; White Paper.* Synonymous with *Single Act.*

single market: see *Single European Act.*

sinking fund: includes the amount of cash, the ledger value of live securities of other companies, and other assets that are held by trustees or by the carrier's treasurer in a distinct fund for the purpose of redeeming outstanding obligations.

Sistema Económico Latinoamericano (SELA): see *Latin American Economic System.*

SITC: see *Standard International Trade Classification.*

sliding scale tariff: a customs tariff in which rates of duty vary according to the price of a given import. Usually, as the price of the merchandise falls, the duty is lowered.

SLL: the international standard code for the currency of Sierra Leone—the leone.

slot charter: the chartering of a vessel by a fleet operator for a particular voyage when none of the ships in the fleet is available.

small- and medium-sized businesses: enterprises of every size—and their workers—will gain from more open trade with Mexico, but NAFTA presents special opportunities for small- and medium-sized business that have been a fertile source of economic growth and new jobs in the United States for the last decade.

By their very nature, small businesses are poised for success in Mexico. Quick reaction times, minimal bureaucracies, and flexibility allow smaller entities to compete in a market that has its own unique challenges. Learning the ropes is going to be critical to any company's success. But fairer trade laws and the superior performance of U.S. workers and technology provide a healthy competitive edge in opening a fast-emerging market. See *small- and medium-sized enterprises.*

small- and medium-sized enterprises (SMEs): in general, SMEs have between 50 and 500 workers, and not more than one-third of the capital is held by a larger company. SMEs enjoy important advantages, including dynamism, flexibility, and readiness to innovate. They also provide an important source of employment creation, and contribute to regional activity. Disadvantages of SMEs are primarily due to size and include keeping track of legislative developments, administrative and fiscal procedures, and tariff barriers; the use of new technology and modern administrative methods remain insufficient. Access for SMEs to major research-and-development programs is usually very limited. See *small- and medium-sized businesses.*

Small Business Act of 1953: as amended, requires executive agencies to place a fair proportion of their purchases with small-business concerns (business located in the United States which makes a significant contribution to the U.S. economy and is not dominant). See *North American Secretariats; side agreements; small- and medium-sized enterprises.*

SMEs: see *small- and medium-sized enterprises.*

Smithsonian Agreement: an agreement of December 1971 by the Group of Ten setting new par values for the dollar (10 percent devaluation). It raises permissible margins of exchange rate fluctuation from ± 1 percent to ±2.25 percent.

Smoot-Hawley Act: 1930 U.S. legislation considered today to be the most protectionist U.S. legislation ever passed by Congress and ratified by the President. By 1932, import duties reached a record high 31 percent in the United States, thus hastening the collapse of global trade and contributing significantly to the Depression of the 1930s. See *column 1 rates; column 2 rates; protectionism; Reciprocal Trade Agreement Program*. Synonymous with *Tariff Act of 1930*.

snake:

(1) a stable exchange rate with 2.25 percent margins. It acts as a step in stabilizing exchange rates.

(2) an international agreement of most Western European nations, linking the currencies of these nations in an exchange rate system. The signatories have agreed to limit fluctuations in exchange rates among their currencies to 2.25 percent above or below set median rates. The snake was designed to be the first stage in forming a uniform Common Market currency. Members maintain fairly even exchange rates among themselves by buying or selling their currencies when the rates threaten to drop or rise beyond the 2.25 percent limits. See *European Monetary System; Maastricht Treaty; swap*.

snap-back: NAFTA contains a bilateral safeguard that permits a snap-back provision to pre-NAFTA tariff rates for up to three years, or four years for extremely sensitive products, should increases in imports of Mexican goods cause or threaten to cause serious injury to U.S. firms or workers. See *free riders; global safeguard; worker protection*.

social charter: international trade agreements are beginning to incorporate rights for workers that have been traditionally neglected. Within the European Union, such rights have been recently debated by leaders of the 15 EU participating nations.

A social charter defines the fundamental social rights of citizens, in particular workers, whether employed or self-employed. Its major principles relating to the rights might include: (a) the right to freedom of movement; (b) the right to employment and remuneration; (c) the right to improved living and working conditions; (d) the right to social protection; (e) the right to freedom of association and collective bargaining; (f) the right to vocational training; (g) the right of men and women to equal treatment; (h) the right to worker information, consultation, and participation; (i) the right to health and safety protection at the workplace; (j) the right to protection of children and adolescents; (k) the rights of elderly persons; (1) the rights of disabled persons.

A social charter calls for rules guaranteeing minimum social conditions and pay for foreign workers on temporary contracts in NAC member nations. Without legislation, firms could use subcontracting to undercut wage levels and conditions set by law. Such so-called social dumping could give companies unfair advantage.

It is more particularly the responsibility of trading partners, in accordance with national practices, notably through legislative measures or collective agreements, to guarantee the fundamental social rights in this Charter and to implement the social measures indispensable to a strategy of economic and social cohesion. See *social dumping.*

social dumping: the shifting of investment and jobs from countries with high wages and high standards to countries with lower wages and less-stringent labor rules. Often results in unemployment in the more developed nations, and might be carefully monitored by trading partners and, if not justified, it would be eliminated voluntarily. For example, to escape unions or environmental regulations alone is not acceptable. However, when a company is forced to decide on bankruptcy, at one extreme, versus shifting to a less costly labor region for survival, this may be a justifiable reason for the action. See *informal economy; North American Secretariats; social charter.*

Society for Worldwide Interbank Financial Telecommunications (SWIFT): an organization having a system for the electronic transfer of funds among participating banks in Europe and North America; organized in 1973 with operations commencing in 1977.

sode-no-shita: (Japanese) an under-the-table payment.

SOEs: see *state-owned enterprises.*

soft currency: the funds of a country that are controlled by exchange procedures, thereby having limited convertibility into gold and other currencies. See *convertibility.*

soft loan: a government or multilateral development bank loan with a long repayment period; given at below-market interest.

softs: (slang) tropical commodities, such as coffee, sugar, and cocoa; sometimes also grains, cotton, and orange juice.

soft terms: financial aid made available at less than the cost of its provision by the donor nation.

sogo shosha: a Japanese general trading company; imports and exports merchandise. See *general trading companies.*

Sol: the monetary unit of Peru.

Solomon Island dollar: monetary unit of Solomon Islands.

Somali shilling: monetary unit of Somalia.

SOS: the international standard code for the currency of Somalia—the Somali shilling.

sound money: a nation enjoying a rock-solid currency with sound money is a government able to sustain popularity. It attracts capital back home from overseas bank accounts. It spurs economic growth and the means to uphold sweeping economic reforms, as well as balancing the budget. In addition, potential investors are reassured by the firmness of sound money, especially when it is fully convertible.

Sound money would always be the primary objective of a nation's leadership, as it is the foundation for all economic productivity. Confidence in a nation's currency is essential in establishing a thriving economy. It brings both political and popular support to a government, as it indicates the termination of currency maneuvering as a part of the power and corruption of its leaders. Sound money increases the value of privatization, and the private arena is encouraged and motivated to invest.

sourcing strategy: strategy that a firm follows in buying materials, components, and final products; can be from domestic and foreign locations and from inside and outside the firm.

Southern Africa(n) Development Community (SADC): formerly South African Development Coordination Conference; a regional economic pact of 1992, composed of Angola, Botswana, Lesotho , Malawi, Mozambique, Namibia, Swaziland, Tanzania, Zambia, and Zimbabwe; focuses on development.

In April 2004, SADC included Angola, Botswana, Democratic Republic of Congo, Lesotho, Malawi, Mauritius, Mozambique, Namibia, Seychelles, South Africa, Swaziland, Tanzania, Zambia and Zimbabwe. The driving force remains South Africa; purports to ensure economic well-being, improve living standards via increased economic cooperation and trade.

South African Development Coordination Conference (SADCC): a regional trade organization formed in 1979 purporting to standardize development programs within the area to reduce dependence on South Africa. Members included Angola, Botswana, Lesotho, Malawi, Mozambique, Swaziland, Tanzania, Zambia, and Zimbabwe;

headquartered in Gabarone, Botswana. Reorganized with name change. See *Southern Africa(n) Development Community (SADC)*.

South American Free Trade Agreement: a twenty-first-century proposed free trade pact between the Southern Cone Common Market (Mercosur) and the Community of Andean Nations (CAN). See *Andean Pact; Community of Andean Nations; Mercosur; Southern Cone*.

South American Quadripartite Common Market: see *Mercosur*.

Southern Common Market (SCM): synonymous with *Mercosur*.

Southern Cone: the countries of Argentina, Chile, Paraguay, and Uruguay, whose combined form resembles an ice cream cone. See *Mercosur*.

Southern Cone Common Market Treaty: see *Mercosur*.

South Pacific Bureau for Economic Cooperation: see *SPEC*.

South Pacific Commission: see *SPC*.

Sovereign Compulsion Doctrine: synonymous with *Doctrine of Sovereign Compliance*.

sovereign credit: borrowing guaranteed by the government of a sovereign nation.

sovereign debt: the debt of a national government. See *sovereign risk*.

sovereign immunity: the immunity of a government from lawsuits in the courts of its own country or other countries unless it submits voluntarily. Such immunity is particularly likely to exist if the government limits itself to "governmental" functions as opposed to economic and trade ones.

sovereign ratings: the assessment of an independent agency of the likelihood that a sovereign government borrower will default on its debt obligations.

sovereign risk: a risk that a foreign government will default on its loan or fail to honor business obligations because of a shift in national policy. It results in banks usually observing limits on the amount of lending they will make to any one government whose borrowing is guaranteed by that government.

sovereign risk limit: a bank's limit on the amount of money in the Euromarkets that it is prepared to lend to one government.

sovereignty risk: see *sovereign risk*.

space arbitrage: simultaneous purchase and sale of identical or similar assets in geographically-separated markets.

space charter: an arrangement where a carrier or shipper commits to a ship owner to fill a specified portion of the ship's hold, on one or more trips.

SPC (South Pacific Commission): established in 1947 by Australia, France, the Netherlands, New Zealand, the United Kingdom, and the United States to deal with mutual economic issues of nations with dependent territories in the region.

SPEC (South Pacific Bureau for Economic Cooperation): formed in 1971 to aid the economic development of smaller nations who trade closely with Australia and New Zealand. Tariff reductions have been negotiated, and there have been attempts to standardize trade and customs of its members, who are Australia, Cook Islands, Fiji, Nauru, New Zealand, Tonga, and Western Samoa.

special and differential treatment (S&D): a provision allowing exports from developing countries to receive preferential access to developed markets without having to accord the same treatment in their domestic markets.

special buyer credit limit: a credit insurance limit on a specified buyer to cover an exporter's shipments when a discretionary credit limit is insufficient.

special cargo policy: a marine cargo policy issued to cover a particular shipment.

special customs invoice: a statement, required by some foreign countries, describing a shipment of merchandise and indicating information such as the consignor, the consignee, and the shipment value.

Special Drawing Rights (SDRs): since 1969, a low-interest-bearing issue of reserve assets by the IMF. The creation of artificial (but gold-backed) international liquidity is intended to make a global money supply independent of the size of the U.S. balance-of-payments deficit and international gold production. SDRs were established at the Rio de Janeiro conference of 1967.

special economic zones: foreign trade zones within the Newly Independent States of the former Soviet Union.

special license: allows for the export of pre-approved commodities and/or technical data to preapproved consignees or destinations.

special service tariff: a tariff containing charges and/or rules governing switching, storage, demurrage, reconsignment, diversion, and so on.

Special 301:   pursuant to section 182 of the U.S. Trade Act of 1974, as amended by the Omnibus Trade and Competitiveness Act of 1988, the U.S. Trade Representative (USTR) must identify those countries that deny adequate and effective protection for intellectual protection rights or deny fair and equitable market access for persons or deny fair and equitable market access for persons that rely on intellectual property protection. Countries that have the most onerous or egregious acts, policies, or practices and whose acts, policies, or practices have the greatest adverse impact, actual or potential, on the relevant U.S. products must be designated as priority foreign countries.

Priority foreign countries are potentially subject to an investigation under section 301 conducted on an accelerated time frame. The USTR may not designate a country as a priority foreign country if it is entering into good-faith negotiations, or marking significant progress in bilateral or multilateral negotiations to provide adequate and effective protection of intellectual property rights.

The USTR must decide whether to identify countries each year within 30 days after issuance of the National Trade Estimate report. In addition, the USTR may identify a trading partner as a priority foreign country or remove such identification whenever warranted.

The USTR has created a "priority watch list" and "watch list" under Special 301. Placement of a trading partner on the priority watch list or watch list indicates that particular problems exist with respect to the protection or enforcement of intellectual property rights or market access for persons relying on intellectual property. Countries placed on the priority watch list are the focus of increased bilateral attention concerning the problem areas. See *National Trade Estimate Report on Foreign Trade Barriers (NTE); Super 301.*

species flow mechanism: see *Hume's species flow mechanism.*

specifications: in foreign exchange, the conditions and terms used with bills of exchange drawn under letters of credit.

specific commodity rate: rate applicable to some classes of commodities; frequently, items moving in volume shipments.

specific duty: customs duty based on weight, quantity, or other physical characteristics of imported items.

specific tariff: a tariff based on a fixed amount charged per unit of the goods imported.

speculation: the attempt to engage in a transaction where there is a degree of foreign exchange risk, with the objective of making a profit as a consequence of the risks surrounding the transactions.

spillover effect: where a company has a marketing program in one nation yet creates an awareness of the items in another nation; occurs when the medium chosen for use in the program is seen on a cross-national basis.

split shipment: shipment divided by the exporting transport firm from the ports where the goods are shipped.

split spread: in the Eurocredit, different spreads over LIBOR for different periods of the credit.

sporadic dumping: the random selling of exported items in foreign markets at a lower price than domestically, thus getting rid of a temporary surplus. The rationalization given is that the excess was "unforeseen." See *dumping.*

spot:
(1) the price at which a currency or physical commodity is selling for immediate or very near delivery (two days in the case of foreign exchange).
(2) the availability of a vessel for charter in the near vicinity of a charterer's requirements for tonnage.

spot against forward: a central bank's limit to control the extent to which banks can hold net current assets in foreign currency against net forward liabilities. The purpose is to prevent a buildup of foreign currency assets outside the official reserves.

spot charger: a ship prepared to begin loading immediately on fixing of the charter.

spot deal: synonymous with *spot exchange transaction.*

spot exchange: the purchase or sale of foreign exchange for immediate delivery.

spot exchange rate: the price of one country's currency in terms of another country's currency that is effective for immediate (today) delivery.

spot exchange transaction: a purchase or sale of foreign currency for ready delivery. In practice, market usage normally prescribes settlement within two working days. For purposes of the International Monetary Fund's Articles of Agreement, the term excludes transactions in banknotes or coins. Synonymous with *spot deal*.

spot/fortnight: see *spot/next*.

spot market: a market in which commodities are sold for cash and delivered quickly. See *destination clauses*.

spot/next: a purchase of currency on Monday for settlement on Thursday, transacted at the exchange rate for spot delivery plus an adjustment for the extra day. The adjustment is referred to as the spot/next (delivery a week after spot). "Spot/fortnight" refers to delivery a fortnight (two weeks) after spot.

spot price: price quotation for immediate sale and delivery of a commodity or currency.

spot rate: exchange rate quoted for immediate delivery, normally within two business days.

spout trimmed (SPT): a ship loaded with a bulk cargo that has been trimmed or leveled off, such as grain commodities, which are often loaded by a spout or chute, thus ensuring level loading.

spread:
(1) a larger than normal difference in currency exchange rates between two markets.
(2) the difference between what is asked for a foreign currency and what is bid for it.

spread effect: the positive impact of international trade on the domestic economic of the trading countries.

SPT: see *spout trimmed*.

square position:
(1) the position in a currency that is balanced, i.e., neither long nor short.
(2) the situation of a trade of foreign currency reflecting that sales of a given currency and purchases of that same currency are in harmony during any accounting period.

squeeze:
(1) the situation when interest rates are high and money is difficult to borrow.
(2) an official action by a central bank or government to lower supply in order to force up the price of money. See *bear squeeze*.

SRG: the international standard code for the currency of Surinam—the Surinam guilder.

Sri Lanka rupee: monetary unit of Sri Lanka.

STABEX: see *Stabilization of Export Earnings.*

Stabilisation des Exports: see *Stabilization of Export Earnings.*

Stability and Growth Pact of the European Union: See *European Union—Stability and Growth Pact.*

stabilization: purchasing and selling of a nation's own currency to protect its exchange value.

Stabilization Fund: a 1934 fund created as a result of the dollar devaluation, with $2 billion to stabilize exchange values of the U.S. dollar for dealing in foreign exchange and gold and to invest in direct government obligations. Under the Bretton Woods Agreement, much of the assets of the Fund were used to contribute to the International Bank for Reconstruction and Development and the International Monetary Fund.

Stabilization of Export Earnings (STABEX): STABEX was introduced in the Lomé I Convention by the European Community. It purports to counter some of the effects on economics and producers' incomes in the African, Caribbean, and Pacific (ACP) states of sudden drops in earnings caused either by fluctuations in world prices or by sharp variations in production resulting from climatic or other conditions. Under Lomé II, the scheme was extended financially. It also lowered the thresholds of dependence on previous exports and relations to earnings over the previous four years, with special concessions to the least-developed, landlocked, and island countries. The Community compensates ACP countries for earnings losses from exports on a range of primary commodities. The transfers (the payments made under STABEX) are used to finance the interests of diversification, in other sectors. A similar system, SYSMIN (the System for Mineral Products) provides financing to help ACP countries maintain their mineral export potential. See *Lomé Conventions.*

stable-valued currency: funds that are stable and come from a country with a low inflation rate.

standard: a document, approved by a recognized body, that provides, for common and repeated use, rules, guidelines, or characteristics for goods or related processes and production methods, or for services or related operating methods, with which compliance is not mandatory. It may also include or deal exclusively with terminology, symbols, packaging, marking, and labeling requirements as they apply to a good, process, or production or operating method.

Standard Industrial Classification (SIC): a standard numerical code system used by the U.S. government to classify products and services. See *International Standard Industrial Classification*.

Standard International Trade Classification (SITC): a system adopted by the United Nations in 1950 as a basis for reporting commodity detail in foreign trade statistics; member nations were urged to make use of it.

standardization: differing technical regulations and national standards in the nations are a very real obstacle to the creation of an effective and unified hemispheric market. The effects are widespread, adding real costs and wasting valuable resources, restricting consumer choice and impeding the full competitive potential.

The existence of different technical regulations in individual Union nations forces manufacturers to concentrate on national rather than trade-wide markets. It is necessary to have different production lines for the different nations, and so the opportunities to reap economies of scale are reduced. As a result, costs are higher, often as much as 10 percent of total product costs.

Greater standards compatibility removes structural barriers to markets and increases the competitiveness of manufacturers. Standards define certain technical specifications which products must meet in order to establish an acceptable level of safety. At the same time, differing standards can have several implications for an exporter. The exporter may have to make costly modifications to a product in order to bring it into line with the other nation's standards. The item may have to be submitted to a laboratory for testing, which can be lengthy and costly. Inexperienced exporters may simply forego the sale, concluding that it is not worth the time and expense. Standards must not create unnecessary barriers to trade.

These barriers result from differences between trading nations in three types of arrangements: (a) Technical regulations lay down the legal requirements enacted by the national parliaments mainly in the interests of health and safety and the environment. Often these regulations refer to standards. (b) Standards are produced by private national standardization bodies. While they are only voluntary codes, they often assume a quasi-legal status because of their use as a reference in technical regulations or insurance claims. (c) Type testing and certification is used to check that a product complies either with voluntary standards or with statutory regulation. A typical problem is that one nation does not recognize another's type test, thus causing the costs and delays of additional testing.

To move toward the goal of removing technical barriers to trade, a new approach to standardization is called for, which would be based on the following principles: (a) a distinction will be drawn in future internal market initiatives between what is essential to standardize legislation and what may be left to be standardized by hemisphere bodies; (b) legislative standardization will in the future be restricted to laying down health, safety, and other essential requirements; (c) industrial standardization will be achieved by the elaboration of standards throughout nations that trade with each other. See *harmonization; ISO; ISO 9000; standards.*

standard money: the money or unit of money on which a particular nation's monetary system is based.

standard rate: in international shipping, a rate established via direct routes from one point to another in relation to which the rates via other routes between the same points are made.

standard route: the line or lines that maintain standard rates.

standards:

(1) harmonization or mutual recognition, which removes technical barriers to trade, irrespective of whether these involve technical rules, standards, tests, or certificates.

(2) technical specifications as defined by a standards code. Germany has some 20,000 standards, France 8,000, and Britain 12,000.

(3) see *CE mark; European Committee for Standardization; harmonization; ISO 9000; mutual recognition; standardization; Standards Code.*

Standards Agreement: see *Standards Code.*

Standards Code: signed by 39 nations in 1988 and initiated on January 1, 1980, as part of an international trade accord evolving from the Tokyo Round of GATT. Its chief purposes are to ensure that national administrative practices related to standards per se do not serve as trade barriers, and to regulate the manufacturing of industrial items to accepted internationally established benchmarks. Synonymous with *Agreement on Technical Barriers to Trade.* See *mutual acceptance of test data.*

standard shipping note: a form used in the United Kingdom to cover deliveries to the docks.

standards (North American Free Trade Agreement): NAFTA preserves each country's right to establish and enforce its own product standards, particularly those designed to promote safety and protect human, animal, and plant life, and health and the environment. Each country has the right to choose the levels of health, safety, and environmental protection it considers appropriate and to conduct assessments of risk and inspections to ensure that those levels are achieved. NAFTA makes clear that a country may establish standards-related measures that achieve a level of protection higher than that afforded by international standards.

At the same time, NAFTA requires that measures to ensure compliance with national standards be carried out in a manner that is timely, predictable, and nondiscriminatory. To this end, NAFTA requires that new standards be developed in an open manner, with ample opportunity for public notice and comment. NAFTA encourages consultation and cooperation on standards as a way to avoid differences that can lead to trade disputes. However, when one NAFTA country believes that another's health or environmental standards-related measure is inconsistent with NAFTA, the burden of proof is on the country challenging the measure to demonstrate the inconsistency. See *ISO 9000; standardization.*

standby agreement: see *standby credit.*

standby credit: form of quasi guarantee opened through a buyer's bank in favor of a seller, allowing them to trade on an open-account basis, with the standby credit lying dormant in the background as security for the seller in case of need.

standstill: an agreement reached during the Uruguay Round. Under the standstill commitment, all participants agreed (a) not to take any restrictive or distorting measures inconsistent with the GATT; (b) not to take any trade restrictive or distorting measure in the legitimate exercise of GATT rights (e.g., safeguard action) that goes beyond that which is necessary to remedy specific situations; and (c) not to take any trade measures in such a manner as to improve their negotiating positions. This commitment only applies to measures taken after the issuance of the Ministerial Declaration on September 20, 1986.

starburst: deposit of dirty money made in a bank with standing instructions to wire it on in small, random fragments to hundreds of other bank accounts around the world.

state aid: see *subsidies.*

state-controlled trading companies: synonymous with *state trading enterprises.*

stateless: (slang) currency deposited in banks outside the country of original issue and used by the banks like any other exchange medium.

State subsidies: see *subsidies.*

State Trading Country: synonymous with *State Trading Nation.*

state trading enterprises: entities established by governments to import, export, and/or produce certain products. Contracting parties are required to operate these entities on the basis of commercial considerations. Synonymous with *state-controlled trading companies.*

State Trading Nation (STN): in Canada, a sovereign entity dependent on government-owned enterprise for foreign trade. Synonymous with *State Trading Country.*

static effects of integration: shifting of resources from inefficient to efficient companies as trade barriers fall.

station order car: a car loaded by a shipper with several less-than-carload shipments destined for different points along the same route, the shipments being loaded in destination order.

statism: where a government plays an active role in running and regulating the economy of the nation, with the compliance of its citizens.

statutory notice: the period of time required by law for giving notice of changes to be made in tariffs.

Statutory Rate of Duty: the rate of duty on the given product specified by the Smoot-Hawley Act. The rates established by this act are applied to column 2 countries (those that do not enjoy most-favored-nation status). Lower rates of duty, as reflected in column 1 of the Tariff Schedules, have been negotiated under the authority of various acts in response to duty reductions on U.S. merchandise. See *column 1 rates, column 2 rates; Smoot-Hawley Act.*

STD: the international standard code for the currencies of Sao Tome and Principe—the dobra.

steamship conference: a group of steamship operators who operate under mutually agreed on freight rates.

steamship freight contract: an agreement between steamship and shipper for space and rate.

stem: subject to availability of cargo.

sterilized intervention: intervention in the foreign exchange market while retaining the existing money supply.

sterling (Stg):

(1) the currency of Great Britain. The unit is the pound sterling.

(2) bills of exchange that are drawn in terms of British currency.

(3) silver that is at least 222 parts out of 240 of pure silver, and no more than 18 parts of an alloy.

sterling balances: sums held in sterling by foreign nations and private persons.

sterling-based gold standards: gold standard in which the British Pound is commonly used as an alternative means of settlement of transactions.

sterling bloc: the British Commonwealth nations that fixed the price of Sterling used in foreign exchange; results in trade within the bloc being favored.

Sterling Exchange: a check or bill denominated in pounds sterling and payable through a bank in the United Kingdom.

sterlizing gold: a strategy for preventing newly imported gold from expanding the credit base of a nation. One method is to have the U.S. Treasury pay for the gold with a draft on a commercial bank in which it has an account, rather than drawing upon the Federal Reserve System and then issuing gold certificates. Cf. *primacy*.

stevedore: the person having charge of the loading and unloading of vessels.

Stg: see *sterling*.

STN: see *State Trading Nation*.

Stockholm Convention (Treaty): the Convention that established the European Free Trade Association on May 3, 1960. See *European Free Trade Association*.

stop charge: a charge imposed by a carrier for stopping en route prior to final destination to deliver part of the shipment.

stoppage in transit: under certain conditions, a shipper's right to halt delivery of a shipment that is already in transit, when payment has not been made. Cf. *carrier's lien*.

stopping in transit: the stopping of freight traffic at a point located between the point of origin and destination, to be stored and reforwarded at a later date.

storage: a tariff charge made on property stored.

storage in transit: stopping of freight traffic at a point somewhere between the point of origin and the destination, to be stored and reforwarded at a later date.

store door delivery: the movement of goods to the consignee's place of business, customarily applied to movement by truck.

stowed: cargo packed and secured for a trip.

straight bill of lading:

(1) a bill of lading that cannot be negotiated, identifying the individual who is to receive goods.

(2) a nonnegotiable bill of lading in which the goods are consigned directly to a named consignee.

(3) a variation of a uniform straight bill of lading.

(4) see *air waybill; order bill of lading.*

straight letter of credit: a letter of credit in which the insurer (e.g., a bank) recognizes only the person named (e.g., an exporter) as authorized under the letter to draw drafts for advances to the named person for whose benefit the letter is issued.

strategic alliance: an agreement between firms that is of strategic importance to one or both firms' competitive viability.

strategic clusters: a means of identifying competitors by the grouping of international firms of overlapping activities within geographic proximity to their primary customers and to their supply networks.

strategic intent: a goal giving an organization cohesion over the long term while it builds global competitive viability.

street name: in international trade, synonymous with *name.*

strong dollar: dollar that can be exchanged for a large amount of foreign currency.

Structural Adjustment Loan Facility: established in 1980 by the World Bank to enhance a country's long-term economic growth through financing projects.

Structural Funds: see *Single European Act.*

Structural Impediments Initiative (SII): bilateral negotiations of September 1989 between the United States and Japan with the specific objective of asking Japanese officials to alter aspects of their economy to assist in the United States' negative trade balance. The Japanese government agreed to deregulate its distribution system and to relax restrictions over time on the establishment of large stores, to allow foreign retailers to open outlets in Japan.

subcontract production: a component of a type of countertrade transaction where a U.S.-origin article usually involves a direct commercial arrangement between the U.S. manufacturer an d a foreign producer, but does not necessarily involves a license of technical information.

subject stem: a vessel that has been chartered for business but without confirmation that the cargo will be available on time.

subject to license being granted: a provision in a vessel offer or charter party that makes the charter conditional on governmental approval.

subsidiaries: firms owned by another firm, which is referred to as the parent company.

subsidiarity:

(1) the principle that member nations of an international economic community, rather than the administrative and larger encompassing body, should be responsible for changes that such members can effectively and efficiently accomplish.

(2) the principle that anything that can be better done at a local, state, or regional level should not be done at a Union level. Following the Danish people's referendum rejection of the Maastricht Treaty in June 1992, the 12 European Union leaders meeting for their regular, biannual summit in Lisbon reiterated their support for subsidiarity, to allay concerns about overly centralized bureaucracy in Brussels. Their plan was to make a separate declaration on subsidiarity rather than change the Maastricht Treaty. See *Maastricht Treaty.*

subsidiary board of directors: board that oversees and monitors the operations of a foreign subsidiary.

subsidiary detriment: the depriving of a subsidiary of a potential advantage so that the multinational organization as a whole may enjoy a greater advantage.

subsidies: financial encouragements provided, usually by a government(s), to support businesses. Such subsidies can take the form of lower taxes, tax rebates, or direct payments. There are two general types: (1) export subsidy: a benefit conferred on a firm by the government that is contingent on exports. (2) domestic subsidy: a benefit not linked to exports, conferred by the government on a specific industry or enterprise or group of industries or enterprises. See *Common Agricultural Policy; export subsidies.*

Subsidies and Countervailing Measures Code: see *Subsidies Code.*

Subsidies Code: a code of subsidies conduct negotiated at the GATT Tokyo Round of 1973-1979. The Code established a mechanism for one nation to inform another of its intention to levy a countervailing duty and to conduct appropriate hearings. See *Tokyo Round.* Synonymous with *Subsidies and Countervailing Measures Code.* Formerly known as the *Agreement on Interpretation and Application of Articles VI, XVI, and XXIII of the General Agreement on Tariffs and Trade.*

subsidy: see *subsidies.*

subsidy discrimination: see *General Agreement on Tariffs and Trade; Super 301.*

subsidy, levy: see *levy subsidy.*

substantial or essential part doctrine: where the imported item lacking a significant part or component essential to its basic function cannot be classified for tariff purposes in the same category as the finished item.

substantial supplier: a country that supplies approximately 10 percent of the trade in a given item imported to a second country.

Substitution Account: a plan of the *International Monetary Fund* that would allow dollar holders to exchange them for assets denominated in a basket of currencies known as Special Drawing Rights. The objective of the plan is to reduce the $500 billion to $1 trillion floating around the world, and thus cut the gyrations of the international financial and trading markets. See *Special Drawing Rights.*

substitution drawbacks: provision allowing domestic merchandise to be substituted for merchandise that is imported for eventual export, thus allowing the U.S. firm to exclude the duty paid on the merchandise in costs and in sales prices.

sucre: the monetary unit of Ecuador.

Sudanese pound: monetary unit of Sudan.

sufferance wharf: a pier where items can be stored temporarily, exempt from taxes or duties, while awaiting transport to another destination or clearance through customs.

summary of international transactions: a revised version of the balance-of-payments accounts, adopted in 1976, that purports to deemphasize the concept of balances and to encourage more detailed assessment of international transactions.

superdeductive: a U.S. Customs procedure in determining the deductive value of merchandise for assessment of ad valorem duties; an alternative valuation method that allows a deduction from the value of the items, for duty purposes, of further processing within the United States prior to sale to the ultimate buyer. Synonymous with *further processing method*.

super gold tranche: the automatic drawing right with the IMF represented by reductions below 75 percent of quota of the Fund's holdings of a given currency. The member country can obtain funds if needed to the full amount represented by the super gold tranche without incurring any conditions. See *International Monetary Fund*.

superimposed clause: a notation on the face of a bill of lading indicating a defect in the cargo or its means of transport.

Super 301: the colloquial name for section 301 of the U.S. Omnibus Trade Act of 1998, which enlarges the authority of the U.S. Trade Representative (USTR). The USTR must identify "priority" foreign countries whose trading practices are thought to curb American exports unfairly. Such identification starts a 36-month negotiating clock, at the end of which there is either agreement to lift the barriers or possible U.S. retaliation.

U.S. trade policy is marked by quotas and preferential rules, often the result of diverse political pressures. The United States still views such actions as necessary evils rather than parts of a coherent strategy to secure stability and growth. Section 301 was the statute under U.S. law dealing with "unfair" foreign trade practices and the measures to be taken to combat them. Major changes were made to Section 301 under the Trade Act of 1988. The Trade Act also introduced a new procedure, the so-called "Super 301," whereby the USTR was required to identify priority unfair trade practices and priority countries and initiate Section 301 investigations with a view to negotiating an agreement to eliminate or compensate for the alleged foreign practice. If no agreement was reached with the foreign country concerned, then unilateral retaliatory action had to be taken. See *General Agreement on Tariffs and Trade; local content; Omnibus Trade Act; retaliation; Special 301; Telecommunications Trade Act of 1988; Trade Act of 1974; Trade Expansion Act of 1962*.

Superzone: see *European Free Trade Association*.

supplemental agreements: synonymous with *side agreements*.

supplier credit: finances available to an exporter by a method that involves the buying, by a financial institution, of promissory notes that are issued in deferred payment to an exporter by a foreign buyer. Credit is extended to it by purchasing the notes at a discount prior to the date of maturity by the institution that runs the risk of collecting on them when they mature.

supply access: assurances that importing nations will, in the future, have fair and equitable access at reasonable prices to raw materials and other needed imports.

supply chain: coordination of materials, information, and funds from the initial raw materials supplier to the ultimate consumer.

supranational organizations: agencies or institutions that plan and implement programs that go beyond or transcend established borders or spheres of influence held by separate nations.

SUR: the international standard code for the currencies of Byelorussian SSR, Ukrainian SSR, Russia—the rouble.

surcharge:
(1) a charge above the usual or customary charge.
(2) an added tax placed on imported goods.

surety:
(1) an individual who agrees, usually in writing, to be responsible for the performance of another on a contract, or for a certain debt or debts of another individual.
(2) a guarantee including a provision for payment of any increased duty that can be found after the merchandise has cleared customs.

surety bond: a guarantee included with each entry, posted with customs to cover any potential duties, taxes, and penalties that may accrue.

surges: see *North American Free Trade Agreement*.

Suriname gulden: monetary unit of Suriname.

surveillance: the monitoring of trade practices to help ensure that governments implement their obligations under trade agreements. One of the objectives of the negotiating group on Functioning of the GATT System (FOGS) is to improve GATT, now WTO, surveillance of trade policies and practices of Contracting Parties.

surveillance body: a body created by the Uruguay Round Trading Negotiating Committee (TNC) to monitor implementation by contracting parties of their standstill and rollback commitments. The surveillance body will transmit its records and reports to the

TNC, so that the latter may conduct periodic evaluations of the implementation of the commitments.

survey: in shipping, the examination of a ship or its cargo by an independent third party for the purpose of establishing condition.

suspense account: an account in which to record an incomplete transaction awaiting additional information or audit for its adjustment, such as interline freight claims paid prior to settlement with the participating lines.

SVC: the international standard code for the currency of El Salvador—the El Salvador colon.

Sveriges Investeringsbank: the Swedish bank (state-owned) that provides, inter alia, finance for exports on commercial terms.

SWAD: saltwater arrival draft.

swap:
(1) to exchange or barter.
(2) an arrangement between central banks of two countries for standby credit to facilitate the exchange of each other's currencies. See *credit.*

swap arrangements: synonymous with *central bank swaps.*

swap contract: an agreement between two parties for the exchange of a series of cash flows, one representing a fixed rate and the other a floating rate. See *interest rate swap.*

swap credits: standby credits established on a reciprocal basis from time to time among major central banks and the Bank for International Settlements, enabling the central bank of a nation to settle a debit balance in its international account with another participating nation by using the latter nation's currency in place of resorting to foreign exchange.

swap curve: a series of fixed rate bids for swaps of various maturities against the standard swap floating rate, six-month London Interbank Offer Rate (LIBOR).

swap line: a mutual credit facility whereby a government buys a foreign currency from a foreign central bank, uses the foreign currency held by foreigners, and agrees to sell the foreign currency back to the foreign central bank at the end of three or six months.

swapped deposit: synonymous with *bank swap.*

Swedish krona: monetary unit of Sweden.

SWIFT: see *Society for Worldwide Interbank Financial Telecommunications.*

swing: in a bilateral trade agreement, the leeway provided for the mutual extension of credit.

Swiss franc: the monetary unit of Switzerland, divided into 100 rappen/centimes.

switch-arrangements: a type of countertrade, where unused purchase rights under government-to-government trade on unwanted merchandise received by a firm in a countertrade transaction are sold at a discount to buyers for cash.

switching: synonymous with *switch trading*.

switch trading: a form of countertrade transaction, where the exporter and importer agree to exchange items and funds that may be "trapped" under bilateral contractual constraints (e.g., shifting items to a different nation importer when the importer is short of U.S. dollars). Synonymous with *switching*.

switch-transactions: see *switch trading*.

syli: the monetary unit of Guinea.

symmetry problem: the problem of devising an international monetary system that will produce equal pressure on countries to revalue or devalue to correct balance-of-payments surpluses or deficits.

syndicate:
(1) an association of two or more individuals, established to carry out a business activity. Members share in all profits or losses in proportion to their contribution to the resources of the syndicate.
(2) a group of investment bankers and securities dealers who, by agreement among themselves, have joined together for the purpose of distributing a new issue of securities for a corporation.

syndicated Euroloans: bank lending of Eurocurrency deposits to nonfinancial funds deficit units.

syndicated loan: a loan in which a number of banks around the world participate.

syndicate release: synonymous with *syndicate termination*.

syndicate termination: the point at which syndicate restrictions are terminated; occurs when a security involved is trading or expected to trade at over its initial offering price. This does not necessarily apply in the Eurobond market. Synonymous with *syndicate release*.

SYP: the international standard code for the currency of Syrian Arab Republic—the Syrian pound.

Syrian pound: monetary unit of Syria.

SYSMIN (the System for Mineral Products): see *Stabilization of Export Earnings*.

System for Mineral Products (SYSMIN): see *Stabilization of Export Earnings*.

systematic risk: the risk of default resulting from a breakdown in the global payments mechanism.

SZL: the international standard code for the currency of Swaziland—the lilangeni.

T

T/A: in shipping, transatlantic.

TAA:

(1) see *Trade Adjustment Assistance.*

(2) see *Trans-Atlantic Agreement.*

Table of Denial Orders (TDO): alphabetical listing of U.S. companies and individuals who may be disbarred with respect to either controlled commodities or general destination exports.

tackle clause: synonymous with *overside delivery clause.*

Taha (Taka): monetary unit of Bangladesh.

take-and-pay contract: a guarantee to purchase an agreed amount of a product or service, provided that it is delivered. Cf. *take-or-pay contract.*

take-or-pay contract: an unconditional guarantee to purchase an agreed amount of the product or service whether or not it is delivered. Cf. *take-and-pay contract.*

takeover regulations: standardized regulations governing takeover bids, which usually apply to large, public limited firms.

Talc: monetary unit of Samoa.

TALISMAN (Transfer Accounting, Lodgment for Investors, Stock Management for Jobbers): The U.K. stock exchange's computerized delivery and settlement system for stocks and shares.

Tanker Owners Voluntary Agreement on Liability for Oil Pollution (TOVALOP): the means by which tanker owners provide compensation on a worldwide basis for damage to the environment, and cleanup costs resulting from oil spills from their tankers. Cf. *Contract Regarding a Supplement to Tanker Liability for Pollution.*

tankoku: Japanese government paper with maturities of six months. Introduced in February 1986 as a means of assisting to smooth out refunding of huge amounts of previously issued 10-year government bonds.

Tanzanian shilling (shilingi): monetary unit of Tanzania.

tap line: a short railroad usually owned or controlled by the industries which it serves.

tare weight:

(1) the weight of a container and packaging materials without the weight of the goods it contains. Cf. *gross weight.*

(2) as applied to a carload, the weight of the car exclusive of its contents.

TARIC: a simplified customs procedure implemented by the European Community on January 1, 1988. It is a new Union tariff applying to goods whose description is harmonized in this way. See *BTN; NIMEXE; Single Administrative Document.*

tarif douanier commun: (French) *common customs tariff.* The tariff between the EU and others.

tariff:

(1) a schedule of taxes on items imported or exported. In the United States, tariffs are imposed on imported goods only.

(2) a published schedule showing the rates, fares, charges, classification of freight, rules, and regulations applying to the various kinds of transportation and incidental services.

(3) see *tariff schedule (North American Free Trade Agreement).*

tariff, alternative: see *alternative tariff.*

tariff, commodity: see *commodity tariff.*

tariff, common: see *common tariff.*

tariff, general: see *general tariff.*

tariff, mileage: see *mileage tariff.*

tariff, scientific: see *scientific tariff.*

tariff, sectional: see *sectional tariff.*

tariff, specific: see *specific tariff.*

Tariff Act of 1930: see *Smoot-Hawley Act.*

tariff anomaly: situation where the tariff on raw materials into the country, regardless of its legitimacy, restricts, impedes, or even forbids the free flow of goods and services.

tariff barrier: a financial restriction imposed by a nation on merchandise being imported into the country, regardless of its legitimacy, that forbids, restricts, or impedes the free flow of goods and services. Cf. *quota.* See *tariff.*

tariff bindings: the agreement by contracting parties to maintain the duty rates on specified goods at negotiated levels or below; provided for in GATT, now WTO. See *bindings.*

tariff escalation: the common situation whereby raw materials and less-processed goods are generally dutied at lower rates than more-processed versions of the same or derivative goods. For instance, the import duty in most countries is generally higher for petrochemicals than for the petroleum and other raw materials necessary for their production. It is argued by primary-commodity-exporting nations that this situation confers a higher degree of protection for the processing industries of importing countries than nominal tariff rates would suggest.

tariffication: to convert quotas and other restrictions to tariffs that would be reduced over time. For example, nations with strict import controls would start with prohibitive tariffs of several hundred percent. Tariffication includes provisions to guarantee a minimum level of imports at reduced tariff rates. Its intent is to permit high tariffs to shrink over a period of time and thus have a minimum tariff quota expanded. Synonymous with *tariffy*.

tariff quota: a tariff that has a lower rate until the end of a specified period or until a specified amount of the commodity has been imported. At that point, the rate increases. See *quota*.

tariff rate: the charge rate or schedule established by the rating organization that has jurisdiction over a given class and territory (e.g., a schedule of freight rates for transporting different items to various cities).

tariff schedule: a full listing of the items that a country may import and the import duties applicable to each item.

tariff schedule (North American Free Trade Agreement): the last three of the five volumes of the *North American Free Trade Agreement* deal with tariff schedules for Canada, for Mexico (written in Spanish), and for the United States. They are each sublabeled Annex 302.2 and concern themselves with tariff eliminations, mostly commencing with January 1, 1994, until January 1, 2003. Duties on many goods (Category A goods) were eliminated and are now duty-free, effective January 1, 1994. Category B were removed in five equal annual stages beginning on January 1, 1994, and became duty-free on January 1, 1998, while Category C goods were removed in ten equal annual stages beginning on January 1, 1994, and became duty-free, on January 1, 2003. See *Tariff-Shift Rule (North American Free Trade Agreement)*.

Tariff Schedules of the United States (TSUS): the official U.S. government nomenclature describing and classifying imported goods and the duty rates applicable to those goods. The TSUS nomenclature is unique to the United States. However, this nomenclature was replaced in 1988 by a new internationally agreed tariff nomenclature called the Harmonized System. See *Harmonized System*.

Tariff-Shift Rule (North American Free Trade Agreement): under NAFTA there are two types of rules of origin; both require substantial North American processing but they measure it differently. Under the Tariff-Shift Rule, all non-NAFTA inputs must be in a different tariff classification from the final product. The rules state the level of tariff-shift required. The rules may require that the non-NAFTA input be in a different Harmonized System chapter, heading or tariff item number. Most goods are subject to this rule. See *tariff schedule (North American Free Trade Agreement)*.

tariff surcharges: an import tax that is usually assessed at a flat rate over and above whatever duties are assessed.

tariff suspension:
(1) the withdrawal of a tariff.
(2) concessions by a nation that there is a reasonable basis for claiming injurious action by a foreign exporter to the allegedly injured nation. The legitimation for tariff suspension is a section in an international agreement referred to as an escape clause. See *escape clause*.

tariff wall: a protective tax barrier used by a protectionist government to: (a) shield domestic industry from global competition; (b) generate government revenues by taking imports; and (c) create an incentive for direct investment by overseas exporters to overcome the tariff wall.

tariff war: a form of competition between nations as evidenced by tariff discrimination of various forms. See *retaliatory duty*.

tariffy: synonymous with *tariffication*.

taxation: see *double taxation*.

tax credit: authorization for a domestic firm to lower taxes payable by the amount of taxes paid to the government in another country.

tax-equalization system: system for ensuring that an expatriate's after-tax income in the host country is comparable to what the person's after-tax income would be in the home country.

tax haven:
(1) a nation that offers low tax rates and other incentives for corporations of other countries.
(2) a nation having little or no taxation on foreign-source income or capital gains, that becomes a source of hiding for those who wish to shelter their funds.

tax haven subsidiary: a division of a multinational firm based in a
tax haven nation so as to
minimize the firm's income tax obligations.

tax incentives: the tax holidays that less-developed countries
sometimes give firms and their managements if they will invest in
the nation, or that developed countries sometimes give to induce
investment in an area of high unemployment or to encourage
exports.

Tax Relief: a July 1985 European Community Amending Directive
allowing tax reliefs on the importation of goods in small consignments of a noncommercial character within the Community. It
would increase the amount of tax relief (from VAT and excise
duties) available on small consignments of a noncommercial character sent from one private individual to another across internal
EC frontiers. This is to keep the real value constant while taking
cost-of-living increases into account.

tax treaty: a treaty between two countries in which each nation
usually lowers certain taxes on residents who are nationals of the
other, and the nations agree to cooperate in tax matters, such as
enforcement.

TCI: see *Third-Country Initiative.*

TDO: see *Table of Denial Orders.*

technical approval: a favorable technical assessment of a product's
fitness for use for a particular purpose, based on its meeting the
specific requirements.

technical barrier to trade: a specification that sets forth characteristics a product must meet (such as levels of quality, performance, safety, or dimensions) to be imported.

technical regulation: a document that lays down goods characteristics or their related processes and production methods, or services characteristics or their related operating methods, including
the applicable administrative provisions, with which compliance is
mandatory. It may also include or deal exclusively with terminology, symbols, packaging, marking, or labeling requirements as they
apply to a good, process, or production or operating method. Cf.
technical specification.

technical specification: lays down goods' characteristics or their
related processes and production methods, or services characteristics or their related operating methods, including the applicable

administrative provisions. It may also include or deal exclusively with terminology, symbols, packaging, marking, or labeling requirements as they apply to a good, process, or production or operating method. Cf. *technical regulation*.

technical transfer: the making available of know-how (patents, operational systems, scientific equipment) from one trading partner to another.

technological dualism: the presence in a nation of industries that use modern technology while others employ more primitive techniques.

technology transfer: transfer, often to another country, of systematic knowledge for the manufacturing of a product, for the application of a process, or for the rendering of a service; does not extend to the mere sale or lease of goods.

TED:
(1) see *Tenders Electronic Daily*.
(2) see *Treasury Bills and Eurodollar Deposits*.

TEE: see *Trans-Europ-Express*.

Telecommunications Trade Act of 1988: federal legislation that is analogous to Super 301 in that it is based on the identification of priority countries for negotiation and the threat of unilateral action (e.g., termination of trade agreements) if U.S. objectives are not met. These objectives are "to provide mutually advantageous market opportunities" to correct imbalances in market opportunities and to increase U.S. exports of telecommunication products and services. See *Super 301*.

telegraphic transfer (T/T): the use of cable or telegraph to remit funds. Physical money does not move, but instead the order is wired to the cashier of a firm to make payment to an identified person or firm.

temporal method: translating financial statements of a foreign affiliate of a U.S. company.

temporary admission of goods (North American Free Trade Agreement) Article 305:
1. Each Party shall grant duty-free temporary admission for: (a) professional equipment necessary for carrying out the business activity, trade, or profession of a business person who qualifies for temporary entry pursuant to Chapter Sixteen (Temporary Entry for Business Persons); (b) equipment for the press or for sound or

television broadcasting and cinematographic equipment; (c) goods imported for sports purposes and goods intended for display or demonstration; and (d) commercial samples and advertising films, imported from the territory of another Party, regardless of their origin and regardless of whether like, directly competitive, or substitutable goods are available in the territory of the Party.

2. Except as otherwise provided in this Agreement, no Party may condition the duty-free temporary admission of a good referred to in paragraph 1 (a), (b) or (c), other than to require that such good: (a) be imported by a national or resident of another Party who seeks temporary entry; (b) be used solely by or under the personal supervision of such person in the exercise of the business activity, trade, or profession of that person; (c) not be sold or leased while in its territory; (d) be accompanied by a bond in an amount no greater than 110 percent of the charges that would otherwise be owed on entry or final importation, or by another form of security, releasable on exportation of the good, except that a bond for customs duties shall not be required for an originating good; (e) be capable of identification when exported; (f) be exported on the departure of that person or within such other period of time as is reasonably related to the purpose of the temporary admission; and (g) be imported in no greater quantity than is reasonable for its intended use.

3. Except as otherwise provided in this Agreement, no Party may condition the duty-free admission of a good referred to in paragraph 1(d), other than to require that such good: (a) be imported solely for the solicitation of orders for goods, or services provided from the territory, of another Party or non-Party; (b) not be sold, leased, or put to any use other than exhibition or demonstration while in its territory; (c) be capable of identification when exported; (d) be exported within such period as is reasonably related to the purpose of the temporary admission; and (e) be imported in no greater quantity that is reasonable for its intended use.

temporary denial order: a U.S. Department of Commerce order for export enforcement for up to 180 days to prevent imminent violation of the export regulations.

temporary entry for business persons (North American Free Trade Agreement): under NAFTA, four categories of business persons from NAFTA countries will be allowed temporary admission to other NAFTA countries. These include: "business visitors" engaged in international business activities related to research and design, growth, manufacture and production, marketing, sales, distribution, after-sales services and other general services; "traders" who carry on substantial trade in goods or services between their country and the country they wish to enter and "investors" seeking to commit a substantial amount of capital in the country; "intra-company transferees" (i.e., executives, managers, and specialists employed by a company operating in a NAFTA country); and certain "professionals" who meet minimum educational requirements or possess alternative credentials and who plan to be active in business at the professional level. There are limits on the number of professionals that may enter the United States from Mexico annually. NAFTA provides entry only for individuals who do not intend to establish permanent residence, and does not impair the normal functioning of U.S. immigration measures.

Entry into the territory of a Party by a businessperson of another Party without the intent to establish permanent residence.

Article 1601—General Principles Further to Article 102

(Objectives) this Chapter reflects the preferential trading relationship between the Parties, the desirability of facilitating temporary entry on a reciprocal basis and of establishing transparent criteria and procedures for temporary entry, and the need to ensure border security and to protect the domestic labor force and permanent employment in their respective territories.

Article 1602—General Obligations

1. Each Party shall apply its measures relating to the provisions of this Chapter in accordance with Article 1601 and, in particular, shall apply expeditiously those measures so as to avoid unduly impairing or delaying trade in goods or services or conduct of investment activities under the Agreement.

2. The Parties shall endeavor to develop and adopt common criteria, definitions, and interpretations for the implementation of this Chapter.

Article 1603—Grant of Temporary Entry

1. Each Party shall grant temporary entry to business persons who are otherwise qualified for entry under applicable measures relat-

ing to public health and safety and national security, in accordance with this Chapter.

2. A Party may refuse to issue an immigration document authorizing employment to a business person where the temporary entry of that person might affect adversely: (a) the settlement of any labor dispute that is in progress at the place or intended place of employment; or (b) the employment of any person who is involved in such dispute.

3. When a Party refused pursuant to paragraph 2 to issue an immigration document authorizing employment, it shall: (a) inform in writing the business person of the reasons for the refusal; and (b) promptly notify in writing the Party whose business person has been refused entry of the reasons for the refusal.

4. Each Party shall limit any fees for processing applications for temporary entry of business persons to the approximate cost of services rendered.

Article 1605—Working Group

1. The Parties hereby establish a Temporary Entry Working Group, comprising representatives of each Party, including immigration officials.

2. The Working Group shall meet at least once each year to consider: (a) the implementation and administration of this Chapter; (b) the development of measures to further facilitate temporary entry of business persons on a reciprocal basis; (c) the waiving of labor certification tests or procedures of similar effect for spouses of business persons who have been granted temporary entry for more than one year under Section B, C, or D of Annex 1603; and, (d) proposed modifications of or additions to this Chapter.

Some union and citizen groups argues that NAFTA ignores the vital issue of immigration except for provisions that allow temporary entry of business and professional persons. They claim that by further freeing corporate mobility while continuing to restrict labor mobility, NAFTA enhances the power of corporations over communities and workers. They state that rules are set in place in the "temporary entry" chapter that further disadvantage U.S. workers without addressing larger immigration issues. Specifically, the term "business persons" is very broad, including a wide range of workers, raising the possibility that employers may rely on this section to bring in strikebreakers. During NAFTA negotiations, the U.S. Department of Labor recommended that the U.S. Trade Representative include language to suspend the temporary entry provisions where a labor dispute was in effect; this suggestion was rejected in place of discretionary language.

Temporary Importation Under Bond (TIB): a U.S. Customs Service bond guaranteeing items imported into the U.S. by an importer temporarily and claimed to be exempt from duty. Items are to be exported within a specified time frame, often within one year from the date of importation.

temporary tariff surcharge: an increased rate of duty on imports temporarily applied, usually to assist in correcting a balance-of-payments deficit.

tender: the offer of goods for transportation, or the offer to place railcars for loading or unloading.

Tenders Electronic Daily (TED): an online database, run by the European Commission, advertising public-sector contracts open to tender.

tenor: the designation of a payment as being due at sight, a given number of days after sight, or a given number of days after date.

term documentary draft: an instrument used for the payment of exports.

term draft: a draft maturing either a certain number of days following acceptance or a certain number of days following the date of the draft. Synonymous with *time draft*.

termes de l'echange: (French) *terms of trade*—the ratio between export and import prices.

terme sec: (French) for outright transaction, in forward foreign exchange.

terminal carrier: the transportation line making delivery of a shipment at its destination.

terminal charge: a charge made for services performed at terminals.

terms currency: exchange rates that are quoted as the number of units of the terms currency per base currency.

terms of sale: synonymous with *terms of trade*.

terms of trade: the relationship between export and import price indexes. If export prices rise more rapidly, or fall at a slower pace than import prices, there is a favorable ratio. Synonymous with *terms of sale*.

territoriality: a principle drawing from the application of national law concerning intellectual, industrial, and commercial property that does not, in general terms, allow the partitioning of markets within trading nations.

territorial tax jurisdiction: the levying of tax on taxpayers while living and working in the territory of the taxing government. Income earned while living and working elsewhere is not taxed or is taxed at a lower rate.

TEU: twenty-foot equivalent units; the measure of the area of a container ship.

THB: the international standard code for the currency of Thailand— the baht.

third-country dumping: a U.S. government belief that it is threatened with material injury by being denied fair market access to a foreign nation when another nation dumps competitive items in the foreign nation. See *dumping*.

Third-Country Initiative (TCI): procedure established to aid nations to create an export control system on critical commodities; the U.S. supports this effort.

third-country nations: expatriates or natives of a country other than the home country or host country.

third flag carriage: shipment of items aboard a ship that flies the flag of neither the exporting nor the importing nation.

third window: an alternative low-interest source of lending to developing countries by the World Bank.

third world:

(1) inaccurate phrase for less-developed nations of Africa, Asia, and Latin America.

(2) underdeveloped countries, where three billion people have an annual income that is lower than the monthly income of most people in industrialized nations. The principal causes for underdevelopment in the Third World are limited or underexploited natural resources and the structure of the world economy.

Threadneedle Street: the financial area of London.

Three-Pillar Strategy: used in Canada, to describe the pivotal trade regions of the world-nations of North America; Japan and the Pacific Rim countries; and the European Community, with Germany at its nucleus.

three-point arbitrage: arbitrage based upon exploiting differences between the direct rate of exchange between two currencies and their cross-rate of exchange using a third currency.

three-tier tariff: see *two-tier tariff.*

three-way arbitrage: an exchange arbitrage among three currencies which involves beginning in one currency, passing through each of the other two, and ending in the initial currency. Synonymous with *triangular arbitrage.*

threshold value: the dollar value of contracts above which government entities are covered by the government procurement code.

through bill of lading: a bill of lading covering items that are moving from the origin point to a final location, even if they are moved from one carrier to another. Cf. *inland bill of lading; ocean bill of lading.*

throughput agreement: an agreement to put a stated amount of merchandise through a production facility in an agreed time period, or if not, to pay for the availability of the facility.

through rate: a transit rate applying on a through shipment between two points. It may be a local rate, a joint rate, or a combination of separately established rates.

TIB: see *Temporary Importation Under Bond.*

tied loan: a foreign loan limiting the borrower to spending the proceeds only in the nation making the loan.

tilt: canvas-sided, road-going trailer.

time charter: a ship charter arranged for a fixed period. Payment is either in dollars per deadweight ton per month or dollars daily, but it excludes voyage costs. The charterer has the use of the ship, with the ship owner supplying crew and provisions.

time draft: a draft that matures either a certain number of days after acceptance or a certain number of days after the date of the draft. Cf. *sight draft.* Synonymous with *term draft.*

time volume rate: the contract between a shipper of cargo and a steamship company or conference in which the shipper promises to ship a specific quantity of cargo aboard the carrier's vessels between agreed ports, during a stated time period, for a fixed sum of money per freight unit.

TIR (Transport International Routier): a carnet issued to international vehicle operators, permitting loaded vehicles to cross international borders with minimum formalities.

Title VII of the Trade Act of 1988: see *Trade Act of 1988.*

TND: the international standard code forte currency of Tunisia—the Tunisian dinar.

tokkin: special money trust accounts operated by Japanese trust banks for institutional investors.

Tokyo Round: a ministerial meeting of GATT held in Tokyo in September 1973. It initiated the process of securing an agreement on a new set of tariff cuts and other barriers to world trade. Negotiators presented a number of propositions aimed at working out a code of conduct for government purchases among the participating nations, designed to grant favored treatment to developing countries without seeking reciprocal concessions. Other codes included customs valuation, norms and standards, and import licensing practices. See *Dillon Round; General Agreement on Tariffs and Trade; Kennedy Round; Montreal Round; Standards Code; Subsidies Code; Uruguay Round.*

tolerances: see *shipping tolerances.*

ton: 2,000 pounds. See *cargo tonnage.*

ton, gross: 2,240 pounds. See *cargo tonnage.*

ton, long: 2,240 pounds. See *cargo tonnage.*

ton, metric: 1,000 kg; 2,204 pounds.

ton, net: 2,000 pounds.

ton-mile: the movement of a ton of 2,000 pounds a distance of one mile.

ton-mile revenue: the amount of freight revenue divided by the number of revenue ton-miles. Synonymous with *revenue per ton-mile.*

tonnage: the number of tons of freight handled. See *cargo tonnage.*

tonnage, net: see *net tonnage.*

tonne: 2,204 pounds. See *cargo tonnage.*

TOP: the international standard code for the currency of Tonga— the pa'anga.

Torkay (Torquay) Round: see *General Agreement on Tariffs and Trade.*

TOVALOP: see *Tanker Owners Voluntary Agreement on Liability for Oil Pollution.*

TPE: the international standard code for the currency of East Timor—the Timor escudo.

TPM: see *Trigger-Price Mechanism.*

trace: to follow the movement of a shipment.

traceability regulations: 2003 regulations of the European Union to keep close records of crop origins to help verify the labels and allow regulators to take action if a biotech strain is later found to be dangerous.

tracer:
> (1) a request on a transportation line to trace a shipment for the purpose of expediting its movement or establishing delivery.
> (2) a request for an answer to a communication, for advice concerning the status of a subject.

trackage right: the right obtained by one carrier to operate its trains over the tracks of another carrier.

tracking: a carrier's procedure for monitoring the movement intervals of shipments from point of origin to point of destination.

track storage: a charge made on railcars held on carrier's tracks for loading or unloading after the expiration of free time allowed. The charge is generally made in addition to demurrage charges.

trade: transactions involving goods and/or services from profit between legal entities. See *mergers; standardization; Trade Bill of 1988 (U.S.); trade reform.*

trade acceptance: a negotiable instrument created when a documentary draft, drawn by an exporter on the importer, is acknowledged by the importer to be the obligation to pay, in consideration for items shipped or services rendered. Synonymous with *accepted bill of exchange.*

Trade Act of 1974: authorized the U.S. to enter the Tokyo Round of Multilateral Trade Negotiations and established the Office of the U.S. Trade Representative; extended the Generalized System of Preferences to developing nations; expanded the definition of international trade to include trade in services.

> **Section 201,** an escape clause of the Act, as amended, provides a wide range of possible relief to a domestic industry when increased imports are a substantial cause of serious injury of a threat of serious injury.

> **Section 301** of the Act, as amended, is an important statutory tool that can help open foreign markets when another nation is violating a trade agreement or is engaging in other unfair practices.

> **Section 304** of the Act, as amended, allows the USTR to take actions against all countries or solely against the country under investigation. The actions taken may include: (a) suspension of trade agreement concessions; (b) imposition of duties or other import restrictions; (c) imposition of fees or restrictions concerning services; (d) entry into agreements with the subject country to eliminate the offending practice or to provide compensatory ben-

efits for the United States; (e) restriction of service sector authorizations. Synonymous with *Omnibus Trade and Competitiveness Act of 1988.* See *Section 201 of the Trade Act of 1974; Section 301 of the Trade Act of 1974; Special 301; Trade Act of 1988 (Title VII); Trade and Tariff Act; Trade Expansion Act of 1962.*

Trade Act of 1988 (Title VII): federal legislation calling for the identification of foreign countries that discriminate in government procurement against U.S. goods and services. The Office of the U.S. Trade Representative is required by section 181 of the Trade Act of 1974 and section 1304 of the Omnibus Trade and Competitiveness Act of 1988 (the 1988 Trade Act) to submit to the President, the Senate Finance Committee, and appropriate committees in the House of Representatives, an annual report on significant foreign trade barriers. Synonymous with *Omnibus Trade and Competitiveness Act.* See *Exon-Florio Amendment; Special 301; Trade Act of 1974.*

Trade Adjustment Assistance (TAA): U.S. government policy that offers aid to workers laid off because of competition from imported goods; attempts to alleviate the burden on people who are hurt by the operation of comparative advantage in international trade, which leads to contraction of some domestic industries and expansion of others.

Trade Agreement Act (1934) (U.S.): federal legislation that gave the President authority to negotiate mutual reductions of tariffs with trading partners under the most-favored-nation principle. See *most-favored nation.*

Trade Agreement Act (1979) (U.S.): federal legislation that implemented the Tokyo Round agreements. See *Tokyo Round.*

Trade and Investment Framework Agreement (U.S. and Pakistan): signed in 2003 between the United States and Pakistan. Came with a Presidential promise of $3 billion in aid for Pakistan.

Trade and Tariff Act (1984) (U.S.): federal legislation giving the President the authority to enter into negotiations with other trading nations to form free trade areas. See *Trade Bill of 1988; Trade Expansion Act of 1962.*

trade balance: see *balance of trade; favorable trade balance; invisible trade balance.*

trade balancing: see *North American Free Trade Agreement.*

Trade Bank of Iraq: created in July 2003 by the U.S. Coalition in

Iraq, making it easier for citizens and firms of Iraq to obtain credit to purchase food, commodities, materials, and other necessities for reconstruction, to ensure that creditors will be paid. The new trade bank will be liable for up to $100 million worth of credit guarantees. Funds backing the bank came from a $1.2 billion Development Fund for Iraq. A consortium of 13 international banks, led by J.P. Morgan Chase & Co., was chosen by the Coalition Provisional Authority to lead the Bank, allowing big-ticket purchases abroad. Commenced in September 2003. Initially the consortium will work with the government of Iraq, but it is expected to expand operations to handle private-sector projects.

trade barrier: an artificial restraint on the free exchange of goods and services between countries, usually in the form of tariffs, subsidies, quotas, or exchange controls. See *barriers*.

Trade Bill of 1988 (U.S.): signed by President Reagan in August 1988. It established new guidelines in critical areas:

(1) **unfair trade:** investigation of countries with "evasive" unfair trade practices; provides for retaliation if their barriers are not eliminated.

(2) **trade relief:** some protection for industries seriously injured by imports if willing to make "positive adjustment" to foreign competition.

(3) **foreign corruption:** clarification of the Foreign Corrupt Practices Act to specify what kind of knowledge makes American corporate officials liable if their foreign employees or agents are involved in bribery.

(4) **worker assistance:** expansion of programs for workers displaced by imports. Creation of a $1 billion retraining program, with most of the money going to states.

(5) **agriculture loans:** a marketing loan provision for grains and oilseeds that was activated in 1990 by a stalemate in trade liberalization talks. Farmers pay such loans at market rates, thus protecting their income while releasing crops to the market.

(6) **securities:** a ban against foreign companies serving as primary dealers in U.S. government securities unless their homeland lets American firms compete against domestic firms.

(7) **negotiating authority:** the provision of special authority to the President to complete international trade negotiations aimed at increasing markets for banking, insurance, etc., by liberalizing

rules of investment and slashing tariffs up to 50 percent.

trade bloc (trading bloc): nations that unite economically to form an international unit for trade with each other.

Trade Commission (Canada Free Trade Agreement): CFTA's central bilateral oversight body is the U.S.-Canada Trade Commission, chaired jointly by the U.S. Trade Representative and the Canadian Minister for International Trade. The Commission has established several working groups and advisory bodies to consider ways to facilitate CFTA's implementation and to examine unresolved issues as appropriate. The Commission in June 1992 instituted a quarterly review of the bilateral trade agenda as a means of further enhancing the effective management of the trade relationship between formal Commission meetings. See *North American Secretariats; Trinational Commission on Labor Standards.*

trade community: groups, firms, and people involved in the sale and transport of international trade; includes importers, exporters, manufacturers, brokers, freight forwarders, freight consolidators, and carriers.

trade concessions: see *General Agreement on Tariffs and Trade; Super 301.*

trade controls: governmental influences that are usually aimed at reducing the competitiveness of imported products or services.

trade creation: the formation of commercial transactions because of the displacement of domestic production by lower-cost imports.

trade deficit: a negative trade balance. Cf. *trade surplus.*

trade deflection: the entrance of imports into nations that offer the lowest tariffs, to avoid the higher tariffs of other member nations in international trade agreements.

trade dispute assistance: a U.S. government activity for aiding firms in adjusting trade disputes as requested by either party; intent is to open communications toward a friendly resolution of conflict.

trade diversion: situation in which exports shift to a less-efficient producing country because of preferential trade barriers. See *free trade.*

Trade Expansion Act of 1962: federal legislation permitting the President to negotiate additional tariff reductions, eliminate or reduce tariffs on items of the European Common Market, reduce tariffs on the basis of reciprocal trade agreements, and grant technical and financial assistance to employers whose business is adversely affected. Protective measures can be taken for an unlimited period of time. The Department of Commerce investigates the effects of import which threaten to impair national security either by a quantity or by circumstances. The purpose of the Act is to be a safeguard of national security. See *Buy American Act; Exon-Florio Amendment; Reciprocal Trade Agreements Program; Trade Act of 1974; Trade Act of 1988.*

trade financing: credit extended to an importer by the exporter, or a commercial bank or some other intermediary, that enables the importer to pay for the merchandise, presumably until it is sold and the importer receives funds to pay.

trade gap: the spread between the value of a nation's merchandise imports and a lesser value of item exports during a fixed time period.

trade in invisibles: (British) denoting trade in services.

trade liberalization: the lowering or elimination of tariffs and nontariff barriers between nations as the result of trade negotiations among such nations.

trademark:
(1) a word or symbol affixed to goods or their package to identify the manufacturer or place of origin.
(2) a distinctive identification of a manufactured product or of a service in the form of a name, logo, motto, etc. A trademarked brand has legal protection, and only the owner can use the mark. See *trademark (North American Free Trade Agreement).*

Trademark, Community: see *Community Trademark.*

trademark (North American Free Trade Agreement):
Article 1708—Trademarks:
1. For purposes of this Agreement, a trademark consists of any sign, or any combination of signs, capable of distinguishing the goods or services of one person from those of another, including personal names, designs, letters, numerals, colors, figurative elements, or the shape of goods or of their packing. Trademarks shall include service marks and collective marks, and may include certification marks. A Party may require, as a condition for registration, that a sign be visually perceptible.
2. Each Party shall provide to the owner of a registered trademark the right to prevent all persons not having the owner's consent

from using in commerce identical or similar signs for goods or services that are identical or similar to those goods or services in respect of which the owner's trademark is registered, where such use would result in a likelihood of confusion. In the case of the use of an identical sign for identical goods or services, a likelihood of confusion shall be presumed. The rights described above shall not prejudice any prior rights, nor shall they affect the possibility of a Party making rights available on the basis of use.

3. Each Party may make registrability depend on use. However, actual use of trademark shall not be a condition for filing an application for registration. No Party may refuse an application solely on the ground that intended use has not taken place before the expiring of a period of three years from the date of application for registration.

4. Each Party shall provide a system for the registration of trademarks, which shall include: (a) examination of applications; (b) notice to be given to an applicant of the reasons for the refusal to register a trademark; (c) a reasonable opportunity for the applicant to respond to the notice; (d) publication of each trademark either before or promptly after it is registered; and (e) a reasonable opportunity for interested persons to petition to cancel the registration of a trademark. A Party may provide for reasonable opportunity for interested persons to oppose the registration of a trademark.

5. The nature of the goods or services to which a trademark is to be applied shall in no case form an obstacle to the registration of the trademark.

6. Article 6 of the Paris Convention shall apply, with such modification as may be necessary, to services. In determining whether a trademark is well-known, account shall be taken of the knowledge of the trademark in the relevant sector of the public, including knowledge in the Party's territory obtained as a result of the promotion of the trademark. No Party may require that the reputation of the trademark extend beyond the sector of the public that normally deals with the relevant goods of services.

7. Each Party shall provide that the initial registration of a trademark be for a term of at least 10 years and that the registration be indefinitely renewable for terms of not less than 10 years when conditions for renewal have been met.

8. Each Party shall require the use of a trademark to maintain a registration. The registration may be canceled for the reason of nonuse only after an uninterrupted period of a least two years of nonuse, unless valid reasons based on the existence of obstacles to such use are shown by the trademark owner. Each Party shall recognize, as valid reasons for nonuse, circumstances arising independently of the will of the trademark owner that constitute an obstacle to the use of the trademark, such as import restrictions on, or other government requirements for, goods or services identified by the trademark.

9. Each Party shall recognize use of a trademark by a person other than the trademark owner, where such use is subject to the owner's control, as use of the trademark for purposes of maintaining the registration.

10. No Party may encumber the use of a trademark in commerce by special requirements, such as a use that reduces the trademark's function as an indication of source or a use with another trademark.

11. A Party may determine conditions on the licensing and assignment of trademarks, it being understood that the compulsory licensing of trademarks shall not be permitted and that the owner of a registered trademark shall have the right to assign its trademark with or without the transfer of the business to which the trademark belongs.

12. A Party may provide limited exceptions to the rights conferred by a trademark, such as fair use of descriptive terms, provided that such exceptions take into account the legitimate interests of the trademark owner and of other persons.

13. Each Party shall prohibit the registration as a trademark of words, at least in English, French, or Spanish, that generically designate goods or services or types of goods or services to which the trademark applies.

14. Each Party shall refuse to register trademarks that consist of or comprise immoral, deceptive, or scandalous matter, or matter that may disparage or falsely suggest a connection with persons, living or dead, institutions, beliefs, or any Party's national symbols, or bring them into contempt or disrepute.

trade mission: an organized group of businesspeople and/or government officials that visit a foreign market in search of business opportunities.

trade preferences: trade concessions, usually preferential tariff treatment, granted by a country to certain nations but not to others.

trade promotion: encouragement of the progress, growth, or acceptance of trade.

trade-promotion authority: gives the President of the United States the authority to negotiate trade accords with limited Congressional involvement, for an up-or-down vote under an expedited timeframe, without further amendment. Formerly called *fast-track authority,* changed to trade-promotion authority soon after the inauguration of President George W. Bush in 2001.

trader:

(1) anyone who is engaged in trade or commerce.

(2) one who buys and sells for his or her own account for short-term profit.

trade reform: a reference to the changes needed to open economies of nations to international trade. Nations involved in such efforts may pull away from quotas as a way of controlling imports. Quotas are usually a damaging condition of protectionism, and distort prices and permit foreigners to collect the implicit tax on consumers. Dropping quotas, even if tariffs replace them, becomes necessary. See *quota.*

Trade-Related Aspects of Intellectual Property Rights (TRIPS): as part of the Uruguay Round GATT negotiations, a proposal to further protect intellectual property rights, with all signatories of GATT having reasonable access to global technology.

Trade-Related Investment Measures (TRIMS): the subject of an Uruguay Round negotiating group. The group's function was to examine the adequacy of GATT rules with respect to investment measures that restricted or distorted trade, and, if necessary, to negotiate additional rules to cover their adverse trade effects. The United States identified 10 types of investment measures for initial examination in the negotiations, including local content and export performance requirements.

Trade Representative: See *U.S. Trade Representative.*

trade secrets (North American Free Trade Agreement):
Article 1711—Trade Secrets

1. Each Party shall provide the legal means for any person to prevent trade secrets from being disclosed to, acquired by, or used by others without the consent of the person lawfully in control of the

information in a manner contrary to honest commercial practices, in so far as: (a) the information is secret in the sense that it is not, as a body or in the precise configuration and assembly of its components, generally known among or readily accessible to persons that normally deal with the kind of information in question; (b) the information has actual or potential commercial value because it is secret; and (c) the person lawfully in control of the information has taken reasonable steps under the circumstances to keep it secret.

2. A Party may require that to qualify for protection a trade secret must be evidenced in documents, electronic or magnetic means, optical discs, microfilms, films, or other similar instruments.

3. No Party may limit the duration of protection for trade secrets, so long as the conditions in paragraph 1 exist.

4. No Party may discourage or impede the voluntary licensing of trade secrets by imposing excessive or discriminatory conditions on such licenses or conditions that dilute the value of the trade secrets.

5. If a Party requires, as condition for approving the marketing of pharmaceutical or agricultural chemical products that utilize new chemical entities, the submission of undisclosed test or other data necessary to determine whether the use of such products is safe and effective, the Party shall protect against disclosure of the data of persons making such submissions, where the origination of such data involves considerable effort, except where the disclosure is necessary to protect the public or unless steps are taken to ensure that the data is protected against unfair commercial use.

trade surplus: a positive trade balance. Cf. *trade deficit*.

trade terms: conditions employed for setting the basis for carrying out the responsibilities and obligations of buyers and sellers in international trade.

trade wars: a program involving legislation to reduce the comparative advantage of a commerce antagonist from another nation. See *comparative advantage; free trade; General Agreement on Tariffs and Trade; protectionism; Super 301*.

trading bloc: see *trade bloc*.

trading companies: firms that develop international trade and serve as intermediaries between foreign buyers and domestic sellers, and vice versa.

trading house: a business that specializes in the import and export of items from overseas nations or regions.

trading paper: certificates of deposit expected to be traded by purchasers on Euromarkets.

Trading-with-the-Enemy Act: U.S. government law that forbids U.S. firms from doing business with countries that are from time to time listed as enemies, for example, North Korea and Cuba.

traffic: persons and property carried by transportation lines.

tramp steamer:

(1) a ship not operating on regular routes or schedules.

(2) a vessel engaged in casual trade, or on charter party fixtures, each of which operates as a separate voyage and does not constitute part of a regular service.

tranche:

(1) an agreed installment of a credit or loan, which may be drawn down as required.

(2) a country's drawings from the IMF, which are made in tranches. See *super gold tranche.*

transactionability: the ease with which currency is accepted in the international arena.

transaction exposure: foreign-exchange risk arising because a company has outstanding accounts receivable or accounts payable that are denominated in a foreign currency.

transaction risk: the risk run in international trade that changes in relative currency values will cause losses.

transaction statement: a document that delineates the terms and conditions agreed on between the importer and exporter.

transaction value: the core of the Customs Valuation Code of GATT, now WTO. It is the price actually paid or payable for goods, when sold for exportation, subject to certain adjustments. It is the preferred method to use in customs valuation. See *customs valuation.*

Trans-Atlantic Agreement (TAA): legislation of 1992 that involves 11 ship lines controlling about 85 percent of the container trade between the United States and North Europe. These container ship firms banded together in this Agreement to withhold substantial cargo capacity from the North Atlantic container trade. The Trans-Atlantic Agreement is a breakthrough for international shipping conferences. It more than doubles the percentage of capacity withheld and increases the power to set prices.

Trans-Atlantic Declaration: an agreement signed by President George H. W. Bush in 1990 formalizing ties between the

European Union and the United States to meet twice a year with the President of the United States and the President of the Commission. The Secretary of State meets biannually with E.U. Foreign Ministers and the E.U. Commission, and relevant U.S. cabinet members meet biannually with the E.U. Commission.

Trans-European Networks: a July 1990 European Union report stating that if people, goods, services, and capital are to move freely throughout the Union once a single market without frontiers is established, adequate infrastructures must be made available. They must be designed from a genuinely trans-European standpoint, with national requirements in mind, and with proper coordination with other networks.

Trans-Europ-Express (TEE): connects major cities in nine European nations by a network of rapid and comfortable trains for which frontier formalities have been lowered to a minimum.

transferable letter of credit: a documentary credit under which a beneficiary has the right to give instructions to the paying or accepting bank or to any bank entitled to effect negotiations, to make the credit available to one or more third parties.

Transfer Accounting, Lodgment for Investors, Stock Management for Jobbers: see *TALISMAN*.

transfer cost: included in a licensing accord, covering (a) the variable costs to a licensor of shipping capital equipment to the foreign-based licensee, or (b) all the ongoing costs to the licensor of maintaining the agreement, including any one-time costs for shipping capital equipment to the foreign-based licensee.

transfer payment: transaction occurring between a parent firm and its subsidiaries consisting of payments of royalties payable to the parent for use of technologies, supplies, equipment, etc.

transfer price: the price charged by one segment of an organization for a product or service it supplies to another part of the same firm.

transfer pricing: see *transfer price*.

transfer risks: government policies that limit the transfer of capital, payments, production, people, and technology in and out of the country.

transit charge: a charge limited in its application to traffic that has been or will be milled, stored, or otherwise specially treated en route.

transitional measures: short-term government decisions introduced for a short time during which a trade accord is implemented.

transition strategies: strategies used to help smooth the adjustment from an overseas to a stateside assignment.

transit privilege: a service granted on a shipment en route, such as milling, compressing, or refining.

Transit Procedure: a major step toward achieving free movement of goods. A 1987 European Community Regulation abolished the requirement for a guarantee of payment of duties and fiscal charges arising from internal transit operations within the Community. However, it does not apply to high-value goods or those subject to high charges. The method used to determine whether or not a guarantee is necessary is intended to reduce the risk of incurred charges not being paid. A guarantee waiver may be granted to operators who are resident in the member state where the waiver is granted, are regular users of the Community transit system, are in a healthy financial position, are not guilty of any serious infringement of customs or fiscal laws, and undertake to pay on demand any claims made on them in respect of their transit operations.

transit rate: a rate restricted in its application to traffic that has been or will be milled, stored, or otherwise specially treated in transit.

transit tariff: a duty or tax imposed by a country on merchandise crossing its territory en route from one nation to another; abolished by most nations today.

transit zone: port of entry in a coastal nation that is experienced as a storage and distribution facility for the convenience of a neighboring nation that lacks adequate facilities and/or access to the sea.

translation (of foreign currencies): the expression of an account denominated in one currency in terms of another currency by use of an exchange rate between the two currencies.

translation exposure: measure of the net asset or liability exposure on the balance sheet of a company's foreign subsidiary; the amount which would be changed in value by a currency-value exchange.

translation loss: an accounting loss reflected in adjustments to accounting statements at the end of an accounting period to record changes in home-country currency values caused by changes in foreign-currency-based receivables, payables, or other assets or liabilities.

translation risk: the apparent losses or gains that can result from the restatement of values from one currency into another, even if there are no transactions, when the currencies change in value relative to each other; common with long-term foreign investments as foreign-currency values are translated to the investor's financial statements in its home currency.

transnationals: organizations variously called global, multinational, or worldwide firms.

transnational team: work teams composed of multinational members whose activities span many countries.

transparency: the extent to which agreements and practices are open, clear, measurable, and verifiable.

transparent: the high degree of visibility and openness to observation of commercial practices and trade measures.

transport:

(1) general: to move traffic from one place to another.

(2) European Union: anticipating the growth of international trade, the Treaty of Rome demanded the creation of a European Community common transport policy. Transport represents more than 7 percent of the Community GNP. In November 1979, the European Commission identified the alternatives in the integration at Community level covering rail, road, air, and sea transport purporting to guarantee free and easy movement of people and items throughout the Community. Driving hours per day and week were legislated in 1977. A Community driving license went into effect in 1983. In addition, the Commission proposed a Regulation permitting Community action against cargo reservation practices that destroy, damage, or threaten to damage Community interests. There is a Regulation for the principle of freedom to provide services of offshore supply services, member states' trades with third countries, the carriage of cargo wholly or partly reserved to the national flag, and, with certain specific exemptions, the carriage of passengers or goods by seas between ports in a member state, including overseas territories of that member state. The Community has adopted a two-phase approach applicable to the main transport sectors: road, sea, and air. In the

first phase, the objective was to liberalize transport services between member states. In the second phase, completed by 1992, the objective was to liberalize transport within member states by opening up the national markets to nonresident carriers. Adoption of all measures permitted the elimination of the border control of the current bilateral quotas in transport and the possibility for a transport carrier to operate in any member state, either occasionally or on a permanent basis. See *Shipping Register; Transport 2000; Truck Transit Pact.*

transportation: the movement of traffic from one place to another.

transportation costs: synonymous with *transportation rates.*

transportation rates:
(1) the rate charged for a line-haul.
(2) charges for freight, loading, unloading, insurance, and interest rates while items are in transit between importer and exporter. Synonymous with *transportation costs.*

Transport International Routier: see *TIR.*

Transport 2000: a group of independent transport policy experts commissioned by the European Union in 1990 to examine the medium- and long-term transport and communication problems within the European Union. Dubbed *Transport 2000,* the group in early 1991 reported the results of its study calling for radical action to prevent an imminent European transport crisis. The group recommended that transport be made more competitive by curtailing member state subsidiaries for weaker transport forms, by deregulating all transport sectors, and by harmonizing applicable taxes. Also, major construction projects should be designed to fill international gaps in infrastructure not at relieving congestion peaks. Also, there should be fair competition between different forms of transport. Transport 2000 also recommended the establishment of a European infrastructure fund to finance urgent construction and maintenance work through a special levy on transport users based on their energy consumption. See *transport.*

traveler's letter of credit: issued by a bank to banks in other countries, authorizing them to cash checks or purchase drafts presented by the bearer.

Treasury Bills and Eurodollar Deposits (TED): dollar-denominated time deposits at banks in Europe.

Treaty of Asunción: see *Mercosur.*

Treaty of Avoidance of Double Taxation: see *Avoidance of Double Taxation, Treaty of.*

Treaty of Nice: see *European Union—Treaty of Nice.*

Treaty of Paris: the treaty that, in 1951, established the European Coal and Steel Community, the first of the European Economic Community institutions. The founder members were Belgium, France, Italy, Luxembourg, the Netherlands, and Germany. It purported to transfer control of the basic materials of war (coal and steel) from individual governments to the ECSC High Authority. See *European Community; Treaty of Rome.*

Treaty of Rome: a reference to two treaties signed in Rome on March 25, 1957. They established the European Economic Community and the European Atomic Energy Community. Founder members were Belgium, France, Italy, Luxembourg, the Netherlands, and Germany. The Treaties identified the constitutions and tasks of the Communities. The Treaty of Rome has been amended several times. See *European Community; Treaty of Paris.*

Treaty of the Union: synonymous with *Maastricht Treaty.*

Treaty on European Union: treaty, signed in 1992, that came into effect on November 1, 1993, furthering economic and political integration of the EU's members; important provisions include the creation of an economic and monetary union, a cohesion fund, a pledge to cooperate on foreign and defense policies, and the renaming of the European Community to the European union. Often synonymous *with Maastricht Treaty.*

Treaty on Monetary and Political Union (EU): synonymous with *Maastricht Treaty.*

triad: principal trade centers of the world—the United States, Asia, and the European Union.

triad strategy: strategy proposing that a multinational corporation should have a presence in Europe, the United States, and Asia, especially Japan.

triangle trade: trade among three countries in which an attempt is made to create a favorable balance for each.

triangular arbitrage: synonymous with *three-way arbitrage.*

triangular trade: see *triangle trade.*

Triffin paradox: paradox that resulted from reliance on the U.S. dollar as the primary source of liquidity in the Bretton Woods systems. For trade to grow, foreigners needed to hold more dollars;

the more dollars they held, however, the less faith they had in the U.S. dollar, thereby undermining the Bretton Woods system.

trigger price: the world price for a commodity or product that is below that charged in the producing nation, set by an international organization.

Trigger Price Mechanism (TPM): an antidumping program formed by the United States in 1978 to protect its steel manufacturers from lower-priced imports. Should the U.S. steelmaker be threatened by steel imports, the mechanism permitted imposing a special countervailing duty, and the U.S. International Trade Commission could investigate allegations. See *snap-back*.

Trilateral Free Trade Agreement: see *North American Free Trade Agreement*.

trilateral trade: commercial trade among three countries.

Trilateral Trade Commission (TTC): under NAFTA, a commission to regularly review trade relations among Canada, the United States, and Mexico to discuss specific problems. The Trade Commission may create bilateral or trilateral panels, as appropriate, of private-sector trade experts to resolve disputes involving interpretations of the NAFTA text. Panelist selection procedures avoid national bias. Dispute resolution must be completed in no more than eight months. Nations must comply with panel recommendations or offer acceptable -compensation. If not, the affected country can retaliate by withdrawing "equivalent trade concessions." See *Countervailing Duty Investigations*.

trimmed: the leveling of a cargo following unloading.

TRIMS: see *Trade-Related Investment Measures*.

Trinational Commission on Labor Standards (NAFTA): in mid-spring 1993, the Clinton administration urged the creation of a Trinational Commission on Labor Standards with independent expert staffs and the authority to review complaints from citizens and nongovernmental organizations. It offers technical assistance in worker safety issues, and provide a clearinghouse for way to improve productivity and labor management cooperation. See *North American Secretariats*.

Tripartite agreement: accord relating to or executed by three nations, as with the *North American Free Trade Agreement*.

TRIPS: see *Trade-Related Aspects of Intellectual Property Rights*.

TRL: the international standard code for the currency of Turkey— the Turkish lira.

tropical products: one of the negotiating subgroups under the Group of Negotiations on Goods; refers to agricultural and other exports indigenous to tropical climates. This issue area is particularly important to the less-developed countries, as the negotiations are aimed at increasing market access for these products, which generally tend to originate in less developed countries.

Truck Transit Pact: the European Union reached an accord with Switzerland and Austria in October 1991 on access to their highways by trucks from EU nations. The pact, which took four years to negotiate, also set out reduced-exhaust-emission standards and urged the improvement of cargo transit facilities for upgraded international trade, such as tunnels. See *transport.*

trunk line: a transportation line operating over an extensive territory.

trust receipt: a receipt in the form of an agreement by which the party signing the receipt promises to hold the imported property received, in the name of the bank delivering the property. It further agrees that the property shall be maintained in a form that can be readily identified. If the property is further fabricated in a manufacturing process, it must be properly identified on the trust receipt. These receipts are used mostly to permit importers to obtain possession of merchandise for resale. Arrangements for this type of financing are usually completed before the issuance of letters of credit. The trust receipt is used as collateral security for the advance of funds by the bank to meet the acceptances arising out of the letter of credit. Under the terms of the agreement, the importer is required to pay to the bank proceeds from the sale of merchandise as soon as they are received. The importer is also required to keep the merchandise insured, and the bank may take possession of the merchandise at any time without due process of law.

TSUS: see *Tariff Schedules of the United States.*

TTC: see *Trilateral Trade Commission.*

TTD: the international standard code for the currencies of Trinidad and Tobago—the Trinidad and Tobago dollar.

tughrik: monetary unit of Mongolia.

Tunisian dinar: monetary unit of Tunisia.

Turkish lira: monetary unit of Turkey, divided into 100 kurus (piastres).

turnaround:

(1) the movement by a freight carrier in which the driver returns

to the point of origin following the unloading and reloading of cargo.

(2) the return to profitability of an ailing company.

turnkey:

(1) a contractual agreement between a customer and an organization to provide full services or a complete product.

(2) a business proposition wherein the seller-exporter plans, organizes, and manages all aspects of the project and hands it over to the buyer-importer following the training of local personnel.

TWD: the international standard code for the currency of Province of Taiwan—the New Taiwan dollar.

twin load: one load that extends over two or more open railcars.

twin plants: typical of some operations along the Mexican-American border. The plant on the U.S. side does the high-tech, capital-intensive part of production, while the Mexican plant does the labor-intensive part. The term is often used synonymously, but incorrectly, with maquiladoras. Cf. *maquiladoras.*

two-point arbitrage: riskless purchase of a product in one geographic market for immediate resale in a second geographic market in order to profit from price differences between the markets.

two-tier gold (price) system: a system devised in 1968 to keep the world's monetary gold from being depleted by speculation and hoarding. International Monetary Fund member nations agreed to keep their present gold reserves for use in settlement of international trade balances only. All gold that was not part of this official tier supply and all newly minted gold would be traded in the open market. The open market gold no longer had any potential monetary value, since all IMF members had promised not to buy any of it for their reserves. See *International Monetary Fund.*

two-tier markets: an exchange rate regime that insulates a nation from the balance-of-payments impact of capital flow while it maintains a stable exchange rate for current account transactions.

two-tier pricing policy: pricing policy under which a firm sets one price for all its domestic sales and a second price for all its international sales.

two-tier tariff: a tariff consisting of two sets of rates for the same items. The United Kingdom has a full rate and a preferential rate for the Commonwealth and, when an *EFTA* member, had a three-tier tariff.

two-transaction approach: procedure used by U.S. firms to account on their income statements for transactions denominated in foreign currencies.

TZS: the international standard code for the currency of the United Republic of Tanzania—the Tanzanian shilling.

U

UA: see *Units of Account.*

UCITS: see *Collective Investment in Transferable Securities.*

UCP400: see *Uniform Customs and Practice for Documentary Credits.*

UCP500: see *Uniform Customs and Practice for Documentary Credits.*

UDEAC: see *Customs and Economic Union of Central Africa.*

Uganda shilling: monetary unit of Uganda.

UGX: the international standard code for the currency of Uganda—the Uganda shilling.

UK (U.K.): United Kingdom.

ullage: the distance between top of cargo and the hatches.

ultimate consignee: the individual located abroad who is the true party in interest, receiving the export for the designated end purpose. Cf. *ultimate consignor.*

ultimate consignor: the individual who is the true party in interest, receiving merchandise for the designate end purpose. Cf. *ultimate consignee.*

ultimate purchaser: as determined by customs officials, the last person who will receive an imported item in the form it was imported.

UN: the United Nations. See listings under *United Nations.*

unbalanced growth: capital investment that grows at different rates in different areas of an economy.

unbalanced traffic: a greater movement of traffic in one direction than in the other.

UNCITRAL: see *United Nations Commission on International Trade Law.*

unclaimed freight: freight that has not been called for by the consignee or owner.

unconditional call money: in Japan, funds lent for an initial period of two days which can then be called for repayment upon one day's notice.

uncovered interest arbitrage: where an investment is made in a foreign currency asset to benefit from a more attractive rate of interest without simultaneously taking out forward exchange cover to protect an investor against the risk of intervening exchange rate changes.

UNCTAD: see *United Nations Conference on Trade and Development.*

under bond: see *Warehouse, U.S. Customs Bonded.*

undercharge: to charge less than the proper amount.

underdeveloped countries: nations in which per capita real income is proportionately low in comparison with the per capita real income of nations where industry flourishes. See *less-developed countries; third world*.

underground economy: the part of a nation's income that, under-reported or unreported, is not measured by official statistics.

underlap: in charters, the period of time by which a charterer prematurely returns a ship to the owner's control in advance of the appointed date.

underselling:
(1) selling at a price lower than that listed by a competitor.
(2) offering import goods for sale in the United States at prices below those of comparable domestic U.S. items.

undertakings: see *multinational disclosure rules; rules of competition*.

undervalued currency:
(1) a currency that has been oversold because of emotional selling.
(2) a currency whose value a government attempts to keep below market to make its nation's exports less expensive and more competitive. Opposite of *overvalued currency*.

underwriter:
(1) an individual or organization that assumes a risk for a fee.
(2) an individual or party that agrees to underwrite a securities issue.

undeveloped countries: see *third world; underdeveloped countries*.

undo: to reverse a transaction.

unfair practices: the discriminatory commercial exchange activities of goods that are either unfairly subsidized or dumped, or are otherwise illegitimate, as with counterfeit items. See *dumping; General Agreement on Tariffs and Trade; priority practices; Super 301*.

unfair trader: as designated by the U.S. Trade Representative or the U.S. International Trade Commission, a nation, organization, or person engaging in "unfair trading practices." See *dumping; snapback*.

unfavorable balance of trade: the condition when the amount of items imported into a country is greater than that exported from the same nation. Cf. *balance of trade*.

unified exchange rates: the condition that prevails when a nation moves from a two- (or more) tier system of exchange rates to a single rate for all transactions. While not necessarily implying convertibility, a unified rate is an important step to establishing credibility on world financial markets. See *convertibility; hard currency.*

Uniform Customs and Practice for Documentary Credits (UCP500): a publication of the international Chamber of Commerce that details the rules, regulations, and responsibilities applying to letters of credit. It superseded UCP400 in 1993.

unilateral transfer: currency transfer from one country to another for the purchase of merchandise. The nation transferring currency does not sell goods to the transferee in return.

Union Douanière et Économique de l'Afrique Centrale (UDEAC): see *Customs and Economic Union of Central Africa.*

United Nations Commission on International Trade Law (UNCITRAL): created in 1966, a permanent subsidiary body of the United Nations dedicated to progressively harmonizing and unifying international trade laws worldwide. UNCITRAL's primary activities include coordinating the work of all international bodies working in the field of international commercial law; preparing international conventions dealing with aspects of the field for signing by nations; and promoting an understanding of international law and of the means of ensuring the interpretation and application of international conventions.

United Nations Conference on Trade and Development (UNCTAD): formed in 1964; headquartered in Geneva; to promote better international trading conditions for developing nations and to help raise their standard of living.

United Nations Convention on Conditions for Registration of Ships: signed in 1986, setting standards of responsibility and accountability in international shipping. Also defines and establishes linkages between ships and the flags they fly.

United Nations Convention on Contracts for the International Sales of Goods: became effective on January 1, 1988; governing contract formation, obligations, risk allocation, and remedies. It applies to contracts for the sale of goods between parties whose places of business are in different nations.

United Nations Convention on International Multimodal Transport of Goods: became effective in 1980; establishes a single set of rules for setting liability when goods are transported multimodally (i.e., with more than one manner of transport).

United Nations Convention on the Carriage of Goods by Sea: adopted in 1978; sets uniform regulations for international buyers and sellers concerning obligations and responsibilities regarding the international physical distribution and movement of items by sea.

United Nations Convention on the Limitation Period on the International Sale of Goods: adopted in 1974; sets a time limit of four years during which parties to an international contract may sue for nonpayment.

United Nations Development Program: see *International Bank for Reconstruction and Development.*

United States (entries): see listings under *U.S.*

Units of Account (European Units of Account) (EUA) (UA): financial instruments of the European Union. They are independent of national currencies but are linked to them by conversion rates, enabling single common prices to be set for the whole Union. Until 1971, the unit had a gold-based value equivalent to 0.88867088 grams of fine gold. Afterward, such conversions had no relation to the real value of national currencies in the world financial market. The Union developed a new unit—the European Unit of Account (EUA)—defined in terms of a "basket" of currencies of the member nations. It varies daily in any one national currency based on movements in all the involved exchange rates. It is used for all Union activities except the Common Agricultural Policy, where the payments retain, in theory, the gold-parity UA conversion rate. This is offset, however, by green currencies and monetary compensation amounts to bring currencies into line with the financial market exchange rate. See *European Currency Unit; European Monetary System.*

unit train: the movement of an entire trainload of items between one shipper and one consignee.

Unit Trusts:

(1) (British) mutual investment; a mutual fund.

(2) the European Community Commission's 1976 proposal on coordinating laws regarding "collective investment undertakings for transferable securities" (CIUTS). It set their organization and activities, their investment policy, and the information to be freely circulated. Its goal is to provide more uniform safeguards for all savers.

Universal Banks: large banks in Germany and Switzerland that have traditionally conducted both commercial and investment banking. They frequently are heavily invested in industrial firms.

unstable exchange rate market: the market for a nation's currency that may go from unsteady to volatile, as a result of political interference or commercial disturbances.

unused license: a current validated export license not having shipments recorded on it. All shipment made against the license must be posted on its reverse side.

up-front authority: see *proclamation authority*.

upstream pricing: forming a market value for commodities from which other items are derived or other by-products are produced.

upstream subsidization: the situation that occurs when a government provides a subsidy to a producer, the producer sells the subsidized product to an unrelated company, and that company performs further processing and ships the product to a foreign country.

urgent consignments: merchandise that, because of its character, requires expeditious release by customs officials (e.g., perishable goods).

Uruguayan peso: monetary unit of Uruguay.

Uruguay Round: on April 8, 1989, more than 100 nations agreed on greater liberalization of trade in goods and agriculture, as well as extending the General Agreement on Tariffs and Trade's authority to such new areas as trade in services and trade-related intellectual property rights. This marked the halfway point to the scheduled completion of the Round—the GATT seventh—at the end of 1990.

On December 7, 1990, the four-year round of talks to establish new rules for world trade broke off in disarray in Brussels. The United States and the European Community remained deadlocked over the issue of reducing subsidies to farmers. The effort to liberalize rules governing $4 trillion in annual world trade among the now 112 nations failed in 15 broad areas of trade, including farming, patents, financial services, telecommunications, and textiles. Although it was not expected to cripple world trade, it was anticipated that trade wars would intensify, and the promising ladder out of poverty would be taken away from the world's poorest nations who are forced to pay the highest prices on subsidized products, especially farm items from member states of the E.C.

The Uruguay Round raised global welfare by at least $120 billion a year, spurred economic growth (especially in the world's poorest nations), and extended competition. It is projected that the United States would gain an annual $35 billion, Japan and Europe nearly $30 billion each, and the rest of the world about $25 billion.

Benefits to the U.S. economy from the completed Uruguay Round included: (a) lower tariff and nontariff barriers to manufactured products and other goods; (b) rules to protect the intellectual property of U.S. entrepreneurs, who lost $60 billion annually through the theft and counterfeiting of their ideas; (c) new markets for U.S. services firms, which export over $163 billion annually and generate 90 percent of new U.S. jobs, and new rules to discipline international services trade; (d) rollback of barriers to trade from restrictive investment rules; (e) fair competition and open markets in agriculture, creating new opportunities for American farmers, who lead the world with almost $40 billion in annual exports; (f) the full participation of developing countries in the global trading system; and (g) strengthened rules on dispute settlement, antidumping, subsidies and trade remedy provisions, that provide predictability and certainty in access to foreign markets and ensure fair trade at home.

See *Draft Final Act; General Agreement on Tariffs and Trade; Montreal Round; Special 301; U.S. Trade Representative; World Trade Organization.*

U.S. Advisory Committee on Trade Policy Negotiations: as provided by the Omnibus Trade Act of 1988, a committee of up to 45 people who serve as primary advisors to the U.S. Trade Representative.

U.S. Agricultural Adjustment Act (1933): early federal legislation allowing for the imposition of restrictions to limit imports into the United States.

usance: the length of time given as credit on a time draft.

U.S.-Australia Free Trade Agreement: on August 13, 2004, Australia's Parliament passed legislation enabling Australia to implement a free trade agreement with the U.S. as of January 1, 2005; to gradually eliminate tariffs and other restrictive barriers of trade between the two nations.

U.S.-Bahrain Free Trade Agreement: In May 2004, Bahrain and the United States signed a free trade accord that would eliminate all duties on consumer and industrial products in their annual two-way trade of $887 million in goods.

U.S. Canada-Free Trade Agreement (FTA): see *Canada Free Trade Agreement.*

U.S. Canada-Trade Commission: see *Trade Commission.*

U.S.-Central America Free Trade Agreement: In December 2003, the Central American nations of El Salvador, Guatemala, Honduras, and Nicaragua (Costa Rica would later sign onto the accord) to strip away barriers to trade, eliminate tariffs, open markets, promote imports, and thus increase economic growth and opportunities for all five nations.

U.S.-Chile Free Trade Agreement: signed by President George W. Bush on September 3, 2003; to be ratified in both countries before it enters into effect on January 1, 2004. It is the first South American free-trade agreement. Creates opportunities for both nations; establishes clear, transparent rules for investors, including an open system for dispute settlement.

U.S. Consular Invoice: a document required on merchandise imported into the United States.

U.S. Customs Service: administers and enforces the Tariff Act of 1930, by assessing and collecting all duties, taxes, and fees on imported items, enforcing customs and related laws, etc.

USD:
(1) the international standard code for the currency of the United States—the U.S. dollar.
(2) the international standard code for the currencies of American Samoa, British Virgin Islands, British Indian Ocean Territory, Guam, Haiti, Johnston Island, Midway Islands, Pacific Islands (Trust Territory), Panama, Panama Canal Zone, Puerto Rico, Turks and Caicos Islands, United States Miscellaneous Pacific Islands, United States Virgin Island, and Wake Island—the U.S. dollar.

U.S. dollar: monetary unit of the United States.

used license:
a validated export license that has expired.
shipment authorized by the license have been made. Shipments made against the license
are posted on the reverse side.

user fee: a fee assessed for a service, required by GATT, now WTO, to be based on the estimated or computed cost of the service. The United States has enacted a Customs User Fee assessed on imported goods to offset some or all of the cost of customs operations.

user's fee: see *user fee.*

U.S. Export Administration Act (1979): legislation authorizing the imposition of export control on goods and services being exported from the United States, empowering the President to order that controls be put in place and to monitor compliance with such controls.

U.S. Inter-Agency Trade Organization: as provided by the Omnibus Trade Act (1988), and chaired by the U.S. Trade Representative, an advisory body to advise the President and the U.S. Trade Representative on matters dealing with international trade policy formation, and the coordinated implementation of international trade policy worldwide.

U.S. International Trade Administration (USITA): a subunit of the U.S. Department of Commerce, formed in 1980; led by an Under Secretary for International Trade. Areas of primary responsibility include international economic policy, import administration, trade development, and U.S. and Foreign Commercial Service.

U.S. International Trade Commission (USITC): created by the U.S. Trade Act of 1974 to regulate and protect U.S. trade in consonance with U.S. laws and international treaties to which the U.S. government is a signatory. The Commission can levy tariffs and duties in response to findings of unfair trading practices and injury.

The Commission's primary responsibilities are to provide: (1) advice concerning trade negotiations; (2) advice on the Generalized System of Preferences; (3) investigations (on petition) for import relief or domestic industries; (4) monitoring of East-West trade; (5) investigations relating to imported manufactured goods or agricultural commodities alleged to be subsidized, unfairly traded, or dumped; and (6) compilation and publication of tariff schedules of the United States, international trade statistics, and tariff summaries.

U.S.-Israel Free Trade Agreement: signed a free trade accord with the United States, on May 22, 1985 purporting to "eliminate duties and other restrictive regulations of commerce in trade between two nations, in products originating therein."

USITA: see *U.S. International Trade Administration.*

USITC: see *U.S. International Trade Commission.*

U.S.-Jordan Free Trade Agreement: signed on October 24, 2000 in Washington, D.C., to eliminate duties on consumer and industrial products. Ten percent of Jordan's imports come from the United States. Although the accord will have minimal impact on the U.S. economy, its significance for Jordan is great. Her exports to the U.S. in 3 years grew 72 percent, with imports from U.S. also increasing.

U.S.-Middle East Free Trade area: projected by the year 2013. Proposed by President George W. Bush in May 2003 as a means of bringing stability to a region bypassed by globalization and torn by terrorism.

U.S.-Morocco Free Trade Agreement: on March 2, 2004, Morocco joined Jordan as the second Muslim nation to sign a free trade accord with the United States, to phase out barriers of trade, including tariffs.

USN: the international standard code for the currency of the United States—the U.S. dollar next-day funds.

U.S. price: as used in dumping inquiries, the price at which items are sold in the U.S. compared to their foreign market value, to determine if the imported goods have been sold at less than fair value.

U.S.-Singapore Free Trade Agreement: signed on May 6, 2003; purports to eliminate duties on bilateral trade; rules of origin for goods and the detailed schedules of commitments in services and investment, including financial services.

USTR: see *U.S. Trade Representative.*

U.S. Trade Representative (USTR): a position authorized in 1963, with powers extended following passage of the Omnibus Trade Act of 1988. It is a cabinet-level position, carrying the title of Ambassador. He or she heads the Office of the U.S. Trade Representative and is responsible to the President for the evolution and coordination of U.S. international trade policy and negotiations. See *Section 301; Super 301.*

usuance: time permitted for payment of an international obligation.

usury: the rate of interest paid for the use of another's money, or for credit extended, which exceeds the legal limit allowed for that type of transaction by the state whose laws govern the legality of the transaction.

UYP: the international standard code for the currency of Uruguay—the Uruguayan peso.

V

valeur mercuriale: an official value, used in the determination of ad valorem duties, assigned by government officials to certain classes of imported items. It is mostly used in Western Africa.

Validated Export License: a required document issued by the U.S. government authorizing the export of specific commodities. This license is for a specific transaction or time period in which the exporting is to take place. Cf. *general export license.*

valuation:

(1) the fixing of value to anything.

(2) the calculation, based on a GATT, now WTO, formula, of the worth of imported items by customs authorities, to determine the amount of duty payable by the importer in the importing nation.

valuation clause: the basis for determining insured value under the open cargo policy.

value-added: that portion of the total value of produced items contributed by an specific firm's manufacturing process or services; determined by subtracting from sales the costs of materials and supplies, energy costs, contract work, etc.; it includes labor costs, administration and sales costs, and other operating profit. See *value-added tax*.

value-added tax (VAT): a turnover or consumption tax payable on items and services from the activities of a business organization. All European Union nations operate a VAT, although the rates vary significantly from one nation to another, with France having the highest. It assists firms operating within the common market and provides the basis for assessing the VAT element of the "own resources" system for financing the Community budget. The first Directive (1967) set the principle of harmonization of legislation concerning turnover taxes. The second Directive (1967) identified the structures and procedures for application. Another Directive (1979) dealt with refunding of VAT to firms operating in a Community nation other than that in which items and services have been invoiced inclusive of taxes. An inevitable prerequisite for the abolition of frontier controls within intra-Community trade is the termination of the present system under which exported goods are relieved of value-added tax and imported goods are subject to it.

A Value-Added Tax Clearinghouse is envisioned. In addition, a uniform Value Added Tax is expected to make duty-free shopping obsolete for travelers between the 12 EC member states, amounting to a loss of $2 billion a year in sales.

On July 29, 1992, EU finance ministers agreed to an interim VAT harmony, which imposed a legally binding minimum standard rate of value-added tax throughout the Union. The standard VAT rate—15 percent for four years from January 1993—was decided upon. During this time, transactions between taxable persons in different member nations were taxed in the importing country. In 1997, a permanent system went into effect; taxation is now levied in the country of origin. See *Europe without Frontiers; excise tax; frontier barriers; value-added.*

value compensated: a purchase or sale of foreign exchange to be executed by cable. The purchaser reimburses the seller for the earlier value on the date of actual payment abroad of the foreign currency, theoretically resulting in no loss of interest to either party.

Value-Content Rule (North American Free Trade Agreement): under the NAFTA, the rules of origin are organized according to the harmonized system classification of the product. There are two types of rules; both require substantial North American processing, but they measure it differently. Under the value-content rule, a set percentage of the value of the goods must be North American (usually coupled with a tariff-shift requirement). Some goods are subject to the value-content rule only when they fail to pass tariff-shift test because of non-NAFTA inputs. Cf. *Tariff-Shift Rule.* See *rules of origin.*

value date:

(1) the date on which a bank deposit becomes effective.

(2) in the Eurocurrency and foreign exchange markets, a reference to the delivery date of funds to settle the transaction. In the Eurobond market, the value date falls seven calendar days after the deal is struck, regardless of holidays.

value for customs purposes only: as stated by the U.S. Customs Service, the value submitted on the entry documentation by an importer, which may or may not reflect information from the producer but in no way reflects Customs officials appraisement of the goods.

variable import levy: a charge levied on certain agricultural items (e.g., some cereals) that is varied so as to raise the price of imports into the European Union broadly to the desired EU price level. During the transitional stage, such levels are applied to trade between member states so that Union suppliers would enjoy a preference over other sources of supply. The intra-EU levies are eliminated when the full Common Market stage is reached. Synonymous with *variable levy*.

variable levy: synonymous with *variable import levy*.

VAT: see *value-added tax*.

VEB: the international standard code for the currency of Venezuela—the Bolivar.

vehicle(s) currency: a currency used in international transactions to make quotes and payments. The U.S. dollar is the currency most frequently used.

velocity of circulation: the rate at which the money supply is spent for a stated time period, usually one year.

venture capital: see *capital; merger*.

VERs (voluntary export restraints): see *voluntary restraint agreements*.

vertical export trading company: an export trading firm that integrates a range of activities taking items from suppliers to consumers; it may also market these items, often via their retail outlets.

very large crude carrier: see *VLCC*.

vessel's manifest: the statement of a vessel's cargo.

vessel ton: 100 cubic feet.

veto: the right, usually under a Treaty or an Agreement, of a member-nation or its representative, to reject an intended act.

VIEs: see *voluntary import expansions*.

virtuous cycle: a concept describing the kinds of actions some bankers think governments should take to minimize the impact of currency fluctuations. The virtuous cycle approach produces a series of sound economic policies to set off a chain of events in which improved economic performance produces sound currencies, which, in turn, further improve economic performance.

Visegrad: a three-member group, named after the place near Budapest where the leaders of Czechoslovakia, Hungary, and Poland met in February 1991 to begin their coordinated efforts to join the European Community and to cooperate on economic, trade, and security issues.

visible items of trade:
  (1) the portion of commerce between nations that is shown by records of transactions involving the exchange of tangible items.
  (2) exports and imports of item and specie. Cf. *invisible items of trade*.

VLCC (very large crude carrier): a tanker capable of carrying a large amount of crude oil.

VND: the international standard code for the currency of Viet Nam—the dong.

Vnesheconombank: the former Soviet Union bank of foreign trade.

volume of freight: the rate applicable in connection with a specified volume (weight) of freight. Cf. *weight/measure*.

voluntary export quota: a quantitative restriction that a country places on the export of a certain item to another nation. Usually evolves from complaints from an importing nation that its domestic industry is being injured by continuing exports of the item from its trading partner.

voluntary export restraints (VERs): see *voluntary restraint agreements*.

voluntary import expansions (VIEs): under which a nation replies to another's threats of trade sanctions by agreeing to buy more of certain items from that country.

voluntary restraint agreements (VRAs): a bilateral arrangement whereby an exporting country agrees to reduce or restrict exports without the importing country having to make use of quotas, tariffs, or other import controls. These agreements are generally undertaken to avoid action by the importing country against imports that may injure or in some way threaten the positions of domestic firms in the industry in question. Cf. *orderly marketing agreements*. See *European Domestic Market*.

vostro account: an account maintained with a depository bank by a bank in a foreign country. Cf. *nostro account*.

voyage charter: a ship charter arranged to carry a cargo on a single voyage between specified ports or areas. Payment, usually on either a cargo ton basis or on a cubic capacity basis, includes voyage costs.

voyage costs: a ship's costs, comprising bunkers, port, and canal charges.

voyage policy: a marine insurance policy issued for one particular voyage only.

VRAs: see *voluntary restraint agreements*.

VUV: the international standard code for the currency of Vanuatu—the vatu.

W

WADB: see *West African Development Bank*.

WAEC: see *West African Economic Community*.

waiver: a legal exception, provided for under GATT, now WTO, whereby the Contracting Parties can vote to allow a WTO signatory to maintain a specified practice that would otherwise violate its WTO obligations.

waiver clause: in marine insurance, a provision enabling either party to take steps to reduce the impact of a loss without prejudice.

watch list: see *Special 301*.

warehouse: a structure where goods are stored prior to distribution.

Warehouse, U.S. Customs Bonded: a federal warehouse where goods remain until duty has been collected from the importer. Goods under bond are also kept there.

warehouse entry: a form declaring merchandise imported and placed in a bonded warehouse. Duty payment may not be required until the items are withdrawn for consumption.

warehouse receipt: a receipt given for goods placed in a warehouse (may be issued as a negotiable or nonnegotiable document).

warehouse to warehouse: an export/import policy statement providing protection from a shipper's warehouse and during the ordinary course of movement to the consignee's warehouse.

warrant: a warehouse receipt containing trust receipt provisions.

warrant Eurobonds: fixed-rate Eurobonds that carry warrants permitting the bondholder to make subsequent purchases of either common stock or other bonds.

waybill: a statement identifying a shipment, showing the shipper, consignee, routing, rate, and weights. It is used by the carrier as an internal record.

waybill, air: see *air waybill*.

waybill destination: the point to which a shipment is waybilled.

Webb-Pomerene Act of 1918: an act exempting from U.S. antitrust laws those associations among business competitors engaged in export trade. They must not restrain trade within the United States or the trade of any other U.S. competitors.

weight agreement: an agreement between shipper and carrier, usually following a series of weighing tests, under which the carrier agrees to accept the shipper's goods at certain agreed weights.

weight breaks: the levels at which the charges per 100 pounds decrease as the shipment increases in weight.

weight cargo: a cargo on which the transportation charge is assessed on the basis of weight.

weight/measure: the correlation of weight to volume for calculation of shipping costs. Cf. *cargo tonnage.*

weights and measures: standards for measuring, analysis, and testing. See *standardization.*

weight sheet: an itemized list furnished by shippers to weighing bureaus, itemizing articles in each consignment.

West African Development Bank (WADB): established in 1973, and operational in 1976; headquartered in Lomé, Togo. Its members include the governments of Benin, Ivory Coast, Niger, Senegal, Togo, and the Upper Volta, plus the Central Bank of the West African States. Its goal is to promote the economic development, trade, and integration of Western Africa.

West African Economic Community (WAEC): a regional international trade grouping, formed in 1973. It is headquartered in Ouadadougou, Burkina Faso, and forms a customs union between its member states of Côte d'Ivoire, Mali, Mauritania, Niger, and Senegal. Synonymous with *Communauté Économique de l'Afrique de l'Ouest (CEAO).*

Western Hemisphere Trade Corporation: a U.S. firm whose business is carried out in any country of North, South, or Central America or the West Indies, and which usually receives certain tax advantages.

wharfage:
(1) a charge levied against a vessel docking at a wharf.
(2) a charge levied against a vessel handling traffic on a wharf.
(3) synonymous with *dockage; moorage.*

White Paper: published in June 1985; the European Community's Commission program for "Completing the Internal Market," which listed over 300 legislative proposals and a timetable for their adoption. It was endorsed by the Heads of State and Government. Its aim was to weld together the 12 separate national economies into a single trading market—a single Europe—by 1992. The White Paper program was approved by the European Community

Heads of State or Government and given a constitutional basis by the Single European Act of 1986. By mid-1988, progress had been made toward achieving the following objectives: an abolition of frontier controls on goods; the freedom of movement and establishment for people; the opening up of public procurement markets; a variety of services, including financial and transport; the liberalization of capital movements; the creation of suitable conditions for industrial cooperation; and the removal of fiscal frontiers, all impacting on trade within the European Community and external to it. Other areas include the second stage of the liberalization of capital movements; public procurement, nonlife insurance; the three direct tax measures designed to improve the fiscal environment for cross-border operations; mutual recognition of diplomas; television without frontiers; road transport; construction products; food law; major shareholdings; second banking directive; and an approximation of indirect taxes. See *internal market; Single European Act.*

wholesale money: money borrowed in large amounts from banks, large firms, or financial organizations.

wholesaler: synonymous with *distributor.*

window dressing: the practice of executing transactions shortly before the end of an accounting period to artificially change the items in the accounting statements of the period.

WIPO: see *World Intellectual Property Organization.*

withholding tax: a tax imposed by a host country on funds that are remitted from the subsidiary to the parent.

without penalty: when the importer, or any other person liable for the payment of duty, is not subject to a fine or threat of fine merely because they chose to exercise their right of appeal in the determination of customs value.

without recourse:
(1) used in endorsing a negotiable instrument where the endorser of a note is no longer responsible, should the obligation not be paid.
(2) an agreement that the purchaser accepts all risk in the transaction, and gives up all the rights to any recourse.

without reserve: indicating that a shipper's agent or representative is empowered to make definitive decisions and adjustments abroad without approval of the group or individual represented. Cf. *advisory capacity.*

won: monetary unit of both Democratic People's Republic of Korea and South Korea.

wordsmith: see *wordsmithing.*

wordsmithing: language creation and the manipulation of terms in a negotiation process; used often as a maneuver in international trade. It has been popularized, and at times is employed in lieu of preferred English by faculty at business universities.

worker protection: temporary protections imposed to ensure a smooth transition for sectors facing increased competition from trade accords. For example, to protect against increased Mexican and Canadian competition, NAFTA provides for (a) long transition periods of up to 15 years for the elimination of U.S. tariffs on the most sensitive U.S. products, such as household glassware, footwear, and some fruits and vegetables; (b) safeguards that permit a temporary hike in U.S. tariff rates to pre-NAFTA levels to protect U.S. workers and farmers from being injured or threatened with injury by increased imports from Mexico; and (c) tough rules of origin to guarantee that the benefits of NAFTA tariff reductions go only to products made in North America. See *free riders; global safeguard; snap-back.*

worker's rights: some union and citizen groups argue that the NAFTA should include provisions to guarantee respect for internationally recognized labor rights, ensuring that workers have the tools they need to demand decent wages and working conditions. As with environmental standards, violations of these labor rights ought to be a legal basis for challenge as an unfair practice. Instead, some believe the NAFTA text undermines existing labor rights standards in U.S. trade law by giving Mexico and all other countries that acceded to the agreement exemption from labor standards now required for countries that seek privileged access to U.S. markets. See *North American Secretariats; side agreements; social charter.*

Working Capital Guarantee Program: an EXIMBANK program that aids small businesses in securing working capital to fund their export interests and activities.

World Bank: synonymous with *International Bank for Reconstruction and Development.* See *International Finance Corporation; World Bank Group.*

World Bank Group: composed of the World Bank (the International Bank for Reconstruction and Development), the International

Finance Corporation, the International Development Association, and the Multilateral Investment Guarantee Agency. See *International Bank for Reconstruction and Development.*

World Intellectual Property Organization (WIPO): one of the 15 specialized agencies of the United Nations system of organizations. WIPO, located in Geneva, is responsible for the promotion of the protection of intellectual property (copyrights, trademarks, patents) throughout the world through cooperation among states, and for the administration of various "unions," each founded on a multilateral treaty and dealing with the legal and administrative aspects of intellectual property.

world price: the price at which a given commodity is selling internationally under market conditions in effect at the time of the sale.

world trade center: city or area providing appropriate services associated with global trade.

World Trade Organization (WTO): replaced *GATT* in 1995, as an international organization that facilitates implementation of trade agreements reached in various Rounds by bringing them together under one institutional umbrella. Requires full participation of all nations in one trading system and provides a permanent forum to discuss new issues facing the international trading system; headquartered in Geneva, Switzerland.

worldwide firms: organizations that are global, multinational, or transnational.

worm: see *snake.*

WST: the international standard code for the currency of Samoa—the tala.

WTO: see *World Trade Organization.*

X

XAF: the international standard code for the currencies of Cameroon, Central African Republic, Chad, Congo, Equatorial Guinea, and Gabon—the CFA franc.

XCD: the international standard code for the currencies of Anguilla, Antigua and Barbuda, Dominica, Grenada, Montserrat, St. Kitts-Nevis, St. Lucia, and St. Vincent and the Grenadines—the East Caribbean dollar.

xenophobia: the fear of foreigners. It can express itself in unfair and illegal trade practices around the world, especially for people living and working within the borders of competing nations.

XOF: the international standard code for the currencies of Benin, Ivory Coast, Niger, Senegal, Togo, and Upper Volta—the CFA franc.

XPF: the international standard code for the currencies of French Polynesia, New Caledonia, and Walls and Futuna Islands—the CFP franc.

Y

Yaoundé Agreements: Yaoundé I was signed in 1963, and Yaoundé II in 1969. They dealt with relations between the European Community and former French, Belgian, Dutch, and Italian colonies that wanted to continue their association with the Community following their independence. Conventions outlined duty-free entry for specific exports from the developing nations, including the output of infant industries; a similar arrangement for exports from the Community into most of the nations; and the creation of a European Development Fund for these associated nations. In 1973, it was replaced by the Lomé Conventions. See *external trade, Lomé Conventions.*

Yemen rial: monetary unit of Yemen.

yen: monetary unit of Japan.

yen-block: investment and trade between Japan and its Asian neighbors: Hong Kong, South Korea, the five ASEAN countries, Australia, and New Zealand.

yen diplomacy: an attempt by Japan to have a trade area dominated by the yen in 2010. To accomplish this, the government of Japan is planning trade agreements with Pacific Rim nations.

York-Antwerp Rules: an organized body of rules relating to the adjustment of claims arising in general average; originally promulgated by world shipping interests. The Rules do not enjoy formal status as law, but are incorporated into virtually all bills of lading.

yuan: monetary unit of People's Republic of China.

Z

zaibatsu: centralized, family-dominated, monopolistic economic groups that dominated the Japanese economy until the termination of World War II in 1945, when they were broken apart. As time passed, however, the units of the old zaibatsu drifted back together, and they now cooperate within the group much as they did before their dissolution. See *keiretsu*.

ZAR: the international standard code for the currencies of Lesotho, Namibia, and South Africa—the rand.

zero-coupon Eurobonds: American company issues that pay no interest but are sold at a steep discount.

zero haven: a tax-haven nation that levies no taxes (or practically none) on income.

zeroing: a practice of overestimating the amount of antidumping fines to be paid by importers. Usually calculated by subtracting the price a company sets for its production in a foreign market from the price it charges at home each month.

zloty (zlotych): monetary unit of Poland.

ZMK: The international standard code of Zambia—Zambian kwacha.

Zollverein: a German term, *Zoll* ("customs"), *Verein* ("union"). It created the economic unification of Germany by allowing the expansion of commerce and industry, the improvement of transport, and the building of railways; it prepared the way for the alignment of commercial and industrial law.

zone: see *zone-restricted merchandise; zone user*.

zone-delivered pricing: a pricing scheme where the supplier equalizes freight on shipments to all customers within a defined geographic area.

zone-restricted merchandise: a category of the U.S. Customs Service when entering imported goods being forwarded into a foreign trade zone. Since these items are considered exported at the time they are entered into the zone, they cannot be brought back into U.S. Customs territory.

zone user: a firm, partnership, or party that utilizes a U.S. foreign trade zone for storage, handling, processing, or manufacturing merchandise in zone status, whether domestic or overseas.

ZRZ: the international standard code for the currency of Zaire—the zaire.

ZWD: the international standard code for the currency of Zimbabwe—the Zimbabwe dollar.